OUTDOORS

NEW ENGLAND BIKING

CHRIS BERNARD

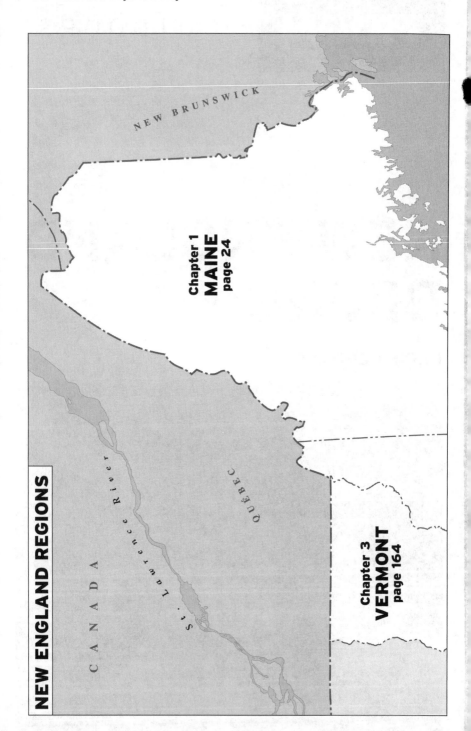

NEW ENGLAND REGIONS

NEW BRUNSWICK

CANADA

St. Lawrence River

QUÉBEC

Chapter 1
MAINE
page 24

Chapter 3
VERMONT
page 164

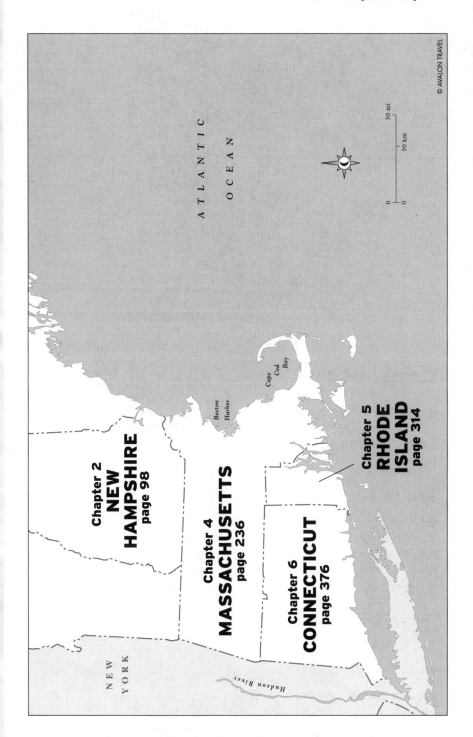

ATLANTIC OCEAN

NEW YORK

Hudson River

Chapter 2
NEW
HAMPSHIRE
page 98

Chapter 4
MASSACHUSETTS
page 236

Chapter 6
CONNECTICUT
page 376

Chapter 5
RHODE
ISLAND
page 314

Boston Harbor

Cape Cod Bay

50 mi

50 km

© AVALON TRAVEL

Contents

How to Use This Book

ABOUT THE MAPS

This book is divided into chapters based on regions; an overview map of these regions precedes the table of contents. Each chapter begins with a region map that shows the locations and numbers of the rides listed in that chapter. Each ride profile is also accompanied by a detailed map that shows the bike route.

Map Symbols

———	Road Route	○	City
········	Unpaved Road Route	○	Town
——————	Trail Route	℗	Trailhead Parking
——·——·—	Optional Route	Start	Start of Ride
············	Trail	▪	Point of Interest
················	Trail (Bikes Prohibited)	★	Natural Feature
	Divided Highway	▲	Mountain
	Primary Road	ⱥ	State Park
	Secondary Road	Λ	Campground
═ ═ ═ ═ ═	Unpaved Road	⸜	Waterfall

ABOUT THE ELEVATION PROFILES

Each profile includes an elevation scale which approximately graphs the hills and dips on the route in height and distance. Please note that the scales on each profile are dramatically different. Scales may not always begin at an elevation of zero feet and height increments and distance can vary.

ABOUT THE RIDE PROFILES

Each profile includes a narrative description of the ride's setting and terrain. This description also includes mile-by-mile route directions, as well as information about the ride's highlights and unique attributes.

The rides marked by the **BEST** ◖ symbol are highlighted in the author's Best Bike Rides list.

Options

If alternative routes are available, this section is used to provide information on side trips or note how to shorten or lengthen the ride.

Driving Directions

This section provides detailed driving directions to the start of the route from the nearest major town.

Route Directions

Each profile includes a mile-by-mile listing of what to expect along the trail or road. Every major turn is noted and nearby sights or supplies are indicated where available.

ABOUT THE DIFFICULTY RATING

Each profile includes a difficulty rating. The ratings are defined as follows:

1: Beginners, families with young children, or anyone seeking a casual, recreational route will like these rides. They're mostly flat and usually less than 15 miles, or offer shorter options. Typically smooth-surfaced, they generally follow bike paths or rail trails with no vehicular traffic. Estimated ride times reflect the slower paces more appropriate for such trails, and more typical of beginner riders.

2: Novices with good fitness, families with older children, or anyone seeking a relatively casual recreational ride will like these rides. They avoid any difficult or technical features, and are generally less than 25 miles with little elevation gain. Off-road rides may involve varied surfaces, like gravel, ballast, or grass, but don't require technical mountain biking skills. Estimated ride times presume a similar pace to the previous category.

3: These rides are appropriate for cyclists with decent aerobic fitness and some cycling experience. Beginners may find them a little daunting. Road rides are generally less than 40 miles, but require moderate hill climbs, and may follow roads with broken pavement and some vehicle traffic. Off-road rides assume basic technical skills and comfort with rough and changing terrain—cyclists should have some experience on a variety of trails, including single-track. Estimated ride times reflect the faster pace of fitter riders.

4: Intermediate riders with excellent aerobic fitness will thrive on these routes, but anyone not used to longer rides with challenging features will be over-matched. Road rides are generally 30–60 miles, with steep climbs and descents, and may include sections with less-than-ideal surfaces or traffic conditions. Off-road rides presume solid technical skills and bike-handling, and involve steep climbs and descents over rough and changing conditions. Bikers should have solid experience on a variety of trails, including single-track. These rides may traverse less-traveled, more remote areas. Estimated ride times presume a faster pace.

5: These rides will challenge even fit riders. They should only be undertaken by experienced cyclists with excellent aerobic fitness. Road rides have several steep or prolonged hill climbs, and cover longer distances. Off-road rides are technical, on a variety of surfaces and types of trails, and require advanced bike handling skills. They will involve steep climbs and descents. Some riders may have to portage their bikes through sections. Estimated ride times presume a fast pace.

INTRODUCTION

Author's Note

My personal journey on a bike began in my parents' backyard more than 30 years ago, and it's never stopped. I still remember wobbling through the yard, weaving between staked tomato plants in my mom's garden, gathering confidence and speed with each stroke of the pedals. My dad had just taken the training wheels off my Huffy. It felt like he'd given me wings.

I've owned a lot of bikes since then, and I've ridden lots of places. I've raced in three disciplines, though I'm rarely in any danger of winning in any of them, and I've ridden for exercise, for transportation, and just for fun. One way or another I try to ride a bike every day—even if just to chase my tireless dog through the Maine woods.

Last March the roads at home were still thick with snow. I drove a couple hours south to Massachusetts, and spring seemed to have beaten me there—the sun shone brightly, the air fresher than it had been for months. On the heels of a brutal winter, the trails had turned to inches of mud. I gritted my teeth against a winter's inactivity and pedaled into the forest on the first ride for this book.

The deeper in I got, to where sun couldn't reach the trails, the more snow I found. I rode around it when I could, straight through it when I couldn't. I passed some dog walkers who looked at me askance, surprised to find me there, and then a pair of snowshoers who seemed skeptical of the provenance of a bike in the snowy woods. Eventually I caught up with a trio of mountain bikers who cheered at my arrival. For the moment we were comrades in arms, united by our mutual love of bikes. We chatted briefly, our conversation bloated with superlatives, and then pedaled off our separate ways. A couple hours later I was in my truck, driving back to Maine, soaking wet, exhausted, and muddy from head to toe. I couldn't stop smiling.

© SARGE BERNARD

Anyone who's had a chance to ride in New England knows how fortunate we are. Many of our bike trails set the standard for those elsewhere in the country. Whether you're a road racer looking for a fast, long lung-buster, a cyclotourist seeking a coastal century, a mountain biker in search of chewed-up single-track to test your skills against, or a family out for a recreational ride in a beautiful setting, you're in luck. You'll find no shortage of options in this book.

You may recognize some trails from the first edition—they've been updated to ensure their accuracy and to reflect any changes—but many are new. They range in surface, terrain, distance, and difficulty, and you'll find them in all corners of New England. The one thing they share is their appeal to riders of all ages, interests, and skill levels—including me. In some ways I've been riding these routes since that long-ago day in my parents' yard.

Biking is healthful, environmentally friendly, and more affordable than driving a car. But if you're reading this book, you already know that. If you're like me—and if you're reading this book, I'll bet you are—that's not why you do it. You ride a bike because you're chasing that same thrill you felt when your training wheels first came off.

See you out there.

Best Bike Rides

❰ Best Bike Paths
Southeast Sojourn, New Hampshire, page 147
Island Line Rail Trail, Vermont, page 174
Nashua River Rail Trail, Massachusetts, page 269
East Bay Bike Path, Rhode Island, page 326
Air Line Trail, Connecticut, page 412

❰ Best Butt-Kickers
Grafton Notch Loop, Maine, page 41
Kittredge Hill Loop, New Hampshire, page 124
Gaps of Glory, Vermont, page 198
Wachusett Mountain, Massachusetts, page 265
Mystic Birthday Ride, Connecticut, page 445

❰ Best Coastal Rides
Schoodic Peninsula, Maine, page 60
Five Lights, Six Beaches, Maine, page 77
Bailey's Three States Bounder, New Hampshire, page 154
Witches to Water's Edge, Massachusetts, page 291
Newport, Rhode Island, page 357
Madison Beach, Connecticut, page 429

❰ Best for Fall Foliage
Bradbury Mountain, Maine, page 63
Two Chiefs and Three Bridges, New Hampshire, page 108
Salt Hill Interstate, New Hampshire, page 111
Green Mountain Peaks and Hollows, Vermont, page 220
Wilmington's Watering Hole, Vermont, page 227
Weeping Willowdale, Massachusetts, page 284
Breakneck Pond Loop, Connecticut, page 385

❰ Best for Families
Carriage Roads, Maine, page 56
Peaks Island Loop, Maine, page 82
Windham Rail Trail, New Hampshire, page 158
Island Line Rail Trail, Vermont, page 174
Ashuwillticook Rail Trail, Massachusetts, page 246
East Bay Bike Path, Rhode Island, page 326
Air Line Trail, Connecticut, page 412

❰ Best Historical Rides
Glass Family Ramble, New Hampshire, page 118
Green Mountain Peaks and Hollows, Vermont, page 220
Reservoir Dogs, Massachusetts, page 261
Blackstone River Bikeway, Rhode Island, page 319
Newport, Rhode Island, page 357

❰ Best Overnight Rides
Carriage Roads and **Schoodic Peninsula,** Maine, pages 56 and 60
Kittredge Hill Loop and **Lovewell Mountain Ride,** New Hampshire, pages 124 and 127
Missisquoi Valley Rail Trail, Island Line Rail Trail, Burlington Bike Path Sampler, and **Shelburne Farms,** Vermont, pages 166, 174, 177, and 184
Farms and Forests, Harold Parker State Forest, Weeping Willowdale, and **Witches to Water's Edge,** Massachusetts, pages 276, 280, 284, and 291
A Point, Two Towers, and the Pier, Conanicut Island Loop, and **Newport,** Rhode Island, pages 349, 353, and 357
Niantic Bay Loop, Bluff Point Loop, and **Mystic Birthday Ride,** Connecticut, pages 437, 441, and 445

❰ Best Scenic Rides
As East As It Gets, Maine, page 33
Schoodic Peninsula, Maine, page 60
Smuggler's Blues, Vermont, page 190
Province Lands Loop, Massachusetts, page 308
Once Around the Block, Rhode Island, page 370

❰ Best Single-Track Rides
Bradbury Mountain, Maine, page 63
Massabesic Lake Loops, New Hampshire, page 143
Kingdom Trails, Vermont, page 194
Vietnam Sampler, Massachusetts, page 296
Breakheart and Shelter Trails, Rhode Island, page 338
Case Mountain Scramble, Connecticut, page 397

❰ Best for Wildlife-Viewing
Baring Division Trail, Maine, page 30
Kittredge Hill Loop, New Hampshire, page 124
Wells River Rail Trail, Vermont, page 207
Plum Island, Massachusetts, page 288
Worden Pond Loop, Rhode Island, page 346
Air Line Trail, Connecticut, page 412

Biking Tips

Most people remember the thrill they felt the first time they rode a bike without training wheels. Part of what draws us to bikes is that each ride gives us the chance to feel that thrill again. Cycling is great exercise, efficient transportation, and a lot of fun—but it also involves risks and dangers. Observing the rules of the road or trail, following simple safety guidelines, and knowing the basics of how to repair and maintain your bike will ensure you many years of happy, trouble-free biking.

Want to get better at bicycling? Want to learn more about rides in your area, or find someone to ride with? Start with local bike shops. Most host group rides a couple days each week, with varied average speeds to attract different riders. Get online and see if there's a cycling club or advocacy group active in your area. Find a local race schedule and go watch, cheer, and mingle—most members of the cycling community like to talk about all things bike-related. Finally, get outside and ride, and say hello when you run into other riders.

BIKE SAFETY TIPS

The following tips can help make your ride safer, both for you and the people with whom you share the roads and trails.

Wear a Helmet

Above all else, helmets should fit properly. According to the Bicycle Helmet Safety Institute (www.bhsi.org), a good helmet should fit "level on your head, touching all around, comfortably snug but not tight. The helmet should not move more than about an inch in any direction, and must not pull off no matter how hard you try." You'll see a lot of riders wearing helmets incorrectly, pushed back off the forehead or with unbuckled straps. These are mistakes that can render the helmet ineffective. Helmets have a life span, and they should be inspected or replaced every few years and after every accident. If you're not sure how to choose a helmet or how to properly fit one, stop in at a bike shop and ask for help.

© CHRIS BERNARD

Rules of the Road

Bicycles and their place on the road is a controversial issue that seems to become more of a problem each year. Our road system was not designed for the shared use of motor vehicles and bicycles, nor was it designed even to handle the numbers of motor vehicles that travel it every day. Entire books have been written about bicycle safety and the rules of the road, but they can be summarized in a few simple rules.

- Bicycles belong on the road or in the bike lane, not on the sidewalk. When riding on a street or road, bicycles are vehicles—just like cars or trucks—and are subject to the same laws and regulations.
- Ride in the same direction as traffic.
- Stop at stop signs, traffic lights, and crosswalks.
- Signal your intention to turn.
- Use the appropriate lanes.
- Treat motorists with respect, because you're asking for theirs in return. In a car-meets-bike matchup, bikes don't stand a chance, so take your own safety seriously.
- Ride predictably. Don't swerve or dodge between cars, and whenever possible, make eye contact with drivers—don't ever assume they see you.
- Watch parked cars for opening doors.
- Use lights when riding at or after dusk.
- State bicycle laws vary, so be sure you're familiar with the laws in the state in which you are riding.

Rules of the Trail

Bicycles and their place on trails can be even more controversial. But a little common courtesy can go a long way.

- When riding off-road, on single- or double-track or fire roads, yield to other bikers and trail users, especially horses. Slow down and use caution when approaching or passing, and let others know you're coming.
- Stay on designated trails. Be aware of your environment—riding trails is a privilege, not a right, and as such is in constant jeopardy of being revoked.
- Don't use overly muddy trails where erosion is a concern, don't build unauthorized trail features or stunts, and stay on marked trails rather than short-cutting or making new trails.
- Don't harass wildlife or domestic animals, and be respectful of private property.

ON THE TRAIL

Riding a bike on rail trails and multiuse paths requires a distinct etiquette built

© CHRIS BERNARD

Keep to the right except when passing.

around common courtesy. Be prepared to share with other trail users: pedestrians, dog walkers, equestrians, in-line skaters, strollers, and other bikers.

Unless separate bike and pedestrian lanes are marked, keep to the right except when passing. Always ride in the direction of traffic, not against it; don't be a bike salmon. Keep your speed to what is safe for the conditions; heavily trafficked paths are not the place to practice your time trial skills. When overtaking another cyclist or pedestrian, call out to him or her well in advance to prevent spooking him or her—startled people have a tendency to veer in front of you. If you don't have a bell, say "On your left" loudly and firmly enough for the person to hear you. Watch for headphones, a sign that he or she hasn't heard you and has no idea you're approaching. Don't wear headphones yourself. If you *do* wear headphones, turn your music low enough to hear what's going on around you.

All cyclists will be judged by your actions, so act responsibly. If you see someone with bike problems, slow down or stop and ask if you can help. Do they need a spare tube or help changing a tire? Do they need a cell phone?

It's also worth noting that many other users will not be as considerate as you'd like them to be. Dog walkers will let their dogs wander to the far side of the path, turning leashes into guillotines; baby strollers will appear suddenly in front of you as the people pushing them make unannounced U-turns; pedestrians and joggers will swerve, veer, or stop without warning or concern for anyone behind them; other cyclists will speed by at leg-busting speeds, talking on cell phones; and in-line skaters will sway side-to-side, hogging the entire path.

Be patient, stay calm, ride defensively, and set a good example. Don't litter. And don't be a jerk. It's that simple.

Be Prepared

Plan your route and make sure you have a good map. Check the weather and dress for the day, and bring extra clothing or rain gear if necessary. Start early enough so you'll have plenty of daylight. If you are riding in a remote area, especially off-road, you'll need a little more preparation. Maps become essential, and you may need a road map as well as a topographic map, a compass, or a GPS device. If you're riding alone, tell someone your trip plans and consider taking a cell phone.

Know Your Bike

The more you get to know your bike, the more fun you'll have with it. Ensure you can make emergency roadside repairs and perform basic maintenance. If you don't know how or have trouble teaching yourself, take a bike repair or maintenance class. Perform a quick safety check before each ride: Check your wheels' quick-release skewers to make sure they're on right and tightly. Check your tire pressure. (Recommended tire pressures are marked on the tires' sidewalls. For mountain biking you'll typically want less pressure in the tires to get more contact with the ground.) Oil your chain. Check your brakes.

Basic Riding Techniques

Several techniques and tricks will help you improve and make it possible for you to ride safely on a wide range of surfaces. Learn to shift properly if your bike has multiple gears. If you don't know how to shift, learn from others, practice in an empty parking lot, or take a class.

Use your brakes wisely: Most of your braking power comes from the front brakes, but use them judiciously to avoid an "endo" (flipping up on your front wheel) or a "superman" (flipping over your handlebars). Learn to use a combination of front and back brakes. Don't squeeze too hard, or you'll lock up the wheels into a skid. Learn to brake before a curve or corner so you can ride through it at the right speed.

For mountain biking, move your weight back to lift the front wheel slightly to get over rocks and roots. On steep downhills, shift your weight back by sliding well back on the seat, or even off the seat and over the rear wheel if possible.

REPAIRS AND MAINTENANCE

Learning the basics of maintenance and upkeep will do more than keep your bike rolling safely and indefinitely; it will enhance your enjoyment. Nothing ruins a ride faster than equipment failure that could have been prevented—except maybe a bike suffering from a multitude of annoying malfunctions that persist throughout the entire ride.

Basic Maintenance

Basic maintenance you can perform on your bike includes learning to change flat tires, regularly checking the tightness of all bolts and connections, and above all, cleaning your bike regularly. As you clean it, inspect it for problems like frayed or rusty cables and nicked tires.

CLEANING

To wash your bike, use a repair stand, tree, or car-mounted bike rack, or hang it over a mailbox. Don't turn the bike upside down; water may get into bearings that need to stay dry. Rinse the bike first, either with a bucket of water or a garden hose on a gentle setting. Then get a bucket of warm, soapy water (dish soap is fine) and use it to scrub the bike gently with a brush or sponge. Don't forget to scrub the wheel rims, either now or with a rag when the bike is dry. Use a separate sponge for the chain and drivetrain. Rinse the bike off, then dry it with a chamois or soft towel. Then clean and lube the chain.

CHAINS

If there's only one thing you ever do to maintain your bike, that's it: clean the chain. This will make riding and shifting smoother and more efficient. It also keeps the chain from wearing down gears and eliminates the dead giveaway of an inexperienced cyclist—a squeaky chain. Wipe the chain off with a clean rag to get at the first layer of grease and grime. Then scrub all parts of the drive train, including the chain, crankset, derailleurs, and cassette (rear cogwheels). Use a citrus degreaser or other biodegradable solvent, and use a rag, small brush (such as an old toothbrush), screwdriver, or whatever tools seem to work. Rinse off the degreaser, and then shake the bike to dry it. When you're done, apply a small amount of lubricant to the chain and wipe off the excess.

Don't overlube the chain. It will only attract dirt and grit. And don't use WD-40—it's not a lubricant, it's a solvent. There are several types of chain lube to choose from, so ask at the bike shop and be sure to mention what type of riding you do.

SHIFTING

Adjusting your bike's shifting is not difficult, and it falls somewhere between art and science. Poor shifting is often the result of cables lacking sufficient tension to shift and hold the proper gears. Most bikes have barrel adjusters, or little knurled knobs, where the cable housings meet the shifters or the derailleurs—turn these adjusters one-quarter turn at a time to shorten the cable, and check the shifting after each turn. If you can't resolve the issue, it may be time for a new cable or an adjustment of the derailleur itself, a fix best made by an experienced mechanic.

BRAKING

Good braking relies on mechanical advantage between the brake lever and the amount of cable it can pull, forcing the brake pads against the wheel's rim. If your brakes don't provide enough stopping power, no matter how hard you squeeze them, you can try shortening the cable using the same method described for adjusting shifting—most brakes have barrel adjusters. You can also dry off your brake pads and see if that helps. If not, it may be time to replace the pads or cables or to have a professional mechanic adjust your brakes. This is not an area in which you can afford to mess up.

Roadside Repairs

The more you ride, the more you'll want to learn to fix your bike, because the more time you spend on it the better the odds that something will go wrong. Every cyclist, beginner or advanced, on- or off-road, needs to know how to fix a flat tire. Mountain bikers in particular should know how to fix a broken chain. From there, you can graduate to replacing broken cables or broken spokes, fixing bent rims, and so on. Many other repairs, adjustments, and fine-tuning can wait until you get home or take it to a bike shop.

FIXING A FLAT

Don't ride with a flat tire, don't rely on others to know how to fix one for you, and don't rely on a cell phone to get you out of a jam. Fixing a flat is quick and easy if you practice a few times. Get a bike repair manual, take a class, or have an experienced cyclist show you how to do it.

The basic steps: 1) Release the brake and remove the wheel. 2) Remove the valve cap, deflate the tire, and use tire levers to unseat the tire and remove the tube. 3) Inspect the tire, tube, and rim to find and remove the cause of the flat. 4) Replace the tube with a new one or patch the old one. 5) Put the tube and tire back on the wheel. 6) Inflate and seat the tire.

REPAIRING A BROKEN CHAIN

This requires a little more skill and knowledge about what type of chain you have on your bike. You'll also need a chain tool. (These are fairly small, inexpensive, and very useful.) If you are serious about cleaning your chain, you'll want one anyway, since the most thorough chain cleaning requires removing the chain from the derailleur. For a trailside repair, use the chain tool to push out the damaged pin or link. Use a replacement pin or link, and then use the chain tool to reconnect the chain. In an emergency, reconnect the chain at the next link, though a shorter chain will mean you will probably not have full use of your gears, so ride home cautiously.

BIKING GEAR CHECKLIST

You can fit the essentials into a small seat bag. If traveling by car to a trailhead, bring additional tools and supplies to leave in your vehicle. Know how to use everything on this list.

If you see another bicyclist stopped, ask if he or she needs help. Maybe someone will do the same for you, but don't count on it: be prepared to self-rescue.

Essential
- Allen wrench set (most bikes use metric bolts, but check yours)
- Cash and ID
- Chain tool (more important if you are mountain biking)
- Food (for longer rides)
- Lights (if riding after dark)
- Map
- Patch kit (replace when needed, as old glue can dry out)
- Premoistened hand wipes (if you need to put a slipped chain back on, you'll be glad you brought them)
- Pump or CO2 cartridge and injector
- Spare tube
- Tire levers

Recommended
- Biking gloves (padded gloves absorb road vibrations and protect your palms in the event of a fall)
- Biking shorts (same as the gloves, but for a different part of your body)
- Cell phone (as long as you don't rely on it to get you out of a tight spot)
- Compass (especially useful for off-road riding)
- Insect repellent (more important for off-road rides in the woods)
- Spare clothing
- Sunglasses or eye protection (essential if you wear contact lenses; nothing's worse than dirt, grit, or a piece of glass in your eye)

Additional
- Bike lock (you never know when you might want or need to leave your bike somewhere)
- Dry clothes (to change into)
- Duct tape (it holds the universe together)
- Extra water and food
- First-aid kit
- Oil and chain lubricant
- Rags or towels (if it's raining or muddy, you'll want to wipe off your frame and tires)
- Sunscreen and lip balm
- Tools (wrenches, a multitool with screwdrivers and a blade, spoke wrench)

MAINE

© CHRIS BERNARD

BEST BIKE RIDES

Summers are blisteringly hot, winters oppressively

cold. Spring brings mud, and a running joke that the state bird is the black fly. So why do so many people love Maine? Start riding these routes and you'll figure it out fast. From the sandy beaches and rocky coastlines in the eastern part of the state to the mountains in the west, and including all the woods, forests, fields, and farmlands in between, Maine is vast, Maine is beautiful, and Maine offers something different at every turn.

It's almost as big as the other five New England states put together. And yet, the population of the entire state is about that of the city of Philadelphia, which makes Maine a good place to get away from crowds and traffic. In fact, even Mainers get away; it's common practice for locals to maintain what they call a "camp" – anything ranging from a rustic shack to a plush cabin, as long as it's in another part of the state – to visit in the summer. You know, some place to get away from the place everyone else goes to get away.

In general, Maine's roads are minimally trafficked and in that way, they're good for cyclists. But long winters wreak havoc on road surfaces, and with such a big state, maintenance crews can't always keep up. Expect some broken pavement, which is worth it for the reward of riding in remote, beautiful places. If you're an off-road cyclist, you've also come to the right state. While Maine offers several options for mountain biking or off-road touring, there are many more than any one guide can cover.

These rides sample a variety of the state's different geographical regions, and if you have time to do them all, you're in for a treat. But because the state is so big, consider weekend trips that piece together different rides in the same region, giving you more time on the bike and less time in the car.

You can wake with the sun on Quoddy Point and be the first person in the United States to do so. This winding ride takes in some of the dramatic coastline and the notoriously rustic back roads for which Maine is famous. Tour the rolling hills around the state capital, past apple orchards and ponds, or leave Freeport, an outlet shopper's paradise, for a ride that visits both the geographic oddity Desert of Maine and the land's end at Casco Bay. Roll for hours on the long tour of potato country in the north, known for its Acadian heritage, or on the much less intimidating – though no less pleasing – Kennebec River Rail Trail along the river through artsy downtown Hallowell.

The mountain bike trails at Bradbury Mountain offer some of the best riding in the state, if not the region. For flatter trails that are no less challenging, check out the unmaintained network of rides in the woods behind the Goodwill-Hinckley School in Fairfield.

Take your time exploring the beaches and lighthouses of southern Maine on the Five Lights, Six Beaches ride or try the Scarborough Marsh route along the East Coast Greenway. Or spend a weekend in Acadia National Park, poking along the unintimidating, scenic carriage roads. The park and nearby downtown Bar Harbor can be crazy-crowded during the summer, so try visiting in late spring, when the weather's good but the tourist season is just warming up.

Better yet, visit in the fall when the foliage sets the landscape ablaze, the nights are cool, and the bugs are less of a menace. In the words of Maine's state slogan, that's "the way life should be."

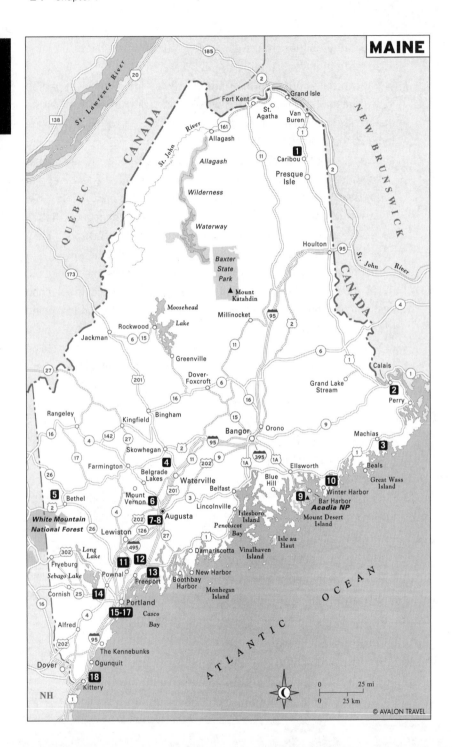

RIDE NAME	DIFFICULTY	DISTANCE	TIME	ELEVATION	PAGE
1 St. John Valley Tour	4	90.4 mi	8 hr	2,526 ft	26
2 Baring Division Trail	2	12.5 mi	3 hr	449 ft	30
3 As East As It Gets	4	90.1 mi	8 hr	1,657 ft	33
4 Hinckley Schoolyard Trails	3	8 mi	2 hr	144 ft	37
5 Grafton Notch Loop	5	66.8 mi	5 hr	2,665 ft	41
6 Summerhaven ATV Loop	3	6 mi	1 hr	283 ft	45
7 Capitol Hills Route	4	59.8 mi	4.5 hr	2,051 ft	49
8 Kennebec River Rail Trail	1	13.2 mi	1.5 hr	100 ft	53
9 Carriage Roads	2	21-28 mi	2.5 hr	256 ft	56
10 Schoodic Peninsula	2	12.8 mi	2 hr	402 ft	60
11 Bradbury Mountain	2-4	7.0 mi	2 hr	457 ft	63
12 Flying Point Loop	3	33 mi	3-4 hr	1,447 ft	67
13 College to Coast: Brunswick Scenic	2	31.2 mi	2 hr	548 ft	71
14 Mountain Division Trail	1	7 mi	1 hr	258 ft	74
15 Five Lights, Six Beaches	3	38.8 mi	3 hr	489 ft	77
16 Peaks Island Loop	1	4 mi	1 hr	96 ft	82
17 Scarborough Marsh Mellow	2	27.2 mi	2.5 hr	243 ft	86
18 The Big A	3	27.7 mi	2.5 hr	692 ft	91

■ ST. JOHN VALLEY TOUR
Caribou, Van Buren, and Madawaska

PAVED ROAD WITH MINIMAL TRAFFIC

Difficulty: 4   **Total Distance:** 90.4 miles

Riding Time: 8 hours   **Elevation Gain:** 2,526 feet

Summary: A long and winding tour through northern Maine's "Big Sky" countryside, this ride can be done in a day or as a comfortable overnight trip.

In the 16th century, French settlers were drawn to the fertile lands of Acadia—now known as Nova Scotia. In 1755, the English government scattered these settlers in what has come to be known as the Great Upheaval, or Le Grand Dérangement, deporting as many as 7,000 Acadians. Thousands died before they reached their destinations, others fled to Quebec or hid in the countryside, and many more died trying to survive the harsh winter that followed.

Some settlers migrated south of the border, to southern New England, the Carolinas, and Louisiana (where "Cajun" is an elided form of "Acadian"), and some settled in northern Maine's St. John Valley, where the Acadian presence and tradition remains strong.

The ride starts at the park and ride on Herschel Street in Caribou. Heading north from Caribou, in Aroostook County, this ride offers cyclists the opportunity to learn more about the Acadians at locations including the Musée Culturel du Mont-Carmel (P.O. Box 150, Lille, ME 04746, www.nps.gov/maac) and the 18th-century Acadian Village (US-1, Van Buren, ME 04785, 207/868-5042), Maine's largest historic site. Split the route in half and stay at one of the local accommodations to experience Acadian hospitality.

History aside, this ride traverses rural acres of potato fields, runs along the shores of several lakes, and tours through a handful of towns and villages. Traffic is light, and the pavement is more or less smooth, though this far north, that can change depending on the severity of the previous winter.

Services are available in Caribou and at several stops along the route. Bicycle services are available at The Ski Shop (31 Main Street, Van Buren, ME 04785, 207/868-2737). Carbon-fiber Argus bicycles are manufactured by hand in Van Buren (287 Champlain Street, Van Buren, ME 04785, 207/868-2200).

For more information, contact the Caribou Chamber of Commerce and Industry, 24 Sweden Street, Caribou, ME 04736, 207/493-4233, www.cariboumaine.net/aboutus.html.

Options

If you want to ride the area but don't have 90 miles in your legs, take a 33-mile ride that visits Stockholm village, home of the Stockholm Historical Society Tri-Cultural Museum (Main Street, Stockholm, ME 04783, 207/896-5759). At Mile 14 of the main route, turn right on Stockholm Road and travel 3.4 miles. Turn left on Jemtland Road, and follow it for 4 miles. Turn right on US-1 and rejoin the main route at Mile 82.

Locals' Tip: You pedaled hard. Reward yourself with an oversized burger at the Irish Setter Pub (710 Main Street, Presque Isle, ME 04769, 207/764-5400).

Places to Stay: Accommodations are available halfway through this route. The Auberge du Lac (Birch Point Road, RR #1, Box 142-1, St. David, ME 04773, 207/728-6047, www.mainerec.com/auberge.shtml) is a reasonably priced bed-and-breakfast with private rooms overlooking Long Lake. To reach it from Mile 45, turn right onto Birch Point Road and travel 1.5 miles.

Camping is available at Lakeview Restaurant and Camping Resort (9 Lakeview Drive, St. Agatha, ME 04772, 207/543-6331, www.lakeviewrestaurant.biz); turn left at Mile 39 onto Flat Mountain/Back Settlement Road.

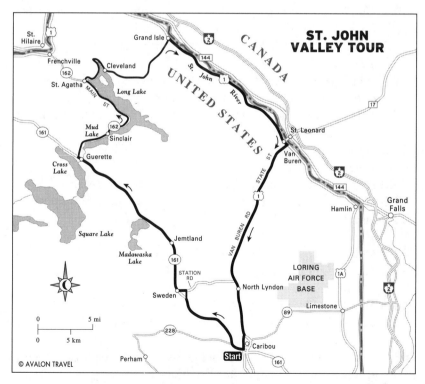

In Caribou, try the Caribou Inn and Convention Center (19 Main Street, Caribou, ME 04736, 207/498-3733, www.caribouinn.com).

Driving Directions

From Bangor, take I-95 North 118 miles north to exit 302 (US-1 toward Houlton/Presque Isle). Turn left at North Street/US-1 to Caribou. In Caribou, turn left at Fort Street, right at Main Street/ME-164, and left onto Herschel Street/ME-161. The route begins at the park and ride, which is on your left.

Route Directions

0.0 Turn LEFT out of the parking lot onto Herschel Street, then LEFT on Prospect Street at a stop sign.

0.2 Turn RIGHT at stop sign on Sweden Street (ME-161).

8.1 Bear RIGHT on Old Route 161; follow signs to New Sweden.

8.8 Turn LEFT at stop sign on Station Road and go 0.5 mile to ME-161. Turn RIGHT at the stop sign and climb the hill for scenic views; retrace your route back to the intersection.

9.3 Turn RIGHT at stop sign onto ME-161. Cross the Little Madawaska River; then Madawaska Lake will be on your left.

14.0 OPTION: Turn RIGHT on Stockholm Road and follow option directions.

17.5 Public boat access to Madawaska Lake. *Turn left for a place to stop, including picnic tables and a convenience store.*

27.1 At Cross Lake, turn RIGHT on ME-162 and ride past Mud Lake on your RIGHT. Enter the village of Sinclair.

31.2 Turn LEFT at stop sign, staying on ME-162 to follow the northern shore of Long Lake.

38.1 Public boat access on the right. *Picnic tables and restroom available.*

38.8 Enter village of St. Agatha. *All services except bicycle repair available.*

39.0 Turn RIGHT on Cleveland Road. *Campground and restaurant available.*

42.5 Make a sharp RIGHT to stay on Cleveland Road.

43.0 Bear RIGHT on Cove Road/Beaulieu Road, which follows the lakeshore.

45.3 Turn RIGHT on Lavertu Road. You're now surrounded by Maine's seemingly endless potato fields, known as Maine's "Big Sky" country. *Accommodations available.*

48.2 Continue STRAIGHT through intersection at Caron Road. Lavertu Road becomes Morneault Road at this point.

51.0 Continue STRAIGHT at four-way intersection, staying on Morneault Road.

52.7 Turn RIGHT at stop sign onto US-1 South. For the next 30 miles or so, you're hugging the Canadian border.

65.6 Enter Van Buren; the Acadian Village is on the right. *All services available in Van Buren. Campgrounds and supplies available in St. Leonard, New Brunswick, Canada, directly across the river from Van Buren.*

69.0 Turn RIGHT on US-1.

82.3 Recreation picnic area on the left, offering scenic views.

88.5 Turn RIGHT on Old Van Buren Road.

89.0 Turn RIGHT on Main Street.

90.0 Turn RIGHT on Herschel Street. Return to start.

90.4 END at parking area.

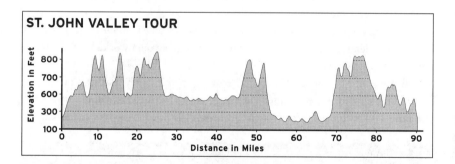

2 BARING DIVISION TRAIL   BEST ◖
Moosehorn National Wildlife Refuge, Baring

DIRT ROADS, PAVED ROAD WITH MINIMAL TRAFFIC

Difficulty: 2   **Total Distance:** 12.5 miles

Riding Time: 3 hours   **Elevation Gain:** 449 feet

Summary: Quiet dirt and gravel trails wind through a remote wildlife refuge, mixing fun with abundant scenic views and opportunities to see wildlife.

Explore the 17,000-plus acres of Moosehorn National Wildlife Refuge on 50 miles of vehicle-free dirt roads. The refuge is split in two, with a northern section (Baring) and a southern one (Edmunds). This short route begins at the Baring Division headquarters, where a well-stocked information kiosk has helpful maps, wildlife checklists, and brochures. The wide dirt roads take you through both woodlands and wetlands and past several ponds and streams with good opportunities to see birds, beavers, and otters.

Mountain bikes are overkill here, but a cyclocross bike is about ideal. The trails rarely challenge, although the soft surface can give you a workout, and they're plenty fast if you want them to be.

But you might not want them to be. If you pedal slowly and stop often, you could see leopard frogs, painted turtles, river otters, muskrat, white-tailed deer, moose, and even black bear. Watch for the rare American woodcock, bald eagles,

© CHRIS BERNARD

Riders are given a sense of what's in store for them right from the get-go when riding the Baring Division Trail.

ospreys, owls, warblers, and dozens of other species that use the refuge as a breeding area and migration rest stop. Early morning or late afternoon riders are most likely to encounter wildlife. Midday, you'll see more black flies and mosquitoes than anything else—bring insect repellent.

These trails are off the beaten path and probably aren't worth the considerable drive for the biking alone. That said, combine the biking with the scenic and wildlife-viewing opportunities, and you've got a trip worth taking.

The refuge is open during daylight hours; the office is open 7:30 A.M.–4 P.M. on weekdays. For more information, contact the Moosehorn National Wildlife Refuge, R.R. 1, Box 202, Suite 1, Baring, ME 04694, 207/454-7161, http://moosehorn.fws.gov.

Options

At Mile 0.54, turn left onto Dudley Swamp Loop for a short single-track loop with a scenic view of Dudley Swamp. There's one short steep downhill and one short set of stairs to climb.

In all, Moosehorn offers 50 miles of trails and roads closed to vehicles, so cyclists seeking longer routes can piece them together with patient exploration and refuge-provided maps. This part of Maine also offers plenty of good long-distance road rides, and those so inclined can cobble together a weekend getaway that includes several varied rides—including Summerhaven ATV Loop, which begins an hour or so south.

Locals' Tip: Because of the remoteness of Moosehorn, the best tip for meals is to pack a good lunch and a cooler full of drinks to keep in your vehicle.

Places to Stay: Nearby Calais, the eighth-busiest United States–Canada border crossing, has shopping and accommodations. Places to stay include the Greystone bed-and-breakfast (13 Calais Avenue, Calais, ME 04619, 207/454-2848) and the International Motel (626 Main Street, Calais, ME 04619, 800/336-7515). For more information, go to www.visitcalais.com.

Driving Directions

From Calais, take US-1 north for 3.3 miles. Turn left onto Charlotte Road and drive 2.5 miles to the main entrance to the National Wildlife Refuge headquarters on the right. The parking lot is a half-mile in on a bumpy dirt road and there are public restrooms, water, and a picnic table. Supplies are available in Calais.

Route Directions

0.0 ENTER trail through gate near information kiosk to left of park headquarters.

0.2 Turn RIGHT onto Barn Meadow Road, heading slightly downhill.

0.5 OPTION: Turn left for Dudley Swamp Loop.

1.6 Turn RIGHT again, onto Barn Meadow Extension. You'll come to the bottom of the hill and start a slight climb, with wetlands to your left. *This is a good place to see wildlife.*

2.5 Turn RIGHT onto wide road, still climbing slightly.

3.2 Turn RIGHT, up slight ascent, then leveling out. Stay STRAIGHT on main road, ignoring intersections and side trails.

4.8 Make a sharp RIGHT, followed by a sharp LEFT. This slight descent crosses a small wetland, and depending on the time of year, you may get wet. *Watch for birds.*

5.9 Turn RIGHT up a small climb, staying with the main road.

8.9 Turn LEFT. There's a gravel pit to your left, and a small stream to your right. You'll pass through more wetlands.

10.5 Stay STRAIGHT, doubling back on a road you traveled earlier.

11.2 Stay STRAIGHT. There's a gravel pit to your right, and you'll be going slightly uphill. When the road ends, take a sharp RIGHT and a quick LEFT.

12.5 END at trailhead.

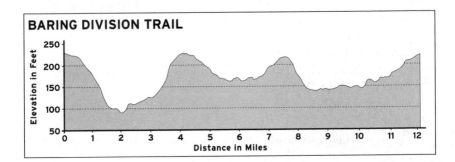

3 AS EAST AS IT GETS   BEST 🅒
Machias, Lubec, and Quoddy Head State Park

PAVED ROADS, MINIMAL TO MODERATE TRAFFIC,
SOME UNPAVED SECTIONS

Difficulty: 4   **Total Distance:** 90.1 miles

Riding Time: 8 hours   **Elevation Gain:** 1,657 feet

Summary: This long, flat ride travels through rural and coastal areas to the country's easternmost point.

This roving ride explores the diverse landscape of Washington County, beginning in downtown Machias, a postcard of a town that's home to one of the University of Maine campuses. From there it travels mostly rural roads to the easternmost point in the continental United States.

A short trip to the sea ends at the famously candy-striped West Quoddy Head Light, keeping watch over Quoddy Narrows, with views of Canada. The photogenic lighthouse was built in 1858 and automated 130 years later.

From Quoddy, the route hugs the dramatically rocky coast much of the way back to Machias, offering a flat ride with lots to see and plenty of ground to cover. To make this a two-day trip, stay overnight in the town of Lubec, on the Canadian border. Visit the Roosevelt Campobello International Park on Campobello Island,

The candy-striped West Quoddy Head Light is a popular, much-photographed piece of the Maine landscape.

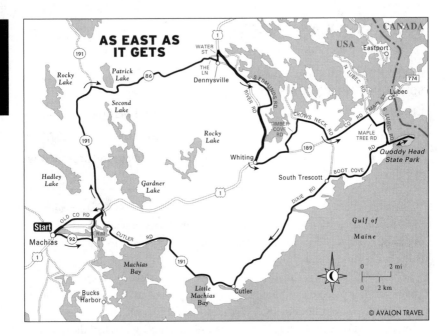

New Brunswick, once the summer residence of President Franklin D. Roosevelt. If you stay overnight in Lubec, you'll see the sunrise before anyplace else in the United States.

Campobello Island sits at the entrance to Passamaquoddy Bay, within the Bay of Fundy, and has its own lighthouse—East Quoddy Light. Though part of Canada, it's connected to Maine by the Roosevelt Bridge. Cyclists who spend time there will find fields of wildflowers, windswept beaches, and lots of fresh seafood. Note that U.S. citizens crossing into Canada are now required to show a passport or another acceptable form of identification.

The Machias Wild Blueberry Festival is held each August in Machias; consider planning your ride to coincide.

This route is a variation of one recommended by the Maine Department of Transportation. For more information, visit the Maine Department of Transportation website at www.exploremaine.org.

Options

If you don't have the legs or the time for this near-century ride, there's no reason not to see the sights. By following US-1 north out of Machias, you can cut the trip nearly in half—no one will judge you. You can also park in Lubec and cobble together a series of shorter rides to West Quoddy and Cutler Cove.

This ride is within reasonable driving distance of Baring Division Trail,

Carriage Roads, and Schoodic Peninsula if you want to make a long weekend of different routes.

Locals' Tip: With nearly 100 miles in your legs, don't feel guilty about the butter you dip your lobster in at the unpretentious Helen's (28 Main Street, Machias, ME 04654, 207/255-8423), where there's a good chance your waitstaff are students at the university. Try the desserts, which favor wild local berries.

Places to Stay: In Machias, hotels include the Bad Little Falls Inn (4 Elm Street, Machias, ME 04654, 207/255-4739, www.badlittlefallsinn.com). If you want to stay in Lubec, the unassuming Cohill's Inn (7 Water Street, Lubec, ME 04652, 207/733-4300, http://cohillsinn.com) offers reasonable rates, rooms with views, and an on-site Irish pub.

Driving Directions

From I-95 North, take exit 182A and merge onto I-395 East, toward ME-15/Bangor-Brewer. Drive 5 miles and take exit 6A, US-1 toward Bar Harbor. Follow US-1 for 83 miles. US-1 becomes Main Street in Machias. A municipal parking area is on your left just before the merge with Court Street.

Route Directions

0.0 From the parking lot, turn LEFT. At the stop sign, turn RIGHT onto US-1 and cross the bridge.

0.2 Make a sharp LEFT on Elm Street/ME-92, following signs to Machiasport.

3.2 Turn LEFT on Rim Road. Stay RIGHT after crossing the Machias River, and turn RIGHT onto US-1.

5.6 Turn LEFT on Jacksonville Road/ME-191.

16.0 Turn RIGHT on ME-86 and ride past Patrick Lake.

25.2 Bear RIGHT on unnamed road, and turn RIGHT on Water Street. Turn LEFT on Old Route 1 across river. Take immediate LEFT onto River Road.

26.8 Turn RIGHT at US-1.

29.4 Turn LEFT on South Edmunds Road.

33.2 Turn LEFT on US-1. Pass the Little Augusta Wildlife Viewing Area.

37.5 In Whiting, turn LEFT on County Road/ME-189. Follow signs for Campobello Island.

40.1 Turn LEFT on Timber Cove Road.

42.7 Turn RIGHT on Crows Neck Road.

45.6 Turn LEFT at stop sign on ME-189. This road has moderate traffic and no shoulders.

49.0 Turn RIGHT on Maple Tree Road/South Lubec Road, following signs for Quoddy Head State Park. Option: Stay straight for the town of Lubec where *lodging and supplies are available.*

50.5 Turn RIGHT on Boot Cove Road.

52.2 Bear LEFT onto Quoddy Head Road in Quoddy Head State Park. West Quoddy Head Light is the easternmost point in the continental United States. From West Quoddy Head, retrace your route for 2 miles out of the park.

56.2 Make a sharp LEFT on Boot Cove Road. The ride passes through blueberry barrens. *There is public access and a trail to the beach at Hamilton Cove.*

61.6 Bear LEFT on Dixie Road/ME-191, and follow it into Cutler village. The road becomes Cutler Road/ME-191, and it hugs the coast for a long time. Scenic views throughout this section.

85.8 Turn LEFT onto US-1. Cross bridge. US-1 has moderate traffic and wide shoulders.

87.8 Bear RIGHT onto Old County Road.

89.2 Merge onto US-1/Court Street and cross bridge.

89.5 Bear LEFT onto Main Street.

90.1 END at parking area.

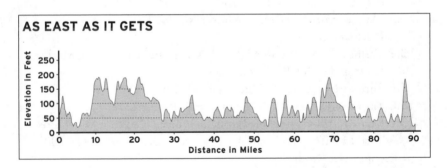

AS EAST AS IT GETS

4 HINCKLEY SCHOOLYARD TRAILS
Fairfield and Skowhegan

SINGLE-TRACK, DOUBLE-TRACK, FIRE ROADS

Difficulty: 3   **Total Distance:** 8 miles

Riding Time: 2 hours   **Elevation Gain:** 144 feet

Summary: Follow New England-style roots-and-rocks fire roads and single-track on this rarely technical, but often challenging ride.

Founded in 1889, the Good Will-Hinckley School for disadvantaged boys and girls has since suspended its boarding program because of financial concerns. The day program continues, and the sprawling, 2,450-acre campus—including a comprehensive trail system used infrequently by hikers, bikers, and snowshoers—remains open to the public.

The trail system, built in the first part of the 20th century, includes several walking-only trails as well as 25 miles of mountain bike trails. Mostly narrow double-track, these are typical New England roots-and-rocks trails. They can get muddy in spring and after rainy periods; they're better-suited to mountain bikes than cyclocross or hybrid bikes.

© CHRIS BERNARD

These trails can get muddy during the spring or a particularly rainy period, and you'll find them harboring ticks during the heat of the summer, so take precautions and enjoy yourself.

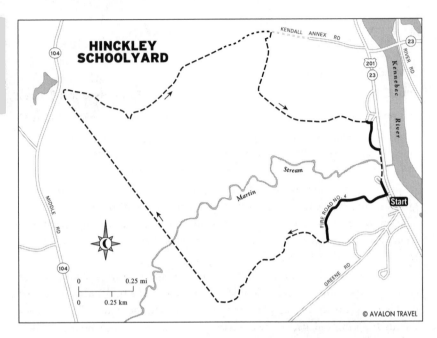

Though trail maps are available at the L. C. Bates Museum on campus, they are not detailed and not to scale. In addition, almost none of the trails are marked. That said, with a general sense of direction, it's difficult to get lost, though a compass or GPS will help.

Here's a little orientation to start out: The paved Middle Road and ME-201 border these trails to the west and east, as do Kendall Annex Road/Hoxie Road and Greene Road to the north and south. If you hit any of these roads, it's easy enough to piece together a route back to base. A power line corridor runs through the campus and intersects with Middle Road, creating an entry back onto campus and the trails system. When in doubt, you can always retrace your steps.

You'll see the occasional blaze marking trails, but they're not coded in any way that makes sense, and they seem to have been painted only halfheartedly at best. No matter, though—these trails are fun to ride, and if you've got even a minimal sense of adventure, you'll let your inner explorer loose to chart your own course.

For more information, contact the Good Will-Hinckley School, P.O. Box 159, ME-201, Hinckley, ME 04944, 207/238-4000, http://gwh.org.

Options

Looking for additional rides in the area? The region's rural nature makes for some phenomenal rides through farm country along the Kennebec River. The campus sits on ME-201, a flat-to-rolling ride with wide shoulders, and is home to a time trial race each year. Seeking something more hilly? Cross the river at the school, head left on River Road and right up Eaton Mountain Road, then turn right on ME-2 and right on Oak Pond Road to rejoin River Road, a 19-mile loop from the campus with a steep climb.

The Capitol Hills Route begins just a half-hour drive from here.

Locals' Tip: Oak Pond Brewery's (101 Oak Pond Road, Skowhegan, ME 04976, 207/474-3233, www.oakpondbrewery.com) 14-barrel system housed in a converted chicken barn is open for tours and always has six beers on tap. The brewery is located right on the option route.

Places to Stay: Nearby Waterville, home to Colby College, has a range of chain hotels, including the Hampton Inn (5 Kennedy Memorial Drive, Waterville, ME 04901, 207/873-0400). The Two Rivers Campground (ME-2, Skowhegan, ME 04976, 207/474-6482) is a short drive from the trailhead.

Driving Directions

From I-95, take exit 133 to Fairfield/Skowhegan. Travel north toward Skowhegan (in the opposite direction from Fairfield) on ME-201. Proceed about 5.5 miles to the Good Will-Hinckley School campus and park behind the Moody Chapel. The trail begins at the information kiosk with maps and trail info.

Route Directions

0.0 From Moody Chapel parking lot, take the dirt and gravel fire road (Fire Road No. 4) heading west, watching for the next trailhead (Trail No. 4, Airport Trail) on your right. The trail is not marked, but it is fairly obvious. Stay with the main trail until you hit a power line corridor.

1.9 Turn RIGHT on the power line corridor, crossing Martin Stream twice. This stream is rideable, but deep enough to make some want to carry their bikes.

3.9 Watch for the entrance to the next trail leg (No. 2, Muskrat Soup Trail) on the RIGHT, also unmarked. On that trail, follow the main trail heading north/northeast. The trail joins Kendall Annex Road/ Hoxie Road.

5.8 Watch for the entrance to the trail (No. 8, 40-Acre Field) on RIGHT. Follow it south/southeast, joining an unnamed paved road that's part of the Good Will-Hinckley campus.

7.3 Turn RIGHT on Pratt Drive. Follow Pratt Drive to Stanley Road, heading south, parallel to ME-201.

8.0 Turn RIGHT at Moody Chapel, and return to parking area.

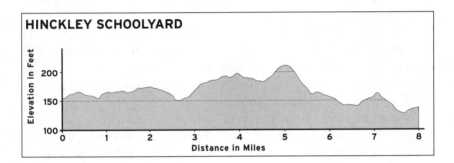

HINCKLEY SCHOOLYARD

5 GRAFTON NOTCH LOOP   BEST [
Bethel, Andover, and Rumford Point

PAVED ROADS WITH MINIMAL TRAFFIC

Difficulty: 5   **Total Distance:** 66.8 miles

Riding Time: 5 hours   **Elevation Gain:** 2,665 feet

Summary: Prepare yourself for a hilly, medium-distance route with panoramic payoffs atop endless climbs.

This is no ride for flatlanders. Neither is it an Alpine stage of the Tour de France, but if you're not used to climbing, you'll learn fast here. Snaking through the Mahoosuc range in western Maine, incorporating the twin peaks of Baldpate, the high point of Old Speck, and the plunging Screw Auger and Mother Walker waterfalls, this ride is a lot of up and down.

The ride begins in Bethel, once the site of an Abenaki village, on the Androscoggin River, and near the popular Sunday River ski area. You'll start on a wide-shouldered highway, but once you turn onto ME-26, everything changes. Traffic disappears. The scenery improves. And the road starts pointing uphill. Passing through protected areas, the trail touches on some true Maine wilderness—which means few services, but spectacular views, rural roads, a covered bridge, and a good chance of spotting moose.

You'll be tempted to descend East B Hill like a bottle rocket, and you should— you'll need your momentum for the climb that follows. A mile and a half long, the climb opens up into a beautiful stretch leading into the town of Andover, a good midway resting point, so don't give up hope.

From there, follow the winding Ellis River through the Lovejoy Covered Bridge, Maine's shortest, but still a scenic photo-op. With the big climbs behind you, the rest of the way is rolling hills with occasional mountain views.

Each year since 1983, the Trek Across Maine—a three-day, 180-mile ride across the state to raise money for the American Lung Association—has begun in Bethel and headed east, ending in the mid-coast region. Cyclists interested in participating can learn more at www.lungme.org.

For more information, contact the Bethel Area Chamber of Commerce, P.O. Box 1247, Bethel, ME 04217, 207/824-2282 or 800/442-5826, www.bethelmaine .com (9 A.M.–5 P.M. Mon.–Sat., noon–5 P.M. Sun.).

Options
If you're in the area and looking for a place to ride your mountain bike, the Sunday River Mountain Bike Park (P.O. Box 4500, Newry, ME 04261,

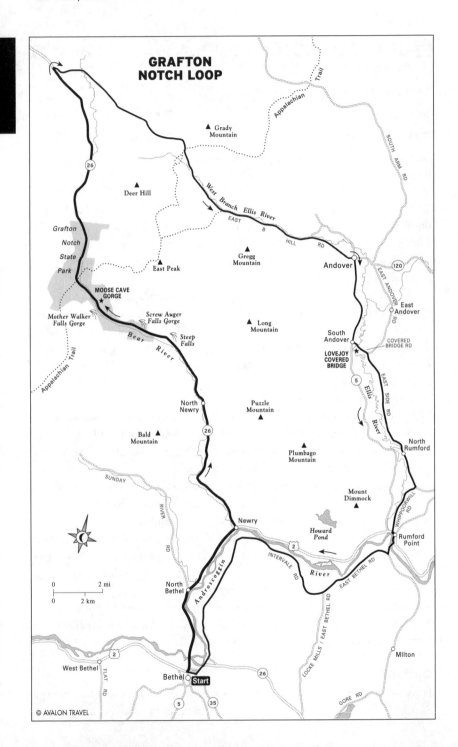

GRAFTON
NOTCH LOOP

© AVALON TRAVEL

207/824-3000, www.sundayriver.com) boasts 15 trails and 20 miles of lift-serviced riding. Terrain varies enough to accommodate everyone from beginners to experts, and rental bikes are available.

Locals' Tip: While in Bethel, grab a meal and start up a conversation with one of the staff at the Crossroads Diner (24 Mayville Road, Bethel, ME 04217, 207/824-3673), a local institution.

Places to Stay: The Briar Lea Inn (50 Mayville Road, Bethel, ME 04217, 207/824-4717) offers comfortable rooms, and the on-site Jolly Drayman, a traditional English pub, is a local hot spot. If you want to camp, try the Pleasant River Campground (800 West Bethel Road, Bethel, ME 04217, 207/836-2000, www.pleasantrivercampground.com), just off ME-26.

Driving Directions

From points north or south on the Maine Turnpike (I-95), take exit 63 in Gray to ME-26. Drive for 50 miles to Bethel. Continue on ME-26 and turn left onto Lincoln Street just before the intersection with US-2 and ME-5. Take an immediate left onto Cross Street and turn right into the Station Place parking lot for the Bethel Area Chamber of Commerce Visitor Information Center. Parking is free. You'll find toilets, water, and cue sheets for dozens of bicycle rides throughout the area. Supplies are available in Bethel and there's a bike shop in Rumford.

Route Directions

0.0 START from the visitor information center. Turn LEFT onto Cross Street and take an immediate RIGHT onto Lincoln Road.

0.1 Turn LEFT onto Parkway (ME-26).

0.2 Turn RIGHT onto ME-26/US-2/ME-5.

6.0 Turn LEFT onto ME-26.

14.2 *Access to Steep Falls, on the right.*

15.8 *Access to Screw Auger Falls Gorge, on the left.*

17.0 *Mother Walker Falls Gorge picnic area is on the right.*

17.8 *Moose Cave Gorge picnic area is on the right.*

27.0 Turn RIGHT onto East B Hill Road.

41.5 Turn RIGHT onto ME-120/ME-5. *Supplies available in Andover, also a good place to rest your legs and lungs.*

44.8 Turn LEFT onto Covered Bridge Road.

45.5 Turn RIGHT onto East Andover Road.

49.5 Turn LEFT onto Andover Road.

50.9 Turn RIGHT onto Whippoorwill Road.

52.8 Turn LEFT onto US-2/ME-5.

53.3 Turn RIGHT onto ME-232 (south) over bridge.

53.8 Turn RIGHT onto East Bethel Road.

56.9 Road curves to the left; go STRAIGHT on Intervale Road.

65.9 Turn RIGHT onto ME-26.

66.3 Turn RIGHT onto Parkway.

66.7 LEFT onto Lincoln Street followed by immediate LEFT onto Cross Street.

66.8 Turn RIGHT to return to parking lot.

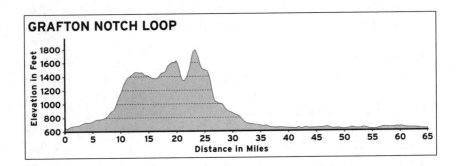

6 SUMMERHAVEN ATV LOOP
Augusta/Belgrade Lakes Region

DOUBLE-TRACK, ATV RUTS, GRAVEL AND SAND

Difficulty: 3   **Total Distance:** 6 miles

Riding Time: 1 hour   **Elevation Gain:** 283 feet

Summary: Grab your mountain bike for this fast double-track through woods and gravel pits – made even more challenging on cyclocross bikes.

Summerhaven is part of the Tyler Pond Wildlife Management Area, and it is maintained by the state as an all-terrain vehicle trail. Just over six miles of trails here swoop through woods, skirting sand and gravel pits, for a fun ride with optional stops at several small ponds.

Double-track or wider the whole way, these trails rarely become technical. They're suitable for nearly all riders, but a few spots require effort or concentration, and the occasional short, steep hill will test your low-end torque on loose surfaces.

This ride starts at an easy-to-miss dirt parking area (the sign marking the Tyler Pond Wildlife Management Area is usually covered by overgrown trees). The first part of the ride begins near the sign and shoots downhill. The banked, looping turns are a blast, and it's easy to build up speed. Don't get lulled into a sense of

Many of the trails at Summerhaven are double-track ATV trails pocked with ruts and grooves, making them chewed up, challenging, and great fun to ride.

complacency, though—the soft dirt trail is littered with loose stones, from grape-sized pebbles up to watermelon-worthy hazards.

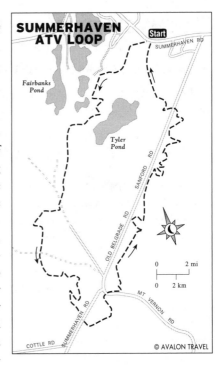

At a small clearing, turn left and, unless it's muddy (which it often is), the trails will turn sandy. They'll also start to turn uphill a bit, with lots of short and steep climbs. You'll be riding on loose gravel in places, but otherwise expect a lot of loose dirt with sections of sand and lots of mud.

Smack in the middle of the ride, you'll come upon a massive sandpit resembling the set from *Ishtar*. There's no good way through it, and no good way around it. The trick is to choose your line wisely and generate enough speed to "float." Or make your way through the unconnected trails along the rightmost rim of the pit to circumnavigate the sand. There are other small sand pits, and you'll cross several roads, most of which are rarely used or abandoned. Watch for gravel trucks, though, when crossing.

The last stretch back to the parking area is perhaps the most fun. After a short climb, the trails level out into a mostly flat, winding sprint through pretty woods. It's a good chance to blow some of the carbon out of your engine and put your legs and lungs to the test.

Trails are largely unmarked. Sporadic signage is maintained halfheartedly by snowmobile clubs and is often easy to miss. Generally, try to follow the main trail, which is well-worn by years of ATV use. There are a multitude of side trails, most of which will eventually rejoin the main trail or dead-end. Listen for approaching ATVs, and give them room to pass.

There are some loose rocks on the trail, and during rainy periods, Summerhaven gets muddy; the trails are closed during the muddiest time in early spring. In the fall, locals use the sandpits to sight in hunting rifles and shoot sporting clays. Use caution, or restrict rides to spring and summer.

For more information, contact Belgrade Lakes Region, P.O. Box 72W, Belgrade, ME 04917, 207/495-2744 or 888/895-2744, www.belgradelakesmaine.com.

Options

The roads heading out past Summerhaven toward Belgrade offer scenic opportunities to extend your ride or to pair it with a longer road ride. The Belgrade Lakes see plenty of tourists during the warmer seasons, and if you're so inclined, you can combine riding with paddling, fishing, golfing, or bird-watching for a getaway weekend. Capitol Hills Route and Kennebec River Rail Trail are a 10-minute drive from Summerhaven, and Hinckley Schoolyard Trails is just over a half-hour north.

Locals' Tip: Start with breakfast at the Sunset Grill (4 West Road, Belgrade, ME 04917, 207/495-2439), a uniquely small-town joint with greasy breakfasts, cheap lobster dinners, and cold drinks.

Places to Stay: Augusta offers plenty of economical accommodations, and Belgrade is full of B&Bs, inns, and campgrounds.

Driving Directions

From points north or south, take the Maine Turnpike (I-95) to Augusta. Take exit 112 to ME-27/Civic Center Drive, the Belgrade Lakes exit. Drive north on ME-27 for 3 miles and take a left onto Summerhaven Road. Bear right where Sanford Road splits to the left, and just under 1 mile from ME-27, turn left onto the gravel access road marked with a boat launch sign. Park in the lot on the left. Accommodations, shopping, and supplies are available just off the highway in Augusta, and bike shops are in nearby Augusta and Farmington.

Route Directions

0.0 START toward Summerhaven Road and turn LEFT at the marked trail before the pavement begins.

0.4 Turn LEFT at the intersection.

0.9 Turn LEFT uphill (follow directional arrows on signage).

1.3 Follow series of downhill bermed turns until LEFT turn at trail to Fairbanks Pond.

1.5 Bear LEFT at T intersection past wetlands on your left; climb a sandy section of road up to loose gravel. Bear RIGHT at the fork, following the marked arrows, instead of continuing straight into the woods. You'll cross a small sandpit and head straight into a climb. Avoid the steep climb to the right (unless you want a challenge).

1.9 Turn RIGHT at the T intersection with rocky, gravel, onto Mount Vernon Road. Bear LEFT immediately, and then LEFT again, staying with the main trail.

2.3 CROSS a gravel road used by heavy trucks. Continue up the short hill "paved" with concrete blocks for erosion control.

2.5 Turn RIGHT at T intersection.

2.9 CROSS Old Belgrade Road and continue following ATV trail.

3.3 At the small gravel pit, continue STRAIGHT across access road and up sandy slope on other side.

3.4 CROSS Mount Vernon Road and stay on the ATV trail. Descend LEFT into the huge sandpit. Plot your own course, or piece together the short trails through the woods to the right of the pit.

4.0 At the far end of the sandpit, look for the trail signs entering the woods on the right. Take trail to the LEFT.

4.8 Turn RIGHT with the trail, and veer LEFT immediately. There's a small gravel pit to your LEFT.

5.1 Turn LEFT at the T intersection, and ignore the upcoming right that breaks off from the ATV trail. Continue across Sanford Road and re-enter the woods. This last stretch is the fastest and perhaps the most fun portion of the entire ride.

6.0 END at parking area.

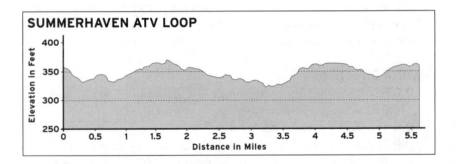

7 CAPITOL HILLS ROUTE
Augusta, Manchester, Winthrop, and Hallowell

PAVED ROADS WITH MINIMAL TRAFFIC

Difficulty: 4   **Total Distance:** 59.8 miles

Riding Time: 4.5 hours   **Elevation Gain:** 2,051 feet

Summary: This mostly rural, hilly route travels along smooth-to-rough pavement, with several good lakeside lunch stops.

This extended loop leaves Capitol Park in Augusta, the easternmost state capital in the United States, and tours the picturesque lakes region to the west, passing through Manchester, Winthrop, and Hallowell. Road conditions are generally good, and the entire route is paved save for one short section of road; expect broken pavement, dirt and sand, uneven surfaces, and soft shoulders. You won't see much traffic except for the occasional main road, which you'll cross to connect to the more rural roads that make up the lion's share of this route.

While most of the route is undulating hills, there are several longer climbs and a handful of short, steep climbs; many pay off with views from the top. Put in the effort, and you're rewarded with vistas of Cobbosseecontee Lake, Kennebec River, and undulating farms and orchards. The route offers several opportunities for scenic, shaded lakeside stops, and a handful of convenient stores and restaurants, but no bike shops. The nearest are Kennebec Bike and Ski in Farmington and Auclair Cycle and Ski in Augusta.

This route is a variation on a bicycle tour recommended by Maine's Department of Transportation. For more information, contact the Bicycle Coalition of Maine, 341 Water Street, Augusta, ME 04330, 207/623-4511, www.bike maine.org.

Options

The Kennebec River Rail Trail intersects this route on Water Street in Hallowell.

Beginning and ending near the Maine State House, this ride follows the rolling hills of the quiet roads surrounding the state capitol.

© KIM BERNARD

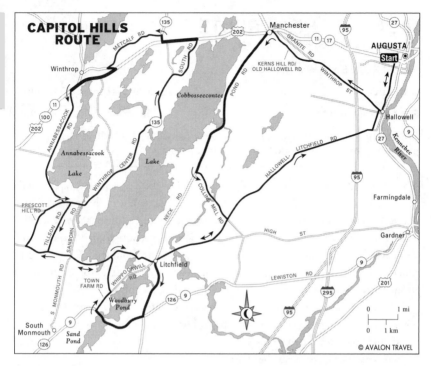

Cyclists seeking an easy cool down to their ride can follow the rail trail south along the Kennebec River.

Locals' Tip: Start your ride with breakfast at the famous A1 Diner (3 Bridge Street, Gardiner, ME 04345, 207/582-4804) in Gardiner.

Places to Stay: Augusta offers plenty of hotels, including the Senator Inn Best Western (284 Western Avenue, Augusta, ME 04330, 877/772-2224, www.senatorinn.com) just off the highway—you may see its owners pedaling their tandem bike on this route. There are several bed-and-breakfasts along the route, including Maple Hill Farm Inn (11 Inn Road, Hallowell, ME 04347, 207/622-2708, www.maplebb.com). Campgrounds include Birches Family Campground (Norris Point Road, Litchfield, ME 04350, 207/268-4330, www.thebirches.com).

Driving Directions

From I-95, take exit 30B. Veer right off the highway and head east on ME-202 (Western Avenue) toward downtown Augusta. Enter the rotary and exit south onto ME-201 (State Street). Take a left at the second set of lights at the far end of Capitol Park. Parking is available at Capitol Park and at the Kennebec River Rail trailhead on Water Street.

Route Directions

0.0 START at the intersection of Sewall and Capitol Streets immediately west of the State House. Continue south to Winthrop Street (Sewall Street becomes 2nd Street).

1.4 Turn RIGHT on Winthrop Street.

4.2 Turn LEFT on Kerns Hill Road. Continue to Manchester.

5.8 Turn LEFT on ME-202/11/100.

5.9 Turn LEFT on Pond Road (becomes Neck Road). Stop for views of Cobbossee Lake.

9.3 Turn RIGHT on Neck Road.

11.2 Turn LEFT on Collins Mill Road.

13.0 Turn RIGHT on Litchfield Road.

13.8 Bear RIGHT on Litchfield Road.

15.1 Litchfield Road becomes Hallowell Road at Cobbossee Stream crossing.

15.8 Bear LEFT on Hallowell Road and continue to Litchfield.

17.7 Turn RIGHT on ME-126/9. Scenic views of Woodbury Pond. *Restaurant and convenience store available.*

19.4 Turn RIGHT on Town Farm Road.

20.1 Turn LEFT on Pease Hill Road (a dirt road).

21.3 Turn LEFT on Cobbosseecontee Road.

24.1 Turn RIGHT on Prescott Hill Road. Scenic views of apple orchards.

25.4 Turn RIGHT on ME-135 (Winthrop Center Road). *Scenic views of Annabessacook and Cobbossee Lakes.*

32.1 Turn RIGHT on South Road.

33.6 Turn LEFT on ME-202/11/100.

34.6 Turn RIGHT on ME-135 (Stanley Road).

34.8 Turn LEFT on Metcalf Road for a long climb. *Scenic views of Maranacook Lake offer a good place to stop and rest.*

36.9 Turn LEFT on Main Street.

37.2 Turn RIGHT on ME-202/11/100.

38.7 Turn LEFT on Annabessacook Road.

41.0 Continue STRAIGHT at intersection. Road becomes Waugan Road.

42.7 Turn LEFT on ME-135.

42.8 Turn RIGHT on Tillson Road.

44.5 Turn LEFT on Cobbosseecontee Road (becomes Hard Scrabble Road).

48.1 Turn LEFT on Hallowell Road (becomes Litchfield Road at Cobbossee Stream crossing).

56.5 Litchfield Road curves sharply LEFT and becomes Middle Street.

56.9 Turn RIGHT on Central Street, and go three blocks to 2nd Street. Turn LEFT on 2nd Street and follow back to starting point.

59.8 END.

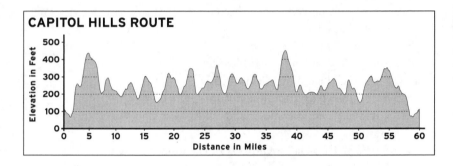

8 KENNEBEC RIVER RAIL TRAIL
Augusta, Hallowell, Farmington, and Gardiner

PAVED ROADS WITH MINIMAL TRAFFIC

Difficulty: 1   **Total Distance:** 13.2 miles

Riding Time: 1.5 hours   **Elevation Gain:** 100 feet

Summary: This easy multiuse path follows the Kennebec River, detouring through artsy downtown Hallowell.

The Kennebec River Rail Trail begins on Water Street in the state capital of Augusta, next door to the Bicycle Coalition of Maine, which was instrumental in the trail's development. The trail offers stunning views of Maine's longest river as it follows the current past the Charles Bullfinch—designed State House, through quaint downtown Hallowell—Maine's smallest city—along the train tracks through Farmington, and into Gardiner, where it ends unceremoniously in a grocery store parking lot.

The trail alternates between paved and hard-packed stone dust, and it is wheelchair-accessible throughout, making it suitable for smooth-tired road bikes. In Hallowell, you'll have to ride on the road for about a half mile. There is a bike lane, but the road can be in tough shape after a rough Maine winter, so ride cautiously.

After Hallowell the trail leaves the road and hugs the train tracks, which are no longer in use. The rest of the trail is paved and offers many spots to stop along

The rail trail runs along the Kennebec River through artsy downtown Hallowell, offering several opportunities for cyclists to stop and take in their surroundings.

the river. Watch for jumping fish and the birds that line the banks to feed on them. The trail also winds through the edges of Vaughn Woods, a cooperatively managed 166-acre private parcel known to locals as "Hobbit Land" because of the miniature stone tables and chairs hidden throughout. You'll pass a waterfall cascading over a granite face as you head into Farmingdale and then Gardiner, where the trail again parallels the busy main road, separated from traffic by a fence. The trail crosses side streets at several intersections, requiring you to stop at marked crossings and pay attention to traffic.

Because of the railway, the trail is flat along its length. It can be heavily used, especially during lunch hours. Expect to share with pedestrians, dog walkers (leash law in effect), in-line skaters, and baby carriages.

The trail will eventually become one segment of the East Coast Greenway. On the trail in Farmingdale you'll find Kennebec Bike and Ski (357 Maine Avenue, Farmingdale, ME 04333, 207/621-4900, http://kennebecbikeski.com), offering ride-in repairs for bicyclists who encounter mechanical difficulties en route. For more information on the Kennebec River Rail Trail, visit www.krrt.org.

Options

Cyclists seeking a challenge can leave the trail in Hallowell and climb Howard Hill via Central or Winthrop Streets, past buildings and homes dating back to the late 1700s and early 1800s. The hill is part of the Capitol Hills Route, which begins less than a mile from the trailhead for this ride.

Locals' Tip: The Liberal Cup (115 Water Street, Hallowell, ME 04347, 207/623-2739, www.theliberalcup.com), on the ride in downtown Hallowell, is known for its craft-brewed beer, but the food—including specials using fresh local ingredients and pub standards like shepherd's pie—is excellent.

Places to Stay: Accommodations in Augusta include the Senator Inn Best Western (284 Western Avenue, Augusta, ME 04330, 877/772-2224, www.senatorinn.com) just off the highway, the Maple Hill Farm Inn (11 Inn

Road, Hallowell, ME 04347, 207/622-2708, www.maplebb.com), and the Birches Family Campground (Norris Point Road, Litchfield, ME 04350, 207/268-4330, www.thebirches.com).

Driving Directions

The Kennebec River Rail Trail begins in Augusta and ends in Gardiner, and it's accessible at a number of points. From I-95, take exit 30B. Veer right off the highway and head east on ME-202 (Western Avenue) toward downtown Augusta. Enter the traffic circle and exit onto Grove Street (ME-104). After the fire station, turn right into the Water Street parking lot.

Route Directions

0.0 START at Water Street parking lot. (At Mile 0.8, you pass the sewage treatment plant. On hot summer days, hold your breath.)

1.8 Make a sharp RIGHT to exit Waterfront Park in Hallowell. CROSS at the corner of Water and Winthrop Streets and turn LEFT in the Water Street bike lane. *Stop in Hallowell for some ice cream or coffee or to check out the many antique and vintage shops.*

2.3 Trail leaves the road via well-marked on-ramp on RIGHT. Slight incline.

2.7 CROSS Greenville Street.

6.5 Trail ends in grocery store parking lot. *Restroom available inside.* TURN AROUND for return trip.

10.0 EXIT bike path. Trail rejoins road via off-ramp. CROSS Water Street at crosswalk and follow bike lane LEFT with traffic for 0.4 mile.

10.4 Trail leaves road via Waterfront Park on RIGHT. Follow 1.8 miles to starting point in Augusta.

13.2 END at parking area.

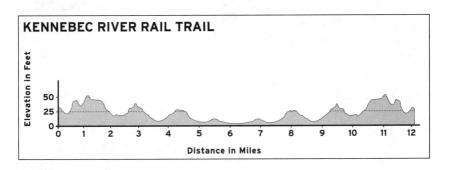

9 CARRIAGE ROADS   BEST [(
Mount Desert Island, Acadia National Park

DIRT AND GRAVEL ROADS

Difficulty: 2   **Total Distance:** 21-28 miles

Riding Time: 2.5 hours   **Elevation Gain:** 256 feet

Summary: Enjoy these nontechnical, vehicle-free, pressed gravel roads looping through gorgeous Acadia National Park.

Philanthropist John D. Rockefeller, Jr., ordered these carriage roads built as a gift to the people, and more than half a century later, they remain just that. Built between 1913 and 1940, these vehicle-free roads offer 45 miles of quiet, scenic, nondemanding riding throughout Acadia National Park on Mount Desert Island.

Of course, Rockefeller wanted to provide vehicle-free roads for horses and carriages, not bicycles, and you'll still see some equestrian activity on these trails. Not to worry—there's plenty of room. No single-track or double-track, these true roads are about 16 feet wide, and the flawlessly maintained broken-stone surfaces make them the best remaining example of the type of road commonly used at the turn of the 20th century. The surface is a little loose for skinny road tires, but there's nothing technical about this ride. A cyclocross bike or wide-tired hybrid is ideal.

© CHRIS BERNARD

The Acadia National Park carriage roads are well marked, well graded, and well maintained, making this one of New England's best rides.

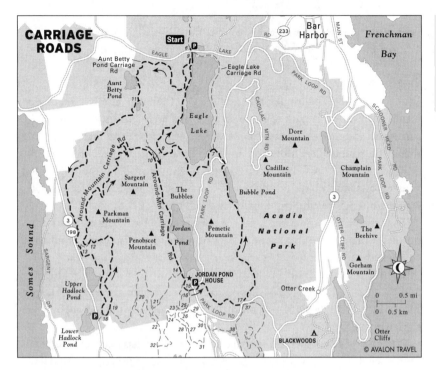

These roads are well-graded and rarely get steep. They're also well marked, with signposts at nearly every turn, and in addition to the stunning natural scenery, they offer photo opportunities with landmarks such as the 17 stone-faced bridges, each different in design, spanning the streams, waterfalls, roads, and cliffs throughout the trail system.

Parking is available at the trailhead, or park in downtown Bar Harbor and bike the short distance. Free Island Explorer shuttles also run from hotels and campgrounds from late June through Columbus Day.

This route starts at the north end of Eagle Lake and makes a big counterclockwise loop to the west and south. At Signpost 13 you'll face a short, steep climb, worth it for the ocean views from the top. Another steady incline comes between Signposts 21 and 14, but after that it's fairly smooth with some good downhills to Jordan Pond.

Bicyclists yield to other users, and the areas around Jordan Pond, Bubble Pond, and Eagle Lake can get crowded. Acadia is the second-most visited national park on the east coast, so try to visit in the off-season (spring and fall). In summer, ride as early in the morning as possible.

Trail maps are available at the visitor center on ME-3. The day-use fee is $20 per vehicle. For more information, contact the National Park Service, P.O. Box 177, Bar Harbor, ME 04609, 207/288-3388, www.nps.gov/acad.

Options

For a longer, more challenging ride, add the Day Mountain climb; this addition begins at the 17-mile mark of the main route and adds 7 miles. At Signpost 17, turn right, and then turn left at Signpost 38. Turn left again at Signpost 36 and follow this road up Day Mountain and back for an elevation gain of 328 feet.

Roadwise, the 27-mile Park Loop is easy riding and incredibly beautiful. Or test your legs and lungs on the north Atlantic coast's highest peak, 1,528-foot Cadillac Mountain, a 3.5-mile heart-pumping climb off the Park Loop Road.

The Schoodic Peninsula ride is just across Frenchman Bay, about an hour's drive. Spend the night in the area at one of the many campgrounds, hotels, or inns and combine the two rides for a weekend on the bike that's difficult to beat.

Locals' Tip: Take part in a tradition more than 100 years old by stopping at the Jordan Park House (Park Loop Road, Acadia National Park, Bar Harbor, ME 04605, 207/276-3316), just off the ride, for afternoon tea and popovers on the lawn.

Places to Stay: Bar Harbor, at the park's entrance, has many overnight options, including the Acacia House Hotel (6 High Street, Bar Harbor, ME 04609, 207/288-8122). Or stay in nearby Southwest Harbor at the Claremont Hotel (P.O. Box 137, Southwest Harbor, ME 04679, 800/244-5036). The National Park Service maintains two campgrounds on Mount Desert Island, Blackwoods and Seawall (for reservations, call 877/444-6777).

Driving Directions

From Ellsworth, take ME-3 to Mount Desert Island. In Bar Harbor, turn right onto ME-233 and drive 2.5 miles. You will pass the entrance to Park Loop Road. Look for the sign for Eagle Lake Carriage Road, and park at the boat ramp in the lot on the left side of the main road. There are restrooms and water in the parking area. Supplies and bike shops are available in Bar Harbor.

Route Directions

0.0 Take the trail to the right of the parking lot, near the restrooms, toward Aunt Betty Pond.

2.9 Turn RIGHT at Signpost 11.

6.2 Continue STRAIGHT at Signpost 13.

8.4 Turn LEFT at Signpost 18 and LEFT again at Signpost 19. CROSS two bridges and continue on trail.

9.7 Turn RIGHT at Signpost 12.

13.3 Turn RIGHT at Signpost 10 toward Jordan Pond.

16.0 Stay to the LEFT at the southern end of Jordan Pond at both Signpost 15 and Signpost 16. CROSS busy Park Loop Road. *The trail to Jordan Pond House is on the left. It's 0.1 mile to the restaurant, gift shop, restrooms, and water.*

17.0 Turn LEFT at Signpost 17, toward Bubble Pond. OPTION: Follow option directions for Day Mountain climb.

19.7 Turn LEFT at Signpost 7, along the southern shore of Eagle Lake.

21.6 Turn RIGHT at Signpost 8.

23.7 Return to parking area.

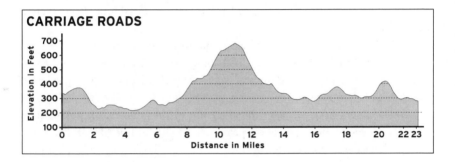

10 SCHOODIC PENINSULA   BEST ◖
Winter Harbor, Acadia National Park

PAVED ROADS WITH MINIMAL TRAFFIC

Difficulty: 2	**Total Distance:** 12.8 miles
Riding Time: 2 hours	**Elevation Gain:** 402 feet

Summary: A quiet road ride suitable for all skill levels and with breathtaking views of Frenchman Bay.

While the bulk of Acadia National Park is on Mount Desert Island, the park also occupies part of the Schoodic Peninsula across Frenchman Bay. The scenery on this side is perhaps even more spectacular, and it's largely ignored by visitors to the park. It's nowhere near as crowded as Bar Harbor and Mount Desert Island, and it's a great place to bike.

This ride starts at Frazer Point Park. From there, you'll immediately hit Acadia's one-way road system. Ride right along the water's edge, basking in the salt breeze, listening to the crashing waves and shorebirds, and keeping your eyes peeled for swimming seals.

You'll know you've reached Schoodic Point by the granite slabs poking into the sea. As you round the tip of the peninsula, you'll see Little Moose Island and then reach a parking area called Blueberry Hill, a good place to stop for photos. A

© CHRIS BERNARD

The views of Frenchman Bay from the Schoodic Peninsula are expansive in places where the Atlantic Ocean meets the dramatic shoreline.

short hiking trail across the road from the parking area leads up to a knob called the Anvil.

The last stretch of park road leaves the exposed coast for quiet Schoodic Harbor. You'll pass the villages of Wonsqueak Harbor and Bunker's Harbor, no more than a few houses and lobster boat moorings, before turning back onto busy ME-186 to return to the entrance road.

Frazer Point Park is open daily 6 A.M.–10 P.M. For more information, contact the National Park Service (P.O. Box 177, Bar Harbor, ME 04609, 207/288-3388, www.nps.gov/acad) or the Schoodic Peninsula Chamber of Commerce (P.O. Box 381, Winter Harbor, ME 04693, 207/963-7658, www.acadia-schoodic.org).

SCHOODIC PENINSULA

Options

The main route is fairly flat, on smooth roads. For an optional workout, take the unmarked left turn at 2.4 miles to climb Schoodic Head. Touring and hybrid bikes will be fine on this bumpy gravel road. It's about a mile to the top of the 440-foot-high mountain, with great views and walking trails as a reward.

The Carriage Roads ride is an hour's drive from here, making it possible to combine these two scenic rides for a spectacular weekend in one of Maine's prettiest areas.

Locals' Tip: Grab breakfast before you start, or a post-ride ice cream, at J.M. Gerrish Provisions Market and Cafe (352 Main Street, Winter Harbor, ME 04693, 207/963-2727).

Places to Stay: Bar Harbor, at Acadia's entrance, has many overnight options, including the Bar Harbor Grand Hotel (269 Main Street, Bar Harbor, ME 04609, 207/288-5226). Campgrounds on the Schoodic Peninsula include Ocean Wood Campground (Ocean Wood Way, Birch Harbor, ME 04613, 207/963-7194), just off the bike route.

Driving Directions

From Ellsworth, take US-1 for 17.2 miles. Turn right on ME-186, signposted for Acadia National Park. Drive 6.5 miles and turn left (a right turn takes you to the village of Winter Harbor). Drive 0.6 mile and turn right onto Moore Road. Drive 1.6 miles and turn right into Frazer Point Park, which has restrooms, water, a picnic area, a dock, and a small beach. Supplies are available in Winter Harbor. The closest bike shops are in Ellsworth or Bar Harbor.

One of the best ways to get to the Schoodic Peninsula is to take the ferry from Bar Harbor to Winter Harbor. The Bar Harbor Ferry (207/288-4585, www .downeastwindjammer.com) runs at least six trips a day. The ride takes about an hour and costs $30 round-trip, plus $6 for a bicycle.

Route Directions

0.0 Leave the parking lot at Frazer Point Park and turn RIGHT onto the main road, immediately entering Acadia National Park and the one-way road system.

2.4 OPTION: Turn LEFT for optional 2.2-mile side trip to the top of Schoodic Head on an unmarked gravel road.

3.4 Turn RIGHT toward Schoodic Point.

4.0 Schoodic Point. TURN AROUND.

4.6 Turn RIGHT onto main road.

5.1 Pass Blueberry Hill parking area.

7.1 Exit Acadia National Park; road becomes two-way.

9.3 *Supplies available in Birch Harbor.*

9.4 Turn LEFT onto ME-186.

11.2 Turn LEFT onto Moore Road.

12.8 Turn RIGHT to return to Frazer Point Park parking lot.

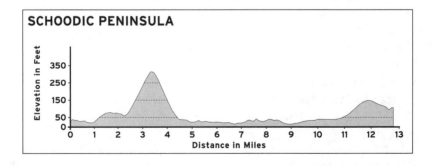

11 BRADBURY MOUNTAIN BEST **C**
Bradbury Mountain State Park, Pownal

SINGLE-TRACK, FIRE ROADS

Difficulty: 2–4   **Total Distance:** 7.0 miles

Riding Time: 2 hours   **Elevation Gain:** 457 feet

Summary: This network of fire roads and single-track is as fun as mountain biking gets.

Bradbury Mountain State Park is a proverbial gem in an unlikely area. Just a short drive from Freeport, known for L.L. Bean and the dozens of outlet stores that line its busy streets, Bradbury is a 590-acre state park that is exceptionally well maintained and warmly welcoming to mountain bikers. Cyclocross bikes are also appropriate for intermediate trails.

For your $3 trail fee, you get access to a growing network of fire roads, double-track, and single-track suitable to all skill levels. Park crews are regularly expanding the trails, so you can return year after year and ride something different.

The route begins in the parking area, and it starts out on easier multiuse trails as it climbs to the summit, offering views of Mount Washington, Casco Bay, and Lake Sebago. It descends the west side of the park—if you don't want the warm-up, an optional descent down the Boundary Trail offers single-track rated "most

© CHRIS BERNARD

Expert riders will find purpose-built single-track at Bradbury Mountain, but more cautious riders will appreciate the miles of fire roads as well.

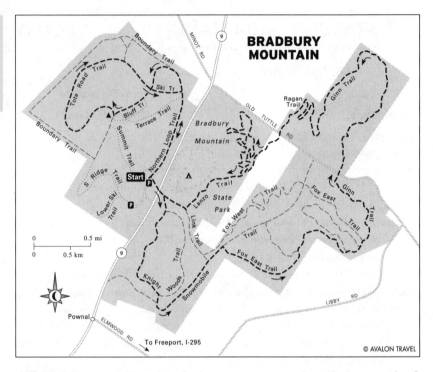

difficult." Crossing ME-9, the ride then zigzags its way through the east side of the park, on fire road and single-track, with lots of rugged climbs, quick descents, and technical terrain.

Most trails are open to ride in May, though the single-track may open later—and may be temporarily closed from time to time—because of rain. Trails are well marked, with wooden signs and colored blazes, and very detailed trail maps are available at the ranger station and online.

For more information, contact Bradbury Mountain State Park, 528 Hallowell Road, Pownal, ME 04069, 207/688-4712, www.state.me.us/doc/parks (daily 9 a.m.–sunset).

Options

For a challenging ride, take the Boundary Trail down from the summit. Rated "most difficult," this route is technical single-track, with lots of rocks and steep sections. Follow the orange blazes 1.2 miles and turn left onto Tote Road Trail, then go 0.4 mile and rejoin Northern Loop Trail, turning right and riding 0.5 mile to parking area.

With the detailed trail maps available at the front gate and so many combinations to link trails, you could visit Bradbury every day for a week and not repeat a route. If you enjoy a downhill run on single-track, challenge yourself to turn around and ride back up it before descending again—in skiing, it's called "earning your turns."

Flying Point Loop and College to Coast are both within 20 minutes.

Locals' Tip: Downtown Freeport does not want for good eateries, but locals favor Gritty McDuff's brewpub (187 Lower Main Street/US-1, Freeport, ME 04032, 207/865-4321). The under-21 crowd can try a frozen custard at Classic Custard (150 US-1, Freeport, ME 04032, 207/865-4417, open seasonally).

Places to Stay: Among the many options for accommodations is the Freeport Clipper Inn bed-and-breakfast (181 Main Street, Freeport, ME 04032, 207/865-9623). More than 30 campsites are available within Bradbury Mountain State Park (207/688-4712, www.campwithme.com).

Driving Directions

From Portland, take I-295 north. Drive approximately 17 miles to exit 22 for Freeport and Durham. Turn right off the exit toward ME-125/136. At the junction, turn left on Durham Road, then right on Pownal Road (which becomes Elmwood Road). Turn right on ME-9. The entrance to Bradbury Mountain State Park is 0.5 mile ahead on the left; the entrance fee is $3 per vehicle. Facilities include restrooms, water, picnic tables, and a campground. Supplies are available in Pownal and nearby Freeport; there are two bike shops in Freeport.

Route Directions

0.0 Northern Loop to summit—follow the main trail, marked with blue blazes, staying STRAIGHT at trail markers 1, 4, 5, 6, and 7.

1.0 Reach the summit. To descend, find Tote Road, marked with white blazes, and follow it to its end, where it intersects with Northern Loop, staying STRAIGHT at markers 15 and 17. OPTION: Take Boundary Trail down from the summit and follow option directions.

2.0 CROSS Northern Loop and pick up Ski Trail, marked with green blazes, descending to its intersection with Northern Loop at trail marker 1.

2.3 Turn RIGHT onto Northern Loop, descending back to start.

2.6 RETURN to parking area, turn LEFT and look for sign to Knight Woods Trail, leading out the east side of the parking lot. CROSS ME-9 and go RIGHT on Knight Woods Trail, marked with signs. Knight Woods is a wide double-track trail with a slight grade.

3.7 Turn RIGHT on Fox East, a narrow single-track with technical challenges. Stay STRAIGHT at trail markers 65, 66, and 67.

4.4 At trail marker 68, cross STRAIGHT to the single-track Ginn Trail. Stay STRAIGHT at markers 69, 70, and 71.

4.2 At marker 72, enter the single-track Ragan Trail, which is technical and challenging.

5.0 At marker 83, cross to the Lanzo Trail, which has some rocky sections and some steep drops and difficult climbs. The trail takes a sharp RIGHT at marker 83 for a challenging loop—if you're tired or ready for a cold drink back at the parking area, stay STRAIGHT and skip the loop.

6.7 Turn RIGHT on wide, easy Link Trail at marker 52. Cross Route 9 into the western section of the park.

7.0 END at parking area.

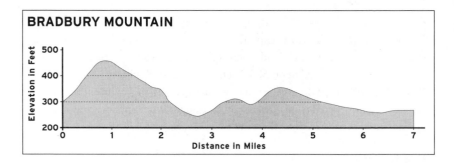

BRADBURY MOUNTAIN

12 FLYING POINT LOOP
Freeport, Brunswick, and South Freeport

PAVED ROADS WITH MINIMAL TO MODERATE TRAFFIC, DIRT ROAD

Difficulty: 3	**Total Distance:** 33 miles
Riding Time: 3-4 hours	**Elevation Gain:** 1,447 feet

Summary: This quiet, scenic ride visits farm roads, coastal vistas, and the desert of Maine.

Freeport is known for three things—being the base of operations for massive retailer L.L. Bean, being situated right on the coast, and being home to a desert.

Created naturally when glaciers of the last Ice Age receded, the layer of glacial silt—as deep as 80 feet in some parts of southern Maine—is hidden by topsoil in most places, which enabled the growth of forest. In a 47-acre stretch of Freeport, poor crop rotation and overgrazing led to soil erosion, which eventually exposed the silt.

OK, so it's not a real desert. But you'd never know that from looking at it.

Dunes pile high, and sand blows with the wind, giving the distinct feel of a desert. This natural tourist attraction draws thousands of visitors every year.

This route begins in downtown Freeport, ducks in at the coast, and heads west

Even the parking areas in Maine involve lighthouses.

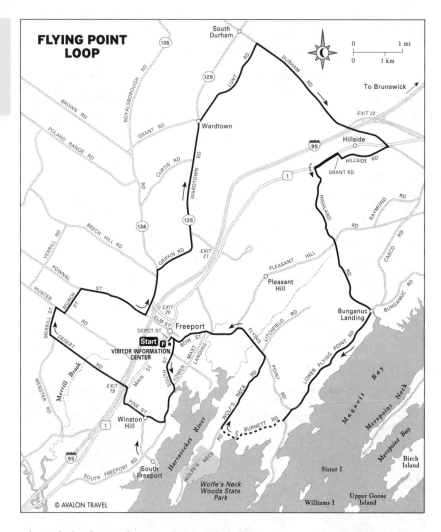

through the desert of Maine, then north, before turning south and east again into beautifully rolling farm country. You'll pass acres of grass, populated only by lazy cows and curious horses that race along their fences as you ride by. From there, the route visits the coast again, offering ocean views and cooling sea breezes, before climbing back to downtown Freeport.

The route follows mostly smooth roads, though there's a short ride on a firmly packed dirt road. From there, a side trip to Wolfe's Neck Woods State Park (426 Wolf's Neck Road, Freeport, ME 04032, 207/865-4465, www.maine.gov) is only two miles out of the way—and worth it.

The Freeport visitor information center is open daily, year-round, and has pamphlets and information; the office is staffed 8 A.M.–5 P.M. Monday–Friday. For more information, contact the Freeport Merchants Association, 207/865-1212 or 800/865-1994, www.freeportusa.com.

Options

This route passes within 3.25 miles of the start of College to Coast; cyclists looking for a 65-mile ride could combine these two. At Mile 18.5, turn left on Greenwood Road, left on Church Road, and then right on McKeen Street. Turn right on Spring Street and left on Columbia Street/Longfellow Avenue, which connects with ME-123; from this point, follow the route directions for the College to Coast ride.

Locals' Tip: If you're going to eat lobster while in Maine, you might as well eat it at Harraseeket Lunch & Lobster Company (Main Street, South Freeport, ME 04032, 207/865-4888), open seasonally and right on the route.

Places to Stay: Freeport has its share of lodging, including the Village Inn (186 Main Street, Freeport, ME 04032, 207/865-3236, www.freeportvillageinn .com), and campgrounds, including Recompence Shore Campground (184 Burnett Road, Freeport, ME 04032, 207/865-9307), which you'll pass on this route.

Driving Directions

From Portland and points south, take I-295 to exit 20 for US-1 to Freeport. Drive north on US-1 for 1 mile and turn right at the light onto West Street. Take the first left onto Depot Street. You will see the lighthouse-shaped Freeport visitor information center; park in any of the lots near the center. Parking is free. The public restrooms at the visitor information center are open May–December. You'll find supplies and bike shops in Freeport.

Route Directions

0.0 Begin at the visitor information center parking lot. Proceed northeast on Depot Street.

0.1 Turn RIGHT onto Bow Street, then make an immediate RIGHT onto South Street.

2.7 Turn RIGHT on Pine Street. *Turn left on Main Street and roll 0.2 mile down the hill to visit the old town landing, the town wharf, and Harraseeket Lunch & Lobster Company.*

4.6 Turn RIGHT onto US-1. Use extreme caution getting into the left lane.

4.7 Turn LEFT at the light onto Desert Road. Cross over I-95.

6.6 Turn RIGHT onto Merrill Street.

7.1 Turn RIGHT onto Hunter Street.

7.3 Turn LEFT onto Murch Street.

7.9 Turn RIGHT onto Pownal Street.

9.3 Sharp left curve. Pownal Street becomes ME-125/136.

10.4 Turn RIGHT onto ME-125 (Griffin Road).

13.8 Turn RIGHT onto Lunt Road. *Supplies available at the corner store.*

15.6 Turn RIGHT onto Durham Road.

18.5 OPTION: Turn left on Greenwood Road and follow option directions.

19.2 Continue STRAIGHT at stop sign across US-1.

19.3 Turn RIGHT onto Hillside Road.

20.3 Turn RIGHT onto Grant Road.

20.4 Turn LEFT onto US-1.

21.2 Turn LEFT onto Highland Road.

24.4 Turn RIGHT onto Flying Point Road (unmarked).

27.0 Turn LEFT onto Lower Flying Point Road. (This easy-to-miss turn comes after a sharp right-hand curve.)

27.3 Turn RIGHT onto Burnett Road, a well-packed dirt road. *Supplies available at the Recompence Campground's general store.*

28.8 Turn RIGHT onto Wolf's Neck Road. *Turn left here for an optional trip to Wolfe's Neck Woods State Park, 1 mile out and back.*

30.4 Turn LEFT onto Flying Point Road; this becomes Bow Street.

33.4 Turn LEFT onto Depot Street.

33.0 Arrive at visitor information center parking lot.

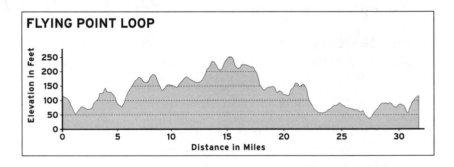

13 COLLEGE TO COAST: BRUNSWICK SCENIC
Brunswick to Harpswell Islands

PAVED ROAD WITH MODERATE TO MINIMAL TRAFFIC

Difficulty: 2

Riding Time: 2 hours

Total Distance: 31.2 miles

Elevation Gain: 548 feet

Summary: A scenic ride that begins at Bowdoin College and crosses two Casco Bay islands to Land's End.

This ride begins in Brunswick on the campus of Bowdoin College, a small, prestigious school chartered in 1794 by Samuel Adams. Consistently ranked among the top 10 liberal arts colleges nationwide, Bowdoin's campus is a stereotypically lovely New England setting with ivy-covered brick and sprawling greens.

Well-known alumni include U.S. president Franklin Pierce, noted researcher Alfred Kinsey, Arctic explorer Admiral Robert Peary, Olympic medalist Joan Benoit Samuelson, and writers Nathaniel Hawthorne and Henry Wadsworth Longfellow. Harriet Beecher Stowe wrote *Uncle Tom's Cabin* here while her husband was a professor.

From Bowdoin the route heads south into Harpswell, traversing both Orrs and Bailey Islands in Casco Bay, offering extraordinary ocean views much of the way—including Mackerel Cove, one of Maine's most-photographed features.

Harbor views along the road as it traverses Bailey and Orrs Islands make the ride scenic, even on overcast days.

The road is mostly smooth, with no shoulders, though traffic is minimal and decreases the farther you get from Brunswick. There are a few good hills, but the payoffs are worth it.

Leave yourself time to visit the Bowdoin College Museum of Art and the Peary-MacMillan Arctic Museum, both on campus. Brunswick's quaint downtown is home to a thriving community of shops, cafés, and restaurants, and to two bike shops.

For more information, contact the Maine Office of Tourism, 59 State House Station, Augusta, ME 04330, 888/624-6345, www.visitmaine.com.

Options

A popular ride in Brunswick is the Androscoggin River Bike Path, a 5-mile route with separate lanes for pedestrians and cyclists. The flat, paved route begins and ends off Water Street. Flying Point Loop is within 20 minutes of this ride.

Locals' Tip: End your ride with lunch on the deck over the Androscoggin River at the Sea Dog Brewing Company (1 Main Street, Topsham, ME 04086, 207/725-0162, www.seadogbrewing.com). As good as the beer is, the food and location make this a worthwhile lunch spot even for teetotalers.

Places to Stay: Rooms at the Daniel Stone Inn (10 Water Street, Brunswick, ME 04011, 207/725-9898) are affordable and the staff is friendly. Camp on the water at Thomas Point Beach and Campground (29 Meadow Road, Brunswick, ME 04011, 207/725-6009, www.thomaspointbeach.com), which also boasts playgrounds, massive lawns for outdoor games and recreation, and an annual bluegrass festival.

Driving Directions

From I-295 North, take exit 28 (US-1/Coastal Route) toward Bath/Brunswick. Merge onto US-1, and after 2 miles, take a slight right at Pleasant Street. After 0.5 mile, turn right at Maine Street/ME-24, and stay on ME-24 as it turns left and becomes Bath Road. Turn right onto Sills Drive/ME-123 and turn right onto Team Drive. Parking is available next to the tennis courts.

Route Directions

0.0 From the parking area, turn RIGHT on Harpswell Road/ME-123.
The road is busiest at the beginning of the ride, though traffic is
moderate. Pass the Brunswick Naval Air Station on your right.

4.0 Harpswell Road becomes Harpswell Neck Road.

6.1 Turn LEFT on Mountain Road. Cross over Harpswell Sound, with
scenic views on both sides. Start a slight climb here at the foot of
Long Reach Mountain.

8.6 Turn RIGHT on Harpswell Islands Road/ME-24. Cross onto Orrs
Island and immediately begin a steep climb, with more beautiful
ocean views to your left, and then Bailey Island. Be careful on the
bridge connecting the islands. The views are spectacular the length
of Bailey Island, including Mackerel Cove, to your right as you near
Land's End.

15.5 At the end of Bailey Island, when the road ends, turn around. *This is
a good place to stop, with a sandy beach, rocky coastline, and a gift shop.*

22.5 Turn LEFT onto Mountain Road.

25.3 Turn RIGHT onto Harpswell Neck Road/ME-123.

27.0 Harpswell Neck Road becomes Harpswell Road.

31.2 END at parking area.

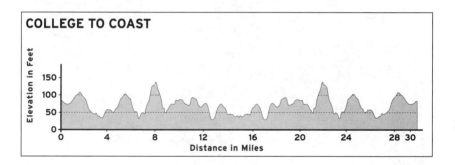

14 MOUNTAIN DIVISION TRAIL
Windham to Standish

PAVED BIKE PATH

Difficulty: 1

Riding Time: 1 hour

Total Distance: 7 miles

Elevation Gain: 258 feet

Summary: An easy, paved path suitable for all skill levels and families with children.

Let's get this out in the open—there's nothing challenging or exciting about this trail. There are no hills to climb or descend, no sharp banked turns to scream through, and no breathtaking vistas or ocean views. Mountain bikers seeking a thrill should look elsewhere.

But since 2003, the Mountain Division trail has offered an ideal route for families or beginners who want a nice, flat path in the woods, with no cars or other concerns. Suitable for all bikes, it's wide enough to ride side by side, but it is a multiuse trail, so watch for people on foot or horseback.

The trail lies alongside the former Mountain Division line of the Maine Central Railroad, abandoned in 1994. Trail planners hope one day to turn the whole

This flat rail trail is accessible and suitable for riders of all skill levels.

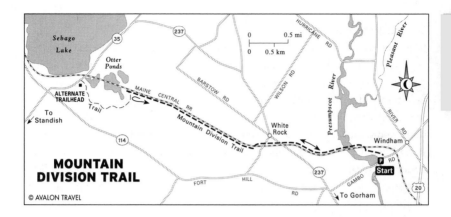

45-mile line from Portland to Fryeburg into a multiuse trail. Currently, another section in Portland connects the Transportation Center with the city's old port, and eventually the two sections will link to create a vehicle-free corridor connecting Portland, Standish, Gorham, Windham, and Westbrook.

For a nice out and back, start at the trailhead in Windham, where a kiosk provides information about the culture and natural history of the area as well as a trail map. Trail markers appear every quarter mile on this mostly straight course, so you'd have to try very, very hard to get lost. The trail crosses the Presumpscot River and heads through woodlands, open fields, and pasturelands.

After 3.5 miles, you'll reach the Otter Ponds area, home to a YMCA day camp and four small ponds, not far from Sebago Lake. Stop for lunch at the pond or take a dip before turning around and heading back.

For more information, contact the Mountain Division Alliance, 207/935-4283, www.mountaindivisiontrail.org.

Options

To extend your ride, continue on from the Otter Ponds area as the Mountain Division Trail leaves the railroad and heads left (uphill) for 1.2 miles to the alternative trailhead in Standish on ME-35.

Five Lights, Six Beaches, Peaks Island Loop, and the Scarborough Marsh Mellow rides are within a half-hour of this one.

Locals' Tip: Visit Burrito! (652 Main Street, Westbrook, ME 04092, 207/854-0040) for lunch after a leisurely morning ride.

Places to Stay: Downtown Portland, half an hour away, offers a wide selection of hotels and other accommodations.

Driving Directions

From the south, take I-95 to exit 48 (Portland/Westbrook). Take ME-25 west approximately 5 miles to Gorham. Turn right onto ME-4/US-202. Drive 5 miles and turn left at the stoplight onto River Road. Go 0.5 mile and turn left onto Gambo Road. Go 0.4 mile and turn right onto the access road; drive 0.1 mile to the parking lot. From the north, take I-95 to exit 63 (Gray). Take ME-4/US-202 south approximately 11 miles to South Windham. At the light, turn right onto River Road, then left on Gambo Road as above. Convenience stores are on River Road. Restaurants and supplies are available in Windham, Gorham, and Standish. The closest bike shop is Ernie's Cycle Shop (105 Conant Street, Westbrook, ME 04092, 207/854-4090).

Route Directions

0.0 Leave the parking lot and turn LEFT onto the trail.

3.5 Reach Otter Pond Day Camp area. TURN AROUND.

OPTION: Continue on the Mountain Division Trail and follow option directions.

7.0 Return to parking area.

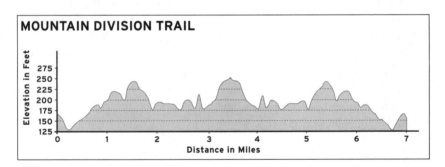

15 FIVE LIGHTS, SIX BEACHES BEST **(**
South Portland, Cape Elizabeth, and Scarborough

PAVED ROADS WITH MINIMAL TRAFFIC

Difficulty: 3	**Total Distance:** 38.8 miles
Riding Time: 3 hours	**Elevation Gain:** 489 feet

Summary: This scenic ride loops around Cape Elizabeth, passing lighthouses and beaches and offering beautiful viewpoints at every turn.

Among other things, Maine is known for its postcard views of lighthouses and beaches. This ride passes four or five lighthouses (depending on how you count them) and six beaches, giving you a jam-packed Maine ride that's best done on a summer day.

The ride starts at historic Fort Williams park, home to the beautiful red-roofed Portland Head Light, commissioned by George Washington and built in 1791. It's Maine's oldest lighthouse, and there's an on-site museum. From there, head along Shore Road, with occasional rocky coast views to your left, eventually coming upon Cape Elizabeth's Two Lights State Park.

The 41-acre park shows off views from the rocky coastline of Casco Bay and the Atlantic. The picnic tables offer scenic vistas, or take a short stroll along the rocky cliffs. Just down the road, you come to the land's edge again, with views of

© CHRIS BERNARD

There's some piece of Maine oceanfront landscape to see all along this ride.

FIVE LIGHTS, SIX BEACHES

Two Lights station—built in 1828 and made famous by a series of Edward Hopper paintings. While it was initially two separate lights—one fixed beam and one flashing—the west tower was discontinued and made into a private residence.

From there, a short climb takes you back to the road. Then the trail heads to diversions to Kettle Cove Beach and the bigger Crescent Beach State Park, and then a few more miles to beautiful Higgins Beach, a favorite among local surfers. Taste the salt in the air as you head out Prout's Neck, past Scarborough State Beach and sprawling Ferry Beach, to the Winslow Homer home. Though the home is not open to the public, the artist lived here for many years, and he painted the seascapes along the cliff walk there.

The ride back takes you into South Portland, past Portland Breakwater Light (known locally as Bug Light and modeled after an ancient Greek monument), past Spring Point Ledge Light (built in the "spark plug" style), and past Willard Beach (where you'll find facilities and a snack bar during beach season) before returning to Fort Williams.

For more information on the lighthouses, contact the Maine Office of Tourism, 59 State House Station, Augusta, ME 04333, 888/624-6345, www.visitmaine.com/attractions/sightseeing_tours/lighthouse/.

Options

This ride can be combined with Scarborough Marsh Mellow, which overlaps by Spring Point Ledge Lighthouse, for a longer ride.

Locals' Tip: The bagels at 158 Pickett Street Cafe (158 Benjamin W. Pickett Street, South Portland, ME 04106, 207/799-8998, www.158pickettstreetcafe.com) are not your typical New York–style bagels, but they're a big hit with local foodies. Check one out with a coffee as you bike past this little café.

Places to Stay: The Higgins Beach Inn (34 Ocean Avenue, Scarborough, ME 04074, 207/883-6684) is right on the route, with nice beach access.

Driving Directions

From I-95, take I-295 to exit 4 and merge onto US-1 toward Portland. After about 2 miles, exit on the left onto ME-77, which becomes Broadway. Turn right onto Cottage Road, bearing left at the lights to stay on Cottage Road, which becomes Shore Road. Turn left at Powers Road, following signs for Fort Williams State Park. Plenty of parking is available.

Route Directions

0.0 From Portland Head Light, follow Fort Williams park road out to Shore Road, and turn LEFT.

2.7 At stop sign, turn LEFT onto Ocean House Road/ME-77.

4.4 Turn LEFT onto Two Lights Road.

5.3 Bear RIGHT into Two Lights State Park. *Facilities available.* TURN AROUND.

5.4 Turn RIGHT onto Two Lights Road, a fast descent to the ocean's edge.

6.0 Road ends, with views of both lighthouses (one is now a private residence). TURN AROUND and begin climbing.

8.0 Turn LEFT onto M-77/Bowery Beach Road.

8.2 Turn LEFT onto Kettle Cove Road, which ends at Kettle Cove Beach. TURN AROUND.

9.4 Turn LEFT onto ME-77/Bowery Beach Road.

10.4 Turn LEFT into Crescent Beach State Park. On hot summer days, there may be a long line of cars waiting to get into the park, so watch for traffic. TURN AROUND.

11.1 Turn LEFT onto ME-77/Bowery Beach Road.

14.6 Turn LEFT onto Ocean Avenue. Road ends at Higgins Beach. Follow the one-way roads and make a loop by turning LEFT onto Bayview, LEFT onto Vesper, LEFT onto Greenwood, and RIGHT onto Ocean Avenue.

16.0 Turn LEFT onto ME-77/Spurwink Road.

17.1 Turn LEFT at the stop sign onto ME-207/Black Point Road, passing Scarborough Beach on your left.

20.2 Road ends at Winslow Homer Road, with views of Saco Bay. TURN AROUND.

20.6 Views to your left of Ferry Beach, of Old Orchard Beach across the bay, and on a clear day, of Mount Washington.

21.0 Turn LEFT onto Ferry Road, following signs for Ferry Beach.

21.5 Road ends at Ferry Beach parking area. *Facilities available.* TURN AROUND.

22.0 Turn LEFT onto ME-207/Black Point Road.

23.7 Bear LEFT to stay on Black Point Road.

25.2 Turn RIGHT onto Fogg Road.

26.8 Turn RIGHT onto Pleasant Hill Road.

27.8 Turn LEFT onto ME-77/Spurwink Road.

28.9 Turn LEFT onto Sawyer Road.

30.9 Turn RIGHT to stay on Sawyer Road.

31.4 Turn RIGHT on Easton Road.

32.2 Turn LEFT on Spurwink Avenue.

33.4 Bear RIGHT onto Sawyer Street.

35.1 Turn RIGHT onto Front Street, which becomes Benjamin W. Pickett Street.

35.9 Turn LEFT onto Fort Road, which ends at Spring Point Ledge Lighthouse. TURN AROUND.

36.8 Turn LEFT at stop sign onto Preble Street.

37.0 Turn LEFT onto Franklin Terrace, down a short, steep hill. Franklin Terrace ends in a traffic circle at Willard Beach. *Facilities available.*

37.2 Head straight through the traffic circle onto Fisherman's Lane, crossing Willard Street onto Willard Haven Road. Turn LEFT at end of road onto Deake Street for views of Willard Beach, Simonton Cove, two historic lobster shacks, and Casco Bay and the islands. Follow the dirt path to the end of the point. Spring Point Ledge Lighthouse is visible to your left, Portland Head Light to your right. TURN AROUND and head STRAIGHT on Deake Street.

37.6 Turn LEFT at stop sign onto Preble Street.

38.0 Turn LEFT onto Shore Road.

38.8 Turn LEFT at sign for Fort Williams and Portland Head Light.

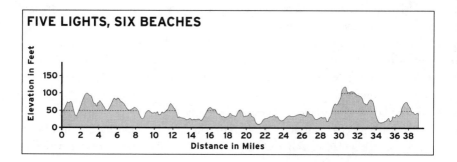

FIVE LIGHTS, SIX BEACHES

16 PEAKS ISLAND LOOP BEST C
Peaks Island, Casco Bay

PAVED ROADS WITH MINIMAL TRAFFIC

Difficulty: 1   **Total Distance:** 4 miles

Riding Time: 1 hour   **Elevation Gain:** 96 feet

Summary: This flat loop follows the coastline of the island, past rock ledges and sandy beaches, back into downtown.

No matter where you're looking from, Casco Bay is beautiful. The more than 300 islands that dot the waters range in size, some home to abandoned military forts, others to year-round communities, others to seasonal homes, and some housing nothing—or next to nothing—at all.

Many of the islands can be visited, and a ferry service from downtown Portland will take you there. If you've ever watched the ferry passengers board, you've seen the bikes lined up one after the other, stacked on the deck of the boat, chained up at the terminal. There's a reason—many of the islands offer fantastic bike rides, with little-to-no traffic, a different pace of life, and a unique perspective on the mainland.

The best biking islands are Great Chebeague Island, Long Island, and Peaks Island, all serviced by the ferry. Peaks is the closest to Portland and has the largest year-round population (about 1,000 people). It's also the most accessible, with the

Bicyclists and beachcombers build stone cairns on the rocky shore of Peaks Island.

PEAKS ISLAND LOOP

most frequent ferries, and offers more services than other islands. This is a great family ride, as there are plenty of things to see and several places to stop, and the bicycling is easy. The roads are paved, and any bike will suffice.

Starting from the ferry terminal, you'll ride in a counterclockwise loop around the island. You have a short climb to get up out of the village, but Seashore Avenue is almost totally flat. Take a side trip to Picnic Point or Sandy Beach if you've got time or inclination, or visit the Fifth Maine Regiment museum for a bit of island history. Once you're riding along the ocean's edge, there are plenty of places where you can pull over to explore the rocky beach, picnic, or beachcomb. The views are outstanding, as the houses are all on the left and there are only rocks, seagulls, islands, and ocean to your right.

Island Avenue takes you past summer homes and down into the village, where more of the year-round residents live. You'll find several restaurants and pubs, a café, a gift store selling ice cream, and a market where you can get supplies or

© CHRIS BERNARD

Island life is welcoming to cyclists right from the moment they arrive at the ferry terminal.

sandwiches. The place gets busy in the middle of summer, so if you hate crowds, try visiting in June or September.

The ferry ride is a scenic 20 minutes, giving you great vistas of Portland, South Portland, and the Casco Bay islands. It's always breezy on the ferry, so bring a windbreaker. All tickets are round-trip; as of October 2009, it was $7.70 for a passenger plus $6.50 for your bike, but rates vary seasonally and from year to year. (You can also rent bikes on the island.) Generally there is one ferry an hour, but the schedule changes with the seasons. For updated ferry schedules, rates, and more parking information, contact Casco Bay Lines, P.O. Box 4656, Portland, ME 04112, 207/774-7871, www.cascobaylines.com.

Options

For an interesting side trip, turn right at Mile 0.3 onto the next dirt road and ride for about 200 feet. You'll see a narrow grassy path on the left. If you walk out on this path, you'll reach Picnic Point, a spit of land jutting into the bay with pebble beaches on either side. Roads crisscross the island—don't be afraid to explore them. It's literally impossible to get lost for long.

Locals' Tip: The Inn on Peaks Island (33 Island Avenue, Peaks Island, ME 04108, 207/766-5100, www.innonpeaks.com) is within sight of the ferry terminal and offers fresh seafood and cold Shipyard beers on tap.

Places to Stay: In addition to good meals, the Inn on Peaks Island (33 Island Avenue, Peaks Island, ME 04108, 207/766-5100, www.innonpeaks.com) also offers Maine-cottage-style luxury guest rooms with private decks.

Driving Directions

From the south, take the Maine Turnpike (I-95) to exit 44, in South Portland, for ME-295. Drive approximately 7 miles and take exit 7 (Franklin Street). From the north, take the Maine Turnpike (I-95) to exit 103, in Gardiner, for ME-295. Drive approximately 44 miles and take exit 7 (Franklin Street). Drive to the end of Franklin and go straight through the intersection; the ferry terminal is on your right. An hourly parking garage is adjacent to the terminal. Supplies are available in Portland and on Peaks Island. A bike shop on the island offers rentals and there are several bike shops in Portland.

Route Directions

0.0 From the ferry pier, walk up a short hill to the main intersection. Turn RIGHT onto Island Avenue.

0.1 Take a sharp LEFT curve, uphill.

0.25 Turn RIGHT onto unmarked Whitehead Street (the second paved road on the right).

0.3 Take a sharp LEFT curve onto Seashore Avenue. OPTION: Turn RIGHT onto the next dirt road and follow option directions.

0.4 Pass Fifth Maine Regiment Museum.

0.5 Turn RIGHT following Seashore Avenue toward the water.

2.4 Curve LEFT uphill.

2.7 Turn LEFT at T junction; go STRAIGHT through next intersection.

2.8 Turn LEFT at stop sign and junction onto Island Avenue.

3.5 Turn RIGHT at junction (the elementary school is on the left).

3.7 *Public restrooms available at the library and community center.*

4.0 Return to start, at corner of Island Avenue and Welch Street. Turn RIGHT for ferry pier and END at parking lot with bike rack.

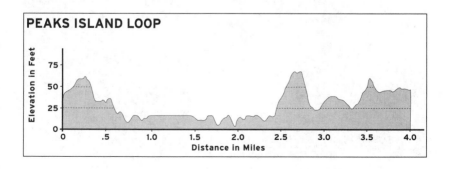

PEAKS ISLAND LOOP

17 SCARBOROUGH MARSH MELLOW
South Portland to Scarborough

BIKE PATH, SOME ROADS WITH MINIMAL TRAFFIC, PACKED DIRT TRAIL

Difficulty: 2   **Total Distance:** 27.2 miles

Riding Time: 2.5 hours   **Elevation Gain:** 243 feet

Summary: Follow the Eastern Trail from South Portland's Willard Beach to the Scarborough Marsh, taking in coastal views and bird-watching opportunities.

Mostly a sheltered bicycle and pedestrian path, though there are some stretches of road, this route connects the Springpoint Shoreway with the Eastern Trail and runs from Casco Bay to the state's largest salt marsh.

The scenery changes repeatedly along this route, which starts at the sandy shores of Willard Beach. The beach is frequented by locals and offers views of Bug Light and Portland Head Light lighthouses and the islands that dot Casco Bay like stars in a watery sky. Watch the tugboats escort the massive tankers into the harbor as you cross the Southern Maine Community College campus, then hop on the South Portland Greenbelt—the northern terminus of the Eastern Trail—and coast

© CHRIS BERNARD

The bike path runs through Maine's largest saltwater marsh, also popular for walking, sightseeing, and fishing.

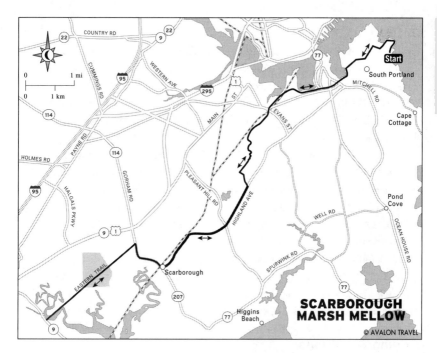

through residential neighborhoods and a shopping district, into a city park, and along the waterfront in the shadow of the Casco Bay drawbridge.

The route takes an industrial turn as you pass oil tanks and train tracks—slow down to read the graffiti on the asphalt—before it dips back into the rural quiet of a beautiful wooded section paralleling a babbling brook. From there it runs through a capped landfill, now grown over with grass and flowers and populated by feeding birds, into the Wainwright Farm Recreation Area, before joining the road system for a short while. Traffic is minimal but can be fast moving. Stick to the bike lane and be careful.

Exiting the Greenbelt, the route stays with the Eastern Trail as it heads into Scarborough Marsh. Here, the trail turns to packed dirt and gravel, though it's suitable for road bikes. Mosquitoes can be vicious around dusk, so be prepared.

The Eastern Trail runs all the way to Kittery in the southern part of the state, though much of it is currently along the road system. Plans are to eventually connect it with similar sections of the East Coast Greenway from Calais, Maine, to Key West, Florida. From Scarborough Marsh, the trail continues south to Old Orchard Beach, a 13-mile round-trip journey.

For more information, contact the Eastern Trail Alliance, P.O. Box 250, Saco, ME 04072, 207/284-9260, www.easterntrail.org.

Options

For those seeking shorter rides, parking is available at the midpoint on Pine Point Road in Scarborough, cutting this route in half. Families riding with children can leave a car at the Wainwright Recreation Area (Gary Maietta Drive, South Portland, ME 04106, 207/767-7650) for a shorter route completely contained within the Greenbelt. The Five Lights, Six Beaches and Peaks Island Loop routes are short distances from this one.

Locals' Tip: The pastry at Scratch Bakery (416 Preble Street, South Portland, ME 04106, 207/799-0668, www.scratchbakingco.com), in Willard Square, draws customers from all over southern Maine. From Benjamin W. Pickett Street, follow Fort Road and turn left on Preble Street. Scratch is on your left.

Places to Stay: Across the bridge, Portland offers a variety of hotels, inns, and B&Bs, including the Inn at St. John (939 Congress Street, Portland, ME 04102, 207/773-6481, http://innatstjohn.com). Camping is available at Wild Duck Campground (39 Dunstan Landing Road, Scarborough, ME 04074, 207/883-4432, www.wildduckcampground.com) or at Bayley's Camping Resort (275 Pine Point Road, Scarborough, ME 04074, 207/883-6043, http://bayleys-camping.com).

Driving Directions

From ME-295, take exit 4, US-1 toward Portland. Exit on the left onto ME-77, and follow over the Casco Bay Bridge. Stay on ME-77 as it becomes Broadway, turning right onto Benjamin W. Pickett Street. Enter parking lot at the end of Benjamin W. Pickett Street. Note that parking is also available at the halfway point of the route, off Pine Point Road in Scarborough, if you'd rather begin there. Food and other supplies are available along the way in South Portland. The nearest bike shops are in Portland.

Route Directions

0.0 Enter the Springpoint Shoreway to your LEFT, following the path north along Willard Beach. Stay RIGHT as the trail forks.

0.26 Dismount and climb the short staircase to your left. Follow the trail RIGHT, and at the end of the path, descend the staircase to your RIGHT to Bug Light Park. At the foot of the stairs, rejoin the path LEFT.

0.8 When the path stops, stay RIGHT toward waterfront. The path resumes and follows a small, rocky beach, adjacent to a boatyard.

1.0 When the path empties onto Adams Street, turn RIGHT at the stop sign onto Benjamin W. Pickett Street.

1.2 At the end of the street, the South Portland Greenbelt begins on your LEFT. Follow the paved trail along the South Portland waterfront and through Mill Creek Park. Watch for vehicle traffic as the trail crosses several streets. *Supplies available.*

3.2 Trail temporarily ends at intersection. Cross Waterman Drive at stoplights, and turn LEFT across ME-77 at same intersection. As soon as you cross ME-77, re-enter the paved Greenbelt path on your right.

4.0 Path empties onto Chestnut Street. Stay straight on Chestnut Street. When Chestnut Street ends, turn RIGHT, and follow to the end of the street, then rejoin paved path on the LEFT at railroad tracks.

4.6 Cross busy Highland Avenue and Evans Avenue, and head down Elizabeth Taylor Lane to rejoin path to the left—watch for signs. This is among the prettiest sections of the trail. While it's strayed from the waterfront, it's a corridor through wooded areas along a running brook. It passes through a capped landfill, which is now covered in grass and flowers. *Supplies available.*

6.1 Pass the soccer fields to your left. *There is a restroom across a small wooden footbridge to your right.*

6.9 The paved trail empties into the parking area at the Wainwright Farm Recreation Area. Follow bike lane markings to the LEFT, and follow Gary Maietta Parkway to the stop sign.

7.3 Turn RIGHT on Highland Avenue, following signs for the Eastern Trail. You're on the road here, so stay in the bike lane and be aware of traffic. At the stop sign, continue through the intersection, remaining on Highland Avenue.

9.3 Follow Highland Avenue as it bears LEFT.

10.2 At the stop sign, turn RIGHT onto ME-207/Black Point Road.

11.0 Turn LEFT on Eastern Road, following signs for the Eastern Trail.

13.5 End at Scarborough Marsh. Turn around.

16.0 Turn RIGHT onto ME-207/Black Point Road.

16.8 Turn LEFT onto Highland Avenue, following signs for the Eastern Trail.

17.7 Bear RIGHT on Highland Avenue. At the stop sign, continue through the intersection, remaining on Highland Avenue.

19.7 Turn LEFT onto Gary Maietta Parkway.

20.1 Rejoin paved South Portland Greenbelt path on the right at the Wainwright Fields Recreation Area.

22.4 Exit the paved path onto Elizabeth Taylor Lane, cross Evans Avenue, and turn LEFT across Highland Avenue. Rejoin paved trail.

23.1 Paved trail empties onto road—turn LEFT onto Chestnut Street, follow it to the end, and watch for signs to rejoin trail.

24.0 Exit trail and cross ME-77, then turn RIGHT across Waterman Drive. Rejoin paved trail.

26.0 South Portland Greenbelt ends. At the stop sign, turn RIGHT onto Madison/Benjamin W. Pickett Street.

26.3 Turn LEFT onto Adams Street.

26.5 Enter Springpoint Shoreway on left, adjacent to marina. When the path ends temporarily at Osprey Lane, bear LEFT along the waterfront toward Bug Light.

26.8 Climb staircase to your RIGHT, and rejoin paved trail LEFT.

26.9 Descend staircase to LEFT, and follow paved trail RIGHT, staying LEFT at fork.

27.2 END at parking area.

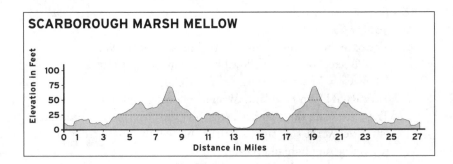

SCARBOROUGH MARSH MELLOW

18 THE BIG A
Kittery, York, and Cape Neddick

PAVED ROADS, HARD-PACKED DIRT ROADS, MODERATE TRAFFIC

Difficulty: 3   **Total Distance:** 27.7 miles

Riding Time: 2.5 hours   **Elevation Gain:** 692 feet

Summary: Leave the Kittery outlets for seaside York, a climb of Mount Agamenticus, and plenty of wildlife along the way.

The titular mountain, Agamenticus, known locally as "Big A," is in truth little more than a hill, but that doesn't stanch local pride in the region's highest peak. You'll climb the summit about halfway through this ride, which starts at the outlet shopping malls in Kittery.

In between, it passes through quaint, touristy York (with an option to visit the rocky coastline of Stage Neck), following mostly quiet roads (with the noted exception of US-1, which can be busy in summer), looping back to Kittery. Along the way, in addition to the hill (or mountain, if you're a local), you'll pass marshlands, rivers, residential neighborhoods, and miles and miles of nothing but scenery.

© CHRIS BERNARD

The summit of Mount Agamenticus is a bit of an uphill slog, but from the top, where this fire tower stands, you can see much of southern Maine and parts of New Hampshire.

The 10,000-acre Mount Agamenticus Conservation Region sits in the midst of a 30,000-acre expanse of conservation land between southern Maine and the New Hampshire seacoast region. This coastal forest supports the greatest diversity of animal and plant species statewide and offers top-notch hiking, biking, and sightseeing opportunities. The area teems with moose, white-tailed deer, black bear, and seldom-seen fishers, giving you a good chance of running across wildlife. Each fall, thousands of migrating birds can be seen in the area, drawing bird watchers from afar.

Legend has it that a chief named Aspinquid was buried atop Mount Agamenticus in 1682 at a funeral service attended by thousands of Native Americans. You'll still find a

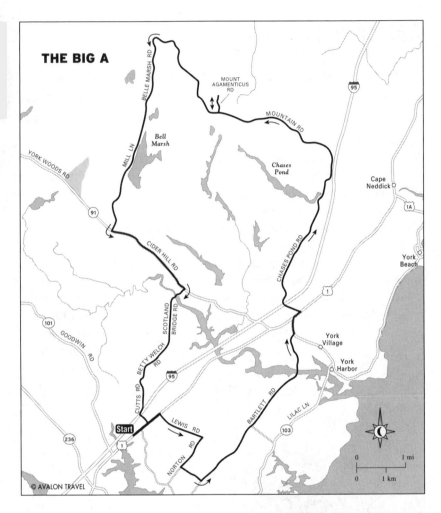

memorial cairn on the summit, and it's said that whoever pays tribute to his soul by adding a rock is assured of luck. Myth or not, it can't hurt.

After the climb, you get to enjoy the descent, the fruit of your labors, and there are no other climbs to speak of—in fact, most of the second half of the ride is downhill or flat. Enjoy it, and end up back at Kittery where you began.

For more information, contact the Greater York Region Chamber of Commerce, 1 Stonewall Lane, York, ME 03909, 207/363-4462, www.gatewaytomaine.org, or the Mount Agamenticus Conservation Program, 186 York Street, York, ME 03909, 207/361-1102, www.agamenticus.org.

Options

Interested in exploring the area further? Try it on a mountain or cyclocross bike—a fun, challenging trail system crisscrosses Mount Agamenticus. Follow the white, yellow, or blue blazes to ensure you stay on the appropriate routes. Watch for pedestrians and horses. Trail maps are available at the summit or online. For a good, short option rideable for most skill levels, follow the signs for the Ring Trail (east/left) to Witch Hazel to Sweet Fern to Ring Trail (west/left), a 1.5-mile loop.

This ride is near several New Hampshire rides, including Bailey's Three States Bounder, which begins just across the border in Portsmouth.

Locals' Tip: Flo's Hot Dogs, north of Pine Loop Road (US-1, Cape Neddick, ME 03902, www.floshotdogs.com), serves dogs steamed the old-fashioned way and often compared to the famous Coney Island ones.

Places to Stay: The Union Bluff Hotel (8 Beach Street, York Beach, ME 03910, 800/833-0721, www.unionbluff.com) offers oceanfront rooms, access to area attractions, and an in-house pub. Or camp at Harborview Oceanside Campground (P.O. Box 1, Cape Neddick, ME 03902, 207/363-4366, www.harbour view.com), located on Shore Road between York and Ogunquit Beaches.

Driving Directions

From I-95 North, take exit 3 toward Coastal Route/Kittery/South Berwick. Keep left at the fork in the ramp, and merge onto US-1 north. The Tidewater Outlet Mall is on your left. Ample parking, supplies, restaurants, and restrooms are all available. The closest bike shops are in York and Portsmouth, New Hampshire.

Route Directions

0.0 START at parking lot at Tidewater Outlet Mall, and head south toward US-1.

0.1 Turn LEFT at US-1. Stick to the shoulders and watch for traffic.

0.4 Turn RIGHT on Lewis Road.

1.5 Turn RIGHT at Norton Road.

2.3 Turn LEFT on Miller Road.

2.8 Turn LEFT on Bartlett Road. Bartlett Road becomes Southside Road.

5.5 Continue STRAIGHT onto Southside Road. Southside Road becomes Seabury Road.

5.9 Slight LEFT at Seabury Road. Seabury Road becomes Organug Road.

6.0 Continue STRAIGHT on Organug Road.

6.9 Turn LEFT on York Street. Option: Turn RIGHT and ride 1.6 miles to Stage Neck Road, then RIGHT again to do a loop of Stage Neck with scenic ocean views along the rocky coast. Turn LEFT on York Street, and follow it 1.6 miles back to rejoin the route, adding 4 miles to the ride.

7.1 Turn RIGHT at US-1. This road can be busy in the summer— stick to the shoulders and watch for traffic.

7.4 Turn LEFT at Spur Road.

8.0 Turn RIGHT at Chases Pond Road.

10.4 Turn RIGHT to stay on Chases Pond Road.

11.7 Slight LEFT at Mountain Road.

14.4 Turn RIGHT at Mount A Road/Summit Road to begin the climb up Mount Agamenticus. At the top you'll find trail maps, tree guides, parking areas, and a lodge open only for special events. Turn around and descend back to Mountain Road. Turn RIGHT on Mountain Road.

18.1 Turn LEFT at Belle Marsh Road, following wetlands to your left. Belle Marsh Road becomes Mill Lane.

22.5 Turn LEFT at Cider Hill Road/ME-91.

24.5 Turn RIGHT on Scotland Bridge Road. Scotland Bridge Road becomes Betty Welch Road.

26.9 Turn LEFT at Cutts Road.

27.7 END at parking lot at Tidewater Outlet Mall.

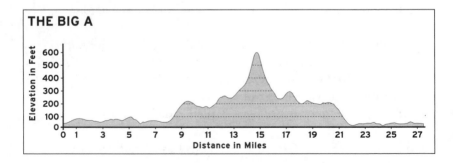

THE BIG A

NEW HAMPSHIRE

© CHRIS BERNARD

BEST BIKE RIDES

There are just six states smaller than New Hampshire,
three of them in New England. But because of New Hampshire's shape – long,
thin, and bottom-heavy, tapering as it nears the border with Quebec – the
state can *feel* very big as you drive its length north-to-south. In one day, you
can leave the stunning scenery and sweeping vistas of the granite-ridged
White Mountains, pass through the rolling hills of the lakes region and the
river valleys, drive by unending cow-studded pastures and farmlands, and
make it to the seacoast to eat dinner while watching the fishing boats return
to the harbors – seemingly a different world from where you began.

Fittingly, New Hampshire's bike rides feel equally big. The road rides can
be sweeping, hilly, and breathtaking, the off-road rides are demanding
and beautiful, and even the short, easy rides can seem disproportionately
impressive. This state has much to offer. Bikes are an excellent way to
take it all in.

Bikes, for example, make for a great half-day's tour of the populous
Seacoast region. Leave thriving, artsy downtown Portsmouth and pedal
past the beaches of Rye, the impressive summer homes of Boar's Head,
and the clam shacks and arcades of Hampton Beach, all the way south
to the Massachusetts border and back. Bikes can open the door to the
lazily twisting roads that climb through the impossibly scenic mountains
of the north, where you can spend an easy day rolling along the Swift
River, admiring the foliage and the covered bridges near popular Conway
village or the rolling hills of the southwest part of the state.

If the feel of dirt beneath your tires is what you want, range far afield on the grizzly Bear Brook trails just north of Manchester, test your brakes on the fire roads and single-track around Massabesic Lake to the south, throw down a blistering pace on the mixed terrain of the Child's Bog Cross Loop, or mud it up on the long, steady off-road ascent into the Pondicherry Wildlife Refuge. Need more adrenaline? Push your limits high above the lakes region on the ridges and descents of Kittredge Hill or the spectacularly steep-and-stony Lovewell Mountain loop.

Prefer the calm to the chaotic? Even easy rollers have plenty of options in New Hampshire. The short, smooth, and wide paved Windham Rail Trail offers recreational riders, beginners, and families a safe and scenic path free from the distractions of vehicle traffic. And any rider with a minimal degree of off-road comfort can manage the ballast-covered path that runs through a variety of terrains from tiny Newfields to the state's most populous city, Manchester.

What's not to love about New Hampshire? As it turns out, not much – except for the early end to the season, which is like a door slamming on the mellow temperatures and brilliant colors of fall. You might also struggle with the biting bugs on some of the woods trails, especially if you ride under the hot, wet blanket of late summer. Additionally, you might prepare yourself for the unpredictability of New Hampshire weather. Many a cyclist has set out on a ride in one extreme only to return in another.

Welcome to northern New England. Enjoy your ride.

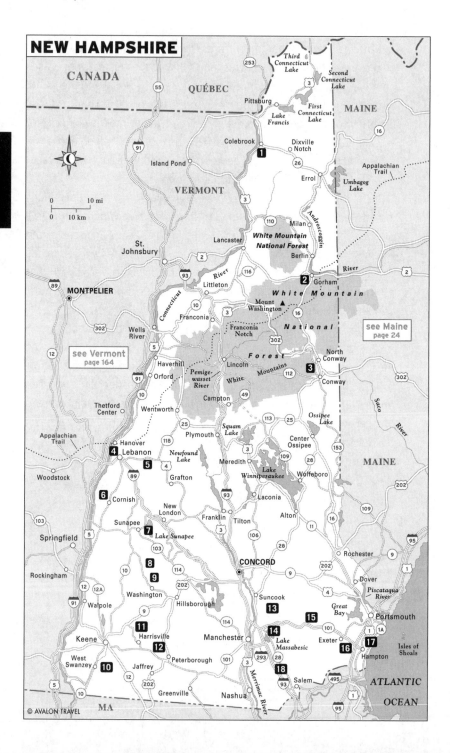

RIDE NAME	DIFFICULTY	DISTANCE	TIME	ELEVATION	PAGE
1 Whistling Dixville	4	83 mi	5 hr	1,890 ft	100
2 Pondicherry Pondering	3	42.5 mi	4.5 hr	1,647 ft	104
3 Two Chiefs and Three Bridges	2	14.5 mi	2 hr	456 ft	108
4 Salt Hill Interstate	3	46 mi	3.5 hr	2,178 ft	111
5 Northern Rail Trail	3	45.2 mi	3-5 hr	724 ft	115
6 Glass Family Ramble	3	30.3 mi	2.5 hr	1,779 ft	118
7 Sunapee Lakes Loop	3	29.2 mi	2.5 hr	1,200 ft	121
8 Kittredge Hill Loop	5	5.5 mi	3 hr	759 ft	124
9 Lovewell Mountain Ride	5	15 mi	3 hr	1,273 ft	127
10 Four Covered Bridges Ride	2	14.8 mi	1.5-2 hr	241 ft	131
11 Child's Bog Cross Loop	3	6.3 mi	1.5 hr	405 ft	134
12 Our Town and the Hancock Hills	3	17.4 mi	2-2.5 hr	1,071 ft	137
13 Kathy's Bear Brook Bounder	3	8.5 mi	1.5 hr	403 ft	140
14 Massabesic Lake Loops	3	5.3 mi	1 hr	174 ft	143
15 Southeast Sojourn	3	52.4 mi	6-7 hr	1,082 ft	147
16 Academy and Atoms Ride	2	37.4 mi	2.5 hr	538 ft	150
17 Bailey's Three States Bounder	3	43.5 mi	3 hr	469 ft	154
18 Windham Rail Trail	1	6.5 mi	1 hr	164 ft	158

1 WHISTLING DIXVILLE
Colebrook, Dixville Notch, and North Stratford

PAVED ROADS AND MINIMAL TRAFFIC

Difficulty: 4   **Total Distance:** 83 miles

Riding Time: 5 hours   **Elevation Gain:** 1,890 feet

Summary: This lovely, long ride through the foliage-heavy mountain region presents one climb – and it's a daunting one.

Nationally, Dixville Notch may be best known for its middle-of-the-night vote during New Hampshire's primary election, the first in the nation, a tradition which began in 1960. Voters gather in a ballroom at the Balsams Grand Resort Hotel and cast their ballots at midnight. Because the population of the entire village is just around 75 people, and the number of eligible voters less than that, the results of the vote are broadcast nationally within minutes.

This ride begins and ends in Colebrook, at the junction of the Connecticut and Mohawk Rivers, passing through Dixville as it climbs to its namesake notch and past the Balsams hotel. One of the few remaining New Hampshire grand hotels, the Balsams is home to both cross-country and downhill ski trails and a championship golf course. Trails are also open to mountain bikers, and on-site facilities rent and repair bikes.

At the top of the ride's biggest climb, the Balsams is one of the few places to stop for supplies on this route, so stock up while you rest. From there, you'll descend through forest and pasture for much of the ride, passing very few signs of life or industry save for a few tiny villages and homes clustered here and there.

You'll follow the winding Androscoggin River for a while, then climb alongside the Connecticut as it parallels the Vermont border north for a ways. Most of this ride is minimally trafficked, except during peak foliage weeks, when leaf peepers clog the roads. If you're riding then to maximize your own foliage intake, be warned—drivers can be distracted by scenery and dangerous.

Around Mile 55, you'll enter the villages of Stark and Groveton. Supplies can be purchased here, just past the midpoint of the ride, and you'll find additional stops farther along the route. Bring enough water and food for the first portion of the trip, though, as facilities are limited.

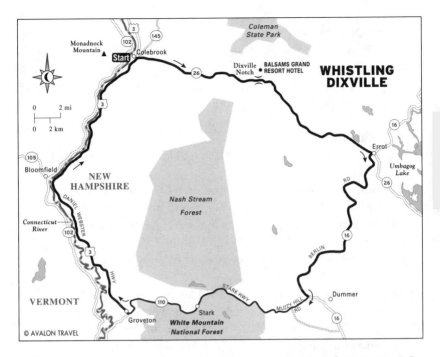

For more information, contact the North Country Chamber of Commerce, P.O. Box 1, Colebrook, NH 03576, 603/237-8939, www.northcountrychamber.org.

Options

To make a weekend out of your visit to Dixville Notch, bring a mountain bike or rent one from the Balsams Grand Resort Hotel (1000 Cold Springs Road, Dixville Notch, NH 03576, www.thebalsams.com) and ride the miles of trails on site, or explore any of the number of forest access roads and other dirt roads.

This ride is an hour from Pondicherry Pondering.

Locals' Tip: The Wilderness Restaurant (181 South Main Street, Colebrook, NH 03576, 603/237-8779) is the locals' favorite for breakfast and is a suitable place to start your calorie-burning ride.

Places to Stay: While the area abounds with campgrounds, inns, and bed-and-breakfasts, no trip to the notch is complete without a night at the Balsams Grand Resort Hotel (1000 Cold Springs Road, Dixville Notch, NH 03576, www.thebalsams.com), which is not just historic, but beautiful.

Driving Directions

From I-93, take exit 35 for US-3/Daniel Webster Highway north. Just after passing NH-26, turn right onto Pleasant Street. Look for parking along Pleasant Street. The ride begins in front of the Colebrook Fire Department at the corner of Pleasant and Cross Streets.

Route Directions

0.0 From Cross Street, turn RIGHT onto Pleasant Street until Pleasant Street ends.

0.25 Turn LEFT onto NH-26/Parsons Street. The climb begins gradually, but immediately as you ride along this thinly settled road.

7.0 The grade steepens here as you begin to climb through trees and pastures.

9.3 You're near the top when you pass the Balsams Wilderness Ski Area on your left.

10.0 Pass through Dixville Notch. The Balsams Resort Hotel is on your left, and the road passes across a pond and begins the descent. You won't see much of anything except scenery for more than 5 miles. *Supplies available.*

19.8 Pass the Errol Airport, a small landing strip, on your right.

21.2 Take a sharp RIGHT onto NH-16/White Mountain Road.

22.0 Ascend the first of three small climbs, the only interruptions in your long, steady descent, as you begin to parallel the Androscoggin River as it runs through Thirteen Woods. The road follows the river's winding path, creating long, endless turns.

37.0 Cross the Androscoggin River at Pontook Reservoir, and begin a short, steep climb up Muzzy Hill.

38.8 Turn RIGHT sharply onto NH 110-A/Muzzy Hill Road.

42.7 Turn RIGHT sharply when NH 110-A ends, onto NH-110/West Milan Road, which becomes the Stark Highway/Berlin Groveton Highway.

54.0 Begin a series of gradual climbs, with several short steep climbs, as the road follows the Upper Ammonoosuc River.

56.3 Turn RIGHT onto US-3/Daniel Webster Highway as it crosses the river. The remainder of the ride is a nearly steady climb, with a few leg-resting descents.

69.0 Follow the Connecticut River as it parallels the border with Vermont, to your left.

69.8 Bear RIGHT to stay on US-3/Daniel Webster Highway along the border.

82.7 Turn RIGHT onto Pleasant Street.

83.0 END at intersection with Cross Street.

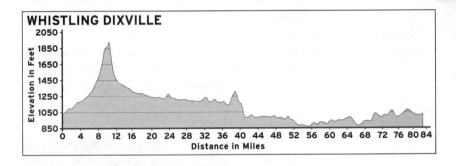

2 PONDICHERRY PONDERING
Gorham, Randolph, Bowman, and Whitefield

DIRT AND GRAVEL PATH

Difficulty: 3   **Total Distance:** 42.5 miles

Riding Time: 4.5 hours   **Elevation Gain:** 1,647 feet

Summary: Follow this hilly, rugged rail trail as it winds and climbs through scenic and remote areas of backwoods New Hampshire.

Sometimes you spend a few hours outdoors and the feeling you get is enough to last you for months. You can't stop talking about it. You tell everyone you meet. And every time you look at the pictures, you're instantly transported back in time. This is one of those rides, especially if you ride it during peak foliage season, which falls sometime in October. You'll be surrounded by colors from start to finish, with views of New Hampshire's stunning Presidential Range around you.

Starting just south of Gorham, the ride follows paved NH-16 for less than 2 miles before picking up the Dolly Copp/Pinkham B Road. This unpaved road is only sporadically maintained in winter, and it's rough in summer. From there, the route joins the 23-mile Presidential (Whitefield-Gorham) rail trail along the old Boston & Maine lines into Pondicherry Wildlife Refuge. The scenery there is breathtaking, with lots of beaver ponds and wildflowers, and you may run into more animal than human trail users. Watch the horizon for Pine Mountain, as well as the more familiar Presidentials, Madison and Adams.

Be warned, this is not your average rail trail. You've got to work on this ride. There's a good amount of climbing, though it's gradual and steady, thanks to the grade work done when the original railroad tracks were laid. And the cinder, rock, gravel, and dirt surfaces can

© ADAM CLOUGH

Though April showers may come your way, they bring mud puddles in which to play.

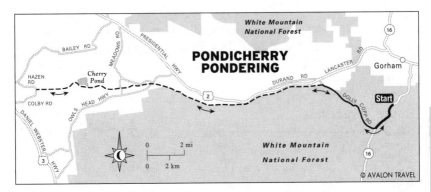

be rough at times, making this ride best-suited for a cyclocross or mountain bike, although you won't need much in the way of suspension. You'll also be more or less in the middle of nowhere, so carry supplies and tools to cover at least the bare necessities.

There's a good climb at the beginning of the ride, and again near the end, but you finish on a descent. Coast right back to your car and end this trip on a good note.

For more information, contact the Androscoggin Valley Chamber of Commerce, 164 Main Street, Berlin, NH 03570, 603/752-6060 or 800/992-7480, www.northernwhitemtnchamber.org.

Options

For an abbreviated version of this ride, start and end at the eastern terminus of the rail trail on US-2, just east of Randolph, at the Moose Brook railroad bridge.

This ride is an hour from Whistling Dixville and Two Chiefs and Three Bridges.

Locals' Tip: Carbo-load retroactively at La Bottega Saladino's Italian Market and restaurant (152 Main Street, Gorham, NH 03851, 603/466-2520, www.saladinositalianmarket.com).

Places to Stay: Rest your weary head under the clouds at the historic, enormous Dolly Copp Campground (NH-16, Gorham, NH 03851, 603/466-2713, www.campsnh.com/dollycopp.htm), a rustic site right on the bike route.

Driving Directions

This ride begins at the U.S. Forest Service Androscoggin Ranger District headquarters (300 Glen Road, Gorham, NH 03581, 603/466-2713). From I-93, take exit 35 for US-3/Daniel Webster Highway North. After 2 miles, turn right onto

NH-115 for 10 miles. Then turn right at US-2/Presidential Highway and continue about 12 miles. Bear right at Main Street to stay on US-2, then turn right onto NH-16/Glen Road. The parking area is about two miles on your right. Facilities are available.

Route Directions

0.0 From the U.S. Forest Service parking lot, turn RIGHT to head south on NH-16/White Mountain Road/Glen Road.

1.7 Turn RIGHT sharply onto Dolly Copp/Pinkham B Road.

2.1 *Dolly Copp Campground is on your left.*

5.6 Enter the rail trail on your LEFT near the old Randolph station parking area. Watch for signs.

8.9 A hiking trail, Lowe's Path, crosses the rail trail. Watch for hikers.

9.8 The trail crosses a small gravel parking area with access to US-2, formerly site of the Bowman station. Hiking trails, including the Castle Trail, head south from here. Watch for hikers. *If you need supplies or facilities or have an emergency, exit the trail here and head east on US-2. After less than a mile will be a gas station and convenience store on your left.*

11.6 The trail crosses a dirt parking area with access to Valley Road. Valley Road is gravel, and it does not see much traffic other than the occasional residential user.

12.1 The trail crosses Jefferson Notch Road at the intersection of Valley Road. Both these roads are gravel, and neither is heavily traveled.

14.9 NH-115 crosses the trail here. Watch for traffic.

16.6 NH-115A crosses the trail.

18.5 The trail passes along the shore of Cherry Pond, part of the Pondicherry Wildlife Refuge to the north.

19.8 Bear RIGHT to stay on the trail.

20.0 Cross a dirt road with access to the Whitefield Regional Airport to the south.

21.0 Pass Hazen Pond to the south.

21.3 TURN AROUND at Hazen Road.

23.4 Bear RIGHT to stay on the trail.
 26.1 Cross NH-115A.
27.5 Cross NH-115.
30.6 Cross Jefferson Notch Road at the intersection of Valley Road.
32.7 Cross Castle Trail.
36.9 Exit trail and turn RIGHT onto Dolly Copp/Pinkham B Road.
38.9 Bear RIGHT to stay on Dolly Copp/Pinkham B Road.
40.7 Turn LEFT onto NH-16/White Mountain Road/Glen Road.
42.4 Turn LEFT into the U.S. Forest Service parking lot.
42.6 END at parking area.

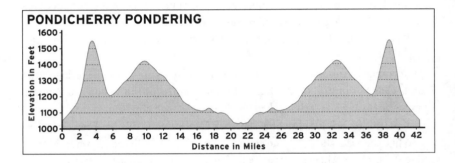

3 TWO CHIEFS AND THREE BRIDGES   BEST (

Conway and Albany

PAVED ROADS AND MINIMAL TRAFFIC

Difficulty: 2	**Total Distance:** 14.5 miles
Riding Time: 2 hours	**Elevation Gain:** 456 feet

Summary: Anyone will enjoy this easy ride along the shady Swift River, passing through Conway Village and three covered bridges.

The Kancamagus Highway, known throughout New England as "the Kanc," stretches nearly 35 miles through the White Mountain region, connecting Conway to Lincoln. Built in 1959, this road is fairly quiet much of the year, but during foliage season it can see a steady procession of leaf peepers.

Picture great convoys of cars, herds of SUVs, and tons of recreational vehicles driving slowly and erratically, stopping with no warning to get out and take pictures. Unfortunately, this is also the best time to ride if you want to see the brilliant reds and yellows of autumn. Fortunately, this ride is also a joy throughout the summer and even during late spring, when you'll have the road almost to yourself.

Kancamagus was a leader of the Penacook Confederacy of Native American tribes, and like the road, the 2,855-foot Kancamagus Pass bears his name—but this ride doesn't climb anywhere near that high. While there are some gently sloping uphills, this ride is suitable for most riders—as long as you're comfortable with the traffic.

Start and end at the Albany covered bridge, first built in 1857. The current 120-foot-long bridge was built a year later for $1,300 to replace the first one,

The scenery along Passaconaway Road is beautiful any time of year, but plan your ride for autumn to encounter peak foliage.

© CHRIS BERNARD

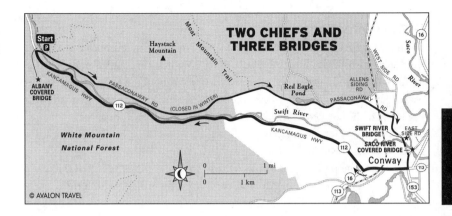

which was destroyed in a windstorm. From there, head east on quiet Passaconaway Road—named for another great Penacook leader—as it ambles along the shady banks of the Swift River, past Red Eagle Pond toward the village of Quint.

Turn south and cross the Swift River past two more covered bridges—the 129-foot Swift River Bridge, rebuilt in 1869 and bypassed by a steel bridge in 1974, and the 225-foot Saco River Bridge, rebuilt for the third time after 1890—into the quaint, busy village of Conway. Then pass west along the Kanc back to the start. If the traffic is not too heavy, or if you ride early in the morning, watch for moose along the road, especially by the banks of the Swift River.

For more information, contact the Conway Village Chamber of Commerce, 250 Main Street/NH-16, P.O. Box 1019, Conway, NH 03818, 603/447-2639, www.conwaychamber.com.

Options

To add a 13-mile loop to this ride, at Mile 6.6 turn left onto West Side Road and follow it to the end. Turn right onto River Road and right again onto NH-116. Turn left onto Kearsarge Road, and right onto North-South Road. At the traffic circle, exit right onto Mountain Valley Boulevard, and turn left onto NH-16 until it meets the Kancamagus Highway at Mile 8.2 on the original ride.

This ride is an hour from Pondicherry Pondering.

Locals' Tip: The Almost There Restaurant (1287 NH-16, Albany, NH 03818, 603/447-2325) is known among locals—and repeat visitors to the region—for its burgers and beer and a rough-around-the-edges atmosphere.

Places to Stay: The Darby Field Inn (185 Chase Hill Road, Albany, NH 03818, 800/426-4147, www.darbyfield.com) is away from the hustle and bustle of Conway village but close enough to be just as convenient. It's a stone's throw from the starting-and-ending area for this ride, too.

Driving Directions

From I-93, take exit 23 for NH-132/NH-104 North. Turn left onto US-3, and a mile later, turn RIGHT onto NH-25. After 23 miles, turn LEFT onto NH-16/White Mountain Highway for 15 miles, then LEFT onto the Kancamagus Highway. About 6 miles down, bear left onto Passaconaway Road. There's a small parking lot near the covered bridge, and the ride starts and ends there.

Route Directions

0.0 From the parking lot of the Albany covered bridge, turn RIGHT onto Passaconaway Road and cross over the bridge. Watch for openings in the floorboards.

4.8 Pass Red Eagle Pond on your left.

6.3 Passaconaway Road ends. Turn RIGHT onto West Side Road.

6.6 OPTION: Turn LEFT onto West Side Road and follow option directions.

7.1 West Side Road becomes Washington Street.

7.3 Turn RIGHT onto NH-16/Main Street/White Mountain Highway. Watch for traffic, and stick to the shoulder.

7.6 Be careful crossing angled train tracks.

8.1 Turn RIGHT onto NH-112/Kancamagus Highway, watching for traffic. Swift River is on your right.

11.0 Stay straight on the Kancamagus Highway. Just across the Swift River is Passaconaway Road.

14.2 Turn RIGHT sharply onto Passaconaway Road.

14.5 Turn RIGHT and end at parking area.

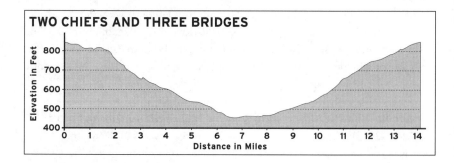

4 SALT HILL INTERSTATE

BEST ☾

Lebanon and Hanover into Vermont

PAVED ROADS AND MINIMAL TO MODERATE TRAFFIC

Difficulty: 3

Total Distance: 46 miles

Riding Time: 3.5 hours

Elevation Gain: 2,178 feet

Summary: Fit riders will thrive on this scenic, hilly interstate ride with two moderate climbs and one monster climb.

If you don't like climbing, this ride is best avoided. But if you don't mind the suffering and rewards a good peak can bring you, saddle up for this interstate tour. The ride begins and ends across from Salt Hill Pub on the Lebanon Green (plenty of parking) and heads along a mix of back roads and main streets through Hanover—home to Dartmouth College—and across the Connecticut River into Vermont.

The first climb begins almost immediately, but it's a mild one followed by a long descent to warm up your legs. From there, the next climb begins, higher than the first, as the ride continues counterclockwise through Goodrich Four Corners, Union Village, and Rices Mills. After a short descent at Mile 16, the real work starts as the route points upward—sharply at times—for the next seven miles.

© CHRIS BERNARD

The hills in the Connecticut River Valley make for some physically demanding, mentally calming rides.

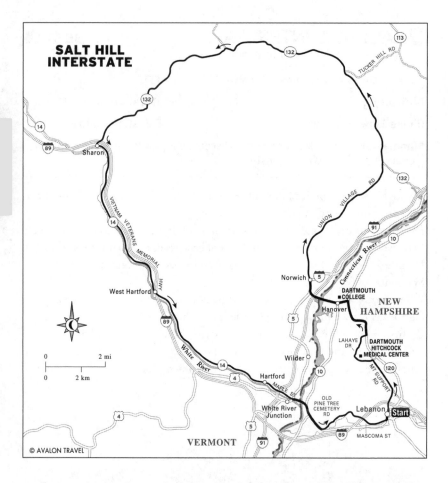

Once you've caught your breath, hold it again as the road drops into a very fast descent. It levels out while remaining mostly downhill for the next 12 miles, as it joins and follows the White River. There's a final push at Mile 40 as you climb back into White River Junction and across the Connecticut River to make your way back to the Lebanon Green, tired and thirsty.

There are bike shops near the start of the ride in Lebanon and in Hanover; supplies can be found at the early and late stages along the way. This ride is good any time of year, but come autumn the hills are alive—not with the sound of music, but with a crayon box of colors when the foliage spreads as far as the eye can see.

For more information, contact the Hanover Area Chamber of Commerce, P.O. Box 5105, Hanover, NH 03755, 603/643-3115, www.hanoverchamber.org.

Options

The Northern Rail Trail ride begins just a few hundred feet from here and offers a challenge much less strenuous while no less scenic. If you're fit and still want more pain, Glass Family Ramble begins about 20 minutes from this ride and could be combined for a long weekend of riding.

Locals' Tip: The trail begins and ends on the green outside Salt Hill Pub (2 West Park Street, Lebanon, NH 03766, 603/448-4532, www.salthillpub.com), a cyclist-friendly pub bursting with tremendous local knowledge. Meat lovers, try the Firehouse burger.

Places to Stay: For affordable, unexciting rooms, the Days Inn Lebanon/ Hanover (135 NH-120, Lebanon, NH 03766, 603/448-5070) is well situated and offers free waffles, the breakfast of cyclists.

Driving Directions

From I-89, take exit 18 south onto NH-120. Turn left at the stop sign and follow Hanover Street to the Lebanon Green. Parking is available around the Lebanon Green (Colburn Park) on Park Street.

Route Directions

0.0 From Park Street, turn RIGHT on Church Street, LEFT on Taylor Street, and RIGHT onto Hanover Street/NH-120 North.

0.4 Bear LEFT to stay on Hanover Street when NH-120 splits.

1.3 Turn LEFT on Mount Support Road/Heater Road.

2.5 Turn LEFT on Lahaye Drive/Medical Center Drive/Hitchcock Loop Road around the hospital campus.

3.5 Turn LEFT on Northern Access Road/Medical Center Drive.

4.1 Turn LEFT on NH-120 North.

6.1 Turn LEFT on North College Street, passing through Dartmouth College.

6.5 Turn RIGHT on an unmarked road along the Dartmouth Green, and then LEFT on North Main Street. *Supplies available.*

6.7 Turn RIGHT on West Wheelock Street/NH-10A. *Bike shop straight ahead.* Cross the Connecticut River into Vermont. NH-10A becomes Main Street/US-5 North.

8.1 Stay STRAIGHT on Main Street when US-5 North splits right. Main Street becomes Union Village Road.

13.5 Union Village Road becomes VT-132.

14.0 Bear LEFT to stay on VT-132. Continue on VT-132.

22.0 Turn LEFT to stay on VT-132.

28.5 Just after passing under I-89, turn LEFT on VT-14 along the White River. Continue on VT-14.

34.5 *Supplies available at the West Hartford Village Store.*

40.4 Pass Watson Park on the right. *This is a good place to rest.*

40.6 Pass under I-91. Continue on VT-14/Maple Street.

41.5 Cross the Connecticut River into New Hampshire. VT-14/Maple Street becomes NH-4/Bridge Street. Watch for bridge traffic.

41.8 Turn RIGHT to stay on NH-4/NH-10.

42.8 Bear LEFT onto Old Pine Tree Cemetery Road, through Old Pine Tree Cemetery.

44.5 Old Pine Tree Cemetery Road becomes Mascoma Street and passes over I-89.

45.7 Mascoma Street becomes Park Street as it meets the Lebanon Green (Colburn Park).

46.0 Return to starting point.

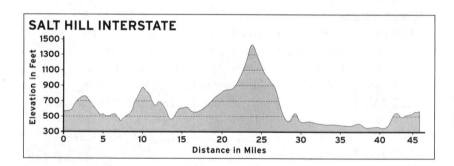

5 NORTHERN RAIL TRAIL
Lebanon to Grafton

RAIL TRAIL WITH BALLAST, DIRT

Difficulty: 3   **Total Distance:** 45.2 miles

Riding Time: 3-5 hours   **Elevation Gain:** 724 feet

Summary: This long, mostly flat, off-road rail trail through varied terrain and scenery is suitable for most riders.

This scenic rail trail wends its way along the Mascoma River, the shores of Mascoma Lake, and the bed of the former Boston & Maine railroad's Northern Line from quaint downtown Lebanon out to Grafton. The foliage along this trail is brilliant in autumn—in fact, that's how the town of Orange got its name.

On the fairly flat ground through the towns of Enfield, Canaan, and Orange, most of the trail's surface is covered with ballast. Road bikes are fine, as are hybrids, comfort bikes, and cyclocross bikes. Mountain bikes are overkill. After passing Mascoma Lake, about four miles in, the trail becomes a little bumpier and a little sandier.

You'll pass under several overpasses and through some large culverts; in East Lebanon you'll pass a dam on the former site of a bustling 18th-century sawmill. Other features include a covered bridge, a few old train depots (one converted into a coin laundry), and seven Mascoma River crossings. A picnic spot at the 4-mile mark provides views and a place to swim in summer.

© CHRIS BERNARD

There's no shortage of places to stop for scenic rests on the Northern Rail Trail.

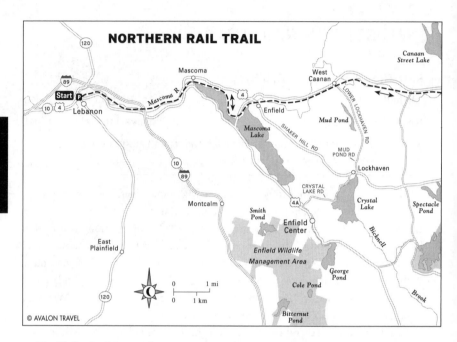

You'll find additional access points (turn around whenever you like) and parking areas in Enfield and Canaan. For up-to-date trail information, contact the Friends of the Northern Rail Trail, P.O. Box 206, Enfield, NH 03748, www.northernrailtrail.org.

Options

If the 45.2-mile out-and-back ride is too long for you, park a car at the end in Grafton or begin at any of the additional access points along the way. Cutting the distance lowers the difficulty of this ride, which is suitable for reasonably fit novices.

This ride is minutes from Salt Hill Interstate and Glass Family Ramble, and they could be combined for a long weekend of riding.

Locals' Tip: The Salt Hill Pub (2 West Park Street, Lebanon, NH 03766, 603/448-4532, www.salthillpub.com), where this trail begins, has a friendly staff with good food and drinks.

Places to Stay: The Trumbull House (40 Etna Road, Hanover, NH 03755, 800/651-5141, www.trumbullhouse.com) is a bed-and-breakfast in nearby Hanover, home to Dartmouth College.

Driving Directions

From I-89, take exit 18 and drive south on NH-120 toward the center of Lebanon. Drive 0.3 mile and turn left onto Hanover Street at the stop sign. Follow Hanover

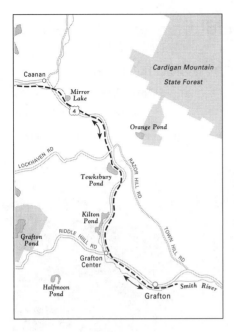

Street 0.5 mile to the town green. Continue around the green on South Park Street and turn left onto School Street. Go straight down Campbell Street, following signs for the Carter Community Building Association (CCBA) and Northern Rail Trail. Parking for the Northern Rail Trail is available at the CCBA in Lebanon. The trailhead is on the right; you'll see an information billboard with a trail map. The Grafton trailhead is at the Grafton Recreation field, Prescott Hill Road, off NH-4 East in Grafton. Services and supplies are available in Lebanon, Enfield, and Canaan; a bike shop is in Lebanon.

Route Directions

0.0 From the parking lot by the Carter Community Building Association (CCBA), ride toward the trailhead on Spencer Street.

3.6 *Picnic bench.*

4.0 *Picnic spot and swimming area on Mascoma Lake.*

6.7 *Supplies available in Enfield.*

13.5 *Supplies available in Canaan. You can leave your bike at a bike rack along the trail.*

22.6 Enter parking lot for Grafton Recreation Field. TURN AROUND.

45.2 Return to CCBA parking area in Lebanon.

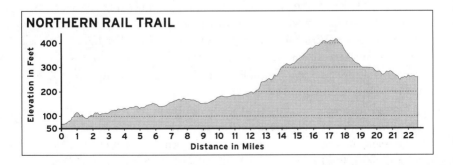

6 GLASS FAMILY RAMBLE   BEST C
Cornish

PAVED, RURAL ROADS WITH LIGHT TO MODERATE TRAFFIC

Difficulty: 3   **Total Distance:** 30.3 miles

Riding Time: 2.5 hours   **Elevation Gain:** 1,779 feet

Summary: Enjoy a hilly ride that runs through beautiful, rural farm country made famous by the artists who've called it home.

Cornish is perhaps best known as the site of the thriving early-20th-century artists' haven, Cornish Colony of New Hampshire. Established by sculptor Augustus Saint-Gaudens—incidentally, one of the first people ever to eat Kellogg's Corn Flakes—the colony attracted such prominent artists as Maxfield Parrish and Herbert Adams, and the area was considered one of the most beautifully gardened villages in the United States.

But Cornish was also home to reclusive novelist J. D. Salinger. While the location of his former residence was a secret maintained by steadfast

Everything about this ride says "quaint New England landscape."

locals, his presence brought the town some notoriety over the last few decades. This ride, named after the Glass family that populates many of Salinger's short stories, showcases the calming rural beauty that likely attracted him to the area in the first place. It's as beautiful a ride as you could ask for.

This ride follows paved roads over one-lane bridges and shady, curvy stretches. You'll ride over meadows and rolling hills, passing farm stands and getting frequent glimpses of Vermont's Mount Ascutney to the west. You'll pass old brick churches and several general stores, spaced out well for refueling. You'll also pass several covered bridges, including the longest in the country, the 460-foot Cornish-Windsor Bridge to Vermont.

On a summer ride, you can stop at Saint-Gaudens National Historic Site to tour the flower gardens or enjoy one of the frequent workshops or concerts.

For more information, contact the Saint-Gaudens National Historic Site, 139 Saint-Gaudens Road, Cornish, NH 03745, 603/675-2175, www.nps.gov/saga.

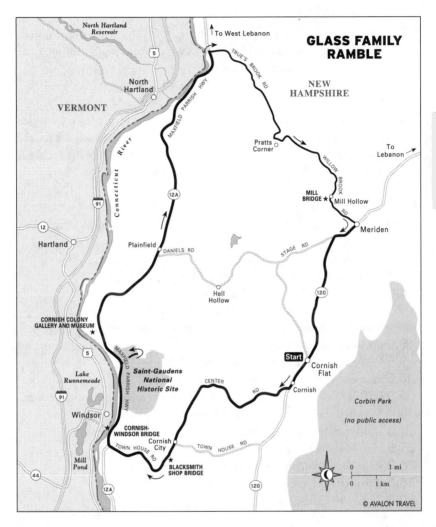

Options

For a shorter route that cuts out most of the hills—but leaves the beauty intact—turn right onto Daniels Road at Mile 13. From there, turn right onto Stage Road at Mile 14, then right onto NH-120 South at Mile 19.2 to return to the parking area.

This ride is minutes from Salt Hill Interstate and Northern Rail Trail.

Locals' Tip: Since you're parking at the Cornish General Store (226 NH-120, Cornish, NH 03745, 603/542-0660), head inside before the ride for cold water and snack food, and again after you've finished for a treat. This traditional shop is anything but, with a new indoor archery range and its own Facebook page.

Places to Stay: Across the river in Vermont, the Juniper Hill Inn

(153 Pembroke Road, Windsor, VT 05089, 802/674-5273, www.juniperhillinn
.com) offers beautiful accommodations in a 29-room converted mansion, right
across from multiple hiking and biking trails.

Driving Directions

From I-89, take exit 18 and drive south through Lebanon town center. Continue
on NH-120 south for approximately 10 miles to Cornish Flat and look for the
Cornish General Store at the intersection with School Street. Supplies are available in Lebanon and West Lebanon; there's a bike shop in Lebanon.

Route Directions

0.0 From Cornish General Store, ride south on NH-120. *Supplies available.*

0.9 Turn RIGHT onto Center Road.

2.8 Pass United Church of Cornish on right.

5.3 Turn RIGHT onto Town House Road.

6.8 Pass Blacksmith Shop Bridge.

7.7 Turn RIGHT onto Route 12A north, also known as Maxfield
Parrish Highway. *Supplies available at convenience store.*

8.0 Pass Cornish-Windsor Bridge.

9.5 Pass Saint-Gaudens National Historic Site.

10.9 Pass Cornish Colony Gallery and Museum.

13.0 OPTION: Turn right onto Daniels Road and follow option directions.

19.4 Turn RIGHT onto True's Brook Road.

21.0 Road becomes Willow Brook Road.

25.5 Pass Mill Bridge (covered).

26.2 Pass Meriden center and Kimball Union Academy.

26.5 Turn RIGHT onto Route 120 south.

30.3 Return to Cornish General Store.

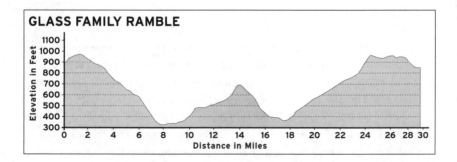

GLASS FAMILY RAMBLE

7 SUNAPEE LAKES LOOP
Sunapee and New London

PAVED ROADS WITH LIGHT TO MODERATE TRAFFIC

Difficulty: 3   **Total Distance:** 29.2 miles

Riding Time: 2.5 hours   **Elevation Gain:** 1,200 feet

Summary: For a breath of fresh air, tour the rural lakes region and take in the fall foliage along this hilly ride.

Less busy than the Lake Winnipesaukee area, the Sunapee Lakes region is every bit as beautiful—or more so—and better-suited to cycling, thanks to the rural roads and the light traffic. Ride in the summer and you'll see a seasonal community of beaches, canoes, and anglers. Ride in the fall and you'll see foliage galore. The area offers plenty of sights to hold your attention, including Sunapee Harbor, several wildlife preserves, a few old cemeteries, and some quaint northern New England towns.

The route climbs gentle rolling hills along paved roads. At times, traffic moves quickly, but only when you're on the major state roads. Once you get onto the rural back roads, you'll see fewer cars.

The lake itself is New Hampshire's fifth-largest, boasting 70 miles of shoreline and three lighthouses. The deep, cold, clean water holds a lot of fish, and you'll see plenty of people trying to catch them. In the winter, when the lake freezes, a micro-community of ice-fishing shanties moves out onto the ice. In winter, it also draws skiers to the modest Mount Sunapee Ski Area. The lakefront is home, at least seasonally, to several names you may recognize, including, most famously, Aerosmith frontman Steven Tyler, who has written about his childhood summers in the area, during which he met the other members of the band.

This route hits some of the more remote stretches of the region, and you'll find few convenience stores along the way. Plan ahead and stock up on any supplies you need before your ride.

For more information, contact the Lake Sunapee Region Chamber of Commerce, P.O. Box 532, New London, NH 03257, 603/526-6575 or 877/526-6575, www.sunapeevacations.com.

Options
For a shorter 19-mile loop around the big lake, at Mile 9 stay straight on NH-103A, and at Mile 13.8 turn left onto NH-11 West back to the starting point.

This ride is not far from Lovewell Mountain Ride and Kittredge Hill Loop.

Locals' Tip: The Quack Shack (74 Main Street, Sunapee, NH 03782,

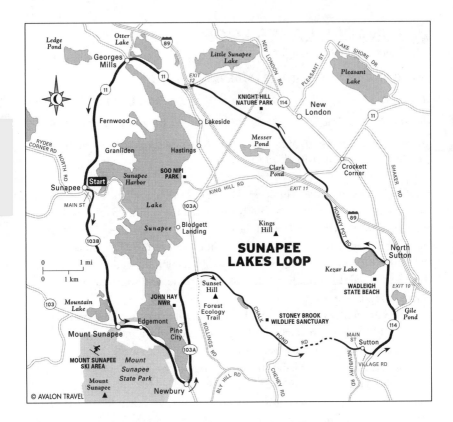

603/763-3084) serves Maine-made Gifford's ice cream from mid-June until Labor Day, just the ticket after a good, hilly ride on a warm day.

Places to Stay: Dexter's Inn (258 Stagecoach Road, Sunapee, NH 03782, 603/763-5571, www.dextersnh.com) is all you could want from a bed-and-breakfast, plus friendly hosts to match.

Driving Directions

From points north, take I-89 to exit 12A toward Georges Mills. Turn right onto Springfield Road and drive about 0.5 mile to NH-11. Turn right onto NH-11 and drive south for about 3.5 miles, until you reach the intersection with NH-103B. From the south and east, take I-89 to exit 12 toward Sunapee. Turn left onto Newport Road/NH-11. Drive approximately 5 miles to the intersection with NH-103B. Parking is available in Sunapee Harbor off NH-11. The ride starts at the information booth at the intersection of Routes 103B and 11. The closest bike shop is in Newbury.

Route Directions

0.0 START at the information booth on NH-11 and ride south on NH-103B.

3.4 Enter a traffic circle. Continue on NH-103 East. Pass Mount Sunapee State Park and beaches.

6.0 Turn LEFT onto NH-103A. Pass Outspokin Bicycle Shop.

9.0 Turn RIGHT onto Chalk Pond Road. Road turns to hard-packed dirt for a mile or so. OPTION: Stay straight on NH-103A and follow option directions.

13.9 Bear LEFT on Main Street in the town of Sutton.

14.1 Bear LEFT onto Village Road. Pass a cemetery on the right.

14.3 Turn LEFT onto NH-114.

16.8 In North Sutton, turn LEFT onto Kezar Street past Kezar Lake.

18.0 Bear RIGHT onto Hominy Pot Road, passing under I-89.

20.0 Cross NH-11/Old King Hill Road onto Old Main Street, which becomes Knights Hill Road and then Burpee Hill Road.

23.8 Turn LEFT onto NH-11/Newport Road, between Lake Sunapee and Otter Lake, through the village of Georges Mills.

29.2 END at parking area.

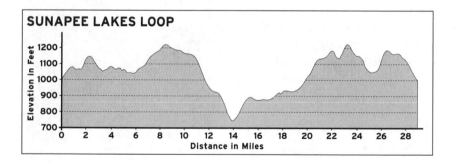

SUNAPEE LAKES LOOP

8 KITTREDGE HILL LOOP BEST **(**

Pillsbury State Park, Washington

SINGLE-TRACK

Difficulty: 5

Total Distance: 5.5 miles

Riding Time: 3 hours

Elevation Gain: 759 feet

Summary: A technical and challenging mountain bike ride for advanced, fit cyclists.

Pillsbury State Park is a beautiful place. The secluded woodland setting surrounds a few gorgeous lakes and ponds, and you'll see and hear wildlife aplenty—but you'll be moving too fast to focus and breathing hard enough to scare anything away. To improve your chances at encountering moose, bear, or other animals, ease off the adrenaline—if you can.

The park attracts hikers from afar, but it's just as well-suited for mountain biking—and maybe better. The Balanced Rock Trail, Five Summers Trail, and Mad Road all offer good options, though these aren't beginner trails. Suspension bikes are recommended.

This particular route starts on the Bear Pond Trail and is among the park's most challenging. One section follows the Monadnock-Sunapee Greenway Trail high on Kittredge Hill, offering a mix of trail conditions and significant obstacles. Don't be surprised to find yourself walking your bike at times.

Overall, it's a rocky, rooty, tough ride. The trails are best described as old jeep roads deeply rutted in sections. Expect steep climbs, roots, logs, ruts, and lots of mud.

The best time to ride this is probably late summer, when the trails are driest and the weather most predictable—and when you've got a summer of riding already in your legs and

© CHRIS BERNARD

Riders, hang on for dear life on the Kittredge Hill trails – they'll challenge even veteran riders with coiled springs for legs.

lungs. If you ride in late fall and maintain some semblance of quiet, you've got a good chance of seeing moose.

For more information, contact Pillsbury State Park, NH-31, Washington, NH 03280, 603/863-2860, www.nhparks.state.nh.us/state-parks/.

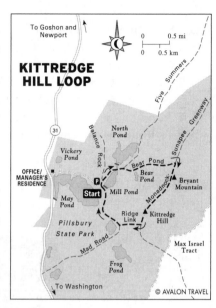

Options

Lovewell Mountain Ride begins in nearby Washington, and it is an equally challenging mountain bike ride that intersects with the Monadnock-Sunapee Greenway Trail. If you spend a little time with a good topo map, you can connect them. Or piece together a longer ride on the marked trails listed above—detailed trail maps are available at the park office.

Locals' Tip: You can't go wrong at the Washington General Store (29 North Main Street, Washington, NH 03280, 603/495-3131); the breakfast sandwiches at the small counter are worth writing home about.

Places to Stay: A number of rustic campsites, including a few canoe-in only sites offering quiet views of the mountains, can be found at Pillsbury State Forest (NH-31, Washington, NH 03280, 603/863-2860, www.nhparks.state.nh.us/state-parks/).

Driving Directions

From the south, take I-89 to exit 5 onto NH-202/9. Follow NH-9 to NH-31 in Hillsborough. Drive approximately 10 miles north on NH-31 and look for signs for Pillsbury State Park. The park is just north of the Franklin Pierce Homestead on NH-31. Stop at the manager's office to pay the $4 entry fee and be sure to get a trail map of the park. Follow the entry road to the far end, where you'll find a parking lot. The ride starts on the trail to the left of the parking lot. Supplies are available in Newport, about 9 miles north of the park, or in Washington to the south.

Route Directions

0.0 Turn LEFT out of the circular parking lot onto trail.

0.1 Continue past gate toward Bear Pond.

0.6 Bear RIGHT onto Bear Pond Trail.

2.0 Turn RIGHT onto Monadnock-Sunapee Greenway Trail (marked with a brown and yellow sign).

3.8 Turn RIGHT onto Ridge Link Trail.

4.5 Turn RIGHT onto Mad Road Trail.

5.4 Turn LEFT after gate and bridge.

5.5 Turn RIGHT onto main road uphill to return to parking lot.

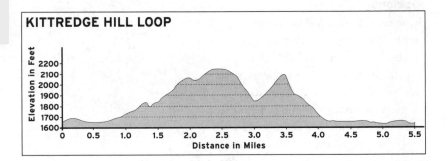

9 LOVEWELL MOUNTAIN RIDE   BEST C
Washington

DIRT ROADS, DOUBLE-TRACK

Difficulty: 5	**Total Distance:** 15 miles
Riding Time: 3 hours	**Elevation Gain:** 1,273 feet

Summary: A demanding, hilly mountain bike ride on rough terrain, this one's not for the faint of heart.

If you're looking for a physically challenging ride that never gets too technical, this fits the bill. This is a highly recommended ride for fit cyclists who like to suffer a little. It also offers excellent wildlife viewing opportunities—watch for moose, deer, and upland birds.

For the first five miles, you're heading steadily uphill—though you gain just a few hundred feet of elevation, the loose, rocky trail and bigger stones scattered throughout make the climbing difficult.

From the top you'll plummet downhill, a raucous descent over bumpy trails that will jar you if you're riding a bike without suspension. (You don't need full suspension, but front suspension definitely helps.) In other words, this is not a challenging single-track descent, but a fun, wild plunge down wide dirt roads.

At the bottom, the route meets a flat, paved road that cuts through a scenic

For one brief stretch, the Lovewell Mountain Ride descends out of the wooded mountainside past an active farm before turning back into the woods.

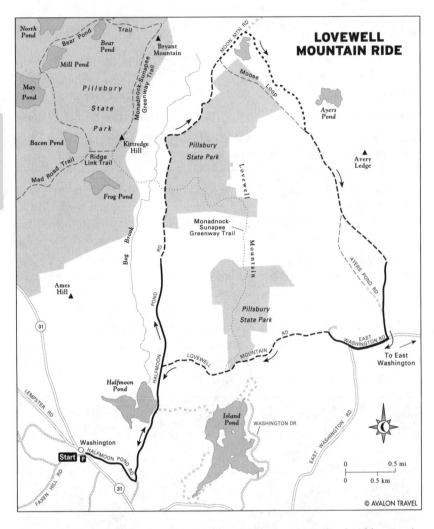

farm with cows, goats, and ostriches penned right up against the shoulder. Don't get too comfortable, though. You're about to start climbing again.

Only this time, it's worse. Much, much worse. The trail regains nearly all the elevation lost coming downhill, but this time over more than 1.5 miles, which pitches the trail at a ridiculously steep grade. This trail is in better shape than the first one, with dirt and mud more common than loose gravel, but even mountain goats with granny gears will be looking for one more cog as the grade worsens with each corner. As you climb, moving very slowly, you're an easy target for the dense clouds of biting insects that hover here.

The trails are mostly well-marked by snowmobile signs and the white blaze of the Monadnock-Sunapee Greenway, a long-distance hiking trail. If you ride during the spring or a particularly rainy summer, expect mud—deep mud. And puddles—deep puddles.

Options
Seeing stars? Gasping for breath? Legs turned to jelly? Cut yourself some slack and trade the final hill for something a little gentler. Around Mile 10, turn left on East Washington Road, and then left onto NH-31 to rejoin your original route.

This ride is minutes from Kittredge Hill Loop and could be combined for a long weekend of riding. It's also a short drive from Sunapee Lakes Loop.

Locals' Tip: While you're without a lot of options in the area, you still can't go wrong at the Washington General Store (29 North Main Street, Washington, NH 03280, 603/495-3131), where breakfast sandwiches at the small counter are worth writing home about.

Places to Stay: Pillsbury State Park (NH-31, Washington, NH 03280, 603/863-2860, www.nhparks.state.nh.us/state-parks/) has a number of rustic campsites, including a few canoe-in only sites offering quiet views of the mountains—including the one climbed on this ride.

Driving Directions
From the north, take I-89 to exit 13 in Grantham. Drive south on NH-10 for approximately 18 miles. Bear left onto NH-31 and drive 9 miles to Washington. From the south, take I-89 to exit 5 onto NH-202/9. Follow NH-9 to NH-31 in Hillsborough and drive 8 miles north on NH-31 to Washington. Parking is available behind the large white church meetinghouse on the hill. The route starts from the tiny green, at the junction of NH-31 (North Main Street) and Halfmoon Pond Road.

Route Directions
0.0 Ride southeast on Halfmoon Pond Road.

0.7 Bear LEFT on Halfmoon Pond Road at T intersection.

1.3 Pass Snow Road. Halfmoon Pond is visible through the trees on the left.

2.0 Pass Lovewell Mountain Road on the right (you will be returning on this road).

3.5 Pass Martin Road on the right.

4.1 Pass Monadnock-Sunapee Greenway Trail on the right.

4.7 Bear RIGHT at fork in road, toward bridge.

6.0 Turn RIGHT at snowmobile trail markers.

7.0 Turn LEFT at small grassy area, onto Ayers Pond Road.

8.2 Continue STRAIGHT. Pass big yellow gate on left.

9.8 Bear RIGHT onto East Washington Road (paved).

10.2 Bear RIGHT onto Lovewell Mountain Road (dirt). OPTION: Turn LEFT on East Washington Road and follow option directions.

10.6 Bear LEFT on Lovewell Mountain Road.

11.0 Begin climbing again. (Don't be afraid to carry your bike—this incredibly steep climb is brutal.) After this hill you're home free.

12.8 Turn LEFT at intersection with Halfmoon Pond Road. (This is the same route you rode in on.)

14.3 Turn RIGHT, continuing on Halfmoon Pond Road.

15.0 Return to starting point.

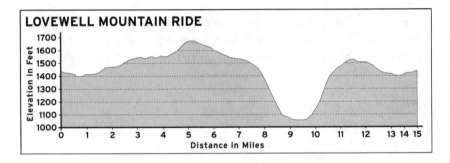

LOVEWELL MOUNTAIN RIDE

10 FOUR COVERED BRIDGES RIDE
Swanzey and Winchester

**PAVED ROADS WITH DETERIORATING PAVEMENT
AND MODERATE TRAFFIC**

Difficulty: 2   **Total Distance:** 14.8 miles

Riding Time: 1.5-2 hours   **Elevation Gain:** 241 feet

Summary: This sightseeing ride follows several covered bridges – the only difficult part is the traffic and the rough pavement.

Of the more than 300 covered bridges built in the state between 1827 and 1912, about 54 still stand. This ride follows paved roads in varying conditions through four of the six bridges in this area near Keene, including the 137-foot Thompson Bridge, built in 1832, and the 67-foot Carlton Bridge, built in 1869.

This lazy ride starts and ends at an old cemetery and the Potash Bowl, a natural amphitheater, and passes through beautiful stands of pine trees in the Yale-Toumey Forest. You'll find gradual, low-level hills and shady terrain, perfect for a mellow Sunday afternoon. Pay attention on the two short stretches on NH-10, where traffic moves fast.

The four wooden covered bridges are in scenic settings, offering lots of visual treats. A note on traversing the bridges: All but Thompson Bridge in West Swanzey are single-lane only. Pay close attention to drivers as you pass through.

© CHRIS BERNARD

New Hampshire's many covered bridges offer endless beautiful photo opportunities for cyclists.

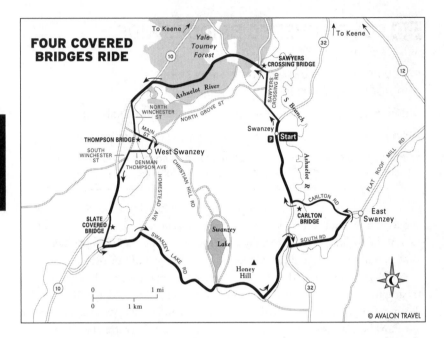

For more information about the area, contact Keene City Hall, 3 Washington Street, Keene, NH 03431, 603/352-0133, www.ci.keene.nh.us.

Options

To add a 2.5 mile loop around Swanzey Lake to this ride, turn left at Mile 9 onto West Shore Road, following it around the lake onto East Shore Road and rejoining the ride on Swanzey Lake Road at Mile 9.2.

Child's Bog Cross Loop and Our Town and the Hancock Hills are nearby.

Locals' Tip: Start your lazy Sunday with breakfast at the Swanzey Diner (515 Monadnock Highway, Swanzey, NH 03431, 603/352-8939).

Places to Stay: The Inn of the Tartan Fox (350 Old Homestead Highway, Swanzey, NH 03431, 603/357-9308, www.tartanfox.com) is a wild place with Scottish themes but all the amenities, dating back to 1833.

Driving Directions

From Keene, take NH-32 south for approximately 5 miles to Swanzey. The ride begins in Swanzey at the town hall, right from NH-32. Parking is available at the town hall. Supplies and bike shops are available in Keene.

Route Directions

0.0 Turn RIGHT out of the town hall parking lot onto NH-32 north.

0.1 Turn LEFT onto Sawyers Crossing Road. Pass Potash Bowl on left.

0.4 Follow signs to Sawyers Crossing Bridge.

1.0 Cross bridge. (Take care crossing one-lane bridges.)

1.2 Bear LEFT. Continue through Yale-Toumey Forest.

3.2 Turn LEFT onto NH-10 south.

3.7 Turn LEFT onto North Winchester Street.

4.2 Turn LEFT onto Main Street. Cross Thompson Bridge; two-way traffic.

4.5 Turn RIGHT onto Homestead Avenue.

4.6 Turn RIGHT onto Denman Thompson Avenue.

5.0 Turn RIGHT onto South Winchester Street.

5.0 Turn LEFT onto NH-10 south.

5.7 *Supplies available at a convenience store and ice-cream stand.*

5.8 Turn LEFT in the direction of Westport Station (unmarked road).

6.3 Cross Slate Covered Bridge.

6.4 Turn LEFT just after bridge onto Swanzey Lake Road (unmarked).

7.2 Bear RIGHT on Swanzey Lake Road.

9.0 OPTION: Turn LEFT onto West Shore Road and follow option directions.

11.1 Turn RIGHT onto NH-32.

11.2 Turn LEFT onto South Road.

12.2 Turn LEFT onto Weber Hill Road.

12.4 Turn LEFT onto Carlton Road.

13.4 Cross Carlton Bridge.

13.6 Turn RIGHT onto NH-32 north.

14.8 Return to Swanzey Town Hall.

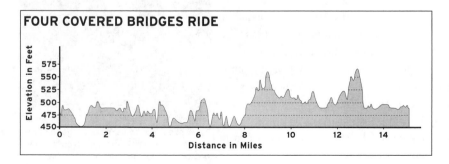

FOUR COVERED BRIDGES RIDE

11 CHILD'S BOG CROSS LOOP
Harrisville

DIRT ROADS, SINGLE-TRACK, PAVED ROADS WITH MINIMAL TRAFFIC

Difficulty: 3   **Total Distance:** 6.3 miles

Riding Time: 1.5 hours   **Elevation Gain:** 405 feet

Summary: An excellent ride for a cyclocross bike, this mix of roads and trails tours a small town and the woods around it.

Old brick mill buildings and waterfalls punctuate the small town of Harrisville, where the mills are reputed to be the country's only surviving unaltered examples of a 19th-century industrial community. Populated by just over 1,000 residents, the town appears on a lot of postcards as an example of what New England used to look like—and here, still does.

The historic, picturesque village is the starting point for a ride that takes you through thickly wooded terrain, a good jaunt for the advanced beginner or intermediate rider.

The route starts in front of the Harrisville General Store, open since 1838 and now run by a local historic nonprofit.

Head down Main Street, then follow a trail varying in width from single-track to a four-wheel-drive road. Cross a paved road, then follow a dirt road before continuing on a rather wide section of the Monadnock-Sunapee Greenway Trail, a long-distance hiking trail. The return ride is on the paved Nelson Road, which takes you by pretty Harrisville Pond.

There's nothing technical about this ride, just fast dirt roads, nondemanding single-track, and quiet paved roads—a good mix for either tearing up the tires with some speed or lazing around on a slow, mellow ride. Cyclocross bikes are ideal, though mountain bikes will work fine. The scenery is at its best in summer and fall. Child's Bog Dam is a great place to stop for lunch.

The Child's Bog trails make for good old-fashioned mountain biking — even for riders on good old-fashioned mountain bikes.

© CHRIS BERNARD

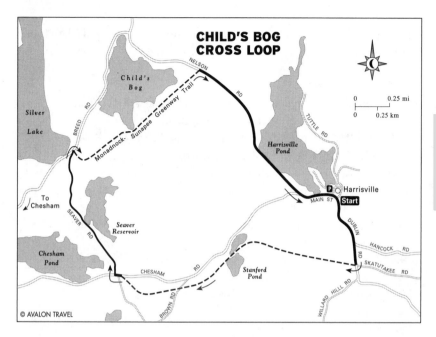

For more information, contact the Harrisville Town Hall, Chesham Road, Harrisville, NH 03450, 603/827-3431, www.keenenh.com/harrisville. For more information on the Monadnock-Sunapee Greenway Trail, contact the Trail Club, P.O. Box 164, Marlow, NH 03456, www.msgtc.org.

Options

This ride is within spitting distance of Four Covered Bridges Ride and Our Town and the Hancock Hills. Make a long weekend of a stay in the area and stack rides for a few days of fun.

Locals' Tip: The Harrisville General Store (29 Church Street, Harrisville, NH 03450, 603/827-3138, www.harrisvillegeneralstore.com), where the ride starts and ends, is also a great place to fill your larder.

Places to Stay: The Hancock Inn bed-and-breakfast (3 Main Street, Hancock, NH 03449, 603/525-3318, www.hancockinn.com), the state's oldest original inn still in operation, is a short distance away.

Driving Directions

From Peterborough, take NH-101 west to Dublin, approximately 7 miles. Turn right onto Dublin Road and follow the signs to Harrisville. Drive approximately 3.5 miles to the center of Harrisville (Dublin Street becomes Main Street). Parking is available throughout this tiny town and supplies are available at the general store. The route begins at Harrisville General Store on the corner of Church and Main Streets. The nearest bike shops are in Keene and Peterborough.

Route Directions

0.0 From the parking lot of the general store, take a RIGHT onto Main Street, which becomes Dublin Road.

0.6 Turn RIGHT onto dirt path, across from Skatutakee Road.

2.0 Turn RIGHT onto Brown Road (dirt).

2.1 Turn LEFT onto Chesham Road.

2.6 Turn RIGHT onto Seaver Road. Pass Seaver Reservoir.

3.6 Bear RIGHT at fork in road.

3.7 Turn RIGHT onto Rosemary Trail, a section of the Monadnock-Sunapee Greenway Trail (marked with a white blaze).

4.2 Pass Child's Bog Dam. *There's a picnic spot on the right side of the dam.*

4.9 Turn RIGHT onto Nelson Road.

6.1 Turn LEFT onto Chesham Road.

6.3 Return to starting point.

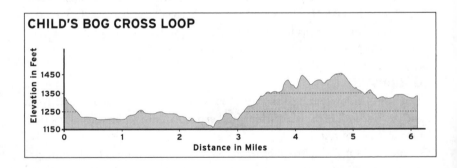

CHILD'S BOG CROSS LOOP

12 OUR TOWN AND THE HANCOCK HILLS
Peterborough and Hancock

DIRT ROAD, PAVED BIKE PATH, PAVED ROADS WITH SOME DETERIORATING PAVEMENT AND MODERATE TO MINIMAL TRAFFIC

Difficulty: 3   **Total Distance:** 17.4 miles

Riding Time: 2–2.5 hours   **Elevation Gain:** 1,071 feet

Summary: A mix of terrain keeps this scenic ride interesting, offering lots to see on a fun, moderately challenging ride.

Peterborough is probably most famous for being the town Thornton Wilder based Grover's Corners on in his play *Our Town,* which he wrote here in the early 1900s. The town remains artist-friendly, and the professional theater of the Peterborough Players, which you'll pass on this ride, offers a variety of productions during the summer.

The route follows the Contoocook River down Summer Street before hooking up with a section of a rail trail bike path. It continues up a long, gradual hill, past farms, and over hilly terrain complete with mountain vistas and erratic boulders. The return route covers similar terrain near the town of Hancock on NH-137, a curvy road with minimal shoulders and fast traffic.

A turn onto Sargent Camp Road provides a pleasant respite along a packed-

The Hancock Hills ride mixes bike paths with dirt and paved roads for a never-boring blend of terrain and scenery.

dirt road. As you pass Halfmoon Pond, reflective views of Hancock's Skatutakee Mountain appear on the left. After Boston University's Sargent Camp, the route continues past a few horse farms and offers glimpses of Pack Monadnock and Temple Mountain to the east and vistas of Mount Monadnock to the west. On MacDowell Road, you'll come across MacDowell Colony, a private artists' colony founded in 1907 to provide artists with a haven where they can pursue their work without interruption. A pleasant downhill coast at the end of the ride brings you back to the starting point in downtown Peterborough.

This route is suitable for any bike, but wide-tired bikes will make the dirt roads and rough pavement easier to pass.

This route could easily be made into a day trip, with a couple of tasty options for lunch in Hancock, about halfway through the ride. For more information about the area, contact the Peterborough Chamber of Commerce, P.O. Box 401, Peterborough, NH 03458, 603/924-7234, www.peterboroughchamber.com; or visit the town's website, www.townofpeterborough.com.

Options

Extend this ride another mile by following the marked bike trail at Mile 1.6 rather than turning left or on your return.

Locals' Tip: The Peterboro Diner (10 Depot Street, Peterborough, NH 03458, 603/924-6710) looks like you want a New England diner to look and serves food that tastes like you want it to taste, all right on the river's edge.

Places to Stay: Book a room at the Jack Daniel's Motor Inn (80 Concord Street, Peterborough, NH 03458, 603/924-7548, www.jackdanielsinn.com) on the Contoocook River, and ask the owners about the name.

Driving Directions

From Manchester and points east, take NH-101 west to Peterborough. After the intersection with NH-202, turn right onto Grove Street. Drive to the end, to the junction with Main Street, and turn right. The route starts at the intersection of Main and Summer Streets. Free parking is available throughout the downtown area, including a municipal parking lot along School Street, just off Grove Street. Supplies are available in Peterborough and a bike shop is on Grove Street.

Route Directions

0.0 Proceed north on Summer Street from the intersection with Main Street, across from Roy's Market.

0.8 Turn RIGHT onto marked bike route.

1.6 Turn LEFT onto Hunt Road, then immediately RIGHT onto Summer Street. Summer Street eventually becomes Middle Road. OPTION: Continue on the marked bike trail.

3.1 Pass Peterborough Players on right.

7.4 Turn LEFT onto NH-137. *A right turn onto NH-137 is a detour to Hancock, where you can find convenience stores and restaurants.*

10.7 Turn LEFT onto Sargent Camp Road (dirt road). Pass Halfmoon Pond.

12.2 Turn RIGHT onto Windy Row (unmarked) at T intersection. Look for a big brown barn on right.

15.4 Turn LEFT onto MacDowell Road. Pass the MacDowell Colony.

15.7 Turn RIGHT onto High Street.

17.1 Turn RIGHT onto Vine Street, then immediately LEFT onto Union Street.

17.4 Return to starting point.

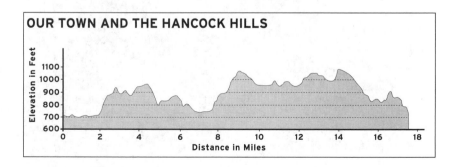

OUR TOWN AND THE HANCOCK HILLS

13 KATHY'S BEAR BROOK BOUNDER
Bear Brook State Park, Allenstown

DIRT ROADS, SINGLE-TRACK, DOUBLE-TRACK, PAVED ROADS WITH MINIMAL TRAFFIC

Difficulty: 3   **Total Distance:** 8.5 miles

Riding Time: 1.5 hours   **Elevation Gain:** 403 feet

Summary: This intermediate off-road ride explores a stunningly scenic park, with options for more difficult rides.

Whether you're new to trail riding or a downhill demon, there's a trail at Bear Brook State Park to amuse you. Among the 40 miles of well-marked trails, which are cross-country ski trails come winter, you'll find wide, rolling double-track and steep, rocky single-track.

If you choose your weather wisely, you'll also find the vibrant colors of fall foliage setting the forest alight around mostly empty trails. Ride earlier, during summer's peak, and you're more likely to see other bikers, hikers, runners, horseback riders, and people using the ponds to swim, paddle, and fish. Off the bike, you can try your skill at the 20-station, 1.25-mile fitness course or visit the antique snowmobile museum and family camping museum.

But why get off the bike? The 10,000-acre Bear Brook State Park, New Hampshire's largest, is a phenomenal place to ride, and it's typically rooty and rocky like many New England trails.

This is a good intermediate ride, offering varying terrain. Not too technical, the route's challenges mostly come in the ascents along the way. This ride is best-suited

The Bear Brook trails can be grizzly, but they provide hours of wild riding.

© CHRIS BERNARD

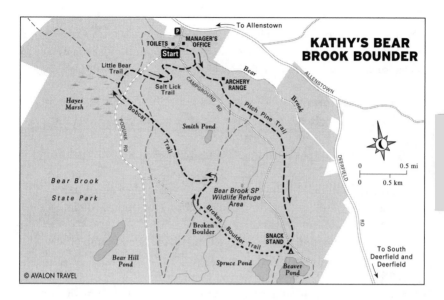

for mountain bikes, but riders comfortable on cyclocross bikes can have some fun. The route is mainly on the side of Podunk Road that comprises the conservation area. The other side is open to hunters, so choose your riding routes wisely during hunting season, which generally runs late September to early December.

Pick up a trail map at the ranger's station May–October, or order a map ahead of time. For more information or to order a biking trail map, contact Bear Brook State Park, NH-28, Allenstown, NH 03275, 603/485-9874, www.nhparks.state .nh.us/state-parks/.

Options

Massabesic Lake Loops is a relatively short drive from here, opening a weekend up to many miles of great mountain bike riding.

Locals' Tip: Visit Meme's Deli and Sandwich Shop (85 Allenstown Road, Allenstown, NH 03275, 603/485-2211) for sandwiches like your grandmother used to make.

Places to Stay: In a place this beautiful, you should camp to make the most of your visit. The park has 96 campsites. To reserve one, call 603/485-9869 or 603/271-3628. Campground is open Memorial Day weekend through Columbus Day weekend.

Driving Directions

From Concord and points north, or from Manchester and points south, take I-93 to Routes 3/28 to Suncook. From Suncook, take NH-28 toward Allenstown. Turn right onto the Allenstown-Deerfield Road and drive approximately 3.1 miles. Turn right onto

Podunk Road and park in the lot immediately to your right. There is a $4 day-use fee. A campground snack stand in the state park is open in summer. Supplies are available in Suncook. The nearest bike shops are in Hooksett, Concord, and Manchester.

Route Directions

0.0 On Podunk Road, by the manager's house, ride STRAIGHT across from parking lot access road.

0.1 Turn LEFT onto Pitch Pine Trail (also marked XC Ski Trail 1).

0.3 Continue STRAIGHT through a sandpit.

0.6 Ride STRAIGHT through an archery area, follow paved trail around pond, bear LEFT through parking lot, and continue STRAIGHT on wide trail.

3.2 Enter campground area, bear RIGHT to far side of camp office. Continue on paved road by ponds.

3.4 Bear RIGHT, away from Beaver Pond.

3.5 Bear RIGHT around gate. Continue through former AmeriCorps cabin site.

4.0 Continue STRAIGHT.

4.6 Bear RIGHT on Broken Boulder Trail toward Smith Pond (also marked XC Ski Trail 10).

5.0 Turn LEFT on Bobcat Trail (also marked XC Ski Trail 7).

6.6 Turn RIGHT on Podunk Road (dirt), then immediately LEFT through Hayes Field onto Little Bear Trail.

7.1 Continue on Little Bear Trail, bearing RIGHT.

7.3 At fork, bear RIGHT on XC Ski connector trail, crossing Podunk Road. Bear LEFT onto Salt Lick Trail.

7.8 Cross Campground Road, bearing LEFT twice onto Pitch Pine Trail.

8.2 Follow trail back to paved road.

8.3 Bear RIGHT toward entry gate on paved road.

8.5 Return to parking lot.

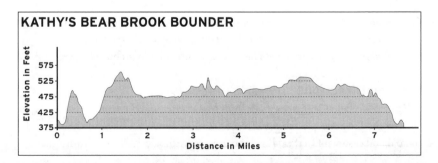

KATHY'S BEAR BROOK BOUNDER

14 MASSABESIC LAKE LOOPS   BEST (

Massabesic Lake State Park, Auburn

DIRT FIRE ROADS, SINGLE-TRACK

Difficulty: 3   **Total Distance:** 5.3 miles

Riding Time: 1 hour   **Elevation Gain:** 174 feet

Summary: These beautifully maintained mountain bike trails through scenic woodlands will challenge riders of all skill levels.

As big and undeveloped as New Hampshire is, some of the best woodland trails are within spitting distance of its largest city. The Friends of Massabesic Bicycling Association (FOMBA) work hard to maintain the 14 miles of trails in this urban watershed, and it shows. The trails are impeccably groomed and thoughtfully laid-out. Riders of all skill levels will find something that appeals to them, from fast fire roads to challenging single-track with well-placed obstacles and stunts for the technically proficient.

That said, most of the trails favor riders with some experience—or at least a lack of fear. Rigid bikes are going to be outgunned here. These rides favor mountain bikes with at least front suspension, though the fire roads are suitable for hardtails and cyclocross bikes.

The Friends of Massabesic Bicycling Association works hard to build and maintain the trails around this southern New Hampshire lake.

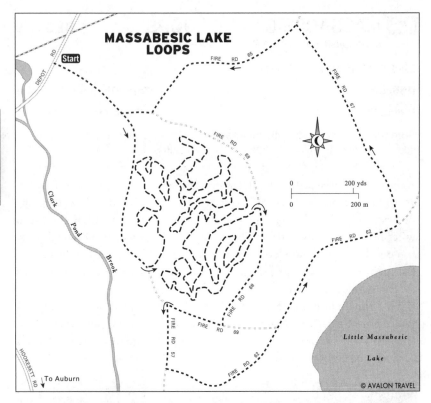

There are no hills to speak of—this is not "mountain" biking in its truest form—but the trails are as good as they get on this coast. This loop follows the Fire Line Trail, with a few extra single-track excursions and a scenic cooldown on fire roads thrown in. The ride barely scrapes the surface of the trails available, so allow yourself plenty of time to explore.

The Friends of Massabesic Bicycling Association (FOMBA; www.fomba.org) puts out a detailed trail map, available at the group's website; be sure to print out a copy before you visit. Volunteer trail crews work regularly to groom existing trails and are always adding new ones to the ever-growing network. It's free to ride here, but consider joining the group or donating to the cause to thank the members for their time and effort. The trails are open to other users as well; yield to hikers or equestrians and be a good ambassador for the sport. We don't want to spoil all the inroads this group has made in the area.

For more information, contact Friends of Massabesic Bicycling Association, P.O. Box 155, Auburn, NH 03032, www.fomba.org.

Options

To extend the ride, at Mile 4.3 continue straight on the fire road for access to additional single-track. Looking for an easier ride? The Woodpecker Trail (not marked on the trail map) is less challenging than many others, with banked berms and sweeping turns. To find the trail, watch for signs along the fire road.

Locals' Tip: No visit to the greater Manchester area is complete without a stop at the 24-hour Red Arrow Diner (61 Lowell Street, Manchester, NH 03101, 603/626-1118, http://redarrowdiner.com), a traditional New England diner. Breakfast, pie, bottomless coffee, and reasonable prices. What's not to like?

Places to Stay: Nearby Calef Lake Camping Area (593 Chester Road, Auburn, NH 03032, 603/483-8282, www.caleflakecampingarea.com) offers 146 seasonal sites and 13 year-round sites. Or stay at any of the dozens of hotels in Manchester.

Driving Directions

From I-93 take exit 7 east on NH-101. Take exit 2 and head south on Hookset Road. Take your second left on Depot Road, about 1,000 feet after crossing a railroad bed. Head north to the parking area on your left. The ride begins there.

Route Directions

0.0 From parking area, cross Depot Road onto gravel and dirt Griffin Road, following signs.

0.2 Bear RIGHT at fork, where you'll find a kiosk with a trail map.

0.4 Watch for Fire Line trailhead on your LEFT. Once on Fire Line, stay on trail. Pay attention to the obstacles, which include several large boulders, lots of small rocks and roots, and a multitude of quick little climbs and descents.

2.0 Here the trail starts to enter a more open, wooded area.

3.4 Fire Line empties onto an unnamed fire road. Turn RIGHT.

3.6 Turn RIGHT onto unnamed fire road at T intersection.

3.7 Turn LEFT onto unmarked fire road at intersection, and LEFT at next fork.

4.3 Turn LEFT on unmarked fire road. OPTION: Continue
     STRAIGHT to extend ride or for access to additional single-track.

4.7 Turn LEFT on unmarked fire road.

4.9 Turn RIGHT on unmarked fire road.

 5.1 Pass kiosk with trail maps where you entered.

5.3 Cross Depot Road and END at parking area.

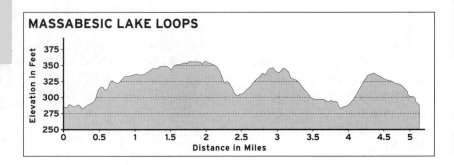

MASSABESIC LAKE LOOPS

15 SOUTHEAST SOJOURN   BEST ℂ
Newfields to Manchester via Rockingham Rail Trail

GRAVEL, DIRT TRAIL

Difficulty: 3	**Total Distance:** 52.4 miles
Riding Time: 6-7 hours	**Elevation Gain:** 1,082 feet

Summary: Travel through varied terrain on this long, flat rail trail, suitable for most riders comfortable off-road.

This is an outstanding example of what an unpaved rail trail can be. It offers flat, easy riding from sleepy Newfields in the Seacoast region all the way to relatively urban Manchester and back. Along the way, you'll pass through scenery that ranges from residential to rural, including forested and semi-industrial sections, twisting rivers, and ponds fit for swimming.

This ride is rich in railroad structures left over from the old Boston & Maine Railroad, which offer great photo opportunities. You'll pass an abandoned railroad car turned into a museum in Raymond, a good place to break for a snack. The turnaround is just outside Manchester city limits on Massabesic Lake.

The surface is a mix of gravel and dirt and can be muddy at times. Mountain or cyclocross bikes will work best here. Sections of loose gravel require a little concentration, and the sometimes-sharp stones mean you should be bring a flat-repair kit. Motorized vehicles are not allowed on this section of the trail, but they use it anyway, so keep your ears open for oncoming ATVs.

The ride from Newfields to Manchester changes from ballast to dirt, and the scenery from pastoral to industrial, but it never stops being fun.

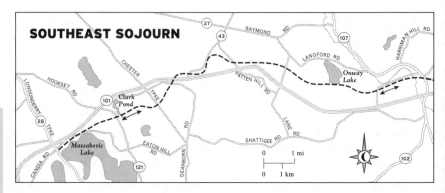

While trail builders have routed the trail through culverts to spare travelers the risk of crossing busy highways, the culverts have low clearance and can be disorienting. Consider walking your bike through them. The wetlands and forests through which long sections of this trail run mean beautiful scenery—and lots of bugs.

For more information, contact the New Hampshire Department of Resources and Economic Development, 172 Pembroke Road, P.O. Box 1856, Concord, NH 03302, 603/271-3556, www.nhparks.state.nh.us.

Options

To cut the ride in half, leave a car at Massabesic Lake in Manchester. From NH-101, take exit 1 to NH-28 Bypass South. At 0.2 mile, enter the rotary and stay on NH-28 South. After the rotary, turn left into Massabesic Lake Park parking area. This option halves the distance of this ride, lowering the difficulty rating to a 2 and making it suitable for reasonably fit novices.

You can also combine this ride with Massabesic Lake Loops, which covers dozens of miles of mountain bike trails and fire roads around Massabesic Lake.

Locals' Tip: Feed your hunger at Rocky's Famous Hamburgers in nearby Newmarket (171 Main Street, Newmarket, NH 03857, 603/292-3393).

Places to Stay: The Hickory Pond Inn (1 Stagecoach Road, Durham, NH 03824, 800/658-0065), dating back to 1783, offers affordable, quaint rooms with breakfast included.

Driving Directions

To get to the Newfields trailhead, from I-95 take NH-101 East, and exit on NH-85 toward Newfields. Turn north onto NH-108 and cross into Newmarket. Turn left onto Ash Swamp Road, across from the athletic club, and when the road forks sharply to the right, stay straight. Park at the abandoned railway depot. The active train tracks are in front of you, and the abandoned Boston & Maine railroad bed starts about 50 yards to the right and behind you—look for the gate.

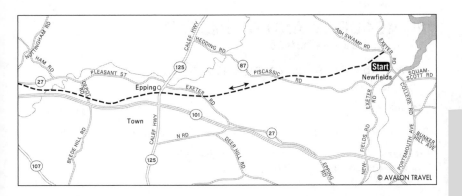

Route Directions

0.0 START at abandoned rail station in Newfields, heading west through gates.

7.6 Cross NH-125 in Epping. After crossing, stay RIGHT when another rail trail bears left.

12.4 Cross NH-108. *Food options available in both directions.*

13.5 Enter Raymond.

20.8 Enter culvert under NH-101. Consider walking your bike, as the overhead clearance is low and the culverts can be dark.

23.7 Cross bridge over Clark Pond, then enter culvert. Consider walking your bike.

25.4 Turn LEFT onto side trail through grove of white pines to parking area.

26.2 TURN AROUND at parking area.

27.0 Turn RIGHT onto main trail.

28.5 Enter culvert, then cross bridge over Clark Pond.

31.2 Enter culvert under NH-101.

44.1 Cross NH-125 in Epping. Stay on main trail.

52.4 END at parking area.

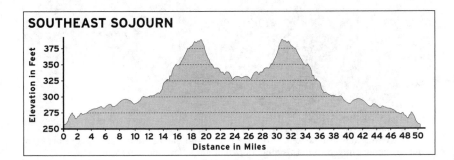

16 ACADEMY AND ATOMS RIDE
Exeter to Massachusetts

PAVED ROADS IN VARYING CONDITIONS WITH MODERATE TO HEAVY TRAFFIC

Difficulty: 2   **Total Distance:** 37.4 miles

Riding Time: 2.5 hours   **Elevation Gain:** 538 feet

Summary: This mostly flat, scenic loop leaves historic Phillips Exeter Academy for the beaches along the coast.

Each summer, a pro-level criterium bike race is held in downtown Exeter, a picture-perfect New England town, with a bandstand, town hall, and shops lining the sidewalks. This ride begins at the bandstand, where public parking is most likely to be found, and dips into Massachusetts to follow back roads and main roads east to the coast. From there, it heads north along the shore before making its way back to the start.

Near its start, the ride passes through the campus of Phillips Exeter Academy, which boasts such alumni as Daniel Webster, Franklin Pierce, Ulysses S. Grant, and more recently, John Irving, Gore Vidal, and Dan Brown. The scenic, storied

© CHRIS BERNARD

A criterium brings professional bike racers to Exeter each summer, and spectators turn out to support the sport in this quaint postcard of a New England town.

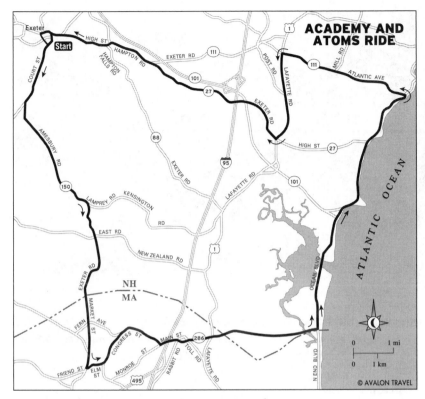

campus was the setting for the John Knowles novel *A Separate Peace* and Irving's *The World According to Garp* and *A Prayer for Owen Meany,* though in each book the school went by a different name.

Crossing the border into Amesbury, Massachusetts, the ride picks up NH-286, which straddles the two states' border all the way to the coast. While NH-286 can see a lot of traffic, it's got wide shoulders, and on busy beach days the traffic moves very, very slowly. Wave as you pass the phalanx of frustrated would-be beachgoers.

It's along this road that, if you look left across the broad, sweeping marsh, you'll see Seabrook Nuclear Power Plant, which went online in 1990. If you think the two domes of the reactor units look like a mismatched set, you're right—funding dried up before the second unit was completed. The plant has been the site of countless protests over the years, and you'll see emergency sirens mounted on telephone poles along the route.

At the end of the road, the route turns left, to the north, and follows the ocean through the busy Seabrook and Hampton Beach areas. Don't expect to maintain fast speeds here. Instead, allow yourself time to coast and watch the people who

© CHRIS BERNARD

flock to these very popular beaches, or stop and sample the food, or even dip your feet in the Atlantic before heading back to Exeter.

For more information, contact the Exeter Chamber of Commerce, 24 Front Street, #101, Exeter, NH 03833, 603/772-2411, www.exeterarea.org.

Options

Start this ride on the seacoast if you're staying in the area—but parking is at a premium there during beach season. If you want a longer ride or a diversion, at Mile 17 turn right into Massachusetts, and follow the coast two miles to Salisbury Center, home to restaurants, arcades, shops, and amusement park rides.

Southeast Sojourn starts nearby in Newfields, and Bailey's Three States Bounder begins less than half an hour away in Portsmouth.

Locals' Tip: After your healthy ride, have a healthy lunch at local favorite Me & Ollie's (64 Water Street, Exeter, NH 03833, 603/772-4600, www.meandollies .com), where sandwiches are made on award-winning bread.

Places to Stay: The Ashworth by the Sea (295 Ocean Boulevard, Hampton, NH 03842, 800/345-6736, www.ashworthhotel.com) is well situated and the hotel of choice for celebrities in town for performances at the nearby Hampton Casino Ballroom. Or try the Exeter Inn (90 Front Street, Exeter, NH 03833, 603/772-5901, www.theexeterinn.com).

Driving Directions

From NH-101, take exit 11 for NH-108 toward Exeter. Follow NH-108 for about 2 miles to the bandstand, on your left, at the intersection of Front Street and NH-108. Park around the bandstand or along Water Street.

Route Directions

0.0 From the bandstand, turn LEFT to head north on Water Street.

0.4 Turn LEFT on Tan Lane at Phillips Exeter Academy.

0.3 Turn LEFT on Front Street and RIGHT onto Elm Street.

1.7 Turn RIGHT onto Court Street/NH-108.

2.7 Bear LEFT onto NH-150/Amesbury Road.

5.8 Bear RIGHT to stay on NH-150/Amesbury Road, which becomes Exeter Road as it enters Massachusetts.

10.4 Turn LEFT on Elm Street in downtown Amesbury.

10.7 Turn LEFT onto Congress Street.

13.2 Pass under I-95. Congress Street becomes NH-286. This road can have a lot of traffic on it, though on summer days the traffic is often at a standstill. There are wide shoulders, but beware of the cars. The power plant is visible to the left, over the marsh.

17.0 When NH-286 ends, turn LEFT onto Ocean Boulevard/US-1A North, which parallels the coast. OPTION: Turn RIGHT into Massachusetts and follow option directions.

24.7 Turn LEFT onto NH-101D/111/Atlantic Avenue.

27.9 Turn LEFT onto US-1 South/Lafayette Road.

30.7 Turn RIGHT onto NH-27/101C/111/Exeter Road.

37.4 END at parking area.

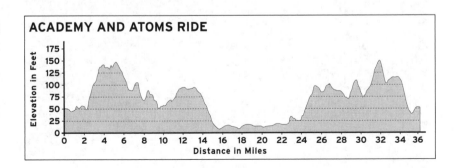

ACADEMY AND ATOMS RIDE

17 BAILEY'S THREE STATES BOUNDER

BEST (

Portsmouth to Kittery and Salisbury

PAVED ROADS, MINIMAL TO MODERATE TRAFFIC

Difficulty: 3

Total Distance: 43.5 miles

Riding Time: 3 hours

Elevation Gain: 469 feet

Summary: This flat ride through coastal areas is best ridden in the off-season, when you can have the beaches, vendors, and views to yourself.

This ride starts in Portsmouth, NH, a thriving, artsy downtown area with no shortage of meal or shopping options. It could just as easily begin a few miles to the north, in Maine, but why not end up in a town with entertainment options? Parking can be difficult to find downtown, so this ride begins at the parking lot for BaileyWorks, home to bicycle advocate Jon Bailey's messenger bag factory.

Alternatively, you can try to find parking in the municipal lot or garage downtown, but cyclists with roof racks, make sure you remove your bikes before entering

This three-state ride starts and ends at bicycle advocate Jon Bailey's headquarters.

© CHRIS BERNARD

the low-clearance garage. You've been warned.

The ride wanders through downtown Portsmouth and across the Piscataqua River separating New Hampshire from its northern neighbor, passing through Badger's Island. The views from there and the bridge are scenic enough to justify this quick diversion across state borders.

Next, the ride winds clockwise south to the coast at Rye Harbor, and more or less hugs the waterfront through Boars Head and Plaice Cove down to Hampton and Seabrook beaches and into Massachusetts's Salisbury Beach. Along the way, you'll pass waterfront mansions and beach cottages, arcades, food vendors, outdoor music stages, and more. Watch for surfers in the wavebreaks, birds in the marshes, and kites in the skies.

From Salisbury Center, which is undergoing a reinvention from a family-friendly amusement park and arcade to a residential area with condos and high-end restaurants, turn around and retrace your route, stopping at will to enjoy the beaches and vendors or just the oceanfront views. You'll pass countless restaurants, shops, and other opportunities to stop and refuel, as well as more than half a dozen different beaches if you're inclined to give yourself a swim break.

During the summer months, you'll find these roads clogged with traffic, and in some areas, pedestrians. But ride it just a week or two after Labor Day and you'll have them almost to yourself. This is a spectacular ride for late September or early October.

For more information, contact the Greater Portsmouth Chamber of Commerce, 500 Market Street, Portsmouth, NH 03802, 603/436-3988, www.portsmouth chamber.org.

Options

Want a long ride that tests your endurance and your climbing? Combine this with Maine's Big A ride, which loops from Kittery out to—and up—Mount Agamenticus—for a 75 miler. This ride also overlaps with the Academy and Atoms Ride.

Locals' Tip: Petey's Summertime Seafood and Bar (1323 Ocean Boulevard, Rye, NH 03870, 603/433-1937, www.peteys.com), now open year-round, is your typical New England clamshack, right on the bike route, about 6 miles from the finish and across the street from public beach access. Try the haddock sandwich and a cold beer.

Places to Stay: Portsmouth is not known for its reasonably priced hotels, but the Anchorage Inn and Suites (417 Woodbury Avenue, Portsmouth, NH 03801, 800/370-8111, http://anchorageinns.com) is competitive.

Driving Directions

From I-95, take exit 3 and turn right onto NH-33. About a mile down the road, turn left at the fork onto Islington Street. About a mile down on your left, you'll see the parking lot for BaileyWorks, with plenty of parking spaces. Supplies are available across the street, and a bike shop is less than 0.25 mile down Islington Street (the ride passes right by it).

Route Directions

0.0 From the parking area, turn LEFT onto Islington Street. *Bike shop at mile 0.25.*

0.8 Just after the Portsmouth Public Library, turn LEFT onto Maplewood Avenue, and take your second RIGHT onto Hanover Street.

1.2 Turn RIGHT onto Market Street, and then LEFT onto Bow Street.

1.4 Turn RIGHT onto Chapel Street.

1.6 Turn LEFT on US-1N onto the Memorial Bridge. Part of the proposed East Coast Greenway, this is the only one of the three Portsmouth bridges open for bicycles. The open gate decking can be slick—cyclists may wish to walk their bikes. *Cyclists who wish to avoid the bridges entirely can skip this portion of the ride, effectively making it a two-state ride.*

1.7 Cross Badger's Island, in Maine, and continue over the Badger's Island Bridge. Stay straight on one-way Hunter Avenue, and turn LEFT onto one-way US-1 South/Newmarch Street, and cross back over the bridges to New Hampshire.

2.8 Turn LEFT onto State Street and RIGHT onto Marcy Street/US-1B south along Prescott Park.

3.4 Bear RIGHT onto South Street when it splits with Marcy Street/US-1B.

4.0 Turn LEFT onto Sagamore Road/US-1A south.

5.5 Bear RIGHT/STRAIGHT, staying on Sagamore Road when it splits from US-1A South.

7.1 Turn sharply to the LEFT onto Wallis Road.

7.7 Turn sharply to the RIGHT onto Brackett Road.

8.7 Turn sharply to the LEFT onto Washington Road, following it to the coast.

8.9 Turn RIGHT onto US-1A/Ocean Boulevard. Stay on US-1A through Rye Beach, passing several beaches and scenic pulloffs.

14.1 Stay on US-1A through North Hampton State Park.

16.7 Stay on US-1A through Boars Head into Hampton Beach.

17.4 Follow one-way traffic down US-1A/Ashworth Avenue, past Hampton Beach Casino Ballroom and over the bridge at Hampton Beach State Park into Seabrook.

20.4 Pass NH-286 and cross into Massachusetts, staying on US-1A/N. End Boulevard into Salisbury.

22.4 At Salisbury Center, turn around. Retrace route through Salisbury, Seabrook, and Hampton, staying on US-1A north along the coast the entire way.

42.6 Turn LEFT onto Lincoln Avenue.

42.9 Turn RIGHT onto Middle Street/US-1.

43.0 Turn LEFT onto Aldrich Road.

43.3 Cross Islington Street.

43.5 END at parking area.

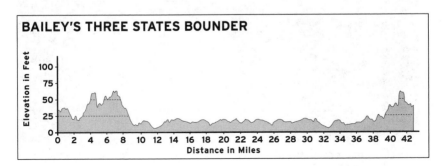

BAILEY'S THREE STATES BOUNDER

18 WINDHAM RAIL TRAIL   BEST 【
Windham and Salem

PAVED RAIL TRAIL

Difficulty: 1   **Total Distance:** 6.5 miles

Riding Time: 1 hour   **Elevation Gain:** 164 feet

Summary: Families and beginners will love this flat, short, paved rail trail that runs through wooded wetlands.

Take the rail bed from the Manchester and Lawrence Branch, built in the 1800s, and tear it out. Replace it with smooth, well-graded pavement. Leave the wooded wetlands through which it passes undeveloped, with habitat for deer, beaver, birds, fisher cats, owls, turtles, and more. Then, add a community of people who—on foot, bikes, strollers, in-line skates, wheelchairs, or cross-country skis—want to get outside and enjoy the natural beauty while getting a little fresh air and exercise.

What do you get? One leg of a growing rail trail with lofty goals of being connected with other rail trails around the state.

Sometimes the joy of riding a bike comes from boiling the act down to basic elements—the Windham Rail Trail is a place where such rides can happen. Easy enough for beginners and children, yet scenic enough to be enjoyable for even jaded

© CHRIS BERNARD

Though the ride is short, the Windham Rail Trail is everything a fun bike ride should be, and suitable for anyone.

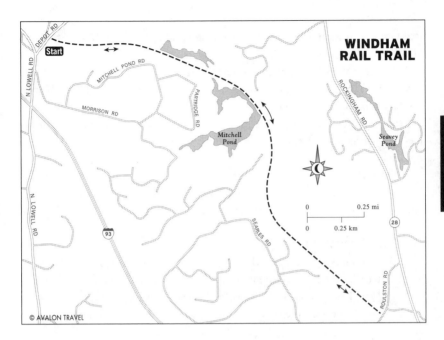

distance cyclists, this trail is a shining example of repurposing for the good of the community.

On any given seasonable day, you'll find people enjoying the trail, but it's never crowded—and to a one, trail users seem friendly and sociable, as if well aware of the gift they've been given.

The parking lot in Windham is open from a half-hour before sunrise to a half-hour after sunset. From there, this section of trail heads south past pastures, orchards, ponds, marshes, and woodlands. It crosses two small bridges and passes along several old stone walls. Ride at your own pace, bring the kids or grandparents, and enjoy the scenery.

For more information, contact Windham Rail Trail Alliance at P.O. Box 4317, Windham, NH 03087, 603/434-0806, www.windhamrailtrail.org.

Options

If you're riding a mountain, hybrid, or cyclocross bike, you can ride an unpaved section of trail north from Windham Depot to Derry Center. Plans call for this section to be paved in the near future, and it may be done by the time this book is published. This trail is part of the longer Rockingham Recreational Trail system, and longer rides can be pieced together. For maps, contact the New Hampshire Department of Resources and Economic Development, Division of

Parks and Recreation, P.O. Box 1856, Concord, NH 03302, 603/271-3254, www .dred.state.nh.us.

This ride is about a half hour south of Massabesic Lake Loops.

Locals' Tip: The Windham Junction Country Store and Kitchen (128 North Lowell Road, Windham, NH 03087, 603/434-7467, www.windhamjunction.com) is a cute traditional country store just a few hundred yards from the Windham Depot parking lot, offering a daily menu of soups and sandwiches for hungry cyclists.

Places to Stay: The unassuming, affordable La Quinta Inn and Suites (8 Keewaydin Drive, Salem, NH 03079, 877/477-5817) is just one of many similar options for overnight accommodations in nearby Salem.

Driving Directions

From I-93, take exit 3 west on NH-111 toward Nashua. Turn right on Church Street after the second set of lights. At the end of Church Street, turn right on North Lowell Road. After the I-93 bridge, turn right on Depot Road. Windham Depot parking lot is on the right. Restroom facilities are located in the parking area.

Route Directions

0.0 From the Windham Depot parking area, head south on the trail at the far right corner of the parking lot, past the old rail car. *Restrooms available.*

1.6 Pond view and access on right.

2.2 Pond view on left.

3.2 At gate (Roulston Road), turn around.

6.5 Return to parking area.

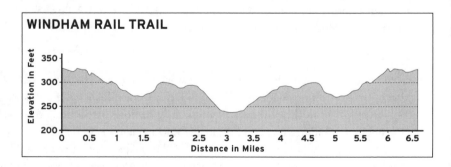

VERMONT

© CHRIS BERNARD

BEST BIKE RIDES

It's possible Vermont is the best of all the

New England states for biking. And that's saying something. Vermont has put a lot of work into constructing bike paths and trails, and it shows. But Vermont's appeal to cyclists doesn't stop with purpose-built routes. Thanks to the landscape and the paucity of population – Wyoming is the only state with fewer people – there are dozens, if not hundreds, of other routes to explore. From the commuter bike paths in and around Burlington and the rail trails scattered throughout the state to the carefully built and groomed mountain bike trails at places such as the Catamount Outdoor Family Center and the Kingdom Trails, cyclists' options are seemingly endless – and very exciting.

The Green Mountain State is a climber's delight, offering rural roads that rise high into the sky as they gain elevation, sometimes by way of short, steep grades. Cyclists come from all over to test their pedal mettle on the well-known Gaps ride, climbing 12,000 feet over 130 miles through six mountain passes. Too much? A route near the popular ski areas of Smuggler's Notch and Stowe gains 2,200 feet over just 42 miles, a ride that might be considered extreme in any other state. Even a relatively short ride out of urban Burlington that offers cyclists a couple of hours of bucolic beauty heads uphill, climbing the short, steep Mount Philo, an aerie with views of the Adirondacks and Lake Champlain.

But to call Vermont strictly a climber's paradise would be misleading. Long rides like Mad River Madness, a meandering century that starts and ends at the state house in Montpelier, highlight the state's other sides. In the southwest, a Peaks and Hollows ride shows off the Green Mountain National Forest's verdant lushness. The Missisquoi Valley Rail Trail, leaving St. Albans for the north country, slices through cornfields and pastures, supplying mountain views and glimpses of forest, all from a flat, hard-packed trail suitable for riders of all skill levels.

Mudders and mountain bikers are in for a treat, too. The Leicester Hollow route follows dirt roads as it rises, posing a challenge for moderately fit riders, while Lamb Brook and Wilmington's Watering Hole, in the southwest, explore rough roads and chewed-up single-track in fun, fast, nontechnical rides. Then there's the Kingdom Trails, well-known and for good reason – they're about as much fun as you can have on a mountain bike, and there are enough them that you could ride for days and never cross your own tire tracks. West of these, closer to Burlington, Catamount offers another series of trails popular with experienced off-roaders. But the outdoor center also runs schools for the next generation of riders – don't be surprised if you're passed by a pack of half-pints carving up single-track like they were born to it.

If you're more of a recreational rider and the cadences and climbs of some of these rides don't call to you, fear not. Just outside Burlington, Shelburne Farms offers a gentle ride in one of the most peaceful settings imaginable. Or roll along the Lake Champlain waterfront as you sample the endless miles of bike paths – rolling past the beaches and the granite monoliths of the Burlington Earth Clock, watching the legendary sunsets over the Adirondack Mountains in New York, perhaps parking your bike at one of the restaurants or bars at the lake's edge for a nightcap.

There are similar rides all over the state. There's also plenty to do and see in your downtime. Be warned, though, that spring can start late in Vermont – and winter early – so plan your trips accordingly. It probably goes without saying that this state can be spectacularly beautiful during foliage season, but it's hard to overstate just how pretty it is during summer, when you can see exactly why it's called the Green Mountain State.

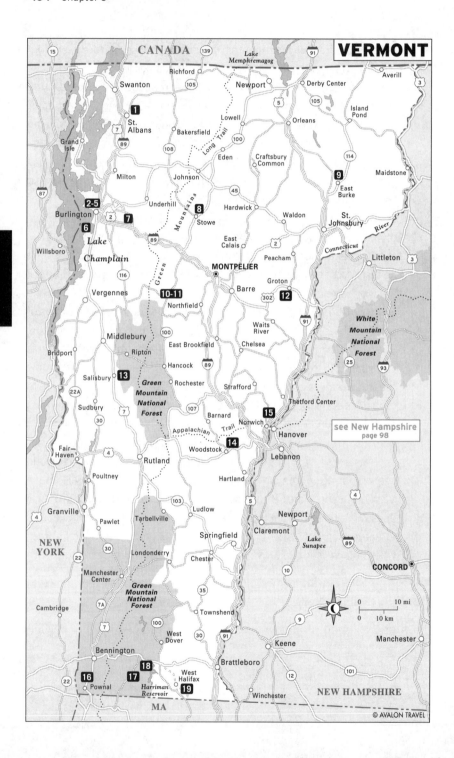

RIDE NAME	DIFFICULTY	DISTANCE	TIME	ELEVATION	PAGE
1 Missisquoi Valley Rail Trail	2	50 mi	5 hr	699 ft	166
2 Hero of Grand Isle	4	66.2 mi	5 hr	1,322 ft	170
3 Island Line Rail Trail	2	19.8 mi	3 hr	220 ft	174
4 Burlington Bike Path Sampler	2	9.2 mi	1.5 hr	404 ft	177
5 Mount Philo Rising	3	33 mi	2 hr	1,200 ft	181
6 Shelburne Farms	1	9 mi	1.5 hr	354 ft	184
7 Catamount Outdoor Center	2	3.1 mi	1 hr	98 ft	187
8 Smuggler's Blues	4	42.6 mi	4 hr	2,182 ft	190
9 Kingdom Trails	3	8.7 mi	1.5 hr	807 ft	194
10 Gaps of Glory	5	131 mi	8-11 hr	11,700 ft	198
11 Mad River Madness	4	102 mi	7 hr	2,208 ft	203
12 Wells River Rail Trail	2	12.4 mi	1.5-2 hr	806 ft	207
13 Leicester Hollow Trail	3	10.8 mi	2.5 hr	1,188 ft	210
14 Woodstock Quechee Gorgeous	3	31.3 mi	2 hr	1,512 ft	213
15 Old Norwich Turnpike Loop	4	20.6 mi	3 hr	2,061 ft	217
16 Green Mountain Peaks and Hollows	3	29.5 mi	3 hr	1,972 ft	220
17 Lamb Brook	3	11 mi	2 hr	900 ft	224
18 Wilmington's Watering Hole	2	15.2 mi	2 hr	940 ft	227
19 Green River Ride	3	13.7 mi	2 hr	1,558 ft	230

1 MISSISQUOI VALLEY RAIL TRAIL   BEST 《
St. Albans to Richford

CRUSHED LIMESTONE RAIL TRAIL

Difficulty: 2

Total Distance: 50 miles

Riding Time: 5 hours

Elevation Gain: 699 feet

Summary: Any cyclist will enjoy this flat rail trail running at length through varied farmlands, woodlands, and wetlands of northern Vermont.

The only challenge to this trail is the distance, which some riders may find daunting. But the conditions and grade make this suitable for nearly anyone comfortable riding on packed unpaved surfaces. Road bikes will work fine, and hybrids or comfort bikes are even better. If the distance is too much, leave a car at one end or at any of the numerous access points along the way—or just turn around when you start to get tired and head back the way you came.

Used by skiers and snowmobilers in the winter and walkers year-round, this trail is yet another example of how a former railroad line can be repurposed into

© CHRIS BERNARD

This northern Vermont rail trail runs past woodlands and farms, giving a subtle taste of the state's standout scenery.

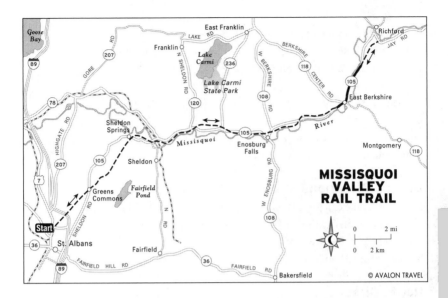

a community gem. It wanders through a changing landscape that shows off much of what northern Vermont has to offer.

This trail runs through agricultural lands and is a multiuse path—cyclists are asked to yield to livestock and other animals and encouraged to use caution at agricultural crossings to avoid mud splatters.

The ten-foot-wide trail is owned by the state and maintained by state workers and volunteers. This ride begins in St. Albans, known as the "maple sugar capital," and it runs north to Richford, passing through several small towns and villages, such as Sheldon Springs, along the way. (Sheldon Springs was a summer resort in the 1800s, and local mineral water was bottled as a remedy for blood disease.) If you're biking in April, your visit may coincide with St. Albans's maple festival, where you can try iced maple sugar and other treats.

For more information, contact the Northwest Regional Planning Commission, 155 Lake Street, St. Albans, VT 05478, 802/524-5958, www.mvrailtrail.com.

Options

Those looking to cut the trip in half can leave a car either on the street behind Mayhew's Corner Store in Richford or at Wetherby's Quick Stop on Main Street. From I-89, take exit 19 toward VT-104/VT-36/St. Albans/US-7. Turn right at Fairfax Road/VT-104, and make a slight right at Sheldon Road/VT-105. After about 16 miles, turn left at Main Street/VT-105.

This ride is about a half-hour north of the Hero of Grand Isle ride.

Locals' Tip: Despite a few diners in town, locals and tourists alike favor the waterfront Bayside Pavilion (10 Georgia Shore Road, St. Albans, VT 05478, 802/524-0909).

Places to Stay: The Back Inn Time (68 Fairfield Street, St. Albans, VT 05478, 802/527-5116, www.backinntime.net) is a lovingly restored Victorian bed-and-breakfast that will make visitors feel like they're being pampered in a time machine.

Driving Directions

From I-89, take exit 19 and follow signs for US-7 North. The St. Albans parking area is at the intersection of US-7/Main Street and VT-105, just north of downtown. The parking area entrance is marked with a green and yellow sign with a bicycle mounted on a post.

Route Directions

0.0 From the parking area, follow the trail north. The first few miles pass through farmland and pastures, with the occasional gravel or dirt road intersection. Traffic is minimal on these roads, but exercise caution when crossing.

3.3 Cross VT-105. The trail meanders through wetlands and woodlands, offering a good probability of seeing some wildlife. The trail also borders on private property at times, so respect neighbors' rights.

5.0 Here the trail begins to parallel Sweet Hollow Road, running into the small village of Sheldon Springs.

7.3 Cross VT-105 again. This section offers views of the eponymous Missisquoi River, which the rail trail begins to follow closely.

12.0 The next 4 miles of trail pass through endless cornfields, stretching as far as you can see. You'll also cross VT-105 again, at a busier intersection outside Enosburg Falls.

16.0 The trail passes through Enosburg Falls, once known as the "dairy capital of the world," with spectacular river and rapids views as well as vistas of the mountains to the east. Here the trail is a false flat (very minimal grade) at times, and you'll ride over the only paved section of the trail.

18.5 *Picnic benches available for a rest stop.*

21.8 *Picnic area, supplies, and restrooms available.*

23.0 After crossing VT-105 again, the trail heads into shaded forests and sunny fields, in and out of shaded forests and sunny fields, with excellent opportunities for bird watching—especially in the wetlands near mile 25.

25.0 The trail ends in Richford, at Troy Street. *Restaurants and shops are available (and receptive to cyclists), as are restrooms.* TURN AROUND and follow the trail back to the start.

50.0 END at parking area.

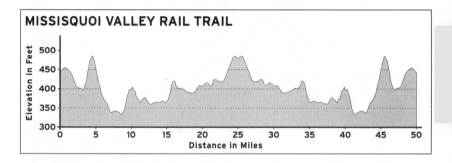

MISSISQUOI VALLEY RAIL TRAIL

2 HERO OF GRAND ISLE

Lake Champlain: Colchester, South Hero, Grand Isle

PAVED ROADS WITH MINIMAL TRAFFIC

Difficulty: 4   **Total Distance:** 66.2 miles

Riding Time: 5 hours   **Elevation Gain:** 1,322 feet

Summary: This long ride along Mallets Bay onto the Champlain Islands and back offers varied and beautiful views around every corner.

For two weeks in March 1998, Lake Champlain joined Huron, Ontario, Michigan, Erie, and Superior as one of America's official Great Lakes. The move came as part of a federal bill that involved funding designations, and it generated enough of an uproar that the lake's status was rescinded.

With a surface area of about 440 square miles, Lake Champlain is significantly smaller than the smallest Great Lake, Ontario (7,450 square miles), but it's hard to imagine it being more important to the people of northwest Vermont. This ride celebrates the lake by riding out to the islands that dominate the northern part of it.

Mostly flat, and mostly minimally trafficked, these roads offer stunning views of the lake and both shorelines. Along the way, a wide variety of stopping points,

© CHRIS BERNARD

Sunsets over Lake Champlain and the Adirondack Mountains are spectacular.

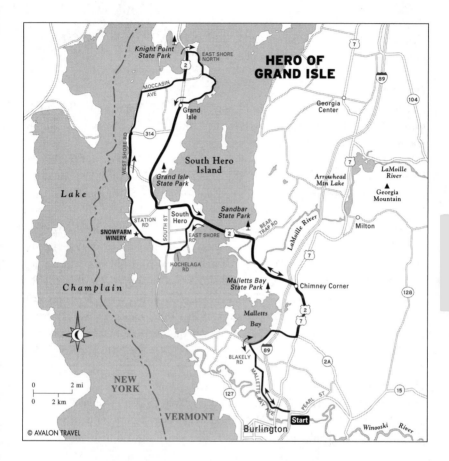

including breathtaking vistas of both New York's Adirondacks to the west and Vermont's Green Mountains to the east, will lure you to make frequent pauses.

Cyclotourists can add as many miles as they want to this ride by expanding it into a multiday tour of the islands, heading north into Quebec, or riding inland a bit, as this ride starts a bit away from the lakeshore, in Winooski.

For the most part, the roads have wide shoulders, though in some sections shoulders are narrow to nonexistent. Use care crossing the many causeways, as the wind coming off the lake can be strong. There are facilities, restrooms, picnic spots, and camping (Grand Isle State Park has a well-placed campground) along this ride.

For more information, contact the Champlain Islands Chamber of Commerce, P.O. Box 213, North Hero, VT 05474, 802/372-8400, www.champlain islands.com. For more on bicycling in the area, contact Lake Champlain Bikeways

Clearinghouse, 1 Steele Street #103, Burlington, VT 05401, 802/652-BIKE (802/652-2453), www.champlainbikeways.org.

Options

Add another 50 miles to this trip by staying on US-2 North and following it through North Hero and Isle La Motte, then taking VT-78 East to VT-7 South, rejoining the ride at mile 54.8.

This ride is about half an hour south of the Missisquoi Valley Rail Trail; just a few minutes north of Island Line Rail Trail and Burlington Bike Path Sampler; and a short drive from Catamount Outdoor Center, Shelburne Farms, and Mount Philo Rising.

Locals' Tip: Sneakers (36 Main Street, Winooski, VT 05404, 802/655-9081, daily 7 A.M.–3 P.M., www.sneakersbistro.com) has been a local favorite for nearly 30 years. Sunday mornings the breakfast line runs down the block.

Places to Stay: It's not fancy, but the Days Inn Burlington/Colchester (124 College Parkway, Colchester, VT 05446, 802/655-0900, www.daysinn.com) is right across the street from the start of this ride; walking distance from downtown Winooski's shopping, bars, and restaurants; and just minutes from downtown Burlington.

Driving Directions

From I-89, take exit 15 and head east (uphill) on VT-15. At the top of the hill, at the lights, turn left into the Saint Michael's College campus and park near the gym on your left. The nearest bike shop is back down the hill in Winooski.

Route Directions

0.0 From campus, head downhill on VT-15/East Allen Street.

0.7 Bear RIGHT onto East Spring Street, and stay on Spring Street as it crosses US-2/US-7.

1.4 When Spring Street ends, bear RIGHT on Mallets Bay Avenue.

4.8 When Mallets Bay Avenue ends, Bear LEFT onto Blakely Road/ VT-127.

5.2 Turn RIGHT onto E. Lakeshore Drive along the lakefront.

6.8 Bear RIGHT onto Bay Road, crossing under I-89.

8.1 Bay Road ends. Turn LEFT onto US-7/US-2 north. There may be traffic on this road, but the shoulders are wide and the roads well paved.

11.1 At Chimney Corner, turn LEFT on US-2 when it splits from US-7.

15.5 Enter Sandbar State Park as you cross onto the islands.

18.2 Turn LEFT onto Landon Road.

19.0 Turn LEFT onto E. Shore Road, which becomes Hochelaga Road.

21.0 Turn RIGHT onto South Street, then make a quick LEFT onto W. Shore Road.

27.0 W. Shore Road merges with Route 314/Ferry Road. Bear LEFT.

28.8 W. Shore Road splits from Route 314. Stay STRAIGHT on W. Shore Road.

30.9 Turn RIGHT onto Moccasin Avenue, which becomes Griswold Road.

33.1 Turn LEFT onto US-2.

34.8 Turn RIGHT onto E. Shore Road North/Point au Roche Road.

36.6 Turn LEFT to stay on E. Shore Road North.

40.0 Turn LEFT onto US-2.

42.2 Enter Grand Isle State Park. *Lakefront camping available.* Stay on US-2, heading back to the mainland.

54.8 At Chimney Corner, turn RIGHT to stay on US-2.

58.0 Turn RIGHT onto Bay Road.

59.3 Turn LEFT onto Lakeshore Drive.

60.8 Turn LEFT onto VT-127/Blakely Road.

61.3 Bear RIGHT onto Mallets Bay Avenue.

64.8 Turn LEFT onto Spring Street.

65.4 Bear LEFT onto VT-15/East Allen Street.

66.0 Turn LEFT into the Saint Michael's College campus and return to parking area.

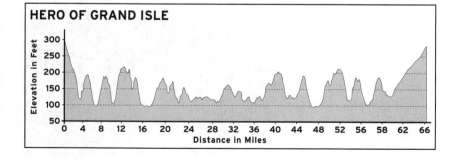

HERO OF GRAND ISLE

3 ISLAND LINE RAIL TRAIL   BEST (

Burlington to Lake Champlain

RAIL TRAIL, WOODEN DECKING, PAVED ROADS, GRAVEL

Difficulty: 2   **Total Distance:** 19.8 miles

Riding Time: 3 hours   **Elevation Gain:** 220 feet

Summary: A rail trail jutting three dramatic miles into Lake Champlain, this lazy ride will please anyone on a bike.

This ride offers a different take on the network of bike paths throughout the Burlington area: it heads north along the waterfront and then three miles out into Lake Champlain on a narrow finger of land. The effect is wonderfully disconcerting, with water on either side of you and spectacular views everywhere you look.

Well-marked the entire way, most of the trail is on pavement, but there are sections on sand, dirt, and wooden boardwalks. Any bike will do, but be warned that once you reach the northern portion of the ride, some of the gravel can be loosely packed.

The Island Line passes through a variety of neighborhoods. Until a few years ago, a seasonal bike ferry was the only way over the Winooski River at Mile 4.7, but now there's a bridge connecting the Burlington Bike Path with Colchester Causeway Trail. If you have time, wait for the ferry—it's a unique experience.

The Colchester Causeway sticks out for three dramatic miles into Lake Champlain. Strong winds are common along these exposed parts of the Island Line, even on hot days.

The next link in the Island Line Rail Trail will be a seasonal bike ferry from the end of the causeway over "The Cut" to Grand Isle, which would extend this ride to the islands in Hero of Grand Isle. Currently, a

On the Island Line Rail Trail, cyclists can travel through some of Burlington's most spectacular scenic areas on an entirely car-free voyage.

ferry runs sporadically during the summer. For a schedule, or for the latest information on the project, contact Local Motion, 1 Steele Street #103, Burlington, VT 05401, 802/652-BIKE (802/652-2453), www.localmotion vt.org.

Options

To extend this ride, combine it with the Burlington Bike Path Sampler and spend an entire day on the local bike path network, or take the ferry across "The Cut" and combine it with the Hero of Grand Isle to explore the Champlain Islands.

Locals' Tip: No trip to Burlington is complete without a meal at Bove's (68 Pearl Street, Burlington, VT 05401, 802/864-6651, http://boves.com), a famously informal Italian restaurant with ridiculously affordable prices. College students have been eating at this family-owned favorite since it opened the day of the attack on Pearl Harbor.

Places to Stay: Burlington has a few hotels on the waterfront, including the Hilton Burlington (60 Battery Street, Burlington, VT 05401, 802/658-6500), but if you spend all your money on bike parts you'll find more affordable rooms in nearby Winooski or South Burlington.

Driving Directions

Take exit 14 off I-89 to US-2 in Burlington. Follow US-2 to the very end (it becomes Main Street), across Battery Street as it curves right. At the next intersection, turn left onto College Street and park in the public lot on your right. Supplies and bike shops are available in Burlington.

Route Directions

0.0 Head north on the bike path, keeping the waterfront to your left.

1.6 *North Beach Park has a campground, a beach, and facilities.*

2.2 Appletree Bay is to your left.

4.7 Arrive at the Winooski River ferry (or ride across the bridge).

7.2 Causeway begins.

10.1 Arrive at end of causeway. TURN AROUND.

19.8 END at starting point.

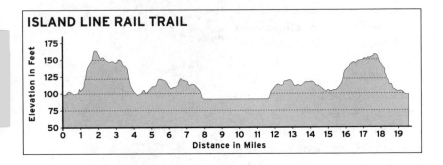

4 BURLINGTON BIKE PATH SAMPLER   BEST (
Burlington

PAVED BIKE PATH, PAVED ROADS WITH MINIMAL TRAFFIC

Difficulty: 2   **Total Distance:** 9.2 miles

Riding Time: 1.5 hours   **Elevation Gain:** 404 feet

Summary: This loop leaves downtown for the suburbs, sampling the excellent local network of bike paths.

From a larger perspective, the best part of this ride is that it highlights the incredibly well-considered bike paths that the city, state, and volunteers have come together to build in Burlington and its suburbs. From the perspective of an individual cyclist, however, the best part may be that a short climb in the first mile of the ride gives you enough elevation that the rest of it is nearly all downhill.

The exception comes before the halfway mark, but that slope is nothing to worry about. Even the least fit riders will make their way successfully to the top. The first climb, however, will give you pause if you're not in some facsimile of fitness. The good news is, it's short enough that most riders will be able either to tough it out or to walk it. Problem solved.

From downtown, this ride crosses the University of Vermont campus and heads south and west through community gardens, cornfields, and beautifully shaded woods before turning north again. From there, it winds along the Lake Champlain

This bike ride passes the Burlington Earth Clock at Blanchard Beach, an amazing place to stop for a rest, a photo, and a bit of intriguing science.

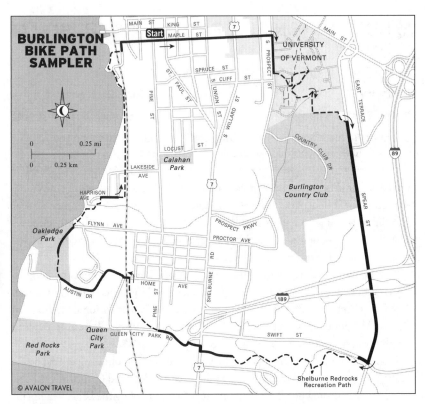

waterfront, offering spectacular views of the Adirondack Mountains and miles of beaches, including Blanchard Beach, home to the Burlington Earth Clock (made of 12 5- to 12-ton granite stones in a 40-foot circle and dedicated to peace).

The scenery is varied and changing, including a brief industrial stretch. Bring a camera for this ride, and allow yourself extra time for stops or side trips.

Nearly three-fourths of the ride follows paved bike paths, and it will make you wish you lived in Vermont and commuted by bike to Burlington. The few roads you encounter don't have much traffic, but exercise caution just the same. Except for the initial hill, this ride is suitable for beginners and families with children. If they can ride the distance, they'll do fine on this route.

For more information, contact Local Motion, 1 Steele Street #103, Burlington, VT 05401, 802/652-2453, www.localmotion.org.

Options

This ride can easily be extended to explore the miles of paths in the area. To find more or to plan a longer ride, visit Local Motion's online Trail Finder at www.localmotion.org/trails.

Turn this ride into one leg of a biking weekend by combining several of the rides in this chapter. From a base in Burlington, try this ride in combination with the Shelburne Farms or Mount Philo Rising rides. Then, follow the Island Line Rail Trail north to the bike ferry, which runs sporadically in the summer. The ferry connects with the Champlain Islands, where you can follow parts of the Hero of Grand Isle ride back to the Burlington area.

Locals' Tip: Ride late in the morning, before the day gets hot and after breakfast at Henry's Diner (55 Bank Street, Burlington, VT 05401, 802/862-9010, www.henrysdiner.net), a traditional New England diner and a Burlington tradition.

Places to Stay: In Burlington, try the waterfront Hilton Burlington (60 Battery Street, Burlington, VT 05401, 802/658-6500). For budget accommodations, better options lie in Winooski or South Burlington.

Driving Directions

From I-89, take exit 14W toward Burlington, and stay straight onto Main Street. After a half mile, turn right onto St. Paul Street, then make a quick right onto College Street. City Hall Park is on the right. Parking is available around the park and on nearby side streets, or stay on St. Paul Street and enter the parking garage on your right. The ride begins at the corner of Maple Street and St. Paul Street.

Route Directions

0.0 From St. Paul Street, turn LEFT on Maple Street to begin. The only real climb starts immediately.

0.6 Turn RIGHT onto South Prospect Street.

1.0 Turn LEFT into the University of Vermont's Redstone Campus at a paved walkway. Follow the painted paw prints, which head southeast toward the playing fields. At the gymnasium, a large domed building, turn RIGHT onto the bike path, which runs alongside a soccer field.

2.1 Path turns sharply to the RIGHT.

3.1 Stay STRAIGHT, exiting the path onto Spear Street downhill when the path turns RIGHT. There's a short, easy climb here.

4.1 Make a sharp RIGHT onto Shelburne Redrocks Recreation Path at the intersection of Spear Street and Swift Street, and follow the path through the community gardens, through a cornfield, and into the woods.

4.7 When the trail splits, turn RIGHT onto the Champlain Bike Path downhill and over a small wooden bridge (the bridge makes a firecracker sound as you cross). Follow it as it arcs left, and stay with it as it hugs a baseball diamond. Do not take the Champlain Bike Path exit to the right.

5.2 Exit the path onto Lindenwood Drive, and stay STRAIGHT.

5.5 Road ends at Shelburne Road/US-7 (this is a busy road). Turn RIGHT, staying on the sidewalk, for 100 feet or so to the crosswalk at the lights, and push the button for the cross signal. Cross Shelburne Road/US-7 onto an unmarked road, and bear LEFT onto Queen City Park Road.

5.8 Turn RIGHT onto the bike path, which follows a fence perpendicular to the road.

6.3 Turn LEFT at the end onto Home Avenue, and stay STRAIGHT onto Austin Drive. This section of the ride runs through an industrial park and is momentarily not scenic.

6.8 Trail begins again on RIGHT at baseball diamond.

7.0 Pass through the parking area, and continue STRAIGHT on path/ Flynn Avenue into Oakledge Park. At the waterfront, the path takes a RIGHT along the waterfront. Do not follow Flynn Avenue to the right.

7.3 On the Lake Champlain waterfront, with Blanchard Beach to your left, the Burlington Earth Clock is to your right. Follow the path past it on the RIGHT.

7.4 Path enters Proctor Place, bearing LEFT, and then bears RIGHT onto Harrison Avenue.

7.6 Turn LEFT onto path at the end of Harrison Avenue, along train tracks.

8.0 Lake Champlain views to your left, including the Adirondacks and islands. Pass through a city park and beaches, then through a marina.

9.0 Turn RIGHT onto Maple Street.

9.2 END at parking area.

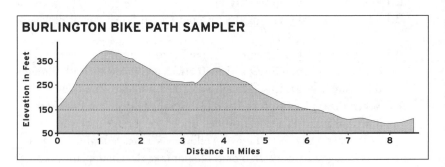

BURLINGTON BIKE PATH SAMPLER

5 MOUNT PHILO RISING
Burlington to Mount Philo State Park

PAVED ROADS WITH MINIMAL TO MODERATE TRAFFIC

Difficulty: 3   **Total Distance:** 33 miles

Riding Time: 2 hours   **Elevation Gain:** 1,200 feet

Summary: Minimally to moderately trafficked roads lead from downtown to – and up – rural Mount Philo, offering stunning views along the way.

Within minutes of leaving Burlington's downtown area, cyclists on this ride find themselves in another world—a more rural world lined with farms and pastures, cornfields and cows, and offering stunning views of the mountains to the east, including Mount Mansfield and the ever-recognizable Camel's Hump.

From there, the ride continues to get more scenic. But it also gets more challenging as it makes its way to Mount Philo State Park and switchbacks its way up Mount Philo itself. Topping out at just under 1,000 feet at its summit, Mount Philo is hardly an alp, but the winding climb will make your legs ask questions you may not have answers for.

If you choose a bright summer weekend or an early fall day, you might find a wedding reception at the top. They're common there, in large part because of the extraordinary views.

The 168-acre state park—Vermont's oldest—looks out over the Champlain Valley, the lake itself, and the Adirondack Mountains on its western shore. The road is narrow and steep at times, and at the summit you'll find a viewing platform and

© CHRIS BERNARD

The Mount Philo climb is steep in parts, and steeper in other parts, but the payoff is a breathtaking vista over Lake Champlain and the Adirondack Mountains.

a shelter to rest your tired legs. After all, you're just a little more than halfway.

The roads leading back to Burlington are quiet and scenic, but after the summit, they can't help but feel like a little bit of a letdown.

For more information, contact Mount Philo State Park, 5425 Mount Philo Road, Charlotte, VT 05445, 802/425-2390, www.vtstateparks.com/htm/philo.cfm (daily 10 A.M.–9 P.M. Memorial Day weekend through Oct. 12, $3 day-use fee).

Options

This ride could be combined with a visit to Shelburne Farms by turning left on Bay Road at Mile 27 and following the Shelburne Farms directions from Mile 0, adding an easy 9 miles to cool down on.

Locals' Tip: Swing by The Little Garden Market (86 Ferry Road, Charlotte, VT 05445, 802/425-5336) for some surprisingly delicious take-out sandwiches and snacks, and carry them up Mount Philo with you for a summit lunch.

Places to Stay: The Inn at Charlotte (32 State Park Road, Charlotte, VT 05445, 802/425-2934) is close to Mount Philo and ideally located on more than a half-dozen cycling loops—and includes easy access to the Lake Champlain ferry to New York state. There's a small campground at Mount Philo State Park (888/409-7579 or 802/425-2390, $16–18) if you want to ride this route in reverse.

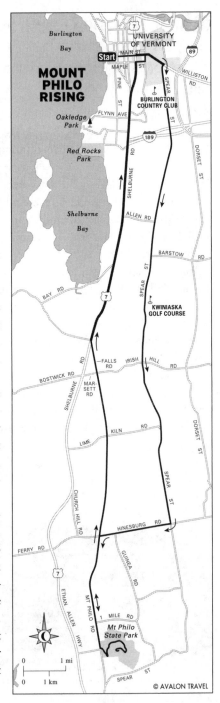

Driving Directions

From I-89, take exit 14W toward Burlington, and continue straight onto Main Street. After halfa mile, turn right onto St. Paul Street, then make a quick right onto College Street. City Hall Park is on the right. Parking is available around the park and on nearby side streets, or stay on St. Paul Street and enter the parking garage on your right.

Route Directions

0.0 From City Hall Park, head east on Main Street, up the hill. Main Street becomes VT-2.

1.0 Turn RIGHT onto Spear Street.

2.9 Pass under VT-189. The road passes into farm country and runs along several pastures and fields.

11.7 Turn RIGHT onto Hinesburg Road.

13.4 Turn LEFT onto Mount Philo Road.

16.2 Turn LEFT onto State Park Road to begin climb. Over the next mile, the road rises sharply upward. At the summit, descend carefully back to the base.

18.4 Turn RIGHT onto Mount Philo Road.

24.8 Mount Philo Road becomes Falls Road.

25.4 Bear RIGHT on Shelburne Road/VT-7. Watch for merging traffic, and stay in the marked bike lane.

27.0 OPTION: Turn LEFT on Bay Road for Shelburne Farms.

31.3 Bear RIGHT on South Willard Street.

31.8 Turn RIGHT on Cliff Street.

32.0 Turn LEFT on South Prospect Street.

32.4 Turn LEFT onto Main Street, downhill.

33.0 END at park.

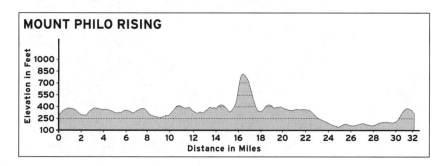

MOUNT PHILO RISING

6 SHELBURNE FARMS BEST [

Shelburne

PAVED, GRAVEL, AND DIRT ROADS AND PATHS

Difficulty: 1   **Total Distance:** 9 miles

Riding Time: 1.5 hours   **Elevation Gain:** 354 feet

Summary: Dirt roads and paths ambling through beautiful farm-oriented conservation land make for a lazy day on two wheels.

Shelburne Farms is a lot of things, including a working farm, a National Historic Landmark, and a nonprofit environmental education center. It's also home to a series of walking and biking trails that, while not technical or challenging, are so beautiful and well-thought-out that you're likely to finish your ride more refreshed than when you began.

Just minutes outside Burlington, and offering an incredible 1,400-acre lakefront setting, Shelburne Farms boasts an inn, a restaurant, vegetable gardens, a children's farmyard, a historical archive, and walking tours, as well as ongoing events. Dairy cows on the property produce milk that in turn is crafted into an award-winning cheese.

Once the private estate of Dr. William Seward Webb, Shelburne Farms was turned into a working nonprofit by his descendants in 1972 as a way to continue the farm's legacy. Conservation easements protect much of the land, and by

A bike ride at Shelburne Farms makes for a quiet, restful day.

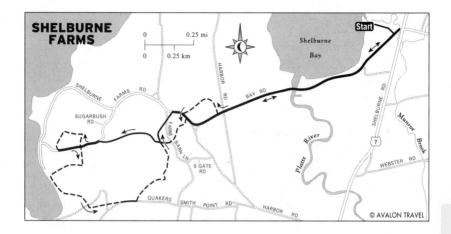

educating new generations about sustainability and farm life, Shelburne Farms continues to contribute.

This ride is suitable for even beginner riders, although it's off-road and some comfort with dirt trail conditions is advisable. Take it as slowly as you care to, and give yourself plenty of time to explore the landscape around you. Mountain bikes are overkill, but hybrid bikes or cyclocross bikes are ideal.

For more information, contact Shelburne Farms, 1611 Harbor Road, Shelburne, VT 05482, 802/985-8686, www.shelburnefarms.org.

Options

At Mile 3.4, a side trail leads to a scenic viewpoint with vistas of the grounds and nearby Mount Mansfield and Camel's Hump. If you're looking to string together a longer ride, check out the trail maps available online (www.shelburnefarms.org) or at the entrance kiosk. This ride is also within a short drive of Island Line Rail Trail, Burlington Bike Path Sampler, and Mount Philo Rising.

Locals' Tip: Right on the Shelburne Farms property at the historic Farm Barn, the Farm Cart serves a fresh and tasty lunch during the summer.

Places to Stay: If you're riding on the property, why not stay at the Inn at Shelburne Farms (1611 Harbor Road, Shelburne, VT 05482, 802/985-8498, www.shelburnefarms.org/comevisitus/inn.shtm)?

Driving Directions

From Burlington, take VT-7 South to the center of Shelburne and turn right onto Bay Road, following signs for Shelburne Farms and Shelburne Bay Park and Recreation Area. Park at the Shelburne Bay Park and Recreation Area, on your right. Restroom facilities are available.

Route Directions

0.0 From the parking area, turn RIGHT onto Bay Road.

1.6 Cross Harbor Road and enter the main gates of Shelburne Farms. *Cyclists aren't required to stop at the entrance kiosk, but it offers maps, guides, and other literature.* Turn RIGHT onto a dirt road, following marked Farm Trail.

3.4 Turn RIGHT to follow signs for Market Garden Trail. Ride along the gardens where produce is grown for use at the Shelburne Inn, on the same property. OPTION: Side trail to scenic viewpoint.

3.8 Turn RIGHT to rejoin Farm Trail.

4.0 Farm Trail turns sharply to the RIGHT and runs to the waterfront, where it follows the shore for four-tenths of a mile before bearing LEFT.

5.2 Trail bears LEFT, and passes several farm buildings. OPTION: Turn LEFT for short Whimsey Meadow Trail, bearing LEFT to rejoin Farm Trail.

6.2 Turn RIGHT onto North Gate Road.

6.4 Cross Harbor Road, staying straight on Bay Road.

8.5 Turn LEFT to return to parking area.

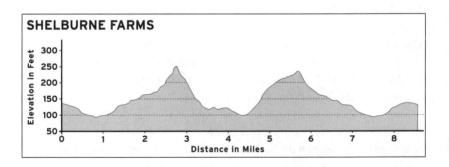

7 CATAMOUNT OUTDOOR CENTER
Williston

DIRT SINGLE-TRACK AND FIRE ROADS

Difficulty: 2

Riding Time: 1 hour

Total Distance: 3.1 miles

Elevation Gain: 98 feet

Summary: Offering miles of wooded, groomed single-track, these trails were designed for mountain bikers of all skill levels.

The first thing you'll notice as you pull into the Catamount Outdoor Family Center parking lot is all the vehicles. Then you'll notice all the people loading and unloading bikes, grouping up for rides, or returning from the trails covered in mud. This place is popular.

You'll also notice that many of them are kids. Catamount offers mountain biking classes for riders of all ages and skill levels, including multiday camps. Pay attention, because these kids are the future of the sport.

Then, as you scan a trail map, you'll notice the options available to you. These trails wander for more than 20 miles over 500 acres, and they are are professionally designed and maintained.

Once you choose a trail and start riding it, you won't notice anything except how much fun you're having until you're done. This place is a blast.

Catamount is a nonprofit created in 1978 as an "ongoing experiment in outdoor

A variety of trails and conditions make the Catamount Outdoor Center trails a great place to spend time on a bike.

recreation." It started as a cross-country ski center, and over the years it has expanded to include mountain biking and trail running. There's a bed-and-breakfast on site, and each fall the center hosts a popular cyclocross race as part of a larger series.

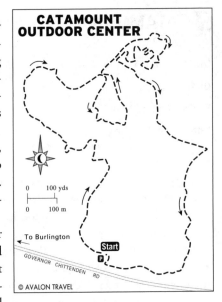

The trails themselves are fast, fun, and scenic, ranging from woods to fields with rolling hills and obstacles. You could easily spend a weekend riding here without getting bored.

If you can't find a trail suitable for your skill level, you're not looking hard enough. When you stop by the front desk to pay the trails fee, ask for recommendations. The friendly and helpful staff will point you in the right direction. The small office also sells supplies and snacks, and restrooms are available.

Catamount is operated by the family that's owned the land—which was a dairy farm until the 1950s—since 1873. Hours vary by season; check online or at the office for the latest schedule.

For more information, contact Catamount Outdoor Family Center, 592 Governor Chittenden Road, Williston, VT 05405, 802/879-6001, www.catamount outdoor.com. Hours and rates vary.

Options

This ride is a short sampler designed to give you a taste for the trails. It's one of the easier routes, and it's short. Grab a trail map and piece together a longer ride, or find another group of cyclists heading in and follow them. You can't go wrong.

This ride is a short drive from Island Line Rail Trail, Burlington Bike Path Sampler, Shelburne Farms, and Mount Philo Rising.

Locals' Tip: Head into downtown Burlington for dinner after a hard day of riding. In a town full of options, the Vermont Pub and Brewery (144 College Street, Burlington, VT 05401, 802/865-0500, www.vermontbrewery.com) holds its own.

Places to Stay: You've come all this way to play; why not stay on site at the Catamount Outdoor Family Center's bed-and-breakfast (592 Governor Chittenden Road, Williston, VT 05405, 802/879-6001, www.catamountoutdoor.com)?

Reasonably priced and well-situated, the B&B is in a historic structure built by the first governor of Vermont.

Driving Directions

Take VT-2 East into Williston Village. At the four-way stop, turn left onto North Williston Road. After 1 mile, turn right onto Governor Chittenden Road. Parking is on the left; check-in and restrooms are on the right.

Route Directions

0.0 From the parking area, with your back to the check-in building, the trailhead is the dirt and gravel road on the far left of the lot. You can also enter from the right side of the lot, following the trail left behind a small fence until it connects with the dirt and gravel road.

0.5 Follow the signs and blue blazes for the trail, which begins on the LEFT. Follow the blue blazes as the trail winds clockwise through the woods.

2.7 Exit the woods into a grassy field, and follow the tracks to the parking area.

3.1 END at parking area.

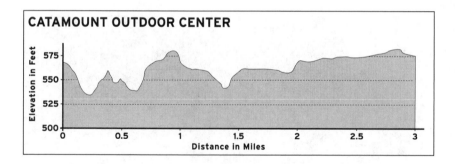

CATAMOUNT OUTDOOR CENTER

8 SMUGGLER'S BLUES   BEST C
   Stowe

PAVED ROADS WITH MINIMAL TO MODERATE TRAFFIC

Difficulty: 4   **Total Distance:** 42.6 miles

Riding Time: 4 hours   **Elevation Gain:** 2,182 feet

Summary: This climbers' loop leaves downtown Stowe and heads up and over the challenging Smuggler's Notch.

The mythology and lore of smugglers holds a certain appeal, and northern Vermont has more than its fair share of legends. This ride celebrates them.

In the early 1800s, under President Thomas Jefferson, the United States halted trade with Great Britain and Canada, bringing undue hardships to Vermonters. Ever resourceful, some locals illegally continued to trade across the border with Montreal, sneaking goods and livestock through the mountains. Later, fugitive slaves used the mountain pass as a means of reaching freedom in Canada, and during Prohibition in the 1920s, others brought liquor to the States through the same pass.

Named Smuggler's Notch in tribute to those who used it, the pass separates Spruce Peak and the Sterling Range from Mount Mansfield. It also separates

© CHRIS BERNARD

While the extensive climbing makes this ride difficult, the scenery makes it worth the lung-busting, leg-quivering effort.

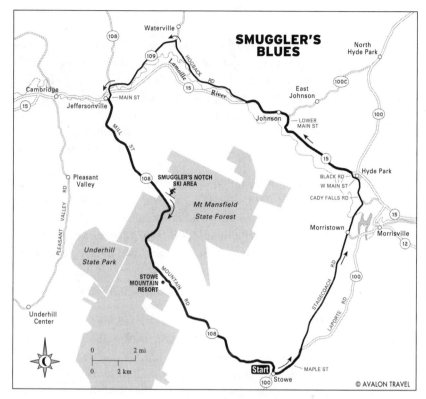

Smuggler's Notch Resort on the north side of the pass from Stowe Mountain Resort on the south, making this area one of the hotbeds of Vermont skiing in winter.

This ride begins amid the shops and restaurants in quaint, touristy downtown Stowe and winds its way counterclockwise through several scenic towns and villages, on a mostly flat route, until about mile 25. At that point, it rises dramatically and makes its way up VT-108 to the notch itself, ending with a fast, breathtaking descent back into Stowe.

Not for the weak of leg, lung, or spirit, this climb is demanding—and yet utterly doable with patience and perseverance. It's also worth it for the views.

End your day with shopping and drinks in Stowe, a tour of the Ben & Jerry's Factory and Flavor Graveyard (VT-100, Waterbury, VT 05672, 802/882-1240) in nearby Waterbury, or a visit to the Trapp Family Lodge (700 Trapp Hill Road, Stowe, VT 05672, 800/826-7000), built and owned by the von Trapps made famous by *The Sound of Music.*

For more information, contact the Lamoille Valley Chamber of Commerce, 34 Pleasant Street, Morrisville, VT 05661, 802/888-7607, www.1-800-vermont .com.

Options

The Stowe Recreation Path is just 5.5 miles long, but its location—and the multitude of picnic and swimming spots along its length—make it a must-ride while in the area. The trailhead is right downtown next to the Stowe Congregational Church. The path crosses the West Branch River on arched wooden bridges 11 times, and it meanders past shops, lodges, and restaurants; consider it a good way to cool down after spending the day climbing in the mountains.

The Gaps of Glory ride and Mad River Madness are within a 40-minute drive, as well.

Locals' Tip: Refuel guilt-free at Frida's Taqueria and Grill (128 Main Street, Stowe, VT 05672, 802/253-0333, www.fridastaqueria.com), located in a historic building and loaded with recipes from artist Frida Kahlo's own collection.

Places to Stay: The Mountain Road Resort (1007 Mountain Road, Stowe, VT 05672, 800/367-6873, http://mountainroadresort.com) is locally owned and operated, with all local employees. The resort shows movies at night on a two-story projection screen in the pool area.

Driving Directions

From I-89, take exit 10 for VT-100 toward US-2/Stowe/Waterbury. Stay on VT-100 for 10 miles, until it becomes Main Street. Parking is available around town. The ride begins at Shaw's General Store (54 Main Street, Stowe, VT 05672, 802/253-4040, www.heshaw.com); supplies are available inside.

Route Directions

0.0 From Shaw's, turn RIGHT onto Main Street/VT-100, which becomes Maple Street and then Morrisville Road.

1.2 Bear LEFT off of VT-100 onto Stagecoach Road.

2.5 The first climb (just a few hundred feet) begins.

4.0 The descent begins, and the route's mostly downhill for the next 20 miles or so.

8.5 Turn LEFT onto Cadys Falls Road.

9.5 Bear LEFT onto Main Street.

10.1 Turn RIGHT onto Johnson Street Extension.

10.3 Turn LEFT onto VT-15/Grand Army of the Republic Highway.

16.1 Bear RIGHT onto Hogback Road.

20.7 Turn LEFT sharply onto VT-109.

24.7 Turn LEFT onto VT-108.

25.1 *Bicycle repair shop.*

25.4 Prepare for the big climb, which begins as you make your way up to Smuggler's Notch Pass.

29.0 Pass Smuggler's Notch ski area on your left. *This is a good place to stop and rest if you need.*

30.0 The climb becomes more difficult as the grade gets steeper—hang on to your helmet.

33.2 Crest the pass at 2,170 feet. Begin the descent, which will carry you all the way to the finish.

35.2 Pass the entrance road for Stowe Resort Ski Area.

42.4 Turn LEFT onto Main Street/VT-100.

42.6 END at parking area.

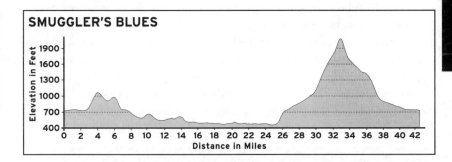

SMUGGLER'S BLUES

9 KINGDOM TRAILS   BEST **C**
East Burke, Northeast Kingdom

SINGLE-TRACK, GRASSY TRAILS

Difficulty: 3   **Total Distance:** 8.7 miles

Riding Time: 1.5 hours   **Elevation Gain:** 807 feet

Summary: Kingdom Trails is home to some of the best mountain biking in the northeast and has something for everyone who loves to get dirty.

Bike Magazine's annual readers' poll named the Kingdom Trails the "Best Trail Network in North America," not the first time these trails have been singled out. And to anyone who's ridden them, the reasons are immediately apparent.

These 100-plus miles of trails include everything from single-track to fire roads, covering some of the most ruggedly beautiful landscape in the northeast. Created and maintained by the nonprofit Kingdom Trails Association, the area is supported by all sorts of agencies, groups, and individuals who have come together to provide some incredible opportunities for outdoor exploration. Each year, existing trails are enhanced and new trails are built, giving the system an ever-changing, evolving character. You can go back every year and not ride the same trail twice.

Marked with purple signs sporting a golden crown in the middle, the trails

© CHRIS BERNARD

Expect mud on the Kingdom Trails early in the season or after heavy rains, and remember – mud makes for a day on the bike.

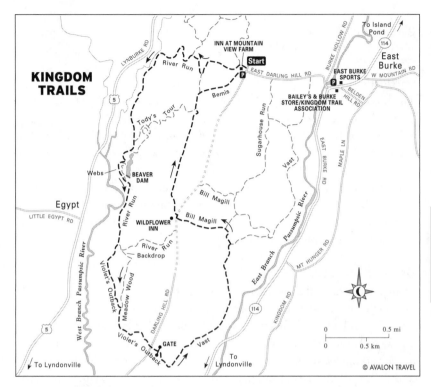

are all assigned degrees of difficulty. This route is a strong intermediate ride on single-track and wide grassy paths, with outstanding views and a good spot to stop for a picnic lunch. The scenery is Vermont at its best, and the trails vary from grassy to sandy, rocky to rooty, with sections of washout. Advanced riders will find more aggressive routes within the trail system.

Local etiquette calls for riding the trails counterclockwise. Trails are open for mountain biking May 1–October 31. Almost three-quarters of the trails remain open during this time regardless of the weather, so expect mud if it's been rainy. Some trails are closed during muddy periods, however, to prevent erosion.

A trail map is a must. Order a map ahead of time from Kingdom Trail Association or East Burke Sports, or pick one up when you arrive in East Burke. Because all the trails crisscross private land, there's a cost to ride them, but the $10 day-use fee is nominal when you consider the work that goes into the system. Pay the trail fee at the Kingdom Trail Association's office in the Bailey's and Burke building (upstairs from the general store) or at an outdoor tent behind the back of the building on summer weekends.

For more information, contact Kingdom Trail Association, VT-114, East

Burke, VT 05832, 802/626-0737, www.kingdomtrails.org and East Burke Sports, VT-114, East Burke, VT 05832, 802/626-3215, www.eastburkesports.com.

Options

The ride detailed here is just one of many in the area. Arm yourself with a trail map and get out in the woods to explore this precious resource.

Locals' Tip: The Pub Outback (466 VT-114/Main Street, East Burke, VT 05832, 802/626-1188) is a favorite hangout of cyclists and skiers in town for the trails.

Places to Stay: Make a weekend of your trip by camping with dozens of other cyclists with the same idea at the Burke Mountain Campground (Burke Mountain Toll Road, East Burke, VT 05832, 802/626-7333, www.skiburke.com/campground.htm), open mid-May through late October.

Driving Directions

From points south, take I-91 to exit 23 north in Lyndon. Take US-5 north to VT-114, and take VT-114 into East Burke. Park in town, behind Bailey's and Burke store at the Pub Outback, and ride up East Darling Hill Road to the Inn at Mountain View Farm, where this ride begins. Alternatively, drive up the hill and park in the parking lot at the inn. The ride starts from the parking lot, heading out to the right behind the red barn and inn to greener, and well-marked, pastures. Supplies are available in East Burke and there's a pub for post-ride refueling. The old general store, Bailey's and Burke, is a treat for trail snacks.

Route Directions

0.0 Turn LEFT out of the parking lot, then make an immediate RIGHT, heading behind the circa-1890 red barn.

0.1 Bear LEFT, continuing through the field.

0.4 Turn RIGHT at view with yellow farmhouse; pass an old barn.

0.5 Bear RIGHT, then make an immediate LEFT on River Run Trail.

2.3 After the bridge, continue to the RIGHT on River Run Trail.

2.6 Bear LEFT.

2.9 Continue STRAIGHT on Violet's Outback Trail (watch for pigs).

3.0 Turn RIGHT on Violet's Outback Trail.

3.8 Continue STRAIGHT.

3.9 Bear LEFT.

4.0 Continue to the RIGHT on Violet's Outback Trail

4.2 *Picnic spot.*

4.3 Cross Darling Hill Road, pass a gate, and continue on a snowmobile trail marked VAST (Vermont Association of Snow Travelers).

6.1 Bear LEFT on Bill Magill Trail.

6.3 Bear LEFT on Bill Magill Trail.

6.6 Turn RIGHT on a dirt road by Wildflower Inn.

6.7 Turn LEFT, then head behind the tennis courts, downhill beyond the fence. At the bottom of the field, bear RIGHT.

8.3 Bear RIGHT on Bemis Trail, toward a big red barn and parking area.

8.7 Return to starting point.

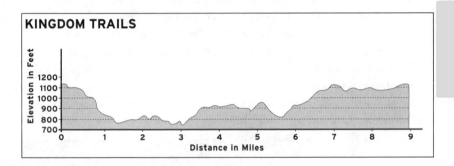

KINGDOM TRAILS

Elevation in Feet

1200
1100
1000
900
800
700

0   1   2   3   4   5   6   7   8   9

Distance in Miles

10 GAPS OF GLORY   BEST ◖

Waitsfield, Warren, Huntington, Rockville, and Fays Corner

PAVED ROADS, SOME DIRT AND GRAVEL ROADS

Difficulty: 5   **Total Distance:** 131 miles

Riding Time: 8-11 hours   **Elevation Gain:** 11,700 feet

Summary: A ridiculously hilly climbers' route, this epic ride is high on scenery and suffering – and it's only for the hardest of the hard core.

Vermont has six notorious mountain gaps accessible by roads. Cyclists have long used them for training grounds, and it's no wonder—all together, they offer more than 130 miles of riding with nearly 12,000 feet of climbing. Collected in one long day's loop, this is as difficult a ride as you'll find in New England, if anywhere. Northeast Cycling (www.northeastcycling.com) has put together a slew of information about this ride on its website and sums it up nicely: "This ride will take a lot out of you."

It goes without saying that this is a ride only for the fittest of cyclists, with good engines for climbing.

Consider the climbs. Lincoln Gap ascends the steepest continuously paved road on the continent (in some sections as much as a 25 percent grade, with sustained grades of about 20 percent) to an elevation of 2,469 feet. The Appalachian Gap has a less punishing grade, but with sections at 18 percent, just barely. The descent on Brandon Gap is wildly fast—and dangerous—and you have to work to get to it. Middlebury Gap gains almost 1,800 feet over 10 miles. Roxbury Gap is scenic and steep, and made more challenging by unpaved, gravel sections. Rochester Gap gains nearly 1,000 feet in just 2 miles.

Afraid? Good. You're using your head for more than just a place to store your helmet.

But don't let that stop you from

At points this ridiculously hilly ride gets twice as steep as the one on the sign, which comes with a warning for drivers.

© CHRIS BERNARD

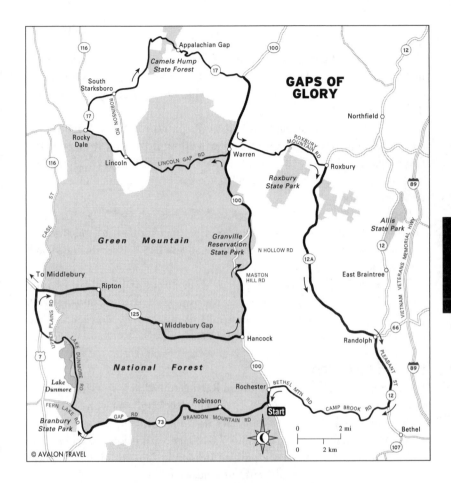

conquering this climbers' delight. Scores of cyclists take on this challenge each year, and you're likely to see some of them when you're out and about.

Alternate gearing is a must, with compact cranks and the biggest rear cog your derailleur will handle a good idea—and a mountain bike derailleur with even bigger cogs is a better bet. Don't be afraid to stop and walk. Better riders than you have broken on these peaks. Just think how good you'll feel when you pull this off.

A few hard-earned tips: Stop every chance you get to refill water bottles and to eat. You'll need the fuel and the rest. On descents, don't ride your brakes—give them time to cool so as not to wear down your pads or superheat your rims, which can blow tires and tubes and break spokes, a very dangerous proposition on a fast descent. And bring a camera—you'll want to remember this ride.

For more information, contact Northeast Cycling, www.northeastcycling .com.

Options

If you're worried about making enemies of your legs, cut 35 miles off the ride, to make it an easy 100 miles or so, by bearing right at Mile 56.6 onto Main Street, and then turning right less than a mile later onto Brook Road, rejoining the ride directions at Mile 92.

Sugarbush Resort (1840 Sugarbush Access Road, Warren, VT 05674, 800/537-8427, www.sugarbush.com) offers 18 miles of lift-served terrain, a pump track, a freeride park, and miles and miles of cross-country trails for all skill levels. Riders looking for a weekend of varied bike rides can bring mountain bikes or rent them at the lodge.

Locals' Tip: The Peavine Family Restaurant and Pub (3657 VT-107, Stockbridge, VT 05772, 802/234-9434, http://peavinerestaurant.com) is family-friendly, but the drinks are cold and the food good, and let's face it, after this ride you'll need a good helping of each.

Places to Stay: The Grunberg Haus Vermont Bed and Breakfast Inn and Cabins (94 Pine Street, VT-100 South, Waterbury, VT 05676, 800/800-7760, http://grunberghaus.com) offers mountainside Tyrolean-style rooms and summer cabins with easy access to trails and other amenities.

Driving Directions

From I-89, take exit 4 for VT-66 toward Randolph. Follow VT-66 for 2.5 miles until it becomes Central Street/VT-12. Follow that for 5.5 miles and turn right onto Camp Brook Road, which becomes Rochester Mountain Road and then Bethel Mountain Road. Turn left onto VT-100, and just before the intersection with VT-73, look for a small dirt parking area to the right side of the road, near Woodlawn Cemetery. The ride starts and ends here.

Route Directions

0.0 Turn RIGHT onto VT-73 toward Brandon.

3.9 Stay on paved road as the steep climb up Brandon Gap begins.

9.2 At the Brandon Gap summit, stay on VT-73 and begin the descent. Some of the turns on this descent can be dangerous, so watch your speed and ride carefully.

14.1 Turn RIGHT on VT-53 toward Lake Dunmore/Middlebury.

19.8 Stay STRAIGHT past Branbury State Park on Lake Dunmore Road.

23.4 Turn RIGHT on VT-7/US-7 toward East Middlebury and pass the lowest elevation of the entire ride.

26.3 Turn RIGHT onto VT-116/Ossie Road.

26.9 Bear RIGHT onto VT-125 toward Hancock. *Supplies and food available.*

27.7 Stay STRAIGHT as the climbing becomes steeper.

30.7 Stay STRAIGHT as you enter the village of Ripton and the climbing levels out—a little.

34.5 Stay STRAIGHT as the climb steepens again toward the summit of Middlebury Gap.

36.2 Summit of Middlebury Gap!

42.3 Turn LEFT onto VT-100 north. *Supplies and food available.*

51.1 Stay STRAIGHT as you pass over the summit Granville Gulf.

56.6 Turn LEFT onto Lincoln Gap Road. OPTION: Bear RIGHT onto Main Street and follow option directions.

58.1 Stay STRAIGHT. The pavement gets rough here and turns to dirt and gravel.

59.5 Stay STRAIGHT as the pavement resumes. The climb reaches its highest grade of the entire ride.

60.9 Lincoln Gap summit, the halfway and high points of the ride.

61.1 Stay STRAIGHT. Road turns to gravel.

64.4 Lincoln Gap Road becomes East River Road/Main Street.

65.5 *Supplies and food available in the village of Lincoln.*

68.9 Turn RIGHT onto VT-116/VT-17 North.

70.6 Turn RIGHT onto VT-17 and begin the ascent to Appalachian Gap.

77.5 Bear RIGHT to stay on VT-17 as the grade increases.

80.2 Appalachian Gap summit! Scenic viewpoint.

80.8 Stay STRAIGHT. Note that the turns here are dangerous.

86.4 Turn RIGHT onto VT-100 south. *Supplies and food available.*

91.2 Turn LEFT onto Main Street.

91.4 Bear LEFT onto Brook Road.

93.9 Turn RIGHT onto Roxbury Mountain Road. Roxbury Gap ascent begins.

94.6 Bear LEFT to stay on Roxbury Mountain Road. Sections of this road are gravel and dirt.

96.1 Roxbury Gap summit! From here, the descent is steep and gravel at times, with bad road conditions and sharp turns. Use caution.

99.7 Turn RIGHT on VT-12A South. *Supplies and food available.*

114.5 Turn RIGHT onto VT-12 South.
120.0 Turn RIGHT onto Camp Brook Road and begin ascent of
Rochester Gap.
125.6 Rochester Gap summit! Begin ascent of second Rochester Gap peak.
128.8 Turn LEFT onto Bethel Mountain Road to resume descent.
130.2 Turn LEFT onto VT-100 south. *Supplies and food available.*
130.8 END at parking area.

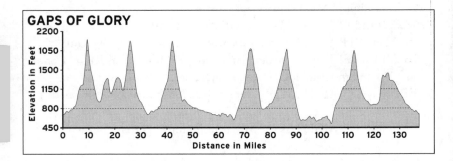

GAPS OF GLORY

11 MAD RIVER MADNESS
Montpelier

PAVED ROADS WITH MINIMAL TRAFFIC

Difficulty: 4	**Total Distance:** 102 miles
Riding Time: 7 hours	**Elevation Gain:** 2,208 feet

Summary: This hilly century through the heart of the state begins and ends at the capital, and it is only for fit riders.

Vermont's capital city, Montpelier, would barely qualify as a city in many states. Just over 10 square miles in size, with a population around 8,000, it's not exactly a bustling metropolis—in fact, it's the smallest state capital—but what would you expect from the second-least populous state in the nation?

If it's not a thriving Gotham, it is a quaint little town that's home to more than the state government. There's a fine arts college, a world-renowned culinary institute, and several galleries and museums, as well as a host of restaurants, cafés, and shops in the downtown area. All of which make Montpelier an excellent place to start and end this century ride that cuts clockwise through the heart of the state.

© CHRIS BERNARD

A bicycle-themed art installation in front of the statehouse marks the starting and ending point for this ride.

Park near the statehouse, a Greek Revival building a block from the Winooski River, and head south on VT-12 to begin this long and winding route that passes through a handful of small towns and villages that will make Montpelier seem downright urban. Pack a lunch, or stop at one of the half dozen general stores you'll pass along the way. Bring a camera. If this is the heart of the state, the beautiful Mad River is the blood that runs through it, and these mostly rural roads wander alongside the river and through the Green Mountain National Forest.

There's a fair amount of climbing, including one gradually increasing ascent up and over the same mountain as one of the state's notorious six gaps, and a few harrowing descents, but if you can't handle the climb, you're probably not ready for a 100-mile ride anyway, right?

Sure, you'll work for it. But the scenery along this route is breathtaking, with stunning mountain views and a lot of opportunities for foliage viewing. If you're up for the challenge, enjoy the ride.

Options

This ride passes right by the start-and-ending point for the Gaps of Glory ride, one of the most difficult rides in this—or any—area. If you combine these two rides in a single weekend, you are truly a cyclist to be feared.

Locals' Tip: Restock lost calories

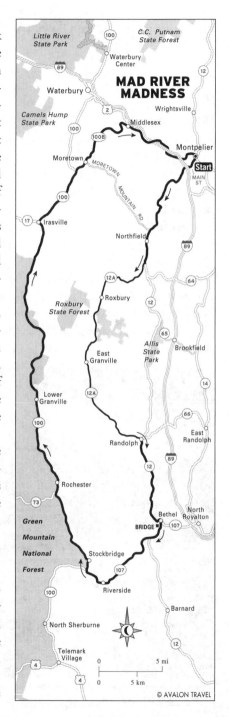

at the Main Street Grill (118 Main Street, Montpelier, VT 05602, 802/223-3188), where students at the New England Culinary Institute learn through on-the-job training. You get great food at reasonable prices and a chance to watch America's up-and-coming chefs at work.

Places to Stay: The Twin City Motel (1537 US-302, Barre, VT 05641, 802/476-3104, www.twincitymotel.com) is a no-frills and no-surprises place to spend a night for a reasonable price.

Driving Directions

From I-89, take exit 8 toward US-2/Montpelier, and merge onto Memorial Drive. Take a quick left onto US-2/Bailey Avenue, and a quick right onto State Street/ US-2 Bridge. The statehouse is on your left at 115 State Street. Parking is available along the street, and supplies are available in town.

Route Directions

0.0 From the statehouse, turn LEFT onto State Street and RIGHT onto Main Street/VT-12.

5.6 Pass through Northfield Center, and bear RIGHT onto Chandler Road.

8.1 Turn LEFT onto Cox Brook Road into Northfield Falls, and make a quick RIGHT onto VT-12.

10.8 Pass through Northfield, and bear RIGHT onto VT-12A. The road starts a gradual ascent into Roxbury.

16.8 Pass through Roxbury and begin a descent.

23.0 Pass through East Granville.

32.6 Turn RIGHT onto VT-12 in the town of Randolph. *Supplies available.*

39.1 Turn LEFT to stay on VT-12 into downtown Bethel. *Supplies available.*

39.6 Turn RIGHT to stay on VT-12/VT-107, across bridge.

41.7 Bear RIGHT to stay on VT-107 when VT-12 splits.

49.9 Turn sharp RIGHT onto VT-100.

50.8 Enter Stockbridge—halfway done! *Supplies available.* Begin a long, gradual ascent that's almost a false flat.

58.5 Enter Rochester. Green Mountain National Forest is to your left. *Supplies and bike shop available.*

67.0 Climb steepens sharply, but the views are worth it.

72.0 Bear LEFT to stay on VT-100, and begin sharp descent. Hang on—it's almost all downhill from here.

82.5 Turn RIGHT to stay on VT-100 in Irasville. *Supplies available.*
83.5 Enter Waitsville. *Supplies available.*
88.0 Bear RIGHT onto VT-100B.
89.0 Enter Moretown. *Supplies available.*
96.0 In Middlesex, turn RIGHT onto US-2.
100.3 Enter Montpelier Junction. Stay on US-2.
102.5 Statehouse on left. END at parking area.

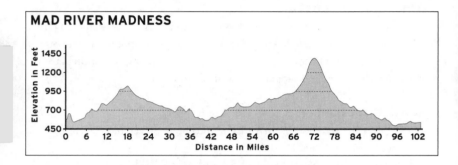

MAD RIVER MADNESS

12 WELLS RIVER RAIL TRAIL

BEST (

Ricker Pond State Park, Groton

RAIL TRAIL WITH BALLAST

Difficulty: 2   **Total Distance:** 12.4 miles

Riding Time: 1.5-2 hours   **Elevation Gain:** 806 feet

Summary: Suitable for anyone comfortable with unpaved surfaces, this pretty ride provides a relaxing way to spend a day in the countryside.

One of the state's lesser-known rail trails in a less-populated section of the state, the Wells River ride is a great way to spend a summer day. You could try it in the fall, when the foliage enhances the already-beautiful scenery, but then you'd miss out on the many opportunities to swim along the length of the ride.

Start south of Ricker Pond State Park, accessing the ride from the campground, and head northwest past Ricker Pond, the first of many which entice and invite sweaty cyclists. From there, you follow the edge of Lake Groton up to Kettle Pond and on, if you want to explore farther, to Marshfield Pond. The hardwood forest through which you ride offers something to see at every turn.

Birders and wildlife enthusiasts will like this trail for its remote location and wildlife-viewing possibilities—moose, deer, black bear, mink, beaver, and otters all call these woods home. Historical remnants lie along the trail, as well, leftovers from the days of logging and railroads. Ricker Pond State Park was among the longest continuously operating sawmills in Vermont. If you stay at Ricker Pond campground, you can ride right onto the trail.

Mostly ballast, dirt, and sand, this trail is flat enough for all riders and rideable with any bike. The ride is a straight out-and-back, so the total riding distance is up to you. The Kettle Pond parking lot is a good place to turn around. If you want more, continue to Marshfield Pond, about 2.7 miles farther up the trail. A section of the trail beyond Marshfield Pond

Most riders, regardless of skill level, will find themselves up to the challenge this ballast-packed rail trail presents.

© CHRIS BERNARD

is more of a walking trail, though long-term plans call for extending this rail trail, officially called the Montpelier and Wells River Rail Trail, all the way to Lake Champlain in Burlington.

For more information on the area, contact Ricker Pond State Park, 526 State Forest Road, Groton, VT 05046, 802/584-3821, www.vtstateparks.com/htm/ricker.cfm.

Options

At Mile 4.4, turn right onto VT-232, and right again onto Owls Head Road. Leave your bike at the small parking lot, and walk the trail to the left to the summit of Owls Head, where you'll find a stone fire tower built by the Civilian Conservation Corps in the 1930s, offering great views of the region. Or bring your mountain bike, as the woods around this rail trail are lined with miles of trails to explore.

This ride is less than an hour from Mad River Madness.

Locals' Tip: While the area options are limited, you'll be pleasantly surprised by the fare at Brown's Market Bistro (1618 Scott Highway, Groton, VT 05046, 802/584-4124).

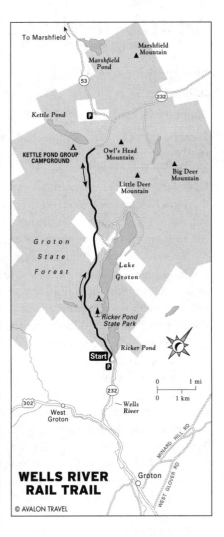

Places to Stay: The Ricker Pond State Park campground (18 Ricker Pond Camp Ground Road, Groton, VT 05046, 802/584-3821, www.vtstateparks.com/htm/ricker.cfm) is open Memorial Day to Columbus Day.

Driving Directions

From I-91, take exit 17, near Woodsville, to VT-302 and drive west to Groton. Drive approximately 2 miles and turn right onto VT-232 north. Drive approximately 1.5 miles to the Ricker Pond Rail Trail terminus (approximately 0.9 mile south of Ricker Pond State Park).

Route Directions

0.0 START from trail terminus at the south end of Ricker Pond.

0.8 Enter Ricker Pond State Park. *Restrooms and water available.*

4.4 OPTION: Turn right onto VT-232 and follow option directions.

6.2 Pass Kettle Pond parking area and group campground, across VT-232. TURN AROUND.

12.4 END at starting point.

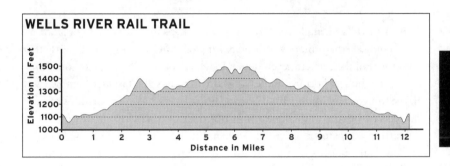

WELLS RIVER RAIL TRAIL

13 LEICESTER HOLLOW TRAIL
Goshen to Branbury State Park

DIRT ROADS, SINGLE-TRACK

Difficulty: 3   **Total Distance:** 10.8 miles

Riding Time: 2.5 hours   **Elevation Gain:** 1,188 feet

Summary: Dirt roads and single-track make this out-and-back a good off-road ride for moderately fit cyclists.

This dirt-road and single-track ride is not overly technical, but it's got a fair bit of climbing. Perhaps more worth preparing for is the stinging wood nettle that lines the trail. It seems to reach out and grab at you as you pass, like something from a low-budget horror film, leaving stinging welts and rashes as reminders of all the fun you had. But the trail is so enjoyable that it's worth the risk. Wear arm warmers and tights, and sally forth.

Starting at the town offices in Goshen, this ride connects with the Leicester Hollow Trail, a lush, green path bathed in filtered sunlight. The mostly single-track trail follows a babbling brook for a long uphill climb that never gets steep, but never seems to end, either. The good news? This is an out-and-back ride, which means smooth sailing home.

© CHRIS BERNARD

While not overtly technical, this trail does get hilly at times as it winds through the Vermont woods.

After about 5 miles, you reach Silver Lake, where—weather permitting—you'll be tempted to swim, or at least sit by the shore and snack. You'll also find pumps offering potable water to refill your bottles. For an added adventure, lock up the bikes and hike about 1.5 miles in, to the scenic overlook at the interestingly named Falls of Lana.

Past Silver Lake, off VT-53, the expansive Lake Dunmore and Branbury State Park have a campground with a sandy swimming beach, hiking trails, boating, and fishing, all within biking distance of the Leicester Hollow Trail.

For more information, contact Branbury State Park, 3570 Lake Dunmore Road, VT-53, Salisbury, VT 05733, 802/247-5925, www.vtstateparks.com/htm/branbury.cfm. For more about the area, contact the Brandon Area Chamber of Commerce, P.O. Box 267, Brandon, VT 05733, 802/247-6401, www.brandon.org.

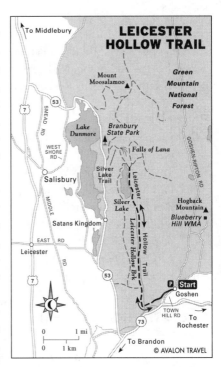

Options

To expand this ride, park instead at the Minnie Baker Trailhead by turning left onto VT-53 off VT-73 just before Goshen and driving 1.6 miles. The Minnie Baker Trail climbs steeply on several ascents from the trailhead to where it joins the Leicester Hollow Trail at Mile 1.7, adding 2.5 miles round-trip and a good amount of climbing.

Locals' Tip: The Brandon Falls Diner (25 Center Street, Brandon, VT 05733, 802/247-5203, www.brandon.org) isn't likely to win any James Beard Awards, but if you're craving traditional New England diner fare, this will satisfy you.

Places to Stay: The Churchill House Inn (3128 Forest Dale Road/VT-73, Brandon, VT 05733, 800/320-5828, www.churchillhouseinn.com) is a bike-friendly place to stay, just minutes from the trailhead.

Driving Directions

From Middlebury, take VT-7 South to Brandon, approximately 17 miles. Just past

Brandon, take VT-73 East to the tiny town of Goshen, approximately 4 miles. Turn left onto Town Hill Road. Parking is available at the town offices. Supplies are available in Killington, Middlebury, and Brandon, and there are bike shops in Middlebury and nearby Rochester.

Route Directions

0.0 Facing the Goshen town offices, ride LEFT onto Fay Road (dirt road).

1.2 Turn RIGHT onto Leicester Hollow Brook Trail.

1.7 Pass Minnie Baker Trail.

4.9 Pass Silver Lake Trail.

5.4 *A left at the dirt campground road will take you to the picnic area, swimming beach, restrooms, and trail to Falls of Lana.* TURN AROUND and retrace route.

10.8 END at starting point.

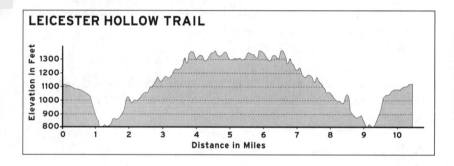

14 WOODSTOCK QUECHEE GORGEOUS
Woodstock, Quechee State Park, and North Pomfret

PAVED ROADS

Difficulty: 3   **Total Distance:** 31.3 miles

Riding Time: 2 hours   **Elevation Gain:** 1,512 feet

Summary: This lovely countryside ride faces a few hills as it loops around historic Woodstock and Quechee.

Hundreds of thousands of people visit Quechee Gorge each year, and while you'll be one of them, the gorge itself is just one of the scenic reasons to ride this route. You also get stunning views from atop a long climb, a 6-mile descent, some rural, wooded areas to pass through, tours of cute Vermont towns, and lungs full of fresh air as you pedal yourself along this hilly 31-mile ride.

Quechee Gorge is the state's deepest, formed glacially about 13,000 years ago. From the bridge above it, you'll have impressive views of the Ottauquechee River 165 feet below. The river once powered the Dewey Company's woolen mills, which made two trademarked types of wool used for, among other things, uniforms for

© CHRIS BERNARD

It's hard to find any faults with this ride through scenic southern Vermont.

both the Boston Red Sox and the rival New York Yankees. While most of the mill and the outbuildings are gone now, you'll see their remains along this ride.

Before Quechee, though, you start in the historic, postcard-perfect, well-to-do town of Woodstock, the site of the state's government before Montpelier became the capital. If the town looks familiar to you, it's because it's been the setting for several films and a popular TV commercial—and it also looks more or less exactly how you'd picture a Vermont town.

From town you hit a good long hill and an even better, longer descent that rolls you past farms and forests, rivers and ridges, and even a covered bridge.

For more information on the area, contact Quechee State Park, 764 Dewey Mills Road, White River Junction, VT 05001, 802/295-2990, www.vtstateparks.com/htm/quechee.cfm.

Options

Shorten this ride by 6 miles by dropping the visit to Quechee Gorge, which will still give you a scenic, hilly ride.

This ride's not too far from the Old Norwich Turnpike Loop.

Locals' Tip: With its giant pie slices and mouthwatering food, Mountain Creamery (33 Central Street, Woodstock, VT 05091, 802/457-1715) seems to always have a line, despite the notoriously prickly service, which somehow adds to the charm.

Places to Stay: Just feet from the town green, and the start and end point for this ride, the Shire Motel (46 Pleasant Street, Woodstock, VT 05091, 802/457-2211, www.shiremotel.com) is a fine choice for local lodging.

Driving Directions

From I-89, take exit 1 and turn left on US-4/Woodstock Road. After 20 miles, turn right onto Pleasant Street/US-4/VT-12. Parking is available along the street. The ride starts at the corner of US-4 and VT-12.

Route Directions

0.0 From Pleasant Street/US-4, turn RIGHT onto VT-12 north, bearing LEFT at the first intersection. Marsh Billings Rockefeller National Historical Park is to your left; Billings Farm and Museum is to your right.

1.1 Bear RIGHT at Pomfret Road.

3.2 The first climb, the biggest of the day, begins here. Bear RIGHT to stay on Pomfret Road. *General store on your left, along with the Suicide Six ski area.*

6.1 Pass Galaxy Hill and Webster Hill roads, staying STRAIGHT on Pomfret Road. Don't let the names worry you—you're at the top of the climb (1,200 feet), with stunning views, and the 6-mile descent begins now.

7.6 Make a sharp RIGHT to stay on Pomfret Road, with fields on your right.

9.9 The landscape becomes more wooded, as the farm fields and pastures give way to forest.

12.0 Bear sharply to the RIGHT to stay on Pomfret Road as it reaches the banks of the White River. Your descent ends here, and with no rest, you start the next climb as the road turns to parallel the river.

12.8 At the iron bridge and stop sign, take a sharp RIGHT onto Quechee/West Hartford Road.

15.8 Right around the time you pass Safford Road/Joe Ranger Road, your climb becomes a descent again.

16.1 Bear LEFT to stay on Quechee/West Hartford Road through this forested stretch.

18.1 As you start the next small climb, the road becomes Quechee Main Street and you head into the town of Quechee. *Supplies available.* OPTION: Turn RIGHT at Mile 18 onto Quechee Main Street/ River Road and skip to mile 24.5 to shorten this ride.

19.2 Bear LEFT on Old Quechee Road.

20.2 Turn RIGHT, sharply, on Softwood Road.

20.4 Turn RIGHT on Hard Road.

21.3 Turn RIGHT, sharply, on Quechee Main Street.

21.6 turn LEFT, sharply, on Dewey's Mills Road around Dewey's Pond (this turn is more than 90 degrees and easy to miss). The road runs along Quechee Gorge.

22.5 Turn RIGHT onto US-4/Woodstock Road, and cross the Quechee Gorge Bridge. The views from here are spectacular.

23.3 Turn RIGHT onto Waterman Hill Road and LEFT onto Quechee Main Street/Quechee West Hartford Road.

24.5 Bear LEFT onto River Road/Quechee Main Street.

27.5 Bear LEFT onto Taftsville Bridge Road.

27.6 Bear RIGHT onto River Road/Gravel Ledge Road along the Ottauquechee River. *Taftsville Covered Bridge is to your left.*

27.9 Merge with Upper River Road.

30.8 Bear LEFT onto VT-12/Elm Street.

31.2 Turn LEFT onto Pleasant Street.

31.3 END at parking area.

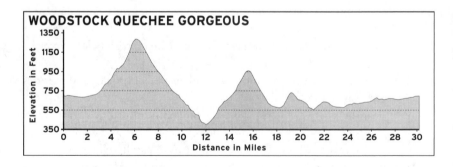

15 OLD NORWICH TURNPIKE LOOP
Norwich

DIRT ROADS, SINGLE-TRACK, PAVED ROADS WITH MODERATE TRAFFIC

Difficulty: 4   **Total Distance:** 20.6 miles

Riding Time: 3 hours   **Elevation Gain:** 2,061 feet

Summary: This mixed-surface ride through beautiful scenery will please everyone – but be warned, it requires a fair amount of fitness.

This ride tackles a variety of conditions and equally disparate scenery. From dirt roads and exposed ledges to tricky descents, you'll traverse terrain most suitable for a strong intermediate rider. Beginners be warned: you may want to look elsewhere.

But just because it's a challenging ride doesn't mean you should fly through it with your head down. You're surrounded by gorgeous scenery, especially if you ride in autumn when the colors seem to set the route on fire. Head from heavily wooded areas to open fields along dirt roads with old country homes, returning along the Norwich Turnpike Road, which is isolated and wooded with few homes to be seen.

Starting in the town of Norwich, ride along Main Street and onto the Norwich Turnpike Road—one continuous climb with broken pavement, a minimal shoulder, and little traffic. The route climbs continuously and relentlessly for the first 6 miles or so, making it a rough way to warm up your legs and lungs. Tackle some rocky, rooty single-track along the Upper Turnpike Road, with great

Mud and mountain bikes seem to go together in Vermont, especially early in the season.

views and challenging riding, before the old, gutted jeep road turns to an even-ground dirt road. Exit the trail at the dirt Rock Ledge Lane, which quickly turns to pavement, a public access point for Upper Turnpike Road.

You've then got a few miles of paved roads, on Mine Road and New Boston Road. Along Mine Road, look for bright orange patches on the ground, all that's left of the copper mines once prevalent in the area. Turn onto the rutted dirt Turnpike Road for the return route. Remember the 6-mile climb? Here's the reward—a downhill coast back to your starting point.

The mixed terrain makes this an ideal ride for a cyclocross bike, but mountain bikes will do fine. Dual suspension is overkill, and conversely, road bikes won't work here.

For more information, contact the Town Clerk, P.O. Box 376, Norwich, VT 05055, 802/649-1419, www.norwich.vt.us.

Options

This ride is a reasonably short drive from Woodstock Quechee Gorgeous and from several New Hampshire rides.

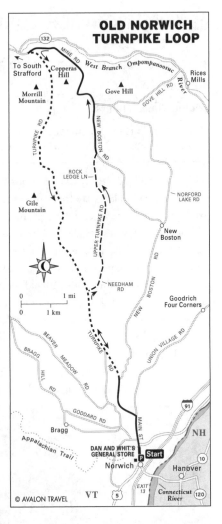

Locals' Tip: Jasper Murdoch's Alehouse in the Norwich Inn (325 Main Street, P.O. Box 908, Norwich, VT 05055, 802/649-1143, www.norwichinn.com) offers pub grub, housebrewed beer, and a relaxed atmosphere, and it's open later than just about any other place in town.

Places to Stay: The Norwich Inn (325 Main Street, P.O. Box 908, Norwich, VT 05055, 802/649-1143, www.norwichinn.com) has been serving guests since 1797. It was a bootlegger's paradise during Prohibition and it reportedly served as the inspiration for the 1980s TV show *Newhart*.

Driving Directions

From points north or south, take I-91 to exit 13 and drive west on VT-5 into Norwich. In Norwich town center, free parking is available near the town green and along the sides of Main Street/VT-5. The ride starts in front of the well-known Dan and Whit's General Store on Main Street, which offers all the food and beverages you might need. A full range of supplies is available in Norwich; the nearest bike shop is just across the Connecticut River in Hanover, New Hampshire.

Route Directions

0.0 From Dan and Whit's General Store, ride north on Main Street (away from I-91).

0.5 LEFT onto Turnpike Road.

3.5 RIGHT onto Needham Road.

4.2 Continue STRAIGHT. The road is a dead end (closed to cars). Continue STRAIGHT (bearing slightly to the left) onto Upper Turnpike Road.

6.7 The dirt road becomes Rock Ledge Lane (paved). Check out the fantastic views.

7.0 LEFT onto New Boston Road from Rock Ledge Lane.

9.0 New Boston Road becomes Mine Road.

10.7 LEFT onto Turnpike Road (dirt road).

13.3 Road turns to double-track jeep road.

13.6 Bear LEFT.

13.7 Bear LEFT at grassy, open space.

13.8 Continue STRAIGHT at four-way intersection marked with a red dot. Gile Mountain is on your right.

14.9 Rough trail becomes dirt road. Pass Gile Mountain parking area.

17.1 Pass Needham Road. Retrace route to Norwich town center.

20.6 Return to starting point.

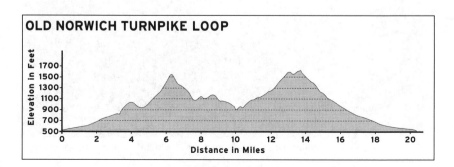

OLD NORWICH TURNPIKE LOOP

16 GREEN MOUNTAIN PEAKS AND HOLLOWS   BEST **C**

Green Mountain National Forest, Bennington

PAVED ROADS WITH SOME UNEVEN PAVEMENT AND MINIMAL TRAFFIC

Difficulty: 3   **Total Distance:** 29.5 miles

Riding Time: 3 hours   **Elevation Gain:** 1,972 feet

Summary: This beautiful, rolling route climbs a bit as it ambles across state lines along the fringe of the Green Mountain National Forest.

The incredibly bucolic Green Mountain National Forest is a great place for mountain bike rides on trails that snake through the dense foliage, but it's just as beautiful seen from outside. The rural roads around it make for great rolling rides and some postcard photo opportunities.

On this route, you'll have to work a bit on the hills. But when you see the landscape open up beneath you onto farmlands, pastures, and rolling meadows, you won't mind at all.

The ride begins in the small, artsy town of Bennington. Come during the fall for Moosefest, when local artists and schoolchildren decorate life-size statues of moose displayed proudly throughout town. You'll find no shortage of options for shopping or eating, and with so much good riding nearby, it's worth making a weekend of.

After a quick tour past some of the town's historic homes and museums and its

© CHRIS BERNARD

Grazing bovines and looming mountains – you'll see lots of both in Vermont, especially from a bicycle.

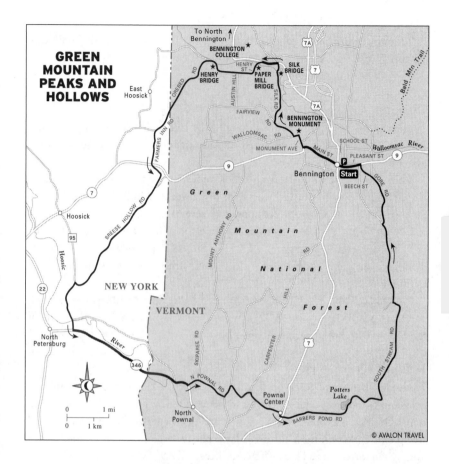

Revolutionary War monument, you'll be in the countryside, crossing two covered bridges and passing a third. That's when the climbing begins, as you hit some uneven pavement and cross into New York.

New York's VT-7 is Vermont's VT-9. Either way, crossing it is difficult, so take it slow and wait for a clear opening. From there, you ride up and over Breese Hollow Road, bringing you within petting distance of cows grazing in front of silos in open fields, with mountains rising in every direction.

Back in Vermont, the 3-mile climb out of North Pownal offers similarly spectacular views. You may feel adrift in a sea of mountains as peaks rise and hollows fold like waves around you.

There's still a bit more climbing, then a ride along a ridge with more spectacular views of farmland with foothills and mountains as far as you can see. This is a great ride to do during fall foliage season, but with the brilliant colors come slow-driving leaf peepers. You'll just have to share the road with them.

For more information, contact the Bennington Area Chamber of Commerce Visitors Center, 100 Veterans Memorial Drive, Bennington, VT 05201, 802/447-3311, www.bennington.com.

Options

To shorten this trip by about half, around Mile 16 turn left onto Skippere Road, and bear left onto Mount Anthony Road. Turn right on VT-9, and right on Main Street toward the parking area.

This ride is close to both Lamb Brook and Wilmington's Watering Hole, as well as several rides in Massachusetts; make it a weekend in Williamstown, Massachusetts, and Bennington, Vermont, with several rides along the way.

Locals' Tip: Get there early to stake your claim in line at the Rattlesnake Cafe (230 North Street, Bennington, VT 05201, 802/447-7018, www.rattlesnakecafe .com), which offers traditional Mexican food with a modern twist—and local beer on tap.

Places to Stay: The Green River Inn Bed & Breakfast (3402 Sandgate Road, Sandgate, VT 05250, 888/648-2212, www.greenriverinn.com) is an old Vermont farmhouse with both charm and amenities.

Driving Directions

From Manchester and points north, take US-7 south to Bennington. From Brattleboro and points east, take VT-9 west to Bennington. VT-9 and US-7 meet at an intersection called Four Corners in the center of downtown Bennington. Several free public parking lots are nearby; a large one is at the corner of Pleasant Street and School Street, one block off Main Street (VT-9), where this route begins. Supplies and a bike shop are available in Bennington.

Route Directions

0.0 From the parking lot, turn LEFT onto School Street and RIGHT onto VT-9 (Main Street).

0.1 STRAIGHT through the Four Corners intersection of VT-9 and US-7.

1.1 RIGHT onto Monument Avenue.

1.5 LEFT at the monument onto Walloomsac Road.

1.6 RIGHT onto Fairview Road.

2.1 RIGHT onto Silk Road.

3.4 Go through the Silk Road Covered Bridge.

3.6 LEFT onto VT-67A.

4.0 LEFT onto Henry Street. Ride through Paper Mill Covered Bridge.

5.5 Turn LEFT just before the Henry Covered Bridge onto Orebed Road. Cross into New York.

7.9 Bear LEFT at unmarked triangular intersection and take an immediate LEFT onto Farmers Inn Road (unmarked).

8.8 Cross VT-7 to Breese Hollow Road, also marked as Rensselaer County VT-100. (Use extreme caution when crossing this busy highway.)

12.7 LEFT at a triangular intersection onto Rensselaer County VT-95.

13.7 RIGHT over a bridge and across railroad tracks.

14.0 LEFT onto VT-346. Cross back into Vermont.

16.0 OPTION: Turn LEFT onto Skippere Road and follow option directions.

16.4 Take care at this diagonal railroad track crossing.

17.2 LEFT at triangular intersection onto North Pownal Road. *Supplies available at general store in North Pownal.*

20.2 Cross US-7 to Barbers Pond Road, just across the road to the right. (Use extreme caution crossing this busy road.)

22.0 Pass Potters Lake. Road becomes South Stream Road.

27.3 RIGHT at fork, staying on South Stream Road.

28.2 LEFT at stop sign onto Gore Road, which becomes Beech Street.

29.0 LEFT at traffic light onto Main Street (VT-9).

29.5 RIGHT onto School Street and RIGHT onto Pleasant Street to return to parking lot.

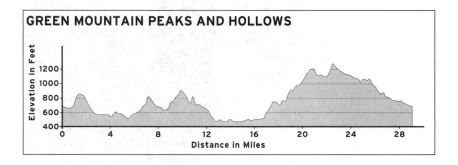

GREEN MOUNTAIN PEAKS AND HOLLOWS

17 LAMB BROOK
Green Mountain National Forest, Heartwellville

UNPAVED ROADS, DOUBLE-TRACK

Difficulty: 3	**Total Distance:** 11 miles
Riding Time: 2 hours	**Elevation Gain:** 900 feet

Summary: This moderately difficult ride climbs rough roads through dense, remote woods.

Heartwellville may not even register on your vehicle's GPS, if you have one, but this ride—which explores one of the more remote sections of the Green Mountain National Forest—is worth the side trip if you're in this part of New England. As you drive to the trailhead, you'll notice a whole lot of nothing in terms of development, and the ride itself is much the same way. Pack a lunch and supplies, because you won't find any nearby.

The Lamb Brook area of the forest has long been the site of a battle between groups on opposing sides of logging. Much of the forest is mature trees, and of great interest to those who would log it, but the area is also considered prime habitat for black bear. Many of the smooth gray beech trees show signs of being climbed by bears seeking to harvest the nuts during the fall. Other bear signs abound: don't be surprised to see such sign—or an actual bear—on this ride.

Running alongside the Deerfield River, this ride includes two climbs made more significant by the trail conditions. You're mostly riding on chewed-up jeep roads. They're tough enough when they're dry, but add in wet weather or a carpet of fallen leaves, and you're fighting for traction. One fast downhill is fun, but it'll have your heart beating in your chest like a caged animal.

Just past the halfway point is the Jewell-Wheeler Hill Cemetery, which is scenic enough, if surprisingly located. On a good fall day, the mist off the streams and the color of the foliage can give the

Despite its peaceful-sounding name, the Lamb Brook ride can challenge out-of-shape riders.

© CHRIS BERNARD

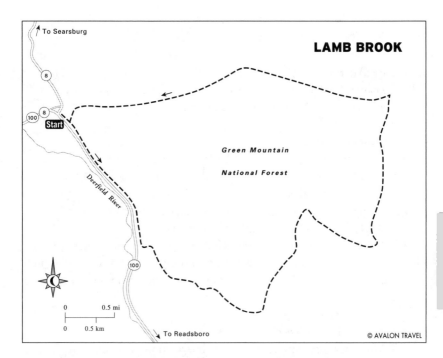

forest an out-of-focus, ghostly feel, which is all the more exciting near the cemetery. From there, the trail crosses Lamb Brook before easing back to Heartwellville to finish.

This route is best ridden on a mountain bike or cyclocross bike, as fitness and comfort with varied terrain are more important than technical bike-handling skills.

For more information, contact the Bennington Area Chamber of Commerce Visitors Center, 100 Veterans Memorial Drive, Bennington, VT 05201, 802/447-3311, www.bennington.com.

Options

This ride can be connected with Wilmington's Watering Hole by turning right at Mile 7.0, picking up that ride at Mile 6.5. It's also a short drive from Green Mountain Peaks and Hollows.

Locals' Tip: The Madison Brewing Company (428 Main Street, Bennington, VT 05201, 802/442-7397) is a typical brew pub, with great housemade beer and decent food.

Places to Stay: The Alexandra Inn bed-and-breakfast (916 Orchard Road, Bennington, VT 05201, 888/207-9386, www.alexandrainn.com) is a farmhouse dating back to the 1850s.

Driving Directions

Outsmart your GPS by following VT-9 East from Bennington to VT-8 South in Searsburg. After 5 miles you'll come to the intersection with VT-100. The best place to park is the lot behind the Door of Hope Church, but please be respectful. The ride starts at the stop sign at the intersection.

Route Directions

0.0 From the stop sign, turn LEFT onto VT-100 north.

1.5 Turn LEFT onto steep uphill dirt road. (There is a signpost, but the sign has been taken, so expect this to be unmarked.)

3.4 At the intersection, turn LEFT, keeping the barn to your left. Trail climbs steadily. Stay straight at next intersection.

4.7 At a fork, turn sharply to the RIGHT onto a jeep road. Follow this along the stone wall to your left, beginning a descent. Pay attention on the descent, which turns fast quickly, and watch for obstacles.

6.5 Turn LEFT at a four-way intersection, then bear RIGHT over Graves Brook.

6.7 Pass the Jewell-Wheeler Hill Cemetery.

7.0 After short descent, bear LEFT at intersection to begin climb. The road gets worse before it gets better, making this uphill a challenge, but a good one. When the route turns downhill again, it gets both smoother and easier. OPTION: Turn RIGHT for option to Wilmington's Watering Hole.

9.7 Turn RIGHT onto gravel and dirt road, and continue downhill.

10.7 Pass a gate.

10.8 Turn RIGHT onto VT-100.

11.0 END at parking area.

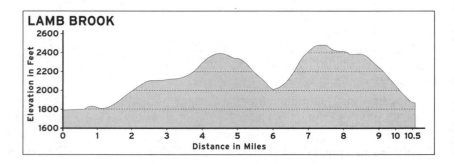

18 WILMINGTON'S WATERING HOLE   BEST (

Green Mountain National Forest, Wilmington

UNPAVED ROADS, BRIEF SINGLE-TRACK

Difficulty: 2	**Total Distance:** 15.2 miles
Riding Time: 2 hours	**Elevation Gain:** 940 feet

Summary: A relatively easy – and relatively flat – ride that is suitable for nearly all cyclists who can handle this distance off-road.

The seven-mile long Harriman Reservoir—also known as Lake Whitingham—is one of a handful of bodies of water in the south-central part of the state. While the reservoir itself is popular with boaters and anglers—the shoreline is a popular place to picnic—the woods around it are home to some fun, winding dirt roads that make for great bicycle rides. When the season is right, the woods become a fiery world of colors as these trails dart through the dense, beautiful foliage.

This route is a good sampler of those trails. You don't have to be an expert mountain biker to make the most of this ride, which follows mostly dirt roads with one brief section of single-track. In fact, this is an excellent route for riders new to the sport or hesitant on more technical terrain. It's also a good ride for a cyclocross bike.

From the start, the ride follows an old railroad bed into the woods. The reservoir was the town of Mountain Mills back in the glory days of the railroad. Now, those days are gone—and so is the town, flooded in 1923 to provide hydroelectric power for the northeast United States. As you ride through the surrounding areas, think of the change that has come to the land and the work that went into it, and

© CHRIS BERNARD

The verdant Vermont countryside is on display throughout the length of this spectacular ride.

keep an eye out for signs of the past, like the old railroad trestles.

The ride is mostly wide and flat, and scenic in a densely forested way. It overlaps with the Lamb Brook ride, a 1.5-mile-long more challenging section that beginners can skip if they choose.

Pack a lunch, and end the day with a picnic on the shoreline. This is a nice place to spend a warm summer or fall afternoon.

For more information, contact the Bennington Area Chamber of Commerce Visitors Center, 100 Veterans Memorial Drive, Bennington, VT 05201, 802/447-3311, www.bennington.com.

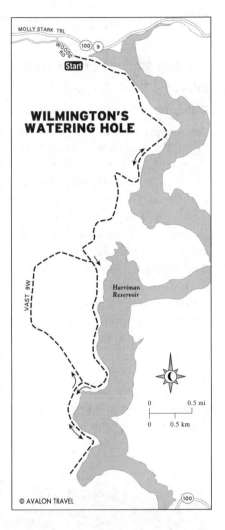

Options

This ride overlaps Lamb Brook. For a slightly shorter ride that skips the only real challenging terrain, continue straight at Mile 8.4 and retrace the trail on which you came in.

Locals' Tip: Fuel up before heading out to the trailhead at the Bean and Leaf Cafe (139 Main Street, Bennington, VT 05201, 802/442-8822, www.beanandleafcafevt.com), where you can order sandwiches and coffee for a picnic lunch along the lake.

Places to Stay: The Green River Inn Bed & Breakfast (3402 Sandgate Road, Sandgate, VT 05250, 888/648-2212, www.greenriverinn.com) is a charming, old farmhouse with plenty of amenities.

Driving Directions

Follow VT-9 east from Bennington into Wilmington, and turn left onto Woods Road. Follow the road over the bridge, and turn left, continuing for about a mile to the picnic area marked Mount Mills West. The ride starts and ends on the same dirt road.

Route Directions

0.0 Continue STRAIGHT on the dirt road to the gate, which marks the start of the railroad bed.

1.2 Pass through the gate (or around it if closed).

3.2 At the intersection in the small clearing, stay STRAIGHT on the trail marked with blue signs (posted by the Catamount Trails Association). *Please respect the trail work done by this group, as this ride is on private land.* Here the trail turns to nontechnical single-track, and then to a muddy groove cut into a rocky ledge.

3.5 Turn RIGHT onto single-track with yellow blazes and wind left and downhill, crossing a small bridge.

3.8 Stay STRAIGHT through intersection on the wide trail along the shoreline. You've got a steep dip and a short, steep climb ahead.

6.0 At the intersection, stay STRAIGHT onto gravel and dirt road.

7.2 The spillway is on your left, offering spectacular reservoir views. TURN AROUND.

8.4 At the intersection, turn LEFT uphill on trail marked VAST (Vermont Association of Snow Travelers) 9W. This is a short, steep, technical climb that overlaps Kingdom Trails. OPTION: Skip this step and continue straight, reversing the directions.

9.8 After a yellow gate, turn RIGHT, then BEAR RIGHT again, crossing Grave's Brook. Jewell-Wheeler Hill Cemetery is on your left.

10.8 At the intersection, turn RIGHT and head downhill, then turn LEFT again to rejoin the trail you came in on.

15.2 END at parking area.

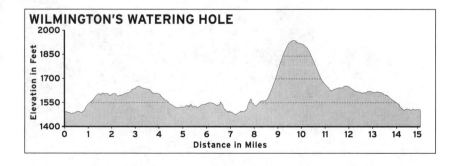

19 GREEN RIVER RIDE
Guilford and Halifax

DIRT ROADS WITH MINIMAL TRAFFIC

Difficulty: 3	**Total Distance:** 13.7 miles
Riding Time: 2 hours	**Elevation Gain:** 1,558 feet

Summary: This dirt-road loop runs through a rural area with constant reminders of the past, including a quaint covered bridge.

Entirely on dirt roads, this loop takes you through a quaint rural corner of southeastern Vermont that seems as if time has passed it by. In fact, the covered bridge where the ride begins warns of a "Two dollars fine to drive on this bridge faster than a walk." Put the modern world behind and pedal into the past along flowing rivers and quiet ponds, through dense stands of maple and birch, past crumbling stone walls marking out homes and farms.

Starting in the tiny village of Green River, you'll parallel the river on a hard-packed, flat dirt road. As you turn onto Deer Park Road, the hill-climbing starts and doesn't quit. You've got to climb your way up the forested Jolly Mountain. This dirt road can be potholed and muddy in spring or in a rainy summer, so choose your weather wisely or plan on getting roostertailed.

Closer to the village of Halifax, you'll see more signs of life, including a large horse farm, a few homes, a traditional white church, an old cemetery, and rows

© CHRIS BERNARD

There's much scenery to see along this beautiful ride through southern Vermont.

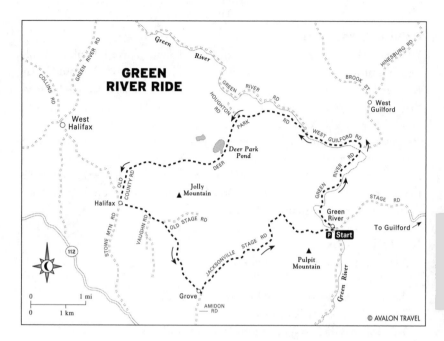

of mailboxes. There's still more climbing ahead before an opening in the woods gives glorious views of a ridge to your right.

From there it's more or less downhill. Scream down the very steep, very fast descent to Green River and back into the modern-day world.

While a mountain bike would work on this ride, it's not necessary. A cyclocross bike is ideal, especially if there's likely to be mud, but a road bike or comfort bike with wide tires would suffice.

For information on the area, contact the Brattleboro Area Chamber of Commerce, 180 Main Street, Brattleboro, VT 05031, 802/254-4565 or 877/254-4565, www.brattleborochamber.org.

Options

This ride is a short drive from Lamb Brook and Wilmington's Watering Hole, and within an hour's drive of several rides in southwestern New Hampshire.

Locals' Tip: Find the locals sampling the wares at the Riverview Cafe (36 Bridge Street, Brattleboro, VT 05301, 802/254-9841, www.riverviewcafe.com) overlooking the scenic Connecticut River.

Places to Stay: Some of the rooms at the Meadowlark Inn (P.O. Box 2048, Brattleboro, VT 05303, 800/616-6359, www.meadowlarkinnvt.com) have double whirlpool tubs, and all come with breakfast, a good way to end—and start—your day.

Driving Directions

From Brattleboro, take I-91 south to exit 1, VT-5 South. Drive 1.3 miles to Guilford and turn right on Guilford Center Road. Go 4.6 miles on Guilford Center Road and turn right on Jacksonville Stage Road. This is a hard-packed dirt road that can be narrow and windy at times, but it is fine for driving and gives you an idea of what's to come on the route; it's a very scenic approach to the starting point. Go 2.5 miles on this road until you come to a triangular intersection with Green River Road. Go left and drive carefully across the one-lane covered bridge. There is room for two cars to park on the left. No supplies are along the route; stock up before you leave the Brattleboro area, where you'll find restaurants, stores, and bike shops.

Route Directions

0.0 Ride through the covered bridge and turn LEFT on Green River Road.

1.9 LEFT on West Guilford Road (unmarked).

3.0 LEFT on Deer Park Road.

4.2 Bear RIGHT, staying on main road at fork.

4.4 Bear LEFT, staying on main road at fork.

7.1 LEFT on Old County Road.

7.8 LEFT on Jacksonville Stage Road.

8.6 Bear RIGHT, staying on main road at fork.

10.2 LEFT on Jacksonville Stage Road.

13.7 Return to bridge.

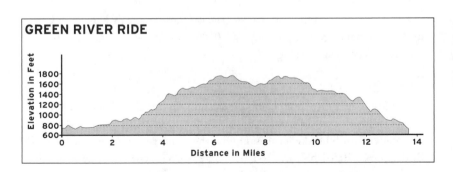

MASSACHUSETTS

© CHRIS BERNARD

BEST BIKE RIDES

During mountain biking's nascent years, the dirt

trails, fire roads, and single-track of Massachusetts's state forests started seeing an influx of fat-tire traffic. These roots-and-rocks trails spawned a lot of recreational cyclists and more than a few pros, including Jesse Anthony and national cyclocross champ Tim Johnson, both of whom grew up in the northeastern part of the state.

As the trails' popularity increased, so did their number, thanks in large part to the New England Mountain Biking Association (NEMBA). The recreational trails advocacy organization is a membership-based group with nearly 20 chapters in New England. Collectively, the group advocates for recreational use, gives grants for trail projects, provides volunteers for trail maintenance and protection, and organizes bicycle patrols. In 2003 NEMBA became the first bike advocacy group in the country to buy, own, and manage property with its purchase of a 47-acre trail network in Milford. Known informally as "Vietnam," these trails draw mountain bikers from all over the region. Mixing a variety of terrains with hardcore natural obstacles and laced with purpose-built stunts and features, they've become the standard by which other trails are judged.

In Massachusetts, Vietnam's no anomaly. You'll find outstanding off-road trails all over the state. Sharpen your skills on the rugged Grizzly Adams and Old Florida Road rides in the mountainous northwest, where you're likely to have miles of single-track and dirt roads to yourself. Tackle the Trail of Tears on Cape Cod, a remarkably wild patch of woods just minutes from both beach and highway. Bomb through the fast corners of the Beaver Pond trail in central Massachusetts or the fire roads and root-strewn single-track of the Harold Parker and Willowdale state forests in the northeast.

If white-knuckle woodland rides aren't your cup of tea, don't worry – the state's roads, rail trails, and bike paths offer a menu of rides to sate the hunger of pedalers of all abilities. Push your legs and lungs to their limits on the ferocious climbs of Wachusett Mountain, a little more than an hour from Boston, or Mount Greylock, which looms over tourist-friendly Williamstown. Tour the scenic coastal stretches between historic Salem and gorgeous Cape Ann, pedaling past famous landmarks and photo opportunities. Try to tear your friends' legs off on the long, fast loops around Quabbin Reservoir, or just spend a relaxing day rolling with the family on the Nashua River or Cape Cod rail trails.

There are many routes not covered here, including the Minuteman Bikeway, an incredibly popular commuter path through Bedford, Lexington, Arlington, and Cambridge, or the new Bruce Freeman Rail Trail in Chelmsford, a promising route still under construction at the time of publication. With so many to choose from, deciding which routes to include proved challenging, and you may find it equally daunting deciding which to ride.

Lest you think Massachusetts an unmitigated cyclists' paradise, a simple caveat: Traffic can be unreasonable, especially in the eastern part of the state, and especially during summer in the many touristy areas.

The good news is that with so many routes available, you can time them so you're on a vehicle-free rail trail or deep in the woods when everyone else is angrily bumper-to-bumper on the roads. You'll be pedaling contentedly into a Berkshire Mountains sunset when the roads are empty.

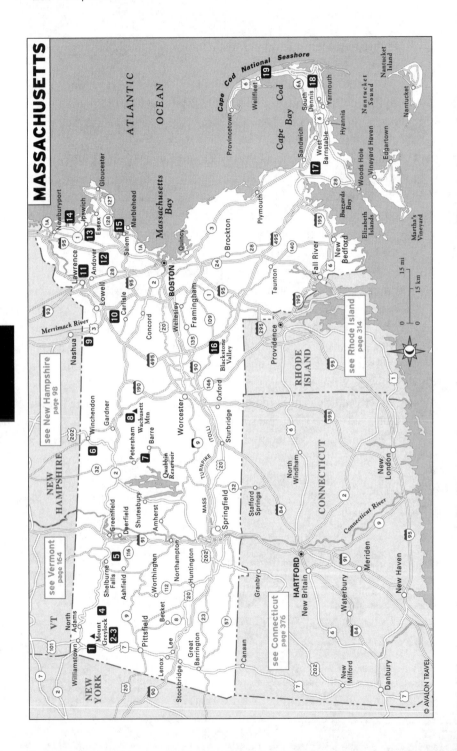

RIDE NAME	DIFFICULTY	DISTANCE	TIME	ELEVATION	PAGE
1 Wandering Williamstown	3	29.1 mi	2.5 hr	1,495 ft	238
2 Grizzly Adams	4	8.5 mi	1.5 hr	1,200 ft	242
3 Ashuwillticook Rail Trail	2	22 mi	3 hr	62 ft	246
4 Old Florida Road	5	7 mi	2 hr	763 ft	249
5 Bardwells Ferry Loop	4	27.5 mi	3 hr	2,440 ft	253
6 Beaver Pond Loop	2	8.7 mi	1.5–2 hr	156 ft	257
7 Reservoir Dogs	4	45.7 mi	3.5 hr	3,260 ft	261
8 Wachusett Mountain	5	20.1 mi	2.5 hr	1,260 ft	265
9 Nashua River Rail Trail	2	22.2 mi	2 hr	108 ft	269
10 Great Brook Farm Tour	2	9 mi	1.5–2 hr	226 ft	272
11 Farms and Forests	2	27.3 mi	2 hr	364 ft	276
12 Harold Parker State Forest	2	7.5 mi	2 hr	300 ft	280
13 Weeping Willowdale	2	6.4 mi	1 hr	102 ft	284
14 Plum Island	2	20.6 mi	2 hr	10 ft	288
15 Witches to Water's Edge	3	54.3 mi	4 hr	775 ft	291
16 Vietnam Sampler	3	6.8 mi	1.5 hr	250 ft	296
17 Trail of Tears	4	12 mi	2.5 hr	302 ft	299
18 Cape Cod Rail Trail	2	44 mi	5 hr	398 ft	304
19 Province Lands Loop	3	8.9 mi	1–2 hr	260 ft	308

1 WANDERING WILLIAMSTOWN
Williamstown

PAVED ROADS WITH MODERATE TRAFFIC

Difficulty: 3   **Total Distance:** 29.1 miles

Riding Time: 2.5 hours   **Elevation Gain:** 1,495 feet

Summary: This hilly ride runs through an artsy college town; it's high on scenery, but also on traffic.

Williamstown is, in many ways, the quintessential college town. The ride starts there, and you're likely to see local cyclists along this popular route. More than most in this book, this ride relies on roads well-traveled by vehicles. While the pavement is generally good and the shoulders wide, if you're not comfortable sharing the road with traffic, skip this one.

That said, the traffic is not bad—Williamstown is not exactly downtown Boston in terms of urban density or population—and the rewards are worth the annoyances on this hilly loop through one of many scenic corners of the Berkshires. Among the payoffs are the stunning views of Massachusetts's highest peak, Mount Greylock.

Leaving Williamstown on MA-43, you'll crisscross the Green River as neighborhoods turn from residential to pastoral. Where MA-43 and US-7 meet, you'll

© CHRIS BERNARD

Mapped out in the shadow of Mount Greylock, this ride explores the popular downtown area of Williamstown and surrounding towns.

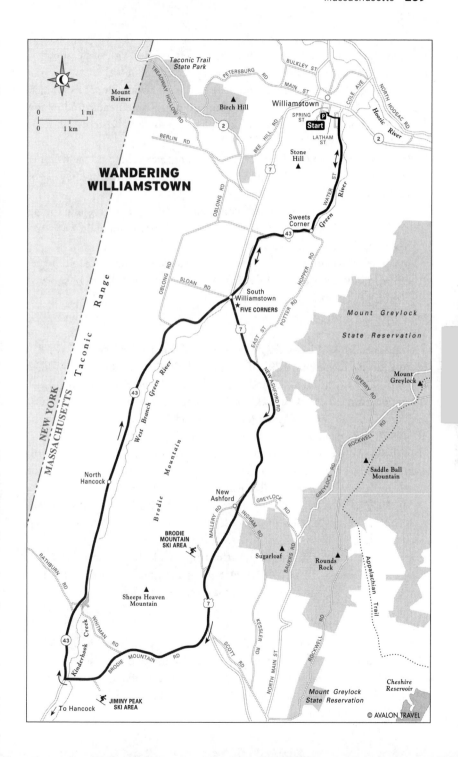

find the historic Store at Five Corners, which dates to 1762, with a café, supplies, restrooms, ice cream, homemade fudge, picnic tables, and more.

You'll then climb US-7, a fast and busy road with a wide, smooth shoulder, making a gradual ascent between two mountain ranges, one smooth and rolling (to the west) and one punctuated with sharp peaks and the 3,491-foot-high summit of Greylock (to the east).

Leave the traffic behind. In its place, face a long, steep climb up the winding Brodie Mountain Road, followed by a long, screaming downhill to the base of ski resort Jiminy Peak.

The return ride on MA-43 starts with a climb, then turns to a gentle rolling up-and-down ride through farmlands and fields with great mountain views and a gentle coast back to where you began.

For more information, contact the Williamstown Chamber of Commerce, P.O. Box 357, Williamstown, MA 01267, 413/458-9077 or 800/214-3799, www .williamstownchamber.com.

Options

Feel like a challenge? A big one? Add the summit of Mount Greylock, with a 2,785-foot ascent and an additional 20 miles or so, to this ride by turning left at Mile 12 onto US-7/New Ashford Road, and bearing left onto Scott Road. At Mile 2.3 of the option, turn left onto Greylock Road, and begin climbing. At Mile 2.75, turn left onto Rockwell Road and enter Mount Greylock State Reservation. Turn right at Mile 10.5 onto the road to the summit, which you'll reach in 0.8 mile. Soak in the views, put on some armwarmers for the descent, and turn around. To return, turn right onto Notch Road for a fast, winding descent. Turn left and then right to stay on Notch Road, eventually turning left to return to MA-2.

Locals' Tip: The Indian food at Spice Root (23 Spring Street, Williamstown, MA 01267, 413/458-5200) is a pleasant surprise and a good, flavorful way to cap a day of riding.

Places to Stay: The (relatively) affordable Maple Terrace Inn (555 Main Street, Williamstown, MA 01267, 413/458-9677, http://mapleterrace.com) is right downtown, near the art museums, and the owners are friendly.

Driving Directions

From points south, take US-7 to Williamstown. From points east, take MA-2 to Williamstown. From MA-2 (Main Street), turn south onto the one-way Spring Street, a busy shopping street. Drive 0.2 mile to the end of Spring Street, where you'll find several public parking lots. Williamstown has plenty of supplies, lodging options, and bike shops.

Route Directions

0.0 From the Spring Street parking lot, turn RIGHT onto Spring Street and bear LEFT onto Latham Street.

0.3 Turn RIGHT onto Water Street (MA-43).

5.0 Turn LEFT onto US-7. *Supplies available at the Store at Five Corners.*

12.0 Turn RIGHT onto Brodie Mountain Road. OPTION: Turn left onto US-7/New Ashford Road and follow option directions.

14.8 *Supplies available at Jiminy Peak ski resort.*

15.4 Turn RIGHT onto MA-43.

24.0 Go STRAIGHT across US-7, staying on MA-43, which becomes Water Street.

28.8 Turn LEFT onto Latham Road.

29.1 Turn RIGHT onto Spring Street and immediate LEFT to return to parking lot.

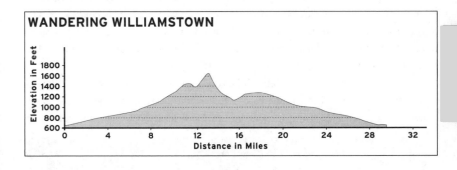

WANDERING WILLIAMSTOWN

2 GRIZZLY ADAMS

Mount Greylock State Reservation, New Ashford

SINGLE-TRACK, DOUBLE-TRACK, DIRT ROADS

Difficulty: 4	**Total Distance:** 8.5 miles
Riding Time: 1.5 hours	**Elevation Gain:** 1,200 feet

Summary: This challenging, climbing mountain route offers rough, remote conditions – definitely not for beginners.

If you're a mountain biker visiting the Mount Greylock area, you're going to want to sample the trails that snake around the mountainside. This ride is a good example of what's there. Almost all double-track, it's not particularly technical, but there's a good, fast descent followed by an equally good climb that will leave most riders fighting for breath—and traction.

The first part of the trail is smooth. It covers wide, grassy trails and loose dirt on what could be considered a road, if it were anywhere a vehicle could access it. But just a mile or so into it, the ride begins dropping obstacles in your path— ruts, tree stumps, rocks, downed branches—that will make any mountain biker worth his or her salt happy.

Then it becomes more difficult. The trail narrows and steepens—first downhill, then up—and obstacles increase in frequency. Decomposing grass and leaves can be slick and hide stumps, roots, and rocks. Pricker bushes seem to reach out

Riders who put in the effort are in for a treat on the Old Adams Road mountain bike trail, beginning high atop Mount Greylock.

© CHRIS BERNARD

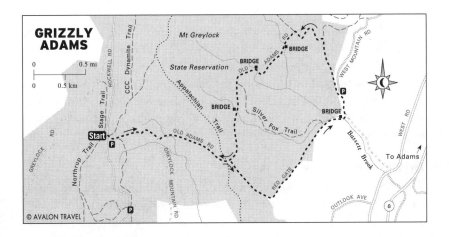

for your legs and wheels. Noises in the woods around you seem louder, closer, and spookier than they should. Bring a spare tube and air pump; you don't want to be stuck here.

A series of climbs begin around the time you hear a noisy mountain stream, which will distract you from the sound of your own panting and gasping. The real challenge is maintaining your momentum—small stones, branches, and roots will fight your traction, and once you're stopped, starting again is very difficult. Near the end of the trail, you'll pass through an area rife with wild raspberry bushes that, in season, are worth stopping for. (After the climb, you'll be grateful for any excuse to stop.)

Note that the road to the parking area is open from late May through November 1, weather permitting. For more information, contact Mount Greylock State Reservation Visitors Center, 30 Rockwell Road, P.O. Box 138, Lanesborough, MA 01237, 413/499-4262, www.mass.gov/dcr/parks/mtGreylock/.

Options

To expand this ride with some serious climbing, park at the base of Goodell Road where it meets US-7, just north of New Ashford, and ride up Goodell Road/Greylock Road to Rockwell Road, taking a right on paved Rockwell Road and riding less than 1 mile to the parking area where this route begins. Goodell Road is a loose dirt road that snakes precipitously up the side of Mount Greylock. Though it's less than 4 miles long, it climbs 1,227 feet over that distance. Riding to and from the route below would add nearly 10 miles of riding—and a lot of climbing. Be careful on the descent.

This ride is near Wandering Williamstown, Ashuwillticook Rail Trail, and Old Florida Road.

Locals' Tip: Grab a bite and a beverage and enjoy a view of Pontoosuc Lake at Matt Reilly's Restaurant (750 South Main Street, Lanesborough, MA 01237, 413/447-9780) just south of Mount Greylock.

Places to Stay: The Lanesborough Country Inn (499 South Main Street, Lanesborough, MA 01237, 413/442-1009, www.lanesboroughcountryinn.com) is a reasonably priced accommodation, with 10 custom-built log cabins in addition to rooms.

Driving Directions

From US-7 North, turn right on North Main Street in Lanesborough, and almost a mile later, right again on Quarry Road, watching for signs for the visitors center. Turn left onto Rockwell Road. The visitors center is half a mile up on your right and has facilities and maps. The parking area for the trail, known as the "Jones Nose" lot, is another 4 miles up Rockwell Road on your right.

Route Directions

0.0 From the far end of the parking area, beside the signs, follow the Old Adams Road Mountain Bicycle Trail, grassy double-track winding around a gate.

0.4 Turn LEFT, and then LEFT again, following signs for Old Adams Road. The trail turns to dirt.

1.5 Stay STRAIGHT at the intersection with the Appalachian Trail. Watch for hikers.

1.6 At the intersection, turn RIGHT onto double-track. This snowmobile trail is called Red Gate Trail.

2.2 Stay STRAIGHT over rough bridge. Crossing the bridge can be sketchy, so be careful.

2.4 At bottom of short descent, stay STRAIGHT past logging road.

2.5 Turn RIGHT onto logging road.

2.6 Enter a clearing, and begin descent. Stay straight past next few trail entrances.

3.2 Turn LEFT (downhill).

3.3 Turn LEFT over a bridge, then RIGHT over second bridge.

3.5 Turn LEFT, sharply, onto West Mountain Road double-track.

4.0 A rocky uphill leads to a large, dirty parking area. Cross the lot into the field and follow the signs to the LEFT for Cheshire Harbor Bicycle Trail.

4.1 Behind a gate, the real climb begins.

4.8 Switchbacks signal that you're nearing the top of the climb.

5.1 Turn LEFT onto Old Adams Road, and cross a bridge.

6.1 Begin another uphill section, this one laced with rocks and other obstacles.

7.8 Turn RIGHT (uphill).

8.5 END at parking area.

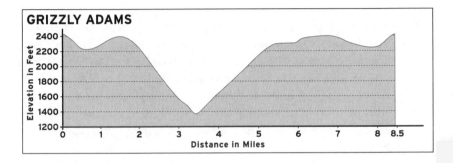

3 ASHUWILLTICOOK RAIL TRAIL   BEST (

Lanesborough, Cheshire, and Adams

WIDE, PAVED RAIL TRAIL

Difficulty: 2   **Total Distance:** 22 miles

Riding Time: 3 hours   **Elevation Gain:** 62 feet

Summary: A wide, flat rail trail through the heart of the Berkshires, this ride is suitable for cyclists of all skill levels.

The 10-foot-wide Ashuwillticook Rail Trail is paved its entire length, paralleling MA-8 and offering cyclists and pedestrians a safe and scenic way to commute, recreate, or just to commune with nature. This is everything a rail trail should be.

The rail corridor began in 1845 when the Pittsfield and North Adams Railroad wanted to connect Rutland, Vermont, with the Housatonic Railroad in the south. Over the years, ownership of the track changed as the rail lines were acquired or merged, until the Boston & Maine bought it in 1981. Rail services were abandoned in 1990.

Since then, the trail has seen a lot of use, and on any given day, you're likely to meet cyclists, runners, walkers, and in-line skaters. In the winter, add snowshoers and cross-country skiers. Ride down the trail on a sunny day in early September,

© CHRIS BERNARD

Paved, smooth, and wide throughout its entire length, the Ashuwillticook Rail Trail is an excellent place for riders of all ages and abilities.

and it's easy to understand its popularity. The paved surface is smooth and flat, the views are spectacular, and the foliage—even this early in the season—adds eye-catching color.

Whether you're on the trail's more rural first third, along the water's edge that hems the Cheshire Reservoir, or the on the final here-and-there sections crossing through downtown, the Ashuwillticook is a perfectly pleasant ride—in fact, the name means "the pleasant river in between the hills."

For more information, contact the Massachusetts Department of Conservation and Recreation in Adams, Massachusetts, 413/442-8928, www.mass .gov/dcr/parks/western/asrt.htm.

Options

This trail is rideable by just about anyone, including beginners and small children. Mileage is marked on the pavement, so can decide exactly how far you want to go before you turn around. Alternatively, leave a car at the far end, in Cheshire (halfway), or just beyond there at Farnam's Causeway on Cheshire Reservoir. Parking is free and available at either end.

This ride is near Wandering Williamstown, Grizzly Adams, and Old Florida Road.

Locals' Tip: The Miss Adams Diner (53 Park Street, Adams, MA 01220, 413/743-5300) is a retro-looking diner that will meet all the expectations of diner lovers and satiate appetites earned after a long, lazy ride on the rail trail.

Places to Stay: The Topia Inn (10 Pleasant Street, Adams, MA 01220, 413/743-9605, http://topiainn.com) is a environmentally friendly inn powered entirely by solar panels and biodiesel. It's a high-end experience for self-indulgence.

Driving Directions

From points north, east, or west, take MA-2 in downtown North Adams to MA-8 south for 5.5 miles to Adams center. (Look for brown Ashuwillticook signs.) Turn left onto Hoosac Street, then immediately right onto Depot Street. Parking is on the left at Discover the Berkshires Visitors Center (3 Hoosac Street, www .berkshires.org, daily 8:30 A.M.–5 P.M.). Access to the rail trail is behind the Visitors Center.

From points south, take I-90 (the Mass Pike) to exit 2 in Lee and follow US-20 west to US-7 North for 11 miles to downtown Pittsfield. At Park Square rotary, follow East Street for 3.25 miles (East Street becomes Merrill Road after 1.5 miles) to the intersection of MA-9 and MA-8. Continue straight through the intersection on MA-8 north for 1.5 miles to the Lanesborough-Pittsfield line. Turn left at lights for the Berkshire Mall Road entrance and rail trail parking.

Route Directions

0.0 From Adams, head south on the rail trail.

2.1 This is one of the quieter sections of the trail.

5.5 Cheshire Reservoir is on your right. (It can be windy here.)

6.9 Cross Farnam's Causeway, which offers trail access and parking. *Restrooms available off the trail to the right. Park benches offer a nice lunch spot with beautiful views of the reservoir.*

11.0 End of rail trail at Berkshire Mall in Lanesborough. *Restrooms available.* TURN AROUND.

15.0 Cross Farnam's Causeway.

22.0 END at parking area.

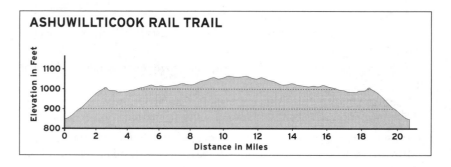

❹ OLD FLORIDA ROAD
Savoy Mountain State Forest

SINGLE-TRACK, DOUBLE-TRACK, DIRT ROADS

Difficulty: 5   **Total Distance:** 7 miles

Riding Time: 2 hours   **Elevation Gain:** 763 feet

Summary: This rugged, backwoods trail will test your endurance, fitness level, and tolerance.

Buggy. Wet. Remote. Poorly marked. Rocky. Muddy. Buggy. Each of those words describes this ride, and that's right, "buggy" gets listed twice. But for those of you who like bushwhacking rides that challenge your sense of adventure as well as your legs and lungs, this is one.

A world apart from some of the state forest rides in the eastern part of the state, this route through Savoy Mountain State Forest—carved out of the Hoosac Range, an extension of the Green Mountains—will have you panting before you even start pedaling. The vertiginous drive along MA-2 to reach the entrance road gives you an idea of the remoteness of the area.

Some of the forest was originally cleared and used as farmland, and there are

© ADAM CLOUGH

Deep in the woods and away from civilization, Old Florida Road can be muddy – and the bugs can be fierce.

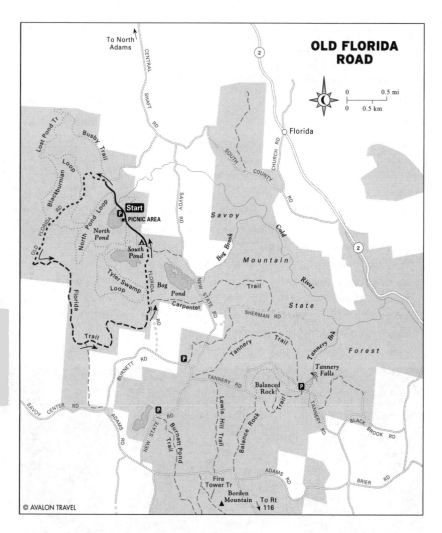

a few concrete dams, as well as some stands of apple trees and secondary forests of Norway and blue spruce mixed in with older hardwoods. You'll find a picnic area, a campground, cabins, two ponds for swimming and fishing, full facilities, and lots of trails to explore.

This route takes you along Old Florida Road counterclockwise from North Pond. From the main entrance road, you pass through Tower Swamp—hence the bugs—before climbing a very rocky trail. After a tough series of downs and ups, the trail heads east. Though most of the trail is technical and rocky, a few late stretches in a pine forest are fun and fast. If you have a GPS unit or a compass, bring it. This is a remote trail that's not well-marked, and it's easy to get lost.

In spring, in early summer, and during exceptionally rainy periods, you're likely to encounter mudpits too deep to ride through. While you're carrying your bike through them, knee deep in the muck, the bugs will feast on you. These trails are designed for all-terrain vehicles, and it shows. You'll also pass several hiking trails. Please don't ride them—they're off-limits to bikes and doing so ruins it for everyone else.

The park is open from 8 A.M. until dusk year-round. For more information, contact Savoy Mountain State Forest, Central Shaft Road, Savoy, MA 413/663-8469, www.state.ma.us/dem/parks/svym.htm.

Options

For a slightly less strenuous ride, follow Florida Road south to a large dirt parking lot, where you pick up the unpaved, rough Tannery Road past Balanced Rock and Tannery Falls, a dramatic plunging waterfall. It's not a bad ride to reach the rock, but it's hilly to Tannery Falls, and you have to leave your bike and hike in a short distance to see them.

Locals' Tip: There's not much food to be had around the park, so packing a lunch is a good bet.

Places to Stay: The campground is open mid-May to mid-October. For reservations, visit www.reserveamerica.com and search for Savoy Mountain State Forest. Some cabins are available.

Driving Directions

From North Adams and points west, take MA-2 east to the small town of Florida. Turn left onto Church Road and follow it to S. County Road. Turn right onto S. County Road and drive to Central Shaft Road, turning left. Drive 3.7 miles to the park's North Pond parking area, just past the boat launch. The parking fee is $5. North Pond has fishing, swimming, and full facilities with water and restrooms. Supplies and a bike shop are available in North Adams.

Route Directions

0.0 From North Pond parking lot, go LEFT on Central Shaft Road (toward park exit).

0.5 Turn LEFT onto Old Florida Road.

0.6 Turn RIGHT at fork.

0.8 Cross a stream on rock slabs.

2.9 Bear LEFT, following snowmobile signs, into a rocky clearing. Trail continues to the right of the clearing, then takes an immediate LEFT.

4.1 Turn LEFT, following the main trail.

5.6 Cross a clearing to a row of boulders, and turn LEFT onto unmarked dirt road. OPTION: To check out Balanced Rock and Tannery Falls, turn RIGHT instead of left onto the unmarked Florida Road. Head south for about 1 mile to a large dirt parking lot and pick up the unpaved, rough Tannery Road that leads to these natural features.

7.0 END at North Pond parking area.

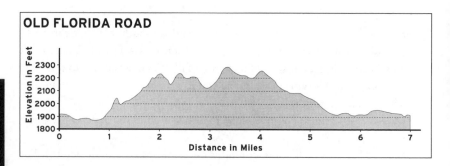

OLD FLORIDA ROAD

5 BARDWELLS FERRY LOOP
Shelburne Falls

PAVED ROADS WITH MINIMAL TO MODERATE TRAFFIC, DIRT ROAD

Difficulty: 4	**Total Distance:** 27.5 miles
Riding Time: 3 hours	**Elevation Gain:** 2,440 feet

Summary: A relatively short – and relatively hilly – climbers' route, this loop highlights the rural backcountry of the river valley.

Shelburne Falls is a fun little place with a thriving downtown, which will catch you off-guard if you've visited some of the other little towns and villages in the region. Artistic and friendly, it's home to galleries, shops, studios, museums, and a handful of restaurants and cafés. And it's actually two towns, blending with the town of Buckland on the other side of the Deerfield River.

Two bridges span the river—the Iron Bridge and the pedestrian-only Bridge of Flowers, said to be the only one of its kind. A former trolley bridge, the concrete span is now completely overcome by gardens and flowers that bloom continuously thanks to volunteer efforts. Before or after your ride, stroll across this landmark, the connecting centerpiece of the towns.

This route gets you into the hills of the Berkshires on some beautiful backcountry roads with few cars or houses. There's a long climb out of Shelburne Falls and

From Shelburne Falls, or neighboring Buckland, the pedestrian-only Bridge of Flowers is worth a stop.

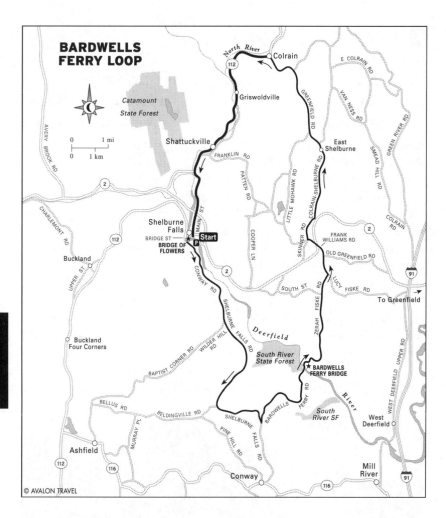

a steep downhill with a sharp backhand turn at the bottom to Bardwells Ferry Road. A few steep hills and some uneven pavement take you from woodlands into more open farmlands, and as you crest the last hill you get outstanding rural views of the river valley. Zip down toward the river and cross high above the water under the red spans of the 1882 Bardwells Ferry Bridge, a Massachusetts Historic Civil Engineering Landmark.

You'll pass farm stands and farmlands, woods and fields, and spend a good amount of time climbing. Savor the view, and savor the downhill that brings you into the village of Colrain.

The route follows the North River all the way back, with a mountain looming on your left and heavy industry (hydropower plants and factories) along the river on your right. You'll cross the river twice before going underneath MA-2 and riding back into Shelburne Falls.

The village information center has maps and restrooms. Make sure you walk across the Bridge of Flowers and look at the glacial potholes (access from Deerfield Avenue), carved out by the river. For more information, contact the Shelburne Falls Area Business Association and Village Information Center, 75 Bridge Street, Shelburne Falls, MA 01370, 413/625-2544, www.shelburnefalls.com.

Options

To extend this ride, from the finish head right on MA-112, following it counterclockwise as it winds its way south to Ashfield. Turn left on MA-116 in Ashfield, left on Baptist Corner Road, and left on Conway Road back to the starting point. This loop adds 18 miles and another 900 feet of climbing to the ride.

Locals' Tip: Christopher's Grinders (55 State Street, Shelburne Falls, MA 01370, 413/625-2345, www.christophersgrinders.com), just north of town on MA-112, is a great place (with a great name) to grab a sandwich or a slice of pizza.

Places to Stay: The Dancing Bear Guest House (22 Mechanic Street, Shelburne Falls, MA 01370, 413/625-9281, www.dancingbearguesthouse.com) is a small, charming bed-and-breakfast in a historic home right downtown.

Driving Directions

From points north and south, take MA-91 to Greenfield and take MA-2 west (exit 26). Drive 9 miles and take MA-2A (at the Sweetheart Restaurant) to Shelburne Falls. MA-2A becomes Bridge Street. Drive 0.3 mile and turn right onto Main Street. There's a public parking lot on the left, where this route begins. Supplies are available in Shelburne Falls. The closest bike shops are in Greenfield.

Route Directions

0.0 From the public parking lot, turn RIGHT onto Main Street.

0.1 Turn RIGHT onto Bridge Street; go across the Iron Bridge.

0.3 Turn LEFT along the river onto Conway Road (this becomes Shelburne Falls Road).

7.5 Make a sharp LEFT onto Bardwells Ferry Road.

10.4 Cross Bardwells Ferry Bridge.

11.8 Turn RIGHT at fork onto Zerah Fiske Road.

13.1 Go STRAIGHT through intersection, continuing on Zerah Fiske Road.

14.1 Continue STRAIGHT at a four-way intersection onto a dirt road.

14.5 Cross MA-2 (use extreme care) to Frank Williams Road.

14.7 Turn RIGHT onto Skinner Road (unmarked).

15.5 Turn LEFT onto Colrain-Shelburne Road.

20.8 Turn LEFT onto MA-112. *Supplies available at general store in Colrain.*

21.8 *Supplies available at general store in Griswoldville.*

26.8 Go under MA-2. Continue on MA-112, which becomes Main Street. OPTION: Head RIGHT on MA-112 and follow option directions.

27.5 Turn RIGHT into public parking lot just before Bridge Street.

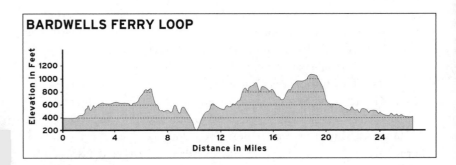

BARDWELLS FERRY LOOP

6 BEAVER POND LOOP
Otter River State Forest, Baldwinville

DIRT ROADS, DOUBLE-TRACK

Difficulty: 2   **Total Distance:** 8.7 miles

Riding Time: 1.5-2 hours   **Elevation Gain:** 156 feet

Summary: A network of fast trails in a surprisingly wild forest, this ride is suitable for most cyclists.

The Otter River State Forest seems like a more wild, remote place than it actually is. For a time, much of the forest was turned to farmland, but the Civilian Conservation Corps reseeded it—be thankful for their work as you meander through the shady woods. And riding the more than 100 miles of dirt roads and trails there, you'll find yourself forgetting you're just minutes from urban civilization. These trails offer riders of all abilities something to savor, and you can pick and choose the difficulty and length of any given ride.

This particular route is suitable for most riders, and begins on the wide, smooth, unpaved New Boston Road. (You can also camp here and begin your ride from the campground.) The first few turns lead deeper into the woods on bumpy roads, then double-track, and eventually nontechnical single-track.

The swampy areas and ponds make mosquitoes a real problem, so don't forget the bug repellent. The trails are not all marked, many small tempting single-track

© CHRIS BERNARD

The Beaver Pond trails are miles of phenomenal single-track in need of mountain bikers seeking a thrill.

BEAVER POND LOOP

trails shoot off the main ones, and it's quite possible to get lost even with a trail map, available from the ranger station.

For the most part, this ride is suitable for a cyclocross bike. A mountain bike would be even better, but dual suspension is overkill.

The park hours are 10 A.M.–8 P.M. For more information, contact Otter River State Forest, New Winchendon Road, Baldwinville, MA 01436, 978/939-8962, www.state.ma.us/dem/parks/ottr.htm.

Options

To extend the ride, or to make it more challenging, around Mile 1.2 follow signs for the Wetmore Trail Loop. Or grab a trail map and explore on your own—there are plenty of options to choose from.

This ride is a reasonable driving distance from Reservoir Dogs and Wachusett Mountain.

Locals' Tip: Since the 1930s, locals have lined up at Lee's Hot Dog Stand (31 Central Street, Baldwinville, MA 01436, 978/939-5346) for foot-long dogs with all sorts of toppings, plus sides from clams to ice cream.

Places to Stay: The campground on site (New Winchendon Road, Baldwinville, MA 01436, 978/939-8962, www.state.ma.us/dem/parks/ottr.htm) offers 85 sites, flush toilets, showers, and out-your-tent-flap access to the trails.

Driving Directions

From points east or west, take MA-2 to exit 20 (Baldwinville Road). Drive 2.5 miles to a flashing red light. Turn right on Maple Street and pass through Baldwinville. Maple Street becomes MA-202. After 1.2 miles you'll see the main entrance to Otter River State Forest; pass this entrance and take the second entrance 1 mile farther down the road. Take the winding access road to Lake Dennison and park in the large parking lot on the right. The $5 day-use fee gets you access to a swimming beach at the lake, a campground, many picnic areas, and restrooms with flush toilets and water. Supplies are available in Baldwinville and the nearest bike shop is in Gardner.

Route Directions

0.0 START from the parking lot along the paved road with the lake on your right.

0.3 Turn LEFT onto wide dirt road.

0.9 Turn RIGHT onto New Boston Road at the intersection.

1.2 Turn LEFT onto Burgess Road. OPTION: Follow signs for the Wetmore Trail Loop.

1.8 Cross the town line into Baldwinville. The road becomes a paved road.

1.9 Turn LEFT onto trail. Follow orange blazes onto Swamp Road (unmarked).

2.2 Continue STRAIGHT on main trail at fork in path.

2.8 Turn RIGHT at intersection following blue trail markers.

3.3 Pass Beaver Pond on right.

3.8 Turn LEFT at the junction.

4.3 The trail comes to an L-shaped junction. Turn LEFT through the yellow gate into a field.

4.4 Follow trail along a chain-link fence; the dam is on the right.

4.7 Turn RIGHT at intersection on River Road (unmarked) through an orange gate. There is a yellow gate to the left.

6.8 Continue STRAIGHT at four-way intersection.

7.2 Turn RIGHT at junction with Goodnow Road (unmarked).

7.8 Turn RIGHT at intersection on New Boston Road.

8.4 Turn RIGHT onto paved road.

8.7 Return to parking lot.

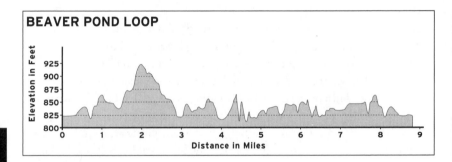

7 RESERVOIR DOGS   BEST **◖**
Barre, Hardwick, and Petersham

PAVED, MOSTLY RURAL ROADS WITH SOME UNEVEN PAVEMENT AND MINIMAL TRAFFIC

Difficulty: 4   **Total Distance:** 45.7 miles

Riding Time: 3.5 hours   **Elevation Gain:** 3,260 feet

Summary: A hilly rural ride popular with road racers, this scenic route will also appeal to any cyclist who can handle the distance and climbs.

In the 1930s, the state flooded four towns in the Swift River valley to create one of the largest manufactured public water supplies in the country. Homes, businesses, and farms were moved, sold, or destroyed. Land was cleared and burned. The central Massachusetts landscape changed forever.

These days, the 18-mile-long Quabbin Reservoir is popular with anglers, but the area surrounding it draws cyclists. The land is hilly and beautiful and the roads untrafficked and rural—especially in the Ware River Reservation watershed area, protected and managed by the state's Metropolitan District Commission.

If you ride slowly, you'll notice the scenery and the wildlife. If you stop often, you can explore the small villages along the route and meet some of the people who give the area its personality. The area seems untouched by time and commercialism,

The ride around Quabbin Reservoir is a hilly treat for racers and confident riders who might feel a little less confident at the end of a long and tiring day.

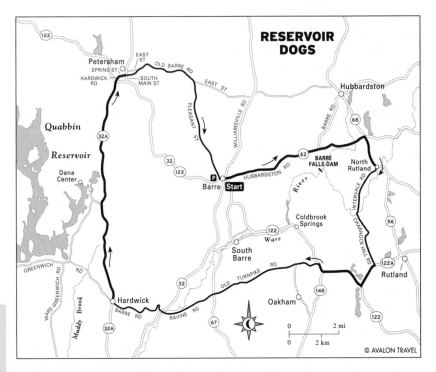

with town commons and general stores that provide just about anything either a cyclist or a community could need.

If you don't ride slowly, you're not alone. The area is training ground for a lot of New England road racers, and home to a race each year. You're likely to see packs of flat-backed, Lycra-clad warriors prowling this route.

The ride begins in Barre, where an expansive town common offers a gazebo and benches surrounded by diners, ice-cream shops, a bike store, and a visitors center. A steep descent takes you out of town into a rural, wooded area, past the entrance to Barre Falls Dam, an Army Corps of Engineers site. (If you're in no rush, ride the mile out and back for great vistas, a look at the impressive dam, and a recreation area with picnic tables and facilities.)

After a short stretch on the fast-moving MA-68, the ride heads onto smooth backcountry roads at the edge of the Ware River Reservation, lined with stone walls and historic markers and old cemeteries. The roads are also hilly—especially on Old Turnpike Road as you pass from woodlands into open pasturelands. The steepest climb comes on the way to Hardwick, but the scenery makes it worthwhile. Closer to town, the views change from farms and pastures to historic white houses with picket fences, impressive gardens, and well-kept stone walls. Hardwick's town common is a great meeting or stopping point, and the general store has restrooms, a deli counter, and a porch where cyclists tend to gather.

The next stretch, on MA-32A, follows the eastern edge of the Quabbin, with occasional views of the 181-mile shoreline, before visiting the town of Petersham. There's one more hilly stretch before finishing the final descent back into Barre.

For more information, contact the Central Quabbin Area Tourism Association, P.O. Box 95, Barre, MA 01005, www.centralquabbin.org.

Options

To extend your ride by 30 miles, in a circle around the reservoir, turn left at Mile 27 onto MA-32 and then bear right onto MA-9 West. After 15 miles, turn right onto MA-202 north. After 20 miles, turn right onto MA-122, rejoining the main route at Mile 45. The entire ride becomes 76 miles long.

Locals' Tip: The Upperdeck Sports Bar and Grille (377 Stetson Road, Barre, MA 01005, 978/355-2224) faces the slopes at Pine Ridge Snow Park.

Places to Stay: The Inn at Clamber Hill (111 North Main Street, Petersham, MA 01366, 978/724-8800, www.clamberhill.com) is a picturesque getaway on conservation land, a relaxing way to end a tiring day.

Driving Directions

From Worcester, take MA-122 west for approximately 20 miles to Barre. As you enter the center of town, bear right around the large town common onto Exchange Street. You'll find free parking lots around the common and a large lot on the eastern edge. Supplies and a bike shop are available in Barre.

Route Directions

0.0 From Exchange Street in the center of Barre, turn RIGHT onto Mechanic Street (this becomes Hubbardston Road/MA-62).

2.5 Continue STRAIGHT. *A right turn will take you on an optional side trip to Barre Falls Dam.*

6.8 Turn RIGHT onto MA-68.

8.2 Turn RIGHT onto Intervale Road.

10.6 Bear LEFT onto Charnock Hill Road.

13.1 Turn RIGHT onto MA-122A.

14.1 Turn RIGHT onto MA-122. *Small roadside picnic area.*

16.6 Turn LEFT onto Old Turnpike Road.

21.7 Continue STRAIGHT through intersection onto Ravine Road.

24.3 Continue STRAIGHT through intersection onto Barre Road. *Supplies available at Cloverhill Country Store farm stand.*

27.0 Turn RIGHT onto MA-32A at Hardwick common. *Supplies and restrooms available at Hardwick General Store.* OPTION: Turn left onto MA-32 and follow option directions.

37.1 Continue STRAIGHT through intersection onto Hardwick Road.

37.3 Bear RIGHT at triangle onto Spring Street.

37.6 Turn LEFT onto South Main Street.

37.8 Turn RIGHT onto East Street. *Supplies available at Petersham Country Store.*

41.0 East Street becomes Old Barre Road.

42.3 Old Barre Road becomes Pleasant Street.

45.6 Turn LEFT at stop sign onto MA-32/122.

45.7 Return to Barre town center.

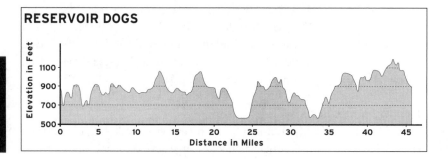

RESERVOIR DOGS

8 WACHUSETT MOUNTAIN   BEST C
Wachusett Mountain State Reservation

**PAVED ROADS WITH SOME DETERIORATING PAVEMENT,
MINIMAL TRAFFIC**

Difficulty: 5	**Total Distance:** 20.1 miles
Riding Time: 2.5 hours	**Elevation Gain:** 1,260 feet

Summary: An uphill battle with incredibly scenic payoffs, this forested ride climbs in the state's rural midsection.

The high point of this ride, both figuratively and geographically, is the summit of Wachusett Mountain, which peaks at 2,006 feet. Some might say the low point is the climb, which is long and slow and hurts. The truth is, it's so beautiful you barely notice the pain.

At least, that's what you should keep telling yourself. That, and that the reason you're panting so hard is not because you're out of shape but because the views are breathtaking.

Wachusett Mountain Ski Area is based at the foot of the mountain, and that's where this ride begins. As you climb, you'll have a chance to crisscross the ski trails, beneath the chairlifts, but first you've got to get there.

The ride heads away from the mountain to start, winding lazily past quiet Noyes Pond and crossing Mare Meadow Reservoir and around the back of the mountain

While you don't want to tackle this ride unless you're willing to climb – a lot – those who do will find the rewards, including the views, worth the effort.

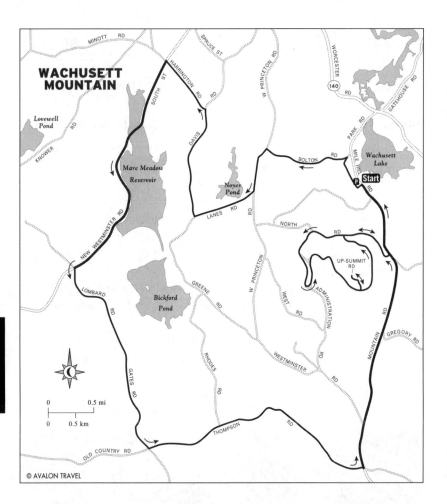

through the beautiful state reservation, a 3,000-acre gem linked with the Leominster State Forest, the Wachusett Meadow Wildlife Sanctuary, and the Minns Wildlife Sanctuary. Some of the trees you'll pass are more than 350 years old.

You get a quick reprieve of a short downhill to the entrance of the reservation before you begin climbing for real up the summit road. Looking down the slopes of the ski area, you'll see the Boston skyline, the Berkshire Mountains, numerous lakes and meadows, and on a clear day, even New Hampshire's Mount Monadnock in the distance. Catch your breath at the visitors center at the summit before descending quickly—and gratefully—back to the start.

Note that the summit road is open from Memorial Day through the last

Sunday in October, 9 A.M.–sunset daily. For more information, contact the Department of Conservation and Recreation at Mountain Road, Princeton, MA 01541, 978/464-2987, www.mass.gov/dcr/parks/central/wach.htm.

Options

Gluttons for punishment can do this ride backward, frontloading two big climbs and making the rest of the ride more or less uphill. This ride is within an hour's drive of Reservoir Dogs.

Locals' Tip: The 1761 Old Mill (69 State Road East, Westminster, MA 01473, 978/874-5941, www.1761oldmill.com) is a rustic restaurant open Tuesday through Sunday, serving locally brewed Wachusett Brewing Company beers.

Places to Stay: The Maguire House bed-and-breakfast (30 Cobb Road, Ashburnham, MA 01430, 978/827-5053, www.maguirehouse.com) is an upscale B&B, built in 1764 and located not far from the ride, with a great location and access to trails and hikes.

Driving Directions

Take MA-2 to exit 25 for Westminster/Princeton. Take MA-140 south, and turn right onto Mile Hill Road. The entrance to the ski area is a half mile down on the right; this ride starts and ends there. Supplies are available in the summer (9 A.M.–5 P.M. Mon.–Fri.).

Route Directions

0.0 From the parking area, exit to the right side of the lot and turn LEFT onto Bolton Road, uphill.

1.3 Turn LEFT onto West Princeton Road, still heading uphill.

1.8 Turn RIGHT onto Lanes Road as the road levels out.

2.4 Turn RIGHT onto Davis Road.

3.7 Turn LEFT onto Harrington Road.

4.5 Turn LEFT onto South Street, cross the Mare Meadow Reservoir, and then follow its shoreline. South Street becomes New Westminster Road and begins a slight downhill.

7.1 Turn LEFT onto Lombard Road. This rural road climbs gradually but steadily through the state reservation.

9.3 Turn LEFT onto Thompson Road.

12.0 Turn LEFT onto Mountain Road, beginning a short downhill to the beginning of the climb.

13.0 Begin the climb.

14.4 Turn LEFT to enter the reservation and follow Up-Summit Road. *The visitors center is on your left.* From here, the climb steepens, but the views improve. The road crosses ski area trails, with chairlifts overhead, and the views to your right go from stunning to breathtaking.

15.8 Follow signs for the summit, bearing RIGHT on Up-Summit Road.

16.2 Stay LEFT on Up-Summit Road, ignoring closed administrative road.

16.5 Stay RIGHT on Up-Summit Road.

17.2 Sharp LEFT to summit.

17.4 Summit! Turn around and bear LEFT onto Down-Summit Road, beginning descent.

18.6 Turn RIGHT onto two-way Summit Road.

19.3 Turn LEFT onto Mountain Road, watching for traffic.

20.1 Turn LEFT into parking area at ski area.

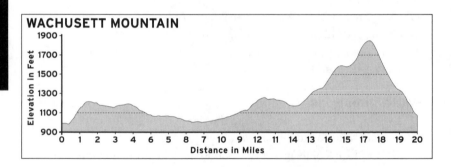

9 NASHUA RIVER RAIL TRAIL   BEST ☾
Ayer to Dunstable

PAVED RAIL TRAIL

Difficulty: 2   **Total Distance:** 22.2 miles

Riding Time: 2 hours   **Elevation Gain:** 108 feet

Summary: This smooth, wide, flat rail trail along the river is a wonderful way to spend a day and is suitable for all riders.

Like many other rail trails, the Nashua River trail is flat and easy to ride. But this one is exceptional in ways not easy to quantify. For one thing, it's beautiful along its length from the New Hampshire border south to Ayer. It's also smoothly paved and 10 feet wide, making it safe and accessible to broad groups of users—including equestrians, who get their own five-foot-wide path paralleling 7 miles of the rail trail.

The trail also offers opportunities to stop and rest along the way, to watch for wildlife, and to take pictures—or just take in the sights—at dozens of scenic overlooks and viewpoints. It's tough to find anything to complain about.

Originally the Hollis Branch of the Boston & Maine railroad, this rail trail was completed in 2002, 20 years after the last train used the tracks. The route's usefulness for transportation continues. The trailhead in Ayer is accessible from

Running south from the New Hampshire border, the Nashua River Rail Trail is wide, smooth, paved, and beautiful.

commuter rail service between Boston and Fitchburg, a move toward a more hopeful future when more bicycle commuting infrastructure is in place.

Flat and smooth as this trail is, it's suitable for bicyclists of all skill levels on any kind of bicycle. Facilities are available at the Ayer trailhead, and you'll find water faucets in front of Groton Town Hall, just off the trail on Station Avenue; watch for signs. Bicyclists should yield to horses on approach and give a verbal acknowledgement before passing.

For more information, contact the Department of Conservation and Recreation, www.mass.gov/dcr/parks/northeast/nash.htm.

Options

Distances are painted on the pavement, so it's easy to piece together a ride of any length—it's all up to you. Additional parking areas can be found along the length of the trail in Groton Center on Court Street, on Groton Sand Hill Road, or in Dunstable on Hollis Street

Locals' Tip: Charlotte's Cozy Kitchen (142 Main Street, Pepperell, MA 01463, 978/433-2693) bills itself as the "rail trail's ice cream stop," and in fact, many trail users do take advantage of its proximity. Charlotte's offers other foods as well, and it's a good place to stop for lunch.

Places to Stay: The Ayer Motor Inn (18 Fitchburg Road, Ayer, MA 01432, 978/772-0797) is a bed on a budget—clean, comfortable, and reasonably priced.

Driving Directions

The Ayer trailhead has more parking than the Dunstable end, so start there. From MA-2, take exit 38B, then follow MA-111 north to the rotary in Ayer. Enter the traffic circle at 6 o'clock and exit at 12 o'clock onto Washington Street (MA-2A). Turn right after Ayer Center and take first right on Groton Street. The parking lot is on the right. Additional parking areas along the trail's length can be found in Groton center on Court Street, on Groton Sand Hill Road, or in Dunstable on Hollis Street.

Route Directions

0.0 Head north on the rail trail.

3.1 Trail parking at Groton Center. *Water available.*

4.8 Trail parking at Sand Hill Road in Groton. Trail runs along the J. Harry Rich State Forest, with scenic views.

11.1 Trail ends at Dunstable parking. TURN AROUND.

22.2 END at parking area.

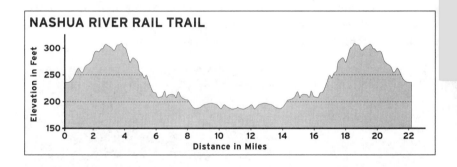

NASHUA RIVER RAIL TRAIL

10 GREAT BROOK FARM TOUR
Great Brook Farm State Park, Carlisle

SINGLE-TRACK, DOUBLE-TRACK, DIRT AND GRAVEL ROADS

Difficulty: 2   **Total Distance:** 9 miles

Riding Time: 1.5-2 hours   **Elevation Gain:** 226 feet

Summary: These shaded, family-friendly mountain bike trails crisscross a state park on the site of a dairy farm.

Locals know there's plenty of good mountain biking to be found within spitting distance of Boston, but Great Brook Farm may not be the first place they think of. For one thing, the trails aren't the primary reason the park is popular—that honor goes to the working dairy farm and its attendant ice-cream stand, the duck ponds and picnic areas, the canoe launch, the cross-country ski touring center, and other family-friendly opportunities. For another, the trails seem to be more well-known among the equestrian crowd than the biking crowd.

But the truth is, the trails here are excellent for mountain biking—in fact, they're maintained by the very active New England Mountain Biking Association (NEMBA)—and are nontechnical enough to be welcoming to even the least-confident off-road riders. This is a great place for beginners.

© CHRIS BERNARD

This ride follows the trails through the woods around Great Brook Farm, but the roads make for popular, bucolic rides as well.

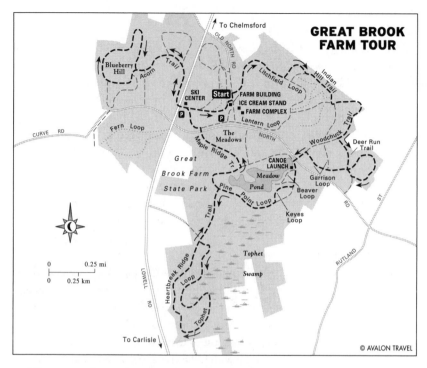

This route takes you all over the park, through fields and meadows, pine forests and woodlands, and past swamps and cornfields. You'll start in the fields, do a little rocky, hilly stretch along the Indian Hill Trail, and ride along some gentle hills on the Woodchuck Trail. It's mostly double- and single-track, but not technical, on this northern side. Across the road, in the southern part of the park, you can find more challenging single-track.

Heartbreak Ridge and Tophet Loop run through the woods along a ridge and past a swamp. The trails are banked nicely to let you gather some speed, and a bridge makes it passable even in wetter seasons. The swamp means mosquitoes, so spray yourself or grit your teeth and bear it.

An easy ride along cornfields brings you to the ski center, where you can cross Lowell Road and take a loop around Blueberry Hill. It's mostly dirt roads and double-track, with a small, more challenging section of single-track that's only hilly and rooty for a short time.

Note that the trails are closed to bikes from December 15 to March 15 and whenever four or more inches of snow cover them. Mountain bikes are the best bet on these trails.

For more information, contact Great Brook Farm State Park, 984 Lowell Road, Carlisle, MA 01741, 978/369-6312, www.state.ma.us/dem/parks/gbfm.htm.

Options

Riders looking for a longer ride can piece together a 5-mile loop around the area by following North Road from Lowell Road east to Rutland Street and turning right. When Rutland Street ends, turn right again on East Street, and right again on Lowell Road to return to the start. The roads are rural and lightly used, and the scenery is beautiful and shaded.

Locals' Tip: If you're riding during the right season, get the ice-cream on site at the stand and general store (984 Lowell Road, Carlisle, MA 01741), where you can see the dairy cows responsible on the premises.

Places to Stay: Concord's Colonial Inn (48 Monument Square, Concord, MA 01742, 978/369-9200, www.concordscolonialinn.com) is a short drive from Great Brook Farm and situated in historic Concord.

Driving Directions

From Lowell, take I-495 to exit 34 and follow MA-110 south for 2.5 miles, to the center of Chelmsford. Follow signs through the one-way system to MA-4 south. Drive 1 mile and bear right onto Concord Road (which becomes Lowell Road). Drive approximately 2.5 miles and turn left onto North Road; look for signs to Great Brook Farm State Park. Turn left into the first parking lot. At the end of this lot, there's a small park building with full facilities, restrooms, water, and trail maps (the main farm building and ice-cream stand are past the pond at the next parking area). The parking fee is $2. The route begins behind this farm building. Supplies and a bike shop are available in Chelmsford.

Route Directions

0.0 START at rear of park building on Litchfield Loop.

0.2 Turn LEFT at fork onto single-track.

0.6 Turn LEFT at edge of field.

0.8 Take the leftmost trail at the three-way intersection onto Indian Hill Trail.

0.9 Turn LEFT onto main trail.

1.2 Stay STRAIGHT through two four-way intersections.

1.3 Cross first bridge and take leftmost trail.

1.6 Turn LEFT at three-way intersection.

1.9 Turn LEFT at four-way intersection.

2.2 Bear RIGHT at junction.

2.3 Turn LEFT at four-way intersection.

2.4 Cross bridge.

2.5 Bear RIGHT on Garrison Loop.

2.8 Turn LEFT onto wide dirt road (Woodchuck Trail, unmarked).

2.9 Cross North Road and pick up Pine Point Loop trail to left of pond.

3.0 OPTION: Take a short, optional side loop left on the Beaver Loop trail.

3.1 Turn LEFT onto Keyes Loop.

3.6 Turn RIGHT back onto Pine Point Loop.

3.9 Turn LEFT onto Heartbreak Ridge trail.

4.2 Turn LEFT at triangular intersection, then make an immediate LEFT onto Tophet Loop trail.

5.0 Turn RIGHT back onto Heartbreak Ridge trail.

5.6 Turn RIGHT at triangular intersection.

5.9 Turn LEFT onto Pine Point Loop.

6.2 Turn LEFT onto Maple Ridge trail.

6.4 Turn LEFT at fork.

6.5 Cross North Road and pick up trail just to the left.

6.7 Arrive at ski touring center parking lot. Cross Lowell Road.

6.8 Pick up Acorn Trail.

7.0 Turn LEFT at fork.

7.3 Turn LEFT at junction on narrow trail.

7.4 Stay STRAIGHT (Acorn South trail goes off to left).

8.2 Turn LEFT at junction onto trail between fields

8.3 Bear LEFT.

8.7 Cross North Road.

8.8 Go through the parking lot and pick up dirt road to left of kiosk.

9.0 END at parking lot.

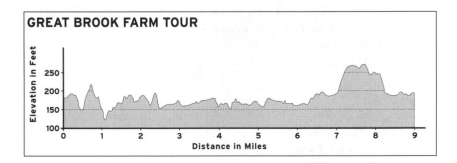

11 FARMS AND FORESTS   BEST ☾
North Andover, Boxford, and Topsfield

PAVED ROADS, MINIMAL TRAFFIC

Difficulty: 2   **Total Distance:** 27.3 miles

Riding Time: 2 hours   **Elevation Gain:** 364 feet

Summary: A flat, winding route through the shady back roads of northeast Massachusetts, with scenic vistas of ponds and forests.

This ride starts and ends at Smolak Farms, a unique and historic spot in the rural fringe of North Andover. The farm stand is a popular meeting spot for local group rides. The lion's share of the farmland is now preserved in cooperation with the state's Agricultural Preservation Restriction Program, which means it will never be developed. The working farm has been around in one form or another for as long as 300 years.

North Andover itself has been around a lot longer—some evidence shows the area has been inhabited for as long as 8,000 years as a Native American encampment, based around Lake Cochichewick. Later, the town was famously sold to a Reverend John Woodbridge for "six pounds and a coat." The town continued to play a part in history—more of its residents were accused of witchcraft during the Salem Witch Trials than residents of the Salem area, and in the 1800s it was home to cotton mills during the textile revolution.

Now it's a town of soccer fields and minivans, but Smolak Farms provides a sense of what the land might once have looked like. This ride heads east on rural, tree-lined roads into Boxford and Topsfield, passing a number of picturesque ponds and lakes, before winding its way clockwise into the verdant Boxford and Harold Parker State Forests. The last stretch passes Lake Cochichewick before arriving through the backdoor at Smolak Farms.

Most of the ride is flat, and there are ample opportunities to stop for snacks or a breather or just to enjoy the archetypal wooded New England setting.

For more information, contact Smolak Farms, 315 South Bradford Street, North Andover, MA 01845, 978/682-6332, www.smolakfarms.com.

Options

To extend this ride by about 15 miles, turn left at Mile 5.8 on Pond Street and right on Killam Hill Road, which becomes Ipswich Road. Bear left onto Boxford Street, which becomes Linebrook Road and skirts the edges of Willowdale State Forest in Ipswich. When Linebrook Road ends, turn right onto MA-133/MA-1A, and

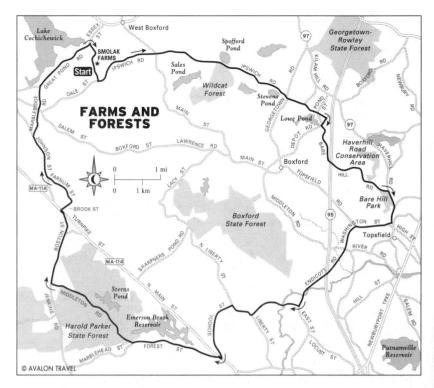

then right onto Market Street/Topsfield Road. Topsfield Road becomes Ipswich Road and rejoins the original ride at Mile 9.

This ride is near the Harold Parker State Forest and Weeping Willowdale off-road rides; combining one or more rides offers a mix of cycling terrain. Witches to Water's Edge, another scenic road ride, is just a half-hour drive away.

Locals' Tip: All the local group rides that start and end at Smolak Farms can't be wrong. Begin your day with a cup of their coffee and a fresh farmhouse doughnut, and end it with pressed apple cider.

Places to Stay: The Killam Hill Cottage (168 Killam Hill Road, Boxford, MA 01921, 978/887-6470) offers no-frills country guest rooms with shared kitchenettes and bathrooms for affordable rates less than a minute from the ride.

Driving Directions

From I-95, take exit 53B for Georgetown/MA-97 north, and turn right at the off-ramp. Take your first left, following the sign for Boxford Village, and take your first right onto Ipswich Road. About 6 miles down, turn right onto South

Bradford Street, following signs for Smolak Farms. A small parking area is available, as are seasonal facilities.

Route Directions

0.0 From the farm parking lot, turn LEFT onto South Bradford Street and LEFT onto Dale Street.

1.0 Stay STRAIGHT on Dale Street, which becomes Ipswich Road (Boxford).

3.5 Pass Spofford Pond on your left. *Take the next left onto Spofford Road to access the pond.*

4.8 Pass Stevens Pond on your right. *A small parking area with water access is available.*

5.8 OPTION: Turn LEFT on Pond Street and follow option directions.

5.9 When road ends, turn RIGHT onto Pond Street and RIGHT onto Depot Road.

6.1 Turn LEFT onto Bare Hill Road.

7.0 Pass over I-95.

8.5 At Bare Hill Park, turn RIGHT onto MA-97/Haverhill Road/ Main Street, past Pine Grove Cemetery.

9.3 Turn RIGHT onto Washington Street (Topsfield).

10.2 Bear LEFT to stay on Washington Street, which becomes Endicott Road.

11.5 Cross over I-95 into Boxford State Forest.

12.5 Turn RIGHT onto Peabody Street.

14.1 Turn LEFT onto School Street.

14.9 School Street ends; turn LEFT onto Essex Street.

15.6 Essex Street ends. Cross MA-114 onto Forest Street. This is a busy road—be careful crossing.

17.6 Forest Street ends. Turn RIGHT onto Salem Street/Middleton Road into Harold Parker State Forest.

20.0 Turn RIGHT onto Jenkins Road/Boston Street (Andover).

21.6 Jenkins Road/Boston Street ends. Turn LEFT onto MA-114. This is a busy road—be careful crossing.

21.7 Turn RIGHT onto Brook Street (North Andover).

22.0 Turn LEFT onto Farnum Street.

22.8 Farnum Street ends. Bear RIGHT onto Johnson Street.

23.9 Turn RIGHT onto Marbleridge Road.

25.0 Bear RIGHT onto Great Pond Road. Lake Cochichewick is on your left.

26.5 Turn RIGHT onto South Bradford Street.

27.3 END at parking area.

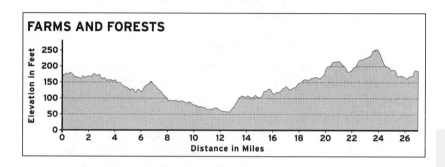

12 HAROLD PARKER STATE FOREST

BEST 🄲

Harold Parker State Forest, Andover

SINGLE-TRACK, DOUBLE-TRACK

Difficulty: 2

Riding Time: 2 hours

Total Distance: 7.5 miles

Elevation Gain: 300 feet

Summary: Enjoy this nontechnical ride through a gorgeous, shady state forest, with opportunities for more intense routes at every turn.

It's possible to piece together 35 miles of riding in Harold Parker State Forest, and the terrain is so well-suited to mountain biking that some of the area's best riders come each year to compete in the "Wicked Ride of the East" race. But the park's real appeal is the seemingly endless winding trails that show off the wooded beauty of Massachusetts's second-oldest state park.

In all, the park covers 3,000 glacially carved acres of rolling hills, grassy wetlands, and rocky outcroppings. Trails range from double-track jeep roads to wooded single-track. This loop is largely nontechnical—the few stretches of

The trails of Harold Parker State Forest are popular with mountain bikers from all over the region.

© CHRIS BERNARD

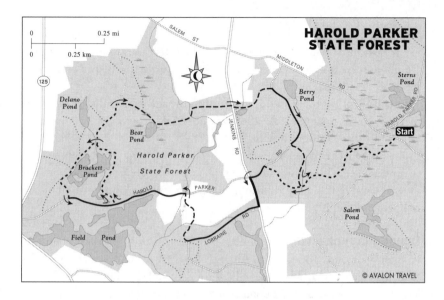

single-track are suitable for beginners who take it slowly, and the entire trail is ideal for cyclocross bikes.

Dense tree cover here prevents much sunlight from reaching parts of the trails, which means they can be muddy in the spring (with snow and ice sometimes lingering) and cool and moist on hot summer days. During the fall, the foliage can be spectacular. Use caution when those leaves end up wet on the ground; they can mask obstacles such as roots or rocks and make trails slippery.

Expect to share the trail with other users, including pedestrians and dog walkers, and be aware that some trails' spurs dead-end into private property. Along the trails, watch for remnants of 18th-century homesteads, sawmills, and stone walls dating back even further. Homes surrounding the forest are said to have been Underground Railroad hideouts, and many still have secret doors and chambers.

For more information on the park, visit the Harold Parker State Forest online at www.mass.gov/dcr/parks/northeast/harp.htm.

Options

For shorter, scenic rides, follow the out-and-back trails around Brackett and Collins Ponds. For more of a challenge, try the three-mile trail in the forest's northernmost section between Middleton and Turnpike Roads (MA-114) or the hilly single-track trails north of Berry Pond.

This ride is near Farms and Forests and Weeping Willowdale. Bicyclists spending a few days in the area might consider combining Harold Parker with the Weeping Willowdale ride for a taste of some of the best state forest trails in the region. Or, put in some road miles on Farms and Forests to give the body a break from the bumps of off-roading.

Locals' Tip: Fuel up for a ride at Harrison's Roast Beef (80 Chickering Road/ MA-125, North Andover, MA 01845, 978/687-9158), a local favorite known for its good food and brusque service.

Places to Stay: Harold Parker State Forest offers nearly 100 well-spread-out campsites, each with picnic table and grill, and with public restrooms with hot water showers, and is open May to mid-October. For more information on the campground, call 978/475-7972.

Driving Directions

From the south, take I-93 north to exit 41. Follow MA-125 north for about 4 miles to the state police barracks on the right. Turn right on Harold Parker Road. Turn left on Jenkins Road and right onto Salem Road, and drive 1.25 miles to forest headquarters, on the left. From the north, take I-495 south to exit 42. Travel east on MA-114 for 6 miles. Take a right at the brown Harold Parker State Forest sign. Follow the road to the end, then take a left to the headquarters.

Route Directions

0.0 START on unpaved road across from park headquarters.
0.3 Turn RIGHT at first fork.
0.5 Turn LEFT at next fork.
  1.1 Turn LEFT sharply at gravel parking area onto single-track.
  1.2 Turn LEFT on Jenkins Road (paved).
  1.4 Turn RIGHT onto paved road into the Lorraine Park campground area.
  1.9 Turn RIGHT along the edges of Field Pond.
2.3 Turn LEFT onto Harold Parker Road (paved).
2.5 Turn RIGHT onto double-track. Trail merges with wider, old road.
2.8 Bear LEFT at first fork.
3.0 Bear LEFT at next fork, circumnavigating Brackett and Collins Ponds.
3.4 Turn LEFT onto Harold Parker Road (paved).
3.9 Turn LEFT onto double-track. Merges with wider, old road.
4.2 Turn RIGHT on trail.

5.7 CROSS Jenkins Road (paved).

6.5 Turn RIGHT on Berry Pond Road (paved).

6.7 Turn LEFT onto unpaved road.

7.0 Turn RIGHT at first fork.

7.2 Turn LEFT at next fork.

7.5 END at park headquarters.

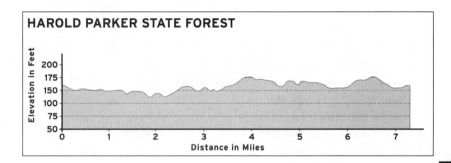

13 WEEPING WILLOWDALE   BEST ◖
Willowdale State Forest, Ipswich

DIRT ROADS, SINGLE-TRACK, DOUBLE-TRACK

Difficulty: 2   **Total Distance:** 6.4 miles

Riding Time: 1 hour   **Elevation Gain:** 102 feet

Summary: Fly along fast, fun cross-country trails and single-track through a shaded, buggy state forest.

Like a lot of state forest trails in this part of Massachusetts, there's a lot of variety in Willowdale. That means riders can pick and choose to their liking, constructing on-the-fly routes that are as fast and challenging or lazy and scenic as they choose.

The fact is, you almost can't go wrong. The forest has no shortage of single-track, which draws experienced mountain bikers from all over the region. In fact, former national cyclocross champions, Massachusetts residents, and husband and wife team Tim Johnson and Lyne Bessette can be seen riding here. You'll find the occasional stunt, but for the most part just well-maintained, nontechnical single-track.

But even the dirt roads and wide double-track are fun here. Ride them at full speed, winding around the corners, or soft pedal your way through the forest

Willowdale State Forest is an appealing mix of single-track and fire roads ideal for a cyclocross bike.

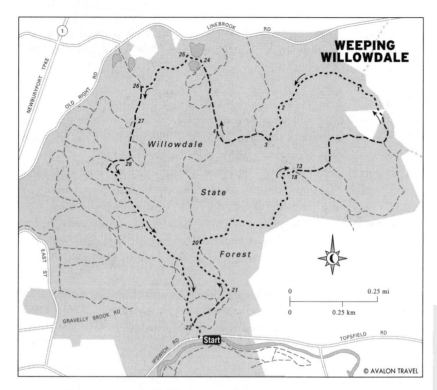

enjoying the swamps and wildlife. Ride in the autumn, during foliage season, for maximum scenic impact. You're not likely to get tired of the rides in Willowdale, but if you do, cross the Ipswich River from your parking area and start all over again exploring the trails at Bradley Palmer State Park.

Ipswich is a beautiful and historic coastal town that seems a world away from the forest on its edge. Just half an hour north of Boston, it's a tourist destination, but Willowdale is a gem that's largely ignored—especially compared to Bradley Palmer. You're likely to encounter a few other bike riders, and the occasional dog walker, but that's it—it's largely, wonderfully uncrowded. You might see riders on horses, but you're more likely to see their leave-behinds, an excellent way to practice your bunny hopping skills on your bike, considering the consequences of failure.

Trails are nominally marked with blazes and signpost numbers, though in reality, markers are faded or missing at many intersections. The forest's not big enough to get truly lost in, however, and riders can always make their way out to one of the roads bordering the woods to find their location.

Mountain bikes and cyclocross bikes are ideal, but recreational riders who stick to the wide, unpaved roads and double-track will do fine on hybrids.

For more information, contact the Department of Conservation and Recreation, 251 Causeway Street, Suite 600, Boston, MA 02114, 617/626-1250, www.mass.gov/dcr.

Options

Extend your ride by following the many trails in the state forest at random, or plan ahead of time using a trail map. Maps of neighboring Bradley Palmer State Park are available at www.mass.gov/dcr/parks/northeast/brad.htm.

Bicyclists in the area should try the Harold Parker State Forest ride, which offers similar trails in the same setting just 45 minutes away. Or, stretch your legs on the roads of the nearby Farms and Forests ride for a varied cycling experience.

Locals' Tip: The Choate Bridge Pub (3 South Main Street, Ipswich, MA 01938, 978/356-2931, www.ipswichma.com) is a comfortable local bar and grill set beside the oldest stone arch bridge in America, built in 1764. Note that the Choate Bridge Pub is cash only.

Places to Stay: The Inn at Castle Hill on the Crane Estate (a property of the trustees of reservations, 280 Argilla Road, Ipswich, MA 01938, 978/412-2555, www.craneestate.org) offers stunning ocean and marsh views from the historic Crane Estate, just a short drive from Willowdale.

Driving Directions

From I-95, take exit 50 to US-1 North. Travel 4 miles and turn right onto Ipswich Road. About 2 miles down, Ipswich Road turns into Topsfield Road. There will be two turn-outs on the right side for parking; park in the second, at the footbridge across the Ipswich River. The ride starts across the street.

Route Directions

0.0 From Ipswich Road, enter the forest at the gate.

0.2 At the intersection at signpost 22, take a RIGHT.

0.4 Turn LEFT at signpost 21 onto an unpaved road.

0.7 Continue right on the fire road at signpost 20.

1.6 Just past signpost 18, turn RIGHT at signpost 13. Bear LEFT at next two forks.

2.4 Turn LEFT on paved road. Ride about a half-mile past the Private Property sign (please respect the homes along the right side of the road).

2.7 Turn LEFT on trail marked by half-buried concrete blocks and signpost 1.

3.3 At the next intersection, signpost 2, turn LEFT, and then RIGHT at signpost 3 onto single-track.

3.9 Turn RIGHT at signpost 4 onto trail marked with white blazes.

4.3 Turn LEFT at signpost 24.

4.4 Turn LEFT at signpost 25.

4.6 Turn LEFT at signpost 26 onto single-track.

4.8 Stay STRAIGHT at signpost 27, and turn RIGHT at signpost 28.

5.3 At the next intersection, turn LEFT on unpaved road (marked with white blazes).

5.9 Bear RIGHT at the next fork onto unpaved road. Stay STRAIGHT past signpost 22, which brings you to Ipswich Road.

6.4 END at parking area.

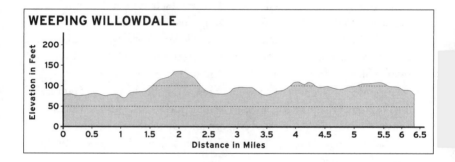

14 PLUM ISLAND   BEST ◖
Parker River National Wildlife Refuge

DIRT ROADS, PAVED ROADS WITH SOME DETERIORATING PAVEMENT AND MODERATE TRAFFIC

Difficulty: 2   **Total Distance:** 20.6 miles

Riding Time: 2 hours   **Elevation Gain:** 10 feet

Summary: This scenic ride brings you close to the water and nature – and traffic. Plan on parking and walking for up-close sights.

The 11-mile-long barrier island off the coast of northeast Massachusetts, Plum Island, was named as far back as 1649. It probably wasn't long after that when hordes of tourists began visiting it each summer, and these days it can be fairly crowded when the weather's nice. Despite the island's provenance being split between four neighboring towns, access to the island is limited to a single road in from Newburyport.

Packed with restaurants, bars, shops, and galleries, Newburyport is a cool little coastal New England town. Leaving from Market Square, downtown, you'll see a lot of vehicles—both moving and parked on the side of the road—on Water Street, so ride smartly. Once you're out of town, the shoulder of the Plum Island Turnpike provides ample riding room. The route itself is flat, and it travels through salt marshes, past the Plum Island Airport, and eventually across a metal-grated bridge before entering the Parker River National Wildlife Refuge (www.fws.gov/northeast/parkerriver/).

This ride through the Parker River National Wildlife Refuge is suitable for riders of all skill levels.

Tourists aren't the only things flocking to the area, which is both good and bad for you. On the good side are the more than 300 species of birds that visit each year. On the other are the nasty, biting greenheads and the mosquitoes that are the banes of the beach come summer. Be prepared from June to August or so to lose a few pounds of flesh.

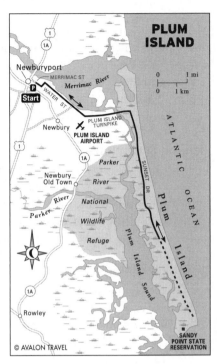

Sadly, bikes are not allowed on the various hiking trails off the main route, but there are some bike racks available at refuge parking lots, allowing you to explore the many walking trails. Please obey posted signs, as the sand dunes are fragile, and observe restrictions around the breeding grounds of the piping plover. Beaches are closed during plover breeding season, which begins in April and sometimes goes as late as August. Bring sunscreen, a windbreaker, and warm clothing in the spring and fall as the weather can change pretty quickly.

The road turns to packed dirt and gravel for about 6 miles at the end of the ride. Morning cycling is recommended, before traffic gets unbearable. The refuge entrance fee is $2 (for bikes and walkers). Maps are available at the gatehouse; public restrooms are available at the gatehouse and farther along inside Parker River National Wildlife Refuge.

For more information, contact the Newburyport Chamber of Commerce, 38R Merrimac Street, Newburyport, MA 01950, 978/462-6680, www.newbury portchamber.org.

Options

To add a 7-mile loop through old Newbury and marshland, on the return trip take your first left after the airport onto Ocean Avenue, and then turn left again onto MA-1A south. At the 3-mile mark, turn right onto Newman Road and right again onto Hay Street, which brings you back to MA-1A. Turn left and follow 1A back to turn right on Ocean Avenue, rejoining the ride by turning left on Water Street and returning to the parking area.

Locals' Tip: The Fish Tale Diner (Bridge Marina, US-1 Bridge, Salisbury,

MA 01952, 978/462-2274, www.bridgemarinasalisbury.com) is a great place to dine while watching the boats come and go in the harbor, with great views of the water. Try the Belgian waffles.

Places to Stay: 167 Water B&B (167 Water Street, Newburyport, MA 01950, 978/255-2386, www.167water.com) is as welcoming as a bed-and-breakfast can be, with river views and friendly hosts.

Driving Directions

From US-1, head east on Merrimac Street for about 0.4 mile into downtown Newburyport. Free parking is available in lots throughout Newburyport, though in summer you'll need to stake your claim early in the day, especially on the weekends. The ride starts downtown at Market Square, at the intersection of Merrimac, State, and Water Streets. Supplies and a bike shop are available in Newburyport.

Route Directions

0.0 START from Market Square. Proceed east down Water Street.

0.2 Bear LEFT, continuing down Water Street. (This eventually turns into the Plum Island Turnpike.)

1.4 Pass Massachusetts Audubon Center.

2.9 Cross metal grated bridge.

3.3 Turn RIGHT on Sunset Drive.

3.8 Enter Parker River National Wildlife Refuge. Pay entry fee.

6.3 Bear LEFT.

7.4 Road turns to gravel.

10.3 Enter Sandy Point State Reservation. *Park your bike on the bike rack and walk to the various beaches.* TURN AROUND and retrace your route back to Newburyport. OPTION: Take the first LEFT after the airport onto Ocean Avenue and follow option directions.

20.6 Arrive at Market Square.

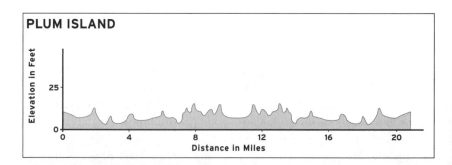

15 WITCHES TO WATER'S EDGE   BEST [

Salem to Cape Ann

PAVED ROADS WITH MODERATE TRAFFIC

Difficulty: 3   **Total Distance:** 54.3 miles

Riding Time: 4 hours   **Elevation Gain:** 775 feet

Summary: This mostly flat road ride leaves historic downtown Salem for the scenic coastal routes of Cape Ann.

Originally named Cape Tragbigzanda by explorer John Smith, Cape Ann—renamed by King Charles I—is everything you'd expect of coastal New England. From working-class fishing town Gloucester to upscale Magnolia with its cliff-front mansions, it's scenic and varied. This ride explores enough of it to get a sense of the variety.

Begin south of Cape Ann, in Salem, best known for being historically unwelcoming to witches. Since then, the city has come to embrace its past, and you'll find evidence of that fact in the shops and museums and even along the streets. The first part of the ride is on the busiest roads, in Salem, and across the bridge in Beverly. There aren't shoulders on all the roads, and during rush hour there can be a lot of traffic. The traffic thins out as you go, but it's present on much of this ride—these aren't the rural farm roads of the central and western part of the state—so be warned, and be careful.

This ride starts and ends in historic Salem, birthplace of Nathaniel Hawthorne, and the site of a pro-level criterium bike race that passes the famous Salem Witch Museum.

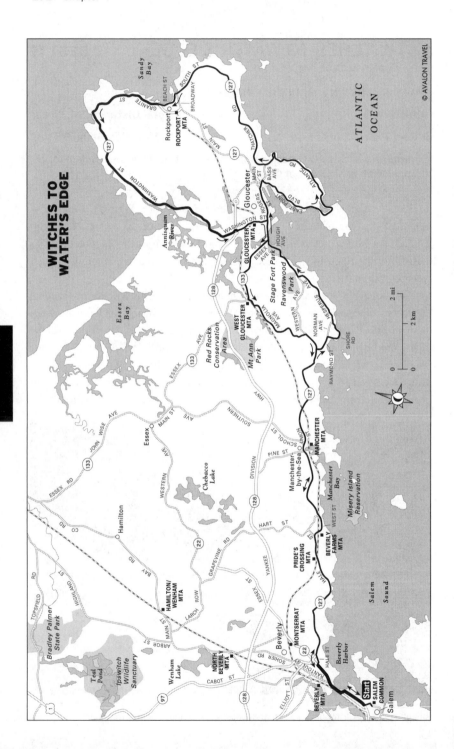

WITCHES TO WATER'S EDGE

North of Beverly, the ride heads through Pride's Crossing and Beverly Farms, where you'll see lots of big impressive gates hiding big impressive homes. John Updike lived there for years, and you'll bike right past his home. Then the route passes through Manchester-by-the-Sea, a cute little waterfront town, and into Magnolia, where it strays off the main road for a loop along the cliffs, offering stunning views of the ocean and the homes along its edge. You'll also pass the medieval-style castle built by inventor John Hammond, creator of, among other things, the remote control.

From there it's north and east to Gloucester, best known by many as the setting for *The Perfect Storm,* but first made famous a century earlier by Rudyard Kipling in *Captains Courageous.* The ride passes through Stage Fort Park, a beautiful oceanfront park that's the site of one of the country's largest cyclocross races each fall, then out to the Bass Rocks area where, on stormy days, the ocean throws rocks onto the road.

Next, head east to Rockport, a postcard of a coastal town surrounded on three sides by ocean. There, a spur road leads to Motif No. 1, a wharf shack considered the most-painted and photographed building in America. The rest of the ride rolls through the scenic neighborhood of Annisquam and the fringes of Essex, where the fried clam was invented, before retracing part of the route back to Salem.

For more information, contact the Cape Ann Chamber of Commerce, 33 Commercial Street, Gloucester, MA 01930, 978/283-1601, www.capeann vacations.com.

Options
Cut 16 miles of the busiest roads off this ride by parking in downtown Manchester-by-the-Sea and picking up the ride at Mile 8, leaving you with an easier distance, less traffic, and just as much beauty.

Locals' Tip: When not being burned at the stake, Salem residents can be found at Red's Sandwich Shop (15 Central Street, Salem, MA 01970, 978/745-3527, www.redssandwichshop.com), where the diner-type breakfasts are worth waiting for.

Places to Stay: The Cape Ann Motor Inn (33 Rockport Road, Gloucester, MA 01930, 800/464-VIEW, www.capeannmotorinn.com) is an inexpensive place to stay right on Gloucester's Long Beach.

Driving Directions
From MA-128 North, take exit 20B and turn right onto MA-1A toward Beverly. Cross the bridge and turn left onto Pleasant Street, and then bear left at Washington Square at the common. Parking is along the street. The ride starts in front

of the Salem Witch Museum at the corner of Hawthorne Boulevard and Brown Street on Washington Square.

Route Directions

0.0 From the Salem Witch Museum, turn LEFT onto Hawthorne Boulevard/MA-1A, and then turn RIGHT at Bridge Street to stay on MA-1A. Follow MA-1A across the bridge into Beverly.

1.3 Immediately after the bridge, bear RIGHT onto Cabot Street/MA-22.

2.1 Turn RIGHT onto Hale Street, which becomes MA-62.

2.6 Stay on Hale Street, which becomes MA-127.

4.3 Along the ocean, Hale Street passes Endicott College on the left.

5.5 Enter Pride's Crossing. Be careful crossing the train tracks.

6.0 Enter Beverly Farms.

7.5 Turn RIGHT onto Boardman Avenue for a short loop out to Tucks Point. After turning around at Tucks Point, turn RIGHT onto Harbor Street and RIGHT onto MA-127, rejoining the ride at Mile 7.8.

8.5 Stay on MA-127. Pass through downtown Manchester-by-the-Sea. *Bike shop and supplies available.*

11.4 Turn RIGHT onto Raymond Street.

11.9 Turn RIGHT onto Shore Road along the cliffs of Magnolia. Shore Road becomes Hesperus Avenue.

13.8 Pass Hammond Castle Museum.

14.5 Turn RIGHT onto MA-127.

15.3 Turn RIGHT onto Hough Avenue, entering Gloucester's Stage Fort Park.

15.6 Turn RIGHT onto MA-127, exiting the park.

17.4 Turn RIGHT onto East Main Street, which becomes Eastern Point Boulevard, loops along Wonson Cove, Lighthouse Cove, Niles Pond, and Brace Cove, and then becomes Atlantic Road.

22.7 Turn RIGHT onto Bass Rocks Road, then RIGHT again onto Atlantic Road.

23.2 Stay STRAIGHT onto MA-127A/Thatcher Road into Rockport.

27.8 Turn RIGHT onto Bearskin Neck Road out to Bradley Wharf to see Motif No. 1. Turn around.

28.2 Turn RIGHT onto Main Street, then bear RIGHT again onto Beach Street past the Old Parish Cemetery on your left.

28.8 Bear RIGHT onto MA-127/Granite Street past Pigeon Cove, Folly Cove, and Halibut Point State Park. *Picnic tables and restrooms available.*

34.0 Pass Lobster Cove on your right, and then Goose Cove on your left.

36.8 Enter traffic circle at 6 o'clock and exit at 12 o'clock onto Washington Street. (Watch for traffic.)

37.8 Turn RIGHT onto Middle Street, and then RIGHT again onto MA-127/Western Avenue.

38.1 Before Stage Fort Park, bear RIGHT onto MA-133/Essex Avenue.

40.0 Turn LEFT onto Magnolia Avenue.

42.2 Turn RIGHT onto MA-127/Western Avenue/Summer Street. Stay on MA-127, retracing the route into Beverly.

51.7 Bear RIGHT onto Hale Street/MA-22.

52.1 Turn LEFT onto Cabot Street/MA-22.

52.8 Merge with MA-1A and cross the bridge into Salem.

53.9 Turn LEFT to stay on MA-1A.

54.3 END at Salem Witch Museum.

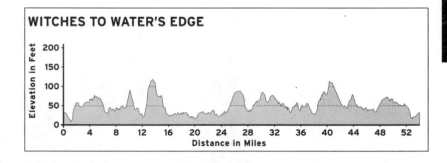

WITCHES TO WATER'S EDGE

16 VIETNAM SAMPLER   BEST ◖
Milford

SINGLE-TRACK, DIRT ROADS

Difficulty: 3   **Total Distance:** 6.8 miles

Riding Time: 1.5 hours   **Elevation Gain:** 250 feet

Summary: Explore some of the best purpose-built mountain bike trails in New England.

The New England Mountain Bike Association (NEMBA) made history in 2003 when it purchased 47 acres of land in Milford and set it aside for nonmotorized vehicles. Land ownership comes with challenges—for one thing, the parcel is largely "landlocked," meaning NEMBA relies on adjacent property owners to allow cyclists to access the land—and the group has been working diligently to meet them.

With NEMBA working to balance trail-building with land stewardship, all while remaining good neighbors, everyone who uses the trails must be on board with the group's mission. The 47-acre parcel connects with nearly 1,000 acres of non-NEMBA–owned land, so it's important to obey land-use and property boundary signs. Please respect property rights.

Now that the caveats are out of the way, on to the good stuff—the trails in this lot, known as "Vietnam," are among the best purpose-built mountain bike trails in New England. They range from fire roads to single-track, covering everything

NEMBA's bike trail-specific property, known informally as Vietnam, is a mountain biker's playground and paradise.

from slick rock to mud pits to ledges in between. You'll find obstacles to overcome, turns to navigate, short climbs to ascend, jumps to take, and endless hours of fun.

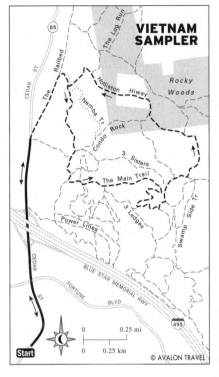

If there's a downside to the area, it's that trails are not well-marked—or, in most cases, marked at all. Perhaps the best way to learn the lay of the land is to join up with an informal guide through the NEMBA membership forum (www.nemba.org) or to ask to join a group of riders at the trails. Rough trail maps are available on the website, as well.

That said, there's nothing wrong with just exploring the area on your own. Trails are easy to find, and they're all fun. Allow yourself plenty of time, and if you have a GPS unit or compass to help yourself find your way back out, all the better. Note that when entering the land, you'll pass several trailheads that are not legal NEMBA access points. Please follow the route directions.

For more information, contact the New England Mountain Bike Association, P.O. Box 2221, Acton, MA 01720, 978/635-1718, www.nemba.org.

Options

With 47 acres of trails and new routes being added or improved all the time, it's possible to return to Vietnam as often as you want without being bored. The route cited here is just a sampler, and it crosses dozens of other networked trails. Riders wishing to lengthen their route or make it more or less challenging should have no trouble doing so.

Locals' Tip: The Alamo (55 Medway Road, Milford, MA 01757, 508/482-0030, http://thealamomexicano.com) is a themed Mexican restaurant that offers a decent, affordable way to end a good day riding Vietnam. Clean the mud off your shoes first, please.

Places to Stay: A half dozen hotels are within biking distance of Vietnam, and you pass every one of them on the route described here, including the Fairfield Inn and Suites (1 Fortune Boulevard, Milford, MA 01757, 508/478-0900).

Driving Directions

From I-495, take exit 20 for MA-85 toward Hopkinton. After about a quarter of a mile, turn right onto Cedar Street. The parking area is on your right, after the cemetery, at Hayward Field.

Route Directions

0.0 From the parking area, turn LEFT onto MA-85/Cedar Street. Traffic can be heavy here, so stick to the shoulder.

1.2 Enter trails via the Railbed on the right side of the road.

1.6 At the first intersection, turn RIGHT onto an unmarked trail.

1.8 Bear RIGHT at the next intersection onto Charles River Trail (unmarked).

2.3 Bear RIGHT at the next intersection, and then LEFT, then RIGHT.

2.6 Bear LEFT at the next intersection onto the Main Trail (unmarked), staying on this trail past the next turn.

3.3 At the intersection, turn RIGHT, and wind your way past the giant, glacially formed rockpile known informally as Teetering Rock.

3.6 At the next three intersections, turn LEFT.

3.9 Bear RIGHT at the next two intersections.

4.2 Turn LEFT, and then LEFT again.

5.0 At the next major intersection of trails, turn LEFT, and stay on this trail until it rejoins the Railbed.

5.2 Turn LEFT on the Railbed.

5.6 Turn LEFT onto Cedar Street.

6.8 END at parking area.

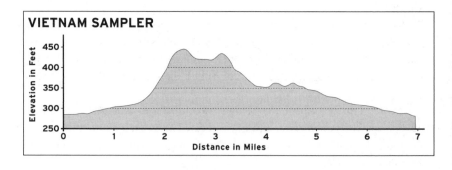

VIETNAM SAMPLER

17 TRAIL OF TEARS
West Barnstable Conservation Area

SINGLE-TRACK

Difficulty: 4   **Total Distance:** 12 miles

Riding Time: 2.5 hours   **Elevation Gain:** 302 feet

Summary: Miles of fun, twisting single-track winds its way through deep scrub pine and oak forest.

The West Barnstable Conservation Area is an oasis in the midst of a desert of traffic on a hot summer day. As the cars line up for miles upon miles, bumper to bumper, waiting to get to Cape Cod destinations, smart cyclists are already on the trails of this 1,000-plus-acre conservation area that offers some of the best mountain biking in the state.

The trails aren't particularly technical, but they'll challenge your aerobic fitness on the short, steep ascents and descents. One minute you're in low gear puffing up a hill, and the next minute you're bouncing off rocks down a steep slope. Most of the time, though, you're twisting through soft pine-covered trails, sliding between slender tree trunks and wondering which way to turn at the upcoming fork in the trail.

This is really fun riding, great for intermediate riders who want a break from the rocky, muddy trails of New England's interior.

A designated 16-mile single-track Trail of Tears is signposted with red and white mile markers. It's not always easy to follow, and up-to-date trail maps are hard to come by. It seems as if new paths are being created all the time, and it's very easy to get lost. There are three types of markers—the red and white Trail of Tears signs, brown signs with white arrows, and small circular patches with reflective arrows. In general, the best bet is to follow what appears to be the main trail—it's usually a little

The Trail of Tears offers Cape Cod cyclists a single-track break from the often-crowded beachfront roads and rail trails.

© CHRIS BERNARD

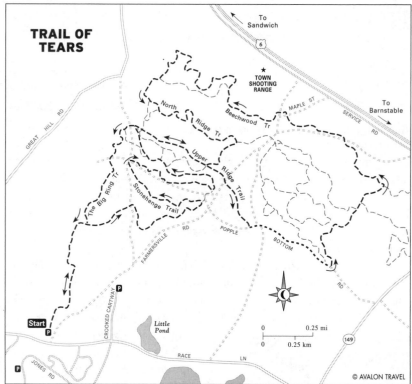

sandier and more packed down. Newer trails are more loamy and have more pine coverage.

This route follows most of the Trail of Tears, starting on some tight single-track with some fun downs and ups on the way to the Walker Point lookout platform. A few rocky patches mix in with the pine trails as you work your way east. The northeast corner is more sandy and you'll ride parallel to the power lines until returning to deeper, leafier forested areas in the northwest corner. Bring a GPS unit if you have one, and be prepared to get lost.

For more information and to obtain a trail map, contact the Barnstable Conservation Commission, 200 Main Street, Hyannis, MA 02601, 508/862-4093, www.town.barnstable.ma.us.

Options

To extend this ride, take a sharp left around Mile 5.8 onto a single-track, called the Broken Arrow Trail, which crisscrosses an area known as the Field of Dreams.

At marker 7.4 turn right, then left at Mile 8.2 to rejoin the main route directions at Mile 6.2.

Locals' Tip: Barnstable Restaurant and Tavern (3176 Main Street, Barnstable, MA 02630, 508/362-235, www.barnstablerestaurant.com) is a local cornerstone, well worth a visit.

Places to Stay: The staff at the Lamb and Lion (2504 Main Street, West Barnstable, MA 02668, 508/362-6823, www.lambandlion.com) bills it as the warmth of an award-winning Cape Cod inn with the spirit of a small luxury hotel. See if they're right.

Driving Directions

From points east and west, take MA-6 to exit 5, MA-149. Drive south on MA-149 for about 1.5 miles; at the intersection, turn right onto Race Lane. Drive 1.8 miles and turn right onto Farmersville Road. Look for the sign for West Barnstable Conservation Area. A gravel parking lot is large enough for about a dozen cars. A trail map is posted at the trailhead, and there is a white Trail of Tears marker. There are no facilities here or at the other two parking lots for the conservation area. Supplies can be found in West Barnstable, Barnstable, and Hyannis; the closest bike shops are in Hyannis.

Route Directions

0.0 START from parking lot.

0.7 Turn RIGHT at the T junction.

0.8 Turn RIGHT at the fork.

1.0 Stay STRAIGHT across the intersection (with wider dirt track) onto single-track.

1.7 Turn LEFT at the intersection.

2.2 Come to a five-way intersection. Look for the single-track going STRAIGHT across the intersection, across a dirt road.

2.8 Turn LEFT at junction.

3.2 Continue STRAIGHT past Spur 2 and Spur 1.

3.4 Arrive at Walker Point lookout platform (you'll see a 3.4-mile marker).

3.4 Continue STRAIGHT at next marker (ignore two trails on left).

3.4 Cross a paved road and turn LEFT, then immediately RIGHT.

3.5 Come to a four-way intersection and go RIGHT (this is marked as a three-way intersection on most trail maps; the newest trail is the one straight ahead). At the next intersection, go RIGHT (ignore small trail on left).

3.6 Continue STRAIGHT at marker, uphill.

4.1 Come to a five-way intersection and go STRAIGHT across (ignore one trail on left and two trails on right; this is marked as a four-way intersection on most trail maps).

4.2 Turn RIGHT onto road, then make an immediate LEFT onto single-track trail.

4.5 Cross road, go STRAIGHT.

4.7 Cross road, go STRAIGHT.

4.9 Turn LEFT at fork and continue STRAIGHT on main trail, ignoring side trails.

5.2 Turn RIGHT onto wide trail.

5.3 Turn LEFT onto dirt road.

5.8 OPTION: Sharp LEFT onto a Broken Arrow Trail and follow the option directions.

6.0 Turn LEFT off wide path onto single-track.

6.2 Go under power lines.

6.3 Stay STRAIGHT across dirt road.

6.7 Turn RIGHT at fork in trail, follow signs.

7.1 Turn LEFT at Trail of Tears sign (marked 11.8).

7.8 Turn LEFT at intersection.

7.8 Turn LEFT at fork.

8.0 Turn RIGHT at intersection.

8.5 Turn LEFT at intersection.

8.7 Trail loops to RIGHT following trail marker.

8.8 Turn LEFT at intersection with wider trail.

8.9 Go STRAIGHT under power lines.

8.9 Turn LEFT back onto single-track trail.

9.0 Turn LEFT at fork.

9.1 Turn LEFT (carrying on main trail).

9.8 Turn RIGHT at fork.

10.0 Turn RIGHT at the five-way intersection.

10.5 Continue STRAIGHT at the four-way intersection, then RIGHT at fork.

10.6 Turn LEFT uphill at fork.

10.8 Continue STRAIGHT across dirt road.

10.9 Follow arrow to RIGHT.

11.2 Turn RIGHT at intersection, then LEFT at unmarked trail to go back to parking lot. (Don't miss this turn!)

12.0 Return to parking lot.

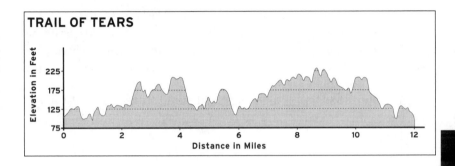

18 CAPE COD RAIL TRAIL
South Dennis to Wellfleet

PAVED BIKE PATH

Difficulty: 2   **Total Distance:** 44 miles

Riding Time: 5 hours   **Elevation Gain:** 398 feet

Summary: A well-thought-out and well-used paved trail cutting through the heart of Cape Cod, this ride will please everyone.

When you think Cape Cod, what do you think of? Maybe it's the beaches or the islands. Maybe it's the seafood, or the fishing, or whale watching. Maybe it's the Kennedys. If you've been to the Cape during the summer season, chances are good you also think of the traffic—there's one main road to and from the Cape, and it's well traveled.

Similarly, the beaches can be crowded, and the small towns, while delightful, can also frustrate with their lines and the people milling about from shop to shop and restaurant to restaurant.

This trail is not immune to those crowds, and it can get busy with cyclists, walkers, joggers, and other trail users, but it will nevertheless offer some respite from the masses—especially if you choose your time to ride wisely. Mornings the

The Cape Cod Rail Trail is well-marked and well-traveled, and provides a safe ride along a good length of the Cape on more than 20 miles of scenic bike path.

trail is slow to fill, and weekdays seem better than weekends. Best of all is the off-season, either late spring or early fall, before the weather turns.

Stretching 22 miles from South Dennis to Wellfleet, this trail is paved and flat throughout. Turn around whenever you like to shorten it, or spend a lazy day exploring its length. You'll find plenty of places to stop and explore as you go. Just 3.2 miles in to the trail, you'll come to a unique feature—a rotary, or traffic circle, for bicycles, where the Cape Cod Rail Trail meets the 8-mile Harwich-Chatham rail trail. In the center of the rotary, a grassy area contains picnic tables and bike racks, a signboard shows maps of the trails, and the trails intersect without difficulty thanks to the roundabout traffic flow.

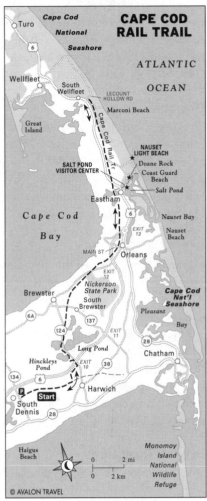

To shorten the trip, start at Nickerson State Park, which also makes a good rest stop about halfway along the trail. Bike rental shops are at many points along the route if you don't have your own bike with you. (The park also offers mountain bike trails.)

Along the route, you'll pass by the shores of Swan Pond, cross many roads, and ride through a few tunnels. You'll find a string of pretty ponds, all of which look inviting for swimming. After some suburban scenery, there's a scenic stretch of typical Cape lowland scrub pine forest, interrupted briefly by the town of Brewster. On either side of Orleans, you'll ride through marshlands, which offer birding opportunities.

Just before the turnaround point, you'll pass an opportunity for a side trip to Marconi National Seashore. The trail ends off LeCount Hollow Road in Wellfleet, where you'll find picnic tables, restrooms, supplies, a general store, a bike shop, and free parking.

For more information, contact the Cape Cod Rail Trail at the Massachusetts

Division of State Parks and Recreation, 508/896-3491, www.mass.gov/dem/parks/ccrt.htm. For more information about the Cape Cod National Seashore, contact the National Park Service, 99 Marconi Station Site Road, Wellfleet, MA 02667, 508/349-3785, www.nps.gov/caco.

Options

To extend this trip with a scenic spur trip from the Cape Cod National Seashore Salt Pond Visitor Center at Mile 17.5, turn right (east) on the Seashore bike trail, following it through the woods, across the bridge, and through the marsh until it ends at the old Coast Guard station on the seashore. You'll find beach access, lots of bike parking, restrooms, and outdoor showers.

Locals' Tip: Along the Cape Cod Rail Trail, you'll pass many opportunities for ice cream, hot dogs, and other snacks, but among the best is Arnold's (3580 State Highway/MA-6, Eastham, MA 02642, 508/255-2575, www.arnolds restaurant.com). The trail runs past the parking lot, about 15 miles into the ride, which hosts air-conditioned restrooms and minigolf. The restaurant offers a full-service lobster and clam bar, and there's excellent homemade ice cream at the outdoor windows and picnic tables.

Places to Stay: The Ocean Park Inn (3900 MA-6, Eastham, MA 02642, 508/255-1132, www.capecodopi.com) is a no-frills, affordable roadside hotel near the midpoint of the Cape Cod Rail Trail, just minutes from the trail. It offers bike parking and a pool. If you have a roof rack for your bikes, don't trust the overhead clearance signs on the front entrance, however—park by the street and bring your bikes into the main lot on their own.

Driving Directions

From anywhere on Cape Cod, take MA-6 to exit 9 (West Harwich and Dennisport). Drive 0.5 mile on MA-134 South. You will go through two traffic lights. Look carefully for the trailhead sign on the left, just past the Cranberry Square shopping plaza. You'll find a parking lot and trail sign but no facilities here. Bike rentals are available at Barbara's Bike and Sport shop, just past the parking lot. Supplies are available all along MA-134 and along the bike path. Bike shops can be found in Brewster, Eastham, North Eastham, North Harwich, Orleans, South Dennis, and South Wellfleet.

Route Directions

0.0 START at Dennis trailhead.

4.4 Gentle incline on bridge over MA-6.

4.7 *Access point and parking lot at Headwaters Drive on the shore of Hinckleys Pond.*

5.2 *Supplies and ice cream available at Pleasant Lake General Store, with bike racks, picnic tables, and portable toilets.*

8.0 *Access point and parking lot along MA-137 in South Brewster. Picnic tables, bike rentals and shops, restaurants, and ice-cream stands available.*

10.7 *Parking with bike rentals, restaurants, and ice-cream stand.*

11.0 Nickerson State Park. *Free parking, picnic tables, lots of side bike trails, campground, and facilities available.*

12.7 Come off bike path onto town road.

12.8 Turn RIGHT onto West Road, cross bridge over MA-6, and turn LEFT to return to rail trail.

13.7 Cross Main Street, Orleans. *Access point with free parking, supplies, restaurants, ice-cream shops, and Orleans Cycles.*

14.1 Bridge over MA-6. (Beginner riders may want to dismount and walk across the bridge, which has a gentle incline.)

17.1 OPTION: For Cape Cod National Seashore Salt Pond Visitor Center, turn RIGHT onto Locust Road, LEFT onto Salt Pond Road, cross MA-6 with caution at traffic lights, and enter the parking area. *Parking, information, maps, and restrooms available.*

22.0 Arrive at Wellfleet trailhead on LeCount Hollow Road. TURN AROUND and retrace route.

44.0 Return to South Dennis trailhead.

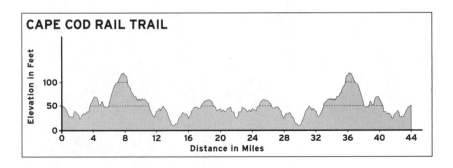

19 PROVINCE LANDS LOOP   BEST ◖
Provincetown

PAVED BIKE PATH

Difficulty: 3   **Total Distance:** 8.9 miles

Riding Time: 1-2 hours   **Elevation Gain:** 260 feet

Summary: A fun ride through a one-of-a-kind town in a spectacular setting.

Even if you've spent your entire life on the coast of Massachusetts, unless it's been in Provincetown, the landscape here will surprise you. It's immediately clear as you drive into town on MA-6. Between the scrub pine and the giant sand dunes, it just doesn't look like any other part of the state's coastline.

And then there's the town itself, and the people who inhabit and visit it, all of which add up to a charismatic spot that's full of surprises. What better way to explore it than on a bike?

Situated at the very tip of Cape Cod, Provincetown traces its roots back to the Mayflower pilgrims. Originally a fishing and whaling town, through the years it's also become known as, among other things, an artists' colony, with a high number of writers and artists living and working there. Notable residents, past and present, include Norman Mailer, Jackson Pollock, and Tennessee Williams. It's also a tourist-friendly town, and on any given day during the summer, the population swells over its year-round numbers.

Before settling down to enjoy some local Wellfleet oysters at a waterfront bar, work up an appetite by pedaling the Province Lands route, which starts at the visitors

You can find people − and bikes − of all kinds in this touristy land's-end town.

© CHRIS BERNARD

center and descends toward Race Point, where you'll find stunningly high sand dunes. Ride through low scrubby pines and bushes in sandy soil, through a low tunnel and a little incline, and toward Herring Cove Beach. The trail comes out at the far end of the parking lot, with seasonal restrooms at the far end. This is a lovely beach, with beach roses and other low-lying shrubs lining the sand dunes.

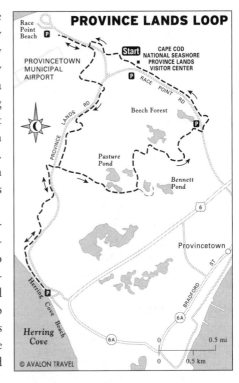

From there you'll ride a steep section followed by a winding downhill past Pasture Pond and into Beech Forest and a totally different ecosystem of trees, swamp, and marshland. On a final short, steep hill, you'll find panoramic views of the dunes and ocean just before you reach the visitors center and the end of the trail.

The Province Lands Visitor Center (daily 9 A.M.–5 P.M., May 1–Oct. 31) offers programs, information, an observation deck, an amphitheater, exhibits, restrooms, a pay phone, a small book and gift store, and trail maps. Parking is free. Restrooms with flush toilets and sinks are available in the parking area year-round. For more information about the Cape Cod National Seashore and the Province Lands Visitor Center, contact the National Park Service, 99 Marconi Station Site Road, Wellfleet, MA 02667, 508/349-3785 or 508/487-1256, www.nps.gov/caco (open May 1–Oct. 31).

Options

This ride can be linked with the Cape Cod Rail Trail. From the Provincelands Visitors Center, head left on Race Point Road and cross MA-6 and MA-6A. Turn left on Commercial Street and then right on 6A/Shore Road. At Mile 7.0, merge with MA-6 and turn right on Castle Road. Castle Road becomes Truro Center Road. Turn right on Depot Road and bear left on Old Country Road. At Mile 14.3, bear left on Bound Brook Island Road and in one 1 mile reach Pole Dike Road; stay straight. Turn left on West Main Street, then bear left on Long Pond Road and cross MA-6. In about 2 miles, turn right at the shore on Ocean View

Drive. In another 2 miles, turn right on Lawrence Road, which becomes LeCount Hollow Road. End at the Cape Cod Rail Trail parking area.

Locals' Tip: Try the Wellfleet oyster shooters—oysters in a shot glass with all the mixings for a Bloody Mary—or any of the other seafood offerings at the Squealing Pig Pub and Oyster Bar (335 Commercial Street, Provincetown, MA 02657, 508/487-5804, www.squealingpigptown.com).

Places to Stay: Stay right downtown in the heart of it at Surfside Hotel and Suites (543 Commercial Street, Provincetown, MA 02657, 508/487-1726, www.surfsideinn.cc).

Driving Directions

From anywhere on Cape Cod, take MA-6 toward Provincetown. You'll pass the intersection with MA-6A. Drive 1.5 miles farther and turn right at the traffic light onto Race Point Road. You'll see signs for Province Lands Visitor Center. Drive 1.4 miles and arrive at the visitors center and parking area. Supplies and bike shops are available in Provincetown.

Route Directions

0.0 START at the trailhead in front of the visitor center.

0.5 Cross the road and come to a T junction. Go RIGHT.

0.9 Arrive at Race Point Beach parking area. *Restrooms available. There is a $3 beach entrance fee for bicyclists.* TURN AROUND.

3.0 Turn RIGHT at intersection toward Herring Cove.

4.1 Arrive at Herring Cove Beach parking area. *Restrooms available. There is a $3 beach entrance fee for bicyclists.* TURN AROUND.

5.3 Continue STRAIGHT at intersection toward Beech Forest.

6.1 *Optional 0.5-mile side trip to Bennett Pond.*

7.4 Arrive at Beech Forest parking lot. *Picnic area and restrooms available.* Turn LEFT, following signs for Province Lands Visitor Center, and cross Race Point Road to continue on bike path.

8.9 END at visitors center parking lot and trailhead.

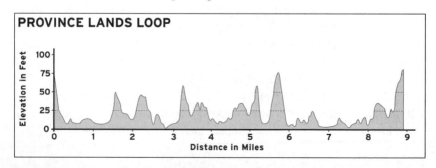

PROVINCE LANDS LOOP

RHODE ISLAND

© CHRIS BERNARD

BEST BIKE RIDES

Rhode Island may be the smallest state in the

nation, but what it lacks in size it makes up for in spirit. That spirit is on display for cyclists at nearly every turn.

By way of example, consider the route that winds counterclockwise around Aquidneck Island from the posh destination town of Newport. It's a near-perfect blend of artificial and natural beauty, as the gigantic, well-appointed mansions lined up like pearls on a necklace tower over dramatic cliffs at the ocean's edge. On a single ride, cyclists are treated to spectacular wave breaks punctuated by surfers, gorgeous beaches, and rural roads. It all starts and ends at a historic waterfront fort on the edge of the trendy, artsy, bustling downtown with its clapboard houses and endless bars, shops, and restaurants.

Moving west across the southern part of the state, you'll find an array of rides exploring Conanicut Island, Point Judith and the surrounding fishing villages and shoreline, the enviable neighborhood of Watch Hill, and the shady, rolling hills of the farmlands that hem the Connecticut border.

Other parts of the state hold their own as well, with the well-planned

Blackstone River Bikeway, which eventually will connect Worcester, Massachusetts, with central Rhode Island, and the East Bay Bike Path that runs along the edge of Narragansett Bay. The state also contains numerous off-road rides ranging in terrain and difficulty. The New London Turnpike is a stretch of abandoned road that makes for an easy, fun ride in the dirt, while the trails at Arcadia Management Area and Burlingame and Lincoln Woods State Parks offer single-track to challenge even the most jaded riders. If you're looking for something in between, try the undulating Trestle Trail or the scenic Worden Pond ride.

If Rhode Island is the jewel of New England, as some people claim, then perhaps the Block Island ride is the jewel of Rhode Island biking. Plan a weekend ferry trip to the island, where bikes are the preferred mode of transport, and ride a peaceful loop past sprawling beaches, lush fields, and rocky coastlines with stunning views of the Atlantic, winding your way through the town and its distinctive Victorian architecture.

Because of the state's small size, it's easy to pack a few rides into a short period of time, but don't get carried away – allow yourself enough downtime to explore all the state has to offer off the bike, as well.

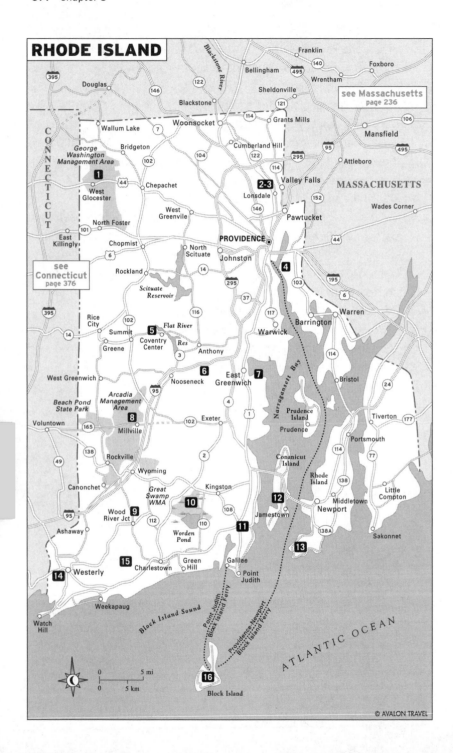

RIDE NAME	DIFFICULTY	DISTANCE	TIME	ELEVATION	PAGE
1 Bits of the Walkabout	4	9.5 mi	2-3 hr	410 ft	316
2 Blackstone River Bikeway	1	11.6 mi	1.5 hr	100 ft	319
3 Land of Lincoln	2	4.2 mi	1 hr	330 ft	323
4 East Bay Bike Path	1	27.2 mi	2-3 hr	17 ft	326
5 Trestle Trail	3	14.4 mi	2.5-3 hr	400 ft	329
6 New London Turnpike	2	13.2 mi	2 hr	574 ft	332
7 Goddard Park	1	4.9 mi	1 hr	220 ft	335
8 Breakheart and Shelter Trails	4	8.7 mi	2 hr	515 ft	338
9 Oh, Chariho!	3	37.9 mi	2-3 hr	1,027 ft	342
10 Worden Pond Loop	2	8.7 mi	1.5 hr	205 ft	346
11 A Point, Two Towers, and the Pier	2	29.1 mi	2-3 hr	466 ft	349
12 Conanicut Island Loop	3	21.6 mi	2-2.5 hr	1,070 ft	353
13 Newport	2	24.7 mi	1.5-2 hr	223 ft	357
14 Watch Hill	3	26.7 mi	2-3 hr	430 ft	362
15 Vin Gormley Trail	4	8 mi	2 hr	315 ft	366
16 Once Around the Block	2	16.5 mi	2 hr	155 ft	370

1 BITS OF THE WALKABOUT
George Washington Management Area, Burrillville

SINGLE-TRACK, DIRT ROADS

Difficulty: 4	**Total Distance:** 9.5 miles
Riding Time: 2-3 hours	**Elevation Gain:** 410 feet

Summary: This rocky single-track offers a challenge for skilled mountain bikers, with dirt road options for the rest of us.

The New England Mountain Biking Association (NEMBA) warns that there are only two kinds of riding in the George Washington State Park and Management Area: technically challenging rock garden single-track and dirt roads. If you like both those types of rides, you'll like this route—it starts and ends on single-track and samples the dirt roads in between, but it's not for the faint of heart.

In 1965, the state forestry division entertained 300 Australian sailors waiting for their ship by encouraging them to help clear an 8-mile walking trail. The sailors apparently had a blast, mingling with the locals and throwing Saturday night barbecues that are still talked about. The state named the trail in honor of the Australian aboriginal tradition of "going walkabout."

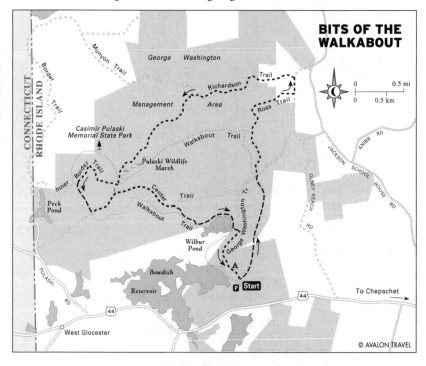

BITS OF THE WALKABOUT

© AVALON TRAVEL

The bike trail winds its way in and around this densely forested wildlife management area, overlapping only bits of the actual Walkabout Trail. You can explore the entire trail or use a trail map to easily find other routes through the management area.

The ride starts with a fairly challenging stretch of single-track through some wet, swampy areas, then leaves it behind in favor of wide dirt roads. From there, you make a loop—first across a little covered bridge and then on some great, woodsy single-track—before heading back on those same dirt roads. The real challenge lies in one last side trip on the Walkabout Trail—narrow, rooty, swampy, steep, and extremely rocky in places. The payback is views of the beautiful and secluded Wilbur Pond.

The trail-marking system on the Walkabout Trail proper uses colored blazes, and each of three colors marks a different length trail. Blue is 2 miles long, red is 6 miles, and orange is 8 miles. If you want to explore more by riding the trail itself, which can be difficult and challenging, use the blaze system to find your way, or use one of the excellent trail maps.

For more information, contact the George Washington Management Area, 401/568-2013, www.riparks.com.

Options

For a shorter ride that cuts out the challenging final section and limits itself mostly to dirt roads, at Mile 5.4 turn left onto Center Trail (unmarked). Then at Mile 6.9, turn right onto the dirt road, and turn right at Mile 7.9, into the parking area.

This ride is a reasonable drive from Blackstone River Bikeway and Land of Lincoln.

Locals' Tip: The area is a little remote, and there aren't a ton of options for food nearby. You could drive to Pasacoag and sample the wares there, or you could bring a lunch for after your ride, which is the recommended option. Don't forget something to drink.

Places to Stay: Spend a night in one of the 45 primitive campsites in the management area on the shores of the Bowdish reservoir, and ride the trails right from your tent. Sites can be reserved by contacting George Washington Campground (2185 Putnam Pike, Chepachet, RI 02814, 401/568-6700, www.riparks .com/georgewashcamp.htm, Apr. 10–Oct. 12).

Driving Directions

From Providence and points east, take RI-295 to RI-44 West (exit 7B). Drive approximately 14 miles and look for the sign for the George Washington Camping Area. Turn right into the camping area and follow the main road for about 0.3 mile. Turn left into the parking area for the beach. There is a beach house with facilities, water fountains, and a pay phone. Trail maps are available in a box by the information kiosk.

There is a small day-use fee in summer. The campground offers primitive campsites and a few camping shelters for a modest fee. Supplies are available in Chepachet or West Gloucester. The closest bike shop is in Putnam, Connecticut.

Route Directions

0.0 Directly across the road from the parking lot, begin on the trail marked with blue, orange, and red blazes.

0.6 Continue STRAIGHT, following orange and red blazes.

1.5 Turn RIGHT onto Center Trail (unmarked).

1.6 Turn LEFT onto Ross Trail (unmarked), through red gate marked GW7.

2.6 Continue STRAIGHT across clearing.

2.7 Continue STRAIGHT through gate marked GW8.

2.8 Turn LEFT onto dirt road.

3.0 Turn LEFT onto Richardson Trail (unmarked), following red arrows.

4.1 Turn LEFT at three-way intersection.

5.3 *A left turn onto the orange-blazed trail makes for a side trip to the lovely Pulaski Wildlife Marsh.*

5.4 OPTION: Turn LEFT onto Center Trail (unmarked) and follow option directions.

5.5 Turn RIGHT onto Inner Border Trail (unmarked), through red gate marked GW10.

5.6 Continue STRAIGHT through covered bridge.

6.0 Turn LEFT onto Walkabout Trail, marked by orange blazes.

6.5 Turn LEFT onto orange-blazed trail.

6.9 Turn LEFT onto dirt road.

7.1 Turn RIGHT onto Center Trail (unmarked).

7.7 Turn RIGHT onto Cut Across Trail (unmarked), following red blazes.

7.8 Turn LEFT onto Walkabout Trail, following red and orange blazes.

9.0 Turn RIGHT onto dirt road.

9.5 Turn RIGHT into parking area.

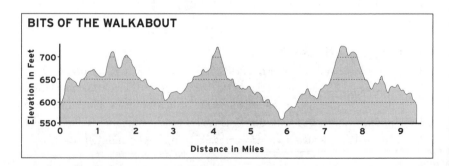

BITS OF THE WALKABOUT

Elevation in Feet

Distance in Miles

2 BLACKSTONE RIVER BIKEWAY   BEST (

Lincoln and Cumberland

PAVED BIKE PATH

Difficulty: 1   **Total Distance:** 11.6 miles

Riding Time: 1.5 hours   **Elevation Gain:** 100 feet

Summary: This trail is everything a purpose-built bike trail should be, offering smooth roads, beautiful scenery, and tranquility.

There are a lot of designated bike routes in this country, and some are better than others. The Blackstone River Bikeway is one of the better ones. The first step in a path that will eventually run nearly 50 miles and connect Providence, Rhode Island, with Worcester, Massachusetts, this almost 12-mile stretch is isolated, paved, flat, and beautiful, and it only has one road crossing to worry about.

The bikeway follows the Blackstone Canal and railway, and considering that this area was once a major cog in the wheels of the Industrial Revolution, it's quite a pretty ride, offering lush vegetation, tasteful stone markers, and good scenery. There's plenty to see. The canal has tinges of industry mixed with hints of wildlife and you might see, for example, a heron flying past a smokestack.

This path is suitable for all riders. The biggest challenge it offers is dodging other riders, in-line skaters, pedestrians, and strollers, but even at its busiest it never gets too crowded.

You don't need to be fit or fast to ride the Blackstone River Bikeway, which is slated to expand in coming years until it connects Worcester, Massachusetts, with Rhode Island.

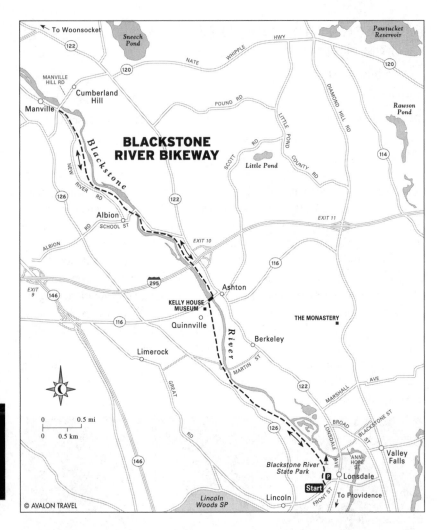

When the East Coast Greenway is completed—that's the proposed bike trail from Florida to Maine—it will include this ride. To check on the progress of the bikeway, contact the Blackstone Valley Chamber of Commerce, 110 Church Street, Whitinsville, MA 01588, 508/234-9090, www.blackstoneriverbikeway.com.

Options

Leave the tranquility of the path for the roads of suburban Rhode Island, including a long, steep hill into the village of Cumberland. Once you're on RI-120, you'll have some nice views of Sneech Pond. Diamond Hill Road gives you a taste of the rural, as you pass a vineyard and farm stand, but then you're back into a 3-mile-long commercial stretch and the historic mill towns of Lonsdale and Valley Falls. This ride is for you only if you don't mind riding in traffic; definitely avoid rush-hour riding. The total distance is 15.9 miles and can be accomplished in an hour or two (elevation gain 470 feet).

Follow the main route directions for 5.8 miles. At Mile 5.8, the bike path ends. Bear left out of the parking area and turn right onto New River Road. Turn right onto Manville Hill Road and in 0.8 mile, turn right again onto RI-120. Get immediately into the left lane. Turn left onto Nate Whipple Highway (RI-120) and in 2.7 miles, turn right onto Diamond Hill Road (RI-114). At Mile 12.3, you'll pass a busy entrance ramp for RI-295; take extreme care. In a little over 2 miles, turn right onto Blackstone Street and then left onto Broad Street (unmarked). Soon, you'll turn right onto Ann-Hope Street; get into the left lane to turn left onto Lonsdale Avenue. Take a right onto Front Street and another right into Blackstone River State Park, returning to the parking area.

Another option is to park at the Blackstone River State Park Visitor Center (open 24 hours) off I-295 North between exits 9 and 10, which has facilities, information, and food. Tuesday afternoons in the summer, there's also a farmers market. A spur trail leads to the bikeway around Mile 2.5 on the route below. This ride also runs near Lincoln State Park, home to Land of Lincoln, and is accessible from the park.

Locals' Tip: Fado Irish Pub (100 Twin River Road, Lincoln, RI 02865, 401/475-8500, www.fadoirishpub.com) is an excellent place to unwind after a ride with a cold drink.

Places to Stay: You'll find a host of hotels nearby, including the Courtyard by Marriott (636 George Washington Highway, Lincoln, RI 02865, 401/333-3400, www.marriott.com).

Driving Directions

From points north, take RI-295 to exit 9A, then RI-146 south toward Lincoln. Drive 3.2 miles and take the Breakneck Hill Road/RI-123 exit. Turn left off the exit ramp onto RI-123 East. Drive 2.9 miles and turn left into Blackstone River State Park.

From Providence, take I-95 to exit 23, RI-146 North. Drive 5 miles and take the Breakneck Hill Road/RI-123 exit. Turn right off the exit ramp onto RI-123 East. Drive approximately 2.8 miles and turn left into Blackstone River State Park. Supplies are available in Lincoln and Lonsdale. The state park has no facilities, only parking lots and an information kiosk. The nearest bike shops are in Providence and East Providence.

Route Directions

0.0 Leave parking lot and start on bike path.

0.2 Bear RIGHT over bridge following bike path.

2.5 *The Kelly House Museum is a transportation history museum with pretty gardens.*

5.8 Bike path ends. TURN AROUND.

11.6 RETURN to parking area.

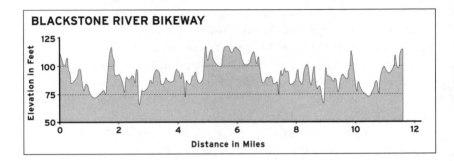

BLACKSTONE RIVER BIKEWAY

3 LAND OF LINCOLN
Lincoln Woods State Park

DIRT TRAILS AND SINGLE-TRACK

Difficulty: 2	**Total Distance:** 4.2 miles
Riding Time: 1 hour	**Elevation Gain:** 330 feet

Summary: These easy-to-moderate mountain bike trails are a rocky, rooty ride in the midst of an otherwise urban piece of the state.

Driving to Lincoln Woods State Park, you'll pass through parts of town that are decidedly urban, especially when held up against the image most people have of Rhode Island as a tiny, touristy New England state. Boarded-up stores, graffiti-marked walls, abandoned cars—and then you enter the park itself, and suddenly everything is green and lush and vivid and you feel like you've been dropped somewhere else entirely.

The park is well used. Picnic sites attract people looking for something more relaxing than the neighborhoods you drove through, ponds draw swimmers, boaters, and anglers, and the trails are used by cyclists, joggers, hikers, and dog walkers. Trails are less crowded in the fall, when the black flies are also mercifully gone, and you can ride until you're tired and only run into a handful of people.

After a while, you may be glad to run into people. The trails are fun to ride, but they're not well-marked, and it's easy to get lost—at least relatively lost, as

the Lincoln Woods

© CHRIS BERNARD

you'll always find your way back to the main road. It can be a challenge to follow a marked route on the trails, even with a map.

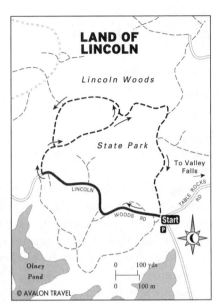

Here are the basics you need to know: The park is split into two halves, or "zones," with north-south Quinsnicket Road the divider. Because of conflicts among user groups, park management has designated all trails west of the road (zone A) as horse-only trails; trails east of the divider (zone B) are multiuse and suitable for bicycles. Don't stray across the road—you don't want to be the rider who wrecks it for everyone.

These trails vary from dirt roads to choked single-track and can be rocky and rooty with the occasional hill. The climbing never gets intense, and this sample route never gets too challenging. You'll pass a lot of spur trails that offer more difficult riding—don't be afraid to explore them.

For more information on the park, contact the Rhode Island State Parks Department, 2 Manchester Print Works Road, Lincoln, RI 02865, 401/723-7892, www.riparks.com/lincoln.htm.

Options

Download a trail map from the park website (www.riparks.com/lincoln.htm) to piece together longer rides, or just explore the trails on a whim as you pass them on this main route.

The Blackstone River Bikeway is accessible from the park.

Locals' Tip: Comfortable, familiar, and nondemanding, the Lodge Pub & Eatery (40 Breakneck Hill Road, Lincoln, RI 02865, 401/725-8510, www.the lodgepub.com) is the kind of place that, once you're inside, could be in any town in the United States.

Places to Stay: There's a slew of chain hotels in the area, especially in nearby Providence. Among them is the Marriot Courtyard (636 George Washington Highway, Lincoln, RI 02865, 401/333-3400).

Driving Directions

From I-95, take RI-146 north to the Lincoln Woods State Park/Breakneck Hill Road exit, and head east on Breakneck Hill Road/RI-123. Lincoln Woods State Park is about 3 miles down the road on the right (follow the signs). Information and maps are available at the office, on the left as you enter the park. There are several parking areas; to reach them, cross the bridge and bear left, then park at the next paved intersection. The bike path begins on the paved road heading to the right.

Route Directions

0.0 From the parking area, start down the paved road, keeping Olney Pond to your left.

0.4 Turn RIGHT onto the trail into the woods, heading east around Tablerock Hill. You'll pass several trail spurs—don't be afraid to explore, as most of them eventually work their way back to the main trail.

1.0 Bear LEFT. This trail loops counterclockwise onto Quinsnicket Hill and doubles back, reconnecting with the trail you rode in on.

2.7 Turn LEFT.

3.5 Bear RIGHT at intersection.

4.0 Bear LEFT on paved road.

4.2 END at parking area.

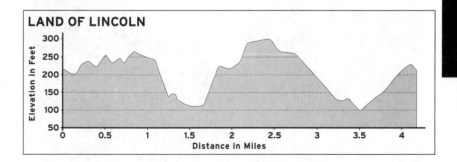

4 EAST BAY BIKE PATH   BEST ◖
Bristol to East Providence

PAVED BIKE PATH

Difficulty: 1   **Total Distance:** 27.2 miles

Riding Time: 2-3 hours   **Elevation Gain:** 17 feet

Summary: This rails-to-trails ride cuts through the city while providing a feeling of being somewhere entirely less urban.

Rhode Island seems to do bike paths right. Like the Blackstone River Bikeway, this route is what you want to find the first time you roll onto a bike path. The East Bay Bike Path somehow manages to slip through urban industrial areas while giving a sense of being in the countryside. You ride along the shore of Narragansett Bay and the Providence River, watching egrets fish in small marshy ponds on one side and waves crash against rocky islands on the other.

There are many access points to the wide, flat, smooth path and plenty of spots along the way for good side trips and picnics, making this a great ride to do with the kids. If you're in Providence, start in East Providence (don't start at the trailhead in India Point Park; it's no fun to cross the bridge over RI-195). You'll get a great breath of fresh air as you ride into the prevailing headwinds toward Bristol. It's a great city escape.

© CHRIS BERNARD

The East Bay Bike Path runs through Providence and the surrounding areas, offering excellent places to stop and rest or snack, like Roger Williams Park in the heart of the city.

If you're just visiting the Ocean State, start in the historic village of Bristol. This route makes an out-and-back from Bristol to Veterans Memorial Parkway in East Providence and then returns.

The path runs through leafy, lush, undeveloped areas and the villages of Warren and Barrington, but if there's a downside, it's the many road crossings—and two bridge crossings—with uneven surfaces. Otherwise the only traffic you'll need to mind are dog walkers, in-line skaters, pedestrians, and other cyclists.

For more information on the bike path, visit the Rhode Island Department of Transportation's website, www .dot.state.ri.us/WebTran/bikeri.html. For information on visiting the area, contact the East Bay Tourism Council, 654 Metacom Avenue, Warren, RI 02885, 401/245-0750 or 888/278-9948, www.eastbayritourism.com.

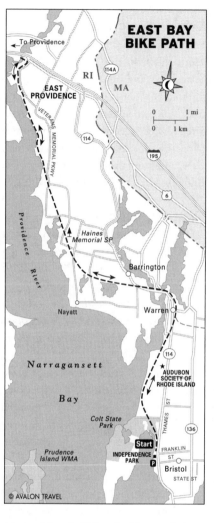

Options

To cut the ride to just under 18 miles, begin in Bristol and follow the route to Haines Memorial Park and back.

This ride is near Blackstone River Bikeway and Land of Lincoln. Eventual plans call for connecting this path with the Blackstone River Bikeway.

Locals' Tip: After riding locally, try locally brewed beer at Trinity Brewhouse (186 Fountain Street, Providence, RI 02903, 401/453-2337, www.trinitybrew house.com), where the food is also good.

Places to Stay: Like most cities, Providence has plenty of overnight options, but one of the fancier is the Edgewood Manor B&B (232 Norwood Avenue, Providence, RI 02905, 401/781-0099), not far from the bike path.

Driving Directions

From Providence and points north, take RI-195 for about 7.5 miles to exit 2 (RI-136). Follow RI-136 through Warren for 7.2 miles. In Bristol, turn right onto State Street and right again at the street's end, onto Thames Street.

From Newport, take RI-114 for approximately 13 miles, to Bristol. In the center of Bristol, turn left onto State Street and right at the end of the street, onto Thames Street. Independence Park is at the corner of Thames and Franklin Streets. A large parking lot is at the harborside park. Supplies are available in Bristol, Warren, and Barrington, and there are a few seasonal ice-cream stands along the bike path. You'll find bike shops and rentals in Providence, East Providence, Riverside, and Warren.

Route Directions

0.0 START on the bike path from Independence Park.

1.0 *A left turn here leads to a highly recommended optional 3.5-mile side trip to Colt State Park, a beautiful, vast oceanside park with bike trails, facilities, and picnic tables.*

2.8 *A right turn leads to an optional side trip through a wildlife refuge and environmental center belonging to the Audubon Society of Rhode Island. There is a bike rack next to the path where you can leave your bike and walk the trails.*

3.9 *Supplies available as you go through Warren.*

4.3 Cross bridge over Warren River.

5.5 Cross bridge over Barrington River.

6.0 *Supplies available as you go through Barrington.*

8.8 *A left turn leads to an optional side trip to Haines Memorial State Park, with picnic tables and restrooms.*

13.6 Arrive at the second of two bike path parking lots along Veterans Memorial Parkway. TURN AROUND.

27.2 Return to Independence Park parking area.

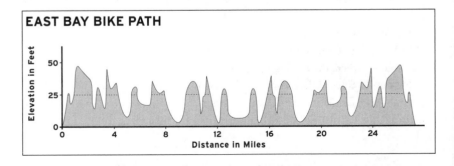

5 TRESTLE TRAIL
Coventry Center

UNPAVED RAIL TRAIL

Difficulty: 3

Riding Time: 2.5-3 hours

Total Distance: 14.4 miles

Elevation Gain: 400 feet

Summary: A roller-coaster of a rail trail with rough, unpaved surfaces, this ride provides a surprising challenge for recreational bike riders.

A kid on a BMX bike might mistake this trail for heaven—it's a reasonable distance to ride, removed from traffic, and in stretches throughout its length it undulates in endless small rollers no more than a pedal stroke long. It rides like a rough-around-the-edges BMX track. But that doesn't mean it's not a great trail for other people to ride, as well. In fact, this trail offers something for everyone but families with the smallest of children, as the path's condition can at times be a bit too challenging.

This trail follows a former railway bed that bisects the state. While there are plans to pave sections of it to extend the Coventry Greenway, a bike path to its east, it's a rough-and-tumble ride in fair to poor conditions that offers a fun trip through some scenic, remote areas.

Start from the eastern end of the Trestle Trail in Coventry Center. The trailhead

The trail's undulations rise and drop in a seemingly endless series of lumps that, after a rainfall, can be marked with puddles gathering in the low spots.

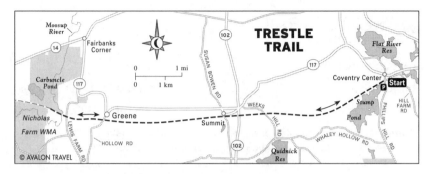

is easy to miss, in an unmarked dirt pulloff angled weirdly to the street. Once you're parked, though, and begin riding, you're rewarded with views of Stump Pond and a cool trestle bridge to cross. Then the lumps begin.

About 1.5 miles into the ride, there's a small stream to cross, followed by a few tricky road crossings and a pretty marshy stretch. There's one more elevated trestle bridge (which may make some riders nervous enough to walk across) before the dirt trails around Carbuncle Pond begin. Explore the shores of this popular fishing spot before turning around and heading back.

Mountain bikes will handle this trail without difficulty, as will cyclocross bikes. Hybrid bikes may struggle a bit.

For more information, contact the Greenways Alliance of Rhode Island, 31 Stanchion Street, Jamestown, RI 02835, www.rigreenways.org.

Options

This ride is near New London Turnpike and Breakheart and Shelter Trails. If overnighting in the area, consider exploring these trails for a few days' worth of exciting off-road riding.

Locals' Tip: While Pete's Pizza Plus (21 Hill Farm Road, Coventry, RI 02816, 401/397-3323) may not inspire you to write home, it's decent pizza just feet from the trail parking area and a great way to end a ride.

Places to Stay: The Wingate Inn (4 Universal Boulevard, Coventry, RI 02816, 401/821-3322, www.winewengland.com) is centrally located, comfortable, and affordable.

Driving Directions

From points east or west, take I-95 to exit 6 (RI-3 North). Drive 1 mile and turn left at the traffic light onto Harkney Hill Road. Drive 0.1 mile and turn right onto Hill Farm Road. After approximately 3 miles, you will reach a junction with Phillips Hill Road. The small dirt parking area is across Phillips Hill Road.

Supplies are available in the small village of Coventry Center and at the general store in Summit, and there's a bike shop in Coventry.

Route Directions

0.0 START at the trailhead from the parking area.

1.6 Cross a small stream.

3.2 Cross RI-102 and pick up trail on the other side.

3.6 Go STRAIGHT on paved road.

3.7 Pick up dirt trail STRAIGHT ahead.

5.8 Trestle bridge (some riders may want to walk across).

6.1 Cross Hollow Road (unmarked dirt road).

6.8 Cross unmarked dirt road.

7.2 *A right turn onto a wide dirt trail will take you to the Carbuncle Pond area, if you choose to explore it.* TURN AROUND.

14.4 Return to parking area.

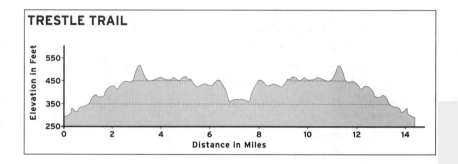

6 NEW LONDON TURNPIKE
West Warwick to Exeter

DIRT AND GRAVEL ROAD

Difficulty: 2   **Total Distance:** 13.2 miles

Riding Time: 2 hours   **Elevation Gain:** 574 feet

Summary: Once a major throughway, the turnpike is now a rough dirt road ideal for off-road touring.

Back in the days when fewer cars plied the roads, roads were constructed differently. Foreseeing the traffic demands was an impossibility, and consequently, some of today's roads are ill-suited for the number of vehicles that travel them daily. Others are constantly under construction in an attempt to retrofit them to the need.

In Rhode Island, as traffic demands grew, new highways were built, and others were relocated to connect with them. In some cases, the old routes were abandoned, either wholly or in part. Such is the case with the New London Turnpike.

The ends of the road are still in use, though not as the major thoroughfare they once were. But for a seven-mile stretch, the New London Turnpike is a rough dirt road that seems purpose-built for bicycles.

On its north end it runs through the state's Big River Management Area, where it connects with miles of unofficial single-track and fire roads. (You can learn more about this area through the New England Mountain Biking Association, www.nemba.org, or through NEMBA's Rhode Island chapter, www .rinemba.org/big-river-cleanup/.) From

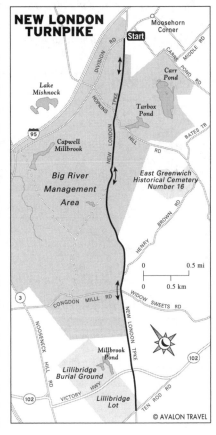

NEW LONDON TURNPIKE

Moosehorn Corner

Start

Lake Mishnock

Carr Pond

Tarbox Pond

Capwell Millbrook

Big River Management Area

East Greenwich Historical Cemetery Number 16

Congdon Mill Rd

Widow Sweets Rd

Millbrook Pond

Lillibridge Burial Ground

Lillibridge Lot

Victory Hwy

Ten Rod Rd

0   0.5 mi

0   0.5 km

© AVALON TRAVEL

there it runs south, past fields and farms and very New England–looking stone walls, until it connects once again with civilization as a paved road. From there, this ride turns around, but you can also head east on paved roads and loop your way north to reconnect with the turnpike.

In places, the road is smooth hard-packed dirt. In others it's chewed up and rutted, with exposed rocks and loose gravel. In every place, it's fun for a mountain bike, or even better, for a cyclocross bike, as the turnpike itself never gets technical enough to require suspension or super-fat tires.

Options

Along the length of the turnpike, you'll pass many access points for single-track. Many of these connect with the Big River trails, an unofficial trail area popular with local mountain bikers. Explore these at will.

To add about 4.5 miles—and 200 feet of climbing—to this ride, turn left at Mile 6.6 onto Ten Rod Road, which becomes RI-102, and left again at Mile 9.1 onto Widow Sweets Road. At Mile 9.6, turn right onto Pardon Joslin Road, then left onto Hopkins Hill Road. Follow this road back to the turnpike, where you'll turn right to return to the parking area about 1.5 miles down the road.

This ride is near Trestle Trail and Breakheart and Shelter Trails.

Locals' Tip: Breakfast at the Phenix Square Restaurant (9 Pleasant Street, West Warwick, RI 02893, 401/828-8110) is fast, cheap, and greasy—the good kind of breakfast greasy.

Places to Stay: Stay at one of the many chain hotels in nearby Providence or at the Warwick Motor Inn (17 Albion Street, West Warwick, RI 02893).

Driving Directions

From I-95, take exit 7 for Coventry/West Warwick. Take the first right immediately from the exit and park in the ride share lot. The ride begins up the same road at a gate with a dirt road behind it.

Route Directions

0.0 From the parking area, enter the New London Turnpike at the gate.

1.3 Stay STRAIGHT across Hopkins Hill Road.

2.6 Bear LEFT at intersection with Sweet Sawmill Road.

4.2 Henry Brown Road merges.

4.5 Stay STRAIGHT.

5.4 Pass Money Swamp Pond.

5.8 Stay STRAIGHT at intersection.

6.6 At intersection, the road continues as a paved road, or heads east on Ten Rod Road. TURN AROUND. OPTION: Turn left onto Ten Rod Road and follow option directions.

13.2 END at parking area.

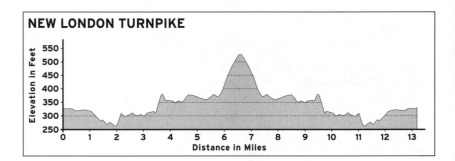

7 GODDARD PARK
Goddard Memorial State Park, Warwick

GRAVEL AND DIRT FIRE ROADS

Difficulty: 1

Riding Time: 1 hour

Total Distance: 4.9 miles

Elevation Gain: 220 feet

Summary: A handful of flat, easy fire roads for beginners or those seeking a calm, relaxing off-road ride.

Mountain bikers, these trails are not for you. They're fast, fun, and beautiful, but if you specifically bought a bike with suspension because you like the abuse and adrenaline of bombing descents, hucking yourself off geographical features, and pounding through thickets and thistles, you'll find these trails anticlimactic.

Everyone else, pay attention, because this short ride is a fun way to spend some time on a bike, enjoying the woods, and these are a decent set of fire roads to get some training miles on if you've got a cyclocross bike.

Just under 950 acres of land on the shores of Greenwich Bay, Goddard Memorial State Park is named for Colonel William Goddard, who bought the land

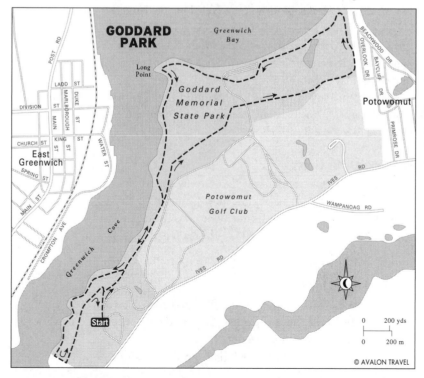

from a philanthropist who literally planted the seeds that turned it from an austere stretch of sand dunes into the woodlands it is today.

According to the state's parks department, this is the state's most popular metropolitan park. The designation may leave some room for interpretation, but there's no arguing that on a good day in the summer, you'll see people there engaged in everything from golfing to equestrian showing to picnicking. You may even see a wedding or a concert at the new performing arts center.

Thanks to Henry Russell, the man who planted the seeds, the park is home to a wide variety of trees from around the globe, not just the ones you see everywhere else in southern New England. Spend some time noticing them as you ride through the park, and you may be surprised.

Trails are open from sunrise to sunset. For more information, contact Goddard Memorial State Park, 1095 Ives Road, Warwick, RI 02818, 401/884-2010, www.riparks.com/goddard.htm.

Options

To expand this ride on similar terrain, explore the park by riding the fire roads that crisscross it at random. You won't get lost.

This ride is a reasonable drive from New London Turnpike.

Locals' Tip: Housed in a former post office, the aptly named Post Office Cafe (11 Main Street, East Greenwich, RI 02818, 401/885-4444, www.pinellimarrarestaurants.com/post_office_cafe.htm) offers Sunday brunch and dinner Tuesday to Saturday.

Places to Stay: Colwell's Campground (119 Peckham Lane, Coventry, RI 02816, 401/397-4614, www.ricampgrounds.com) is a reasonable drive from Goddard Memorial State Park.

Driving Directions

From I-95, take RI-4 south to the East Greenwich exit, and turn right onto Division Street (RI-401). After about 2 miles, turn right onto RI-1 South, and then turn left at the traffic signal. Bear left onto Ives Road. The park will be on your left, and the parking area will be down the main park road on your left. The ride leaves from there.

Route Directions

0.0 From the parking area, bear LEFT past the equestrian area winding out along the shore of the bay. Stay on the main fire road past the boat ramp to the intersection.

1.3 At the intersection, bear RIGHT, heading into the woods.

1.6 Cross the dirt road and stay STRAIGHT.

2.0 Bear RIGHT on paved road.

2.4 Bear RIGHT. The trail loops to the left toward the bay.

2.8 At the intersection, stay STRAIGHT between two small ponds, heading west.

3.6 Pass beach parking. Watch for traffic.

3.5 Long Point, with views of Greenwich cove to your left and Potowomut Rocks to your right.

4.7 Bear LEFT.

4.9 END at parking area.

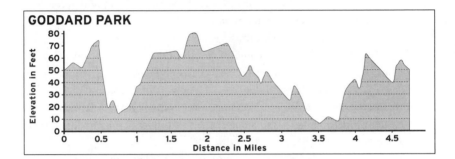

8 BREAKHEART AND SHELTER TRAILS

BEST 🌙

Arcadia Management Area, Millville

DIRT ROADS, DIRT TRAILS, SINGLE-TRACK

Difficulty: 4

Total Distance: 8.7 miles

Riding Time: 2 hours

Elevation Gain: 515 feet

Summary: Explore off-road trails running through gorgeous New England forests.

Arcadia draws mountain bikers from all over the region. The 15,000-acre Arcadia Management Area contains more than 50 miles of single-track, and you can literally ride for days without repeating yourself.

This route is a small sampler, combining technical and easy single-track with dirt roads. Start on the easy Deion Trail, a wide, overgrown trail strewn with pine needles. Take dirt roads around the Frosty Hollow fishing area, and pick up the J. B. Hudson Trail for fast, tight, winding, rooty trails to Breakheart Pond. Follow an easy, wide woodland trail along the western shore of the pond, and then turn onto Yellow Dot (Breakheart) Trail.

The next 1.5 miles are rocky and technical, the hardest stretch of this route. Follow the double yellow blazes through deep woods until you reach a bridge

© CHRIS BERNARD

The trails of the Arcadia Management Area draw mountain bikers from all over New England, and whatever your skill level, you'll find a trail to suit you.

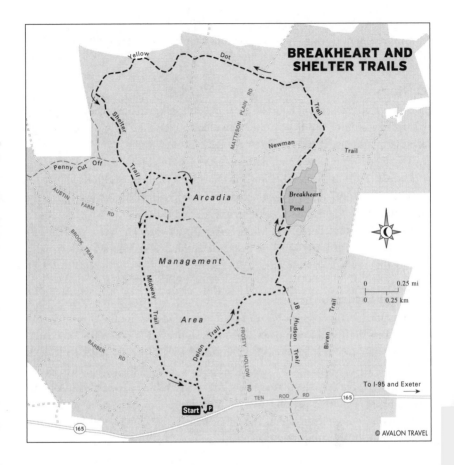

built by the Appalachian Mountain Club. Don't miss the left turn right after the bridge.

From there, you face a tricky climb and a few log bridges before you reach the Shelter Trail, which starts with a very narrow, fun stretch that turns into dirt roads and, eventually, the Midway Trail, a wide path through an area where hunters train bird dogs.

These are mountain bike trails—any other bike will be outgunned. With so many trails, it's easy to get lost, so grab a trail map or join a group ride. The trail map boxes at the parking lot empty fast, so get one at local bike shops (try Victory Cycles, 271 Post Road, Wyoming, RI 02891, 401/322-6005) or online from the state (www.state.ri.us/dem/maps/wma.htm).

The Rhode Island chapter of the New England Mountain Biking Association (RINEMBA; www.rinemba.org) provides trail maintenance and bike patrols and leads group rides in Arcadia. For information on Arcadia, contact the Department of Environmental Management, Arcadia Management Area, 401/539-1052, www.dem.ri.gov.

Options

Arcadia's trails run throughout the area, and cyclists can piece together extended trips. Poke around and have fun or download a trail map (www.rinemba.org/arcadia-management-area) to follow the local experts' routes.

This ride is near New London Turnpike and Watch Hill.

Locals' Tip: The Middle of Nowhere Diner (222 Nooseneck Hill Road, Exeter, RI 02822, 401/397-8855, www.themiddleofnowherediner.com) is a surprisingly good stop in, as the name suggests, an unexpected location.

Places to Stay: The Classic Motor Lodge (859 Victory Highway, West Greenwich, RI 02817, 401/397-6280) is well-situated for cyclists who want to spend a weekend in the woods at Arcadia.

Driving Directions

From points north, take exit 5A off I-95 South to RI-102 South. Drive 0.8 mile and make a sharp right turn onto RI-3 south. Drive 1.2 miles on RI-3 and turn right onto RI-165 west (also marked Ten Rod Road). Drive 1.4 miles on RI-165 to Arcadia Road. Turn left, following Arcadia Road for 3 miles, and turn left at the stop sign. The Arcadia Management Area and Midway parking lot are on the right. There is another parking area 0.4 mile farther down the road on the left, with an outhouse, picnic tables, and canoe launch. Parking is free. The nearest bike shop is in Wyoming, Rhode Island.

Route Directions

0.0 From the parking lot, turn RIGHT onto the main dirt road.

0.2 Turn RIGHT onto Deion Trail, marked by blue blazes. Ride around the low red gate.

0.8 Turn LEFT onto a dirt road (Frosty Hollow Road; unmarked).

1.0 Turn RIGHT into parking area for Frosty Hollow Fishing Area. Trailhead is at far end of parking area; pass around a red gate to access the trail. Go RIGHT at immediate fork.

1.3 Turn LEFT at junction.

1.4 Turn LEFT onto J. B. Hudson Trail, marked by double yellow blazes. Go LEFT again after about 500 yards, following yellow blazes.

1.6 Turn LEFT at fork, following yellow blazes.

2.0 Pass Breakheart Pond. Ride around the southwest corner of the pond into the dirt parking area.

2.1 Pick up trailhead at far end of parking lot, riding around red gate. The pond will be on your right.

2.7 Turn RIGHT at junction.

2.8 Turn LEFT just before brook onto Yellow Dot Trail (also called Breakheart Trail), marked by double yellow blazes. The trailhead is marked by big boulders.

3.7 Make a dogleg turn, LEFT then RIGHT, following the yellow blazes.

4.3 Make a dogleg turn, RIGHT then LEFT, following the yellow blazes.

4.4 Cross bridge and take an immediate LEFT, following the yellow blazes.

5.4 Turn LEFT onto Shelter Trail, marked by white blazes.

6.0 Continue STRAIGHT, staying on main trail.

6.2 Turn LEFT at four-way intersection.

6.5 Bear RIGHT at the fork.

6.8 Emerge onto a dirt road (Austin Farm Road; unmarked). Go RIGHT.

7.1 Turn LEFT into clearing. Join Arcadia Midway Trail. *There is a portable toilet and a picnic table here.*

8.1 End of Midway Trail. Bear LEFT onto main dirt road.

8.2 Continue STRAIGHT on main road.

8.7 Return to parking lot.

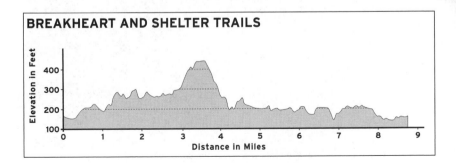

BREAKHEART AND SHELTER TRAILS

❾ OH, CHARIHO!
Richmond, Hopkinton, and Charlestown

PAVED ROADS, MINIMAL TO MODERATE TRAFFIC

Difficulty: 3   **Total Distance:** 37.9 miles

Riding Time: 2-3 hours   **Elevation Gain:** 1,027 feet

Summary: This moderately hilly ride visits state parks, rural back roads, and downtowns, offering a good mix of roads in varied conditions.

Rhode Island may be full of good Native American place names, like Narragansett, Woonsocket, and Tomaquag, but Chariho isn't one of them. Chariho is actually an acronym for Charlestown-Richmond-Hopkinton used by the school district and less formally, by area residents. Fittingly, this ride starts at Chariho High School and explores all three towns comprised within the name.

Adapted from a Narragansett Bay Wheelmen ride, this route heads first onto rural back roads through the hilly dairy farm country of southwestern Rhode Island, bumping right up against the edge of the state—and across it at times—before looping back into more residential areas for a bit. After that, it moves once more into the rural, passing first through Burlingame State Park (home of the Vin

The roads in this corner of the state provide a pleasant respite for cyclists more familiar with the urban conditions of city streets.

© CHRIS BERNARD

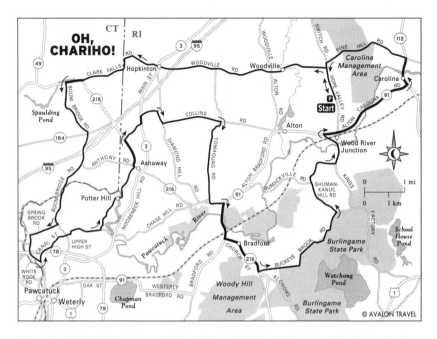

Gormley Trail), where you will head first uphill and then quickly down, before entering the Carolina Management Area.

This ride can challenge the legs of novice cyclists, but it's completely manageable given time to complete it at your own pace—and a few rest stops. You'll find plenty of reasons to stop along the way.

For more information, contact the Narragansett Bay Wheelmen, P.O. Box 41177, Providence, RI 02940, www.nbwclub.org.

Options

This ride overlaps with Watch Hill. To combine these rides, turn right on Canal Street at Mile 13.3, joining Watch Hill at the start once you reach Broad Street. At Mile 18.2 of Watch Hill, turn right onto RI-91, rejoining this ride at Mile 23.4.

Locals' Tip: Sit down at Lucky House Restaurant (32 Main Street, Ashaway, RI 02804, 401/596-3922) for a Chinese feast after burning some calories on this ride.

Places to Stay: The Willows Resort (P.O. Box 1260, Charlestown, RI 02813, 401/364-7727, www.willowsresort.com), run by the same family for decades, offers casual, affordable accommodations on 15 acres.

Driving Directions

From I-95, take exit 3B onto Main Street/RI-138 toward Hope Valley. Continue to follow Main Street for 2 miles, and bear left at Nichols Street. Nichols Street turns slightly left and becomes Mechanic Street. Less than 1 mile later, it becomes Switch Road. Chariho High School (453 Switch Road, Wood River Junction) is on your right. Park at the high school on weekends or during the summer, or at any of the small dirt pull-offs along Switch Road.

Route Directions

0.0 Turn LEFT onto Switch Road.

0.8 Turn LEFT onto Woodville Road.

5.0 As you cross RI-3, stay STRAIGHT onto Clarks Falls Road.

7.8 Turn LEFT onto Boom Bridge Road.

9.2 Cross RI-184.

11.8 Turn RIGHT onto Spring Brook Avenue.

12.6 Turn LEFT onto White Rock Road, paralleling the Connecticut state line.

13.3 Turn LEFT onto Canal Street. OPTION: Turn RIGHT on Canal Street and follow option directions. *Supplies and food available.*

14.3 At the stop sign, stay STRAIGHT onto Potter Hill Road.

16.3 Turn LEFT onto Maxson Street and LEFT again onto Laurel Street.

17.2 Turn LEFT onto High Street/RI-216.

17.8 Turn RIGHT onto Wellstown Road.

18.6 Turn LEFT onto RI-3.

18.8 Turn RIGHT onto Frontier Road.

19.2 Turn RIGHT onto Maxson Hill Road.

19.4 Turn LEFT onto Collins Road.

21.0 Turn RIGHT onto Tomaquag Road.

23.1 Bear LEFT, and then turn LEFT onto RI-216/Ashaway Road.

23.4 Turn RIGHT onto RI-216/RI-91.

24.0 *Supplies and restrooms available along the shore of the Pawcatuck River.*

24.4 Turn LEFT onto RI-216/Church Street.

25.6 Turn LEFT onto Buckeye Brook Road, which leads into Burlingame State Park.

28.5 Turn LEFT onto Shumankanuc Hill Road.

30.5 Turn LEFT onto Kings Factory Road.

31.1 Bear LEFT onto New Kings Factory Road.

31.5 Turn RIGHT onto RI-91, passing Meadow Brook Pond on your left.

34.0 Turn LEFT onto RI-112.

34.6 Turn LEFT onto Pine Hill Road.

35.5 Pine Hill Road enters Carolina Management Area.

36.8 Turn LEFT onto Switch Road.

37.9 END at parking area.

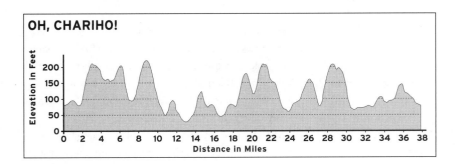

10 WORDEN POND LOOP BEST ◖

Great Swamp Wildlife Management Area, Kingston

DIRT ROADS, BIKE PATH

Difficulty: 2   **Total Distance:** 8.7 miles

Riding Time: 1.5 hours   **Elevation Gain:** 205 feet

Summary: An easy off-road ride through shady swamplands suitable for all but the youngest of riders.

This is not a difficult or exciting ride, but the tranquil setting and pleasant scenery—as well as the opportunities to see wildlife—make this a fun, and popular, choice. If you're looking for a slow, meandering, peaceful off-road stretch, or if you're new to mountain biking, this is the trail for you, offering grassy and sandy stretches on mainly overgrown dirt roads with no technical riding. Cyclocross bikes will work fine, as will any bike with wide, off-road tires.

The trail begins on the paved South County Bike Path, but before long it splits off and heads down a long dirt access road before entering Great Swamp. Low, scrubby vegetation lines the edges of the swamp, and lily pads float on the surface. You'll make a big loop around the pond, watching for wildlife—ospreys nest on top of the power line poles, turtles amble along the path, and ducks splash in the water.

As you leave the swamp, there's a small incline into a series of fields, and the

© CHRIS BERNARD

This ride ends up off-road, but starts on the accessible, paved South County Bike Path.

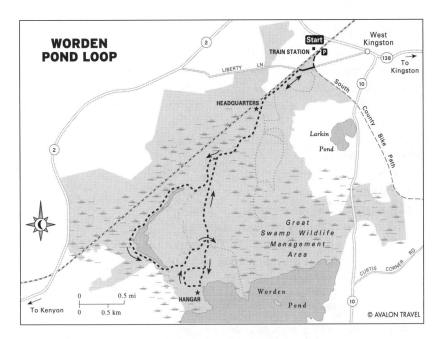

trail becomes grassier. Toward Worden Pond you enter a more wooded area, with a sandy beach and a float plane hangar. Take a left as you leave the pond to make a small loop, which goes up and down a small hill, before rejoining the path.

For more information, contact the Department of Environmental Management, Fish and Wildlife Division, Liberty Lane, West Kingston, RI 02891, 401/789-7481. Hunting and fishing are allowed here, so though most hunting seasons are in the winter, you should be aware of hunters.

Options

To lengthen this trip, on the way back from the pond turn right at Mile 8.5 and ride east along South County Bike Path, which continues for almost 6 smooth flat miles into Narragansett.

This ride is a reasonable drive from A Point, Two Towers, and the Pier and the Vin Gormley Trail, and the three could easily be turned into a weekend of Rhode Island exploration.

Locals' Tip: The Caliente Mexican Grill (Kingston Emporium, 99 Fortin Road, Kingston, RI 02881, 401/284-2816, www.calientemexicangrill.com) is often voted best in the state, and if you eat their burritos, you'll see why.

Places to Stay: Eden Manor (154 Post Road, Wakefield, RI 02879, 401/792-8234, ww.edenmanorbandb.com) is well reviewed and a short drive away.

Driving Directions

From points east or west, take I-95 to exit 3A. Drive about 8.3 miles on RI-138. Turn right, then left onto Railroad Avenue, following signs for the Amtrak train station and parking lot. There are facilities at the train station and supplies available along RI-138 in West Kingston. The nearest bike shops are in North Kingstown and Narragansett.

Route Directions

0.0 START on bike path.

0.2 Turn RIGHT on Liberty Lane (unmarked).

0.4 Bear LEFT onto dirt road.

1.0 Pass Great Swamp Headquarters.

1.5 Go to the end of the large dirt parking area and ride around the red gate next to the information sign.

1.9 Turn RIGHT at fork.

2.3 Turn RIGHT onto grassy trail.

4.3 Turn RIGHT at the fork into wooded area.

4.5 Turn RIGHT at triangular intersection.

5.1 Pass float plane hangar and arrive at Worden Pond. *A tiny sandy beach is just to the left.* TURN AROUND. Take immediate LEFT on narrow trail.

5.5 Turn RIGHT at the junction and RIGHT again downhill.

5.7 Turn LEFT on trail.

5.9 Bear RIGHT at the triangular intersection.

6.6 Continue STRAIGHT under power lines.

6.8 Bear RIGHT at triangular intersection.

7.2 Return to dirt parking area. Go STRAIGHT on dirt road.

8.5 Turn LEFT onto South County Bike Path.

8.7 Return to train station parking lot.

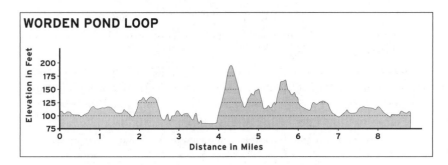

WORDEN POND LOOP

11 A POINT, TWO TOWERS, AND THE PIER

Wakefield to Point Judith

BEST C

PAVED ROADS WITH MODERATE TRAFFIC

Difficulty: 2   **Total Distance:** 29.1 miles

Riding Time: 2-3 hours   **Elevation Gain:** 466 feet

Summary: An easy ride along scenic, oceanfront roads, this route visits villages, landmarks, and beaches.

Contrary to its name, Narragansett Pier is a village, not a landmark. Point Judith, however, is a point—actually, a cape—as well as a village, named after Judith Thatcher, a passenger on a ship that once ran aground. It's also the site of the last sinking of an Allied ship in the Atlantic Ocean during World War II—the S.S. *Black Point* was torpedoed by a German submarine just after she passed the Point Judith lighthouse.

This Narragansett Bay Wheelmen ride heads south from Wakefield to Point Judith, taking a side trip through the fishing village of Galilee, before heading north again to Narragansett Pier. En route, it passes through the stone arch of the Towers, an impressive stone archway that served as the gateway to the Narragansett Pier Casino in the 1800s. The casino burned down in 1900.

© CHRIS BERNARD

The scenery this ride offers includes sweeping ocean views of the Rhode Island coastline.

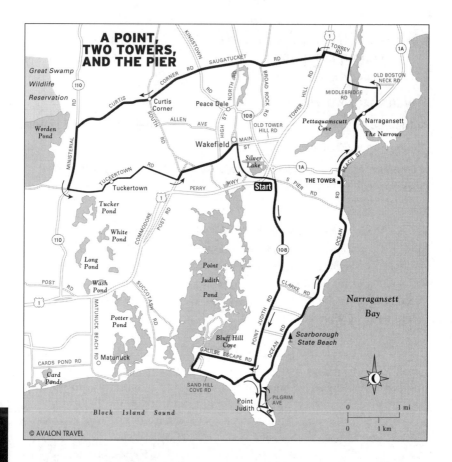

From the archway, the ride loops north and west before turning east again through Tuckertown on its way back to the start. Along the way, you'll pass several beaches, museums, and places to stop, with ocean views along much of the ride and no real climbing to speak of. Though this isn't a difficult ride, if it's too long for you, there's a way to cut it in half without losing most of the ride's visual appeal.

For more information, contact the Narragansett Bay Wheelmen, P.O. Box 41177, Providence, RI 02940, www.nbwclub.org.

Options

For a 14.5-mile ride, turn left onto South Pier Road at Mile 13. Or, to add a few miles, turn right at Galilee at Mile 4.8 and ride out to Great Island, looping back to rejoin the ride where you left it.

This ride is just one bridge over from Conanicut Island Loop, is another bridge over from the Newport ride, and passes the ferry to the Once Around the Block trail.

Locals' Tip: Don't miss out on Crazy Burger Cafe and Juice Bar (144 Boon Street, Narragansett, RI 02882, 401/783-1810, www.crazyburger.com), a place most often described as "unique."

Places to Stay: Pitch a tent at Fisherman's Memorial State Park (1011 Point Judith Road, Narragansett, RI 02882, 401/789-8374), right on the ride (and the ocean).

Driving Directions

From I-95, take RI-4 South for 10 miles. Turn right onto US-1 South. Take the Salt Pond Road exit, and turn right at Salt Pond Road, then right at Woodruff Avenue. Park at the Salt Pond Shopping Center at Woodruff Avenue and RI-108.

Route Directions

0.0 Turn RIGHT onto RI-108/Point Judith Road.

3.8 Turn RIGHT onto Galilee Escape Road at Fisherman's Memorial Park.

4.8 Turn LEFT on Great Island Road, past the Block Island Ferry terminal. Great Island Road becomes Sand Hill Cove Road and passes Roger Wheeler State Beach.

6.6 Turn RIGHT onto RI-108, and RIGHT again onto Ocean Road. At the end of the road, which becomes Follett Street, TURN AROUND.

7.4 Point Judith Light. *This is a beautiful place to stop for a scenic break.* When ready, turn around and head back on Ocean Road.

8.1 Turn RIGHT onto Pilgrim Avenue, and LEFT onto Calef Avenue.

8.8 Turn RIGHT onto Ocean Road, bearing RIGHT where it meets RI-108.

10.0 Pass Scarborough State Beach.

13.0 Enter Narragansett Pier. OPTION: Turn left onto South Pier Road and follow option directions.

13.8 Ocean Road becomes US-1A/Beach Road/Boston Neck Road and heads into Narragansett.

14.0 *This beautiful beach is a good place to stop for a snack or a rest.*

15.5 Turn LEFT onto Old Boston Neck Road, and then LEFT onto Middlebridge Road.

16.8 Turn LEFT onto Torrey Road.

17.5 Turn RIGHT onto US-1 North/Tower Hill Road, and use the U-turn pulloff to reverse direction onto US-1 South. Turn immediately RIGHT onto Saugatucket Road.

20.1 Saugatucket Road becomes Curtis Corner Road as you cross RI-108.

22.9 Turn LEFT onto RI-110.

24.2 Turn LEFT onto Tuckertown Road.

26.7 When Tuckertown Road ends, turn LEFT onto Post Road, and bear RIGHT to stay on Post Road, which becomes Main Street.

28.0 Turn RIGHT onto Woodruff Avenue

29.1 END at parking area.

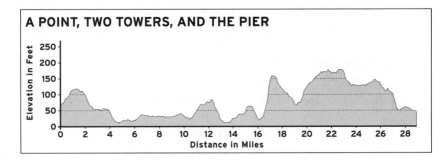

A POINT, TWO TOWERS, AND THE PIER

12 CONANICUT ISLAND LOOP　　　BEST ◖

Fort Wetherill State Park, Jamestown

PAVED ROADS WITH MINIMAL TRAFFIC

Difficulty: 3　　　　　　　　　　**Total Distance:** 21.6 miles

Riding Time: 2-2.5 hours　　　　　**Elevation Gain:** 1,070 feet

Summary: Explore a quiet, touristy island, with ocean views, some good climbs, and a quaint village.

This beautiful island in the mouth of Narragansett Bay is a great place for a half-day trip, and it can be easily combined with a visit to Newport to make a weekend of riding. With spectacular ocean views, very little traffic, moderate hills, a pretty beach, a historic lighthouse, and a pleasant village to explore, Conanicut draws cyclists from around New England.

This route begins at Fort Wetherill State Park and loops counterclockwise around the island. You'll pass coffee shops and ice-cream stands in the village, and once you pass the highway and bridge access roads, the traffic and noise fade. The ocean views become more sporadic on this half of the ride, and there's no shoulder on the road, but it's peaceful and fairly flat and easy, stress-free riding.

Round the tip of the island and heading south, pedal up a slight incline past the

From Conanicut Island, the views of Newport and the connecting Pell Bridge are spectacular, but the bridge – like the Jamestown Bridge to the mainland – isn't open to bikes.

creek and marsh at Mile 11. You'll have a view of the impressive Pell Bridge rising in the background, linking Newport. You'll pass the outskirts of town again before reaching a narrow strip of land called Town Beach. Only residents are allowed to park here, but cyclists can stop and beachcomb. You'll face a steep hill up Beavertail Road and some prevailing headwinds before you arrive at Beavertail State Park, home to America's third-oldest lighthouse, perched right at the rocky island's edge. There are picnic tables, walking trails, and a seasonal museum.

Retrace your route past Town Beach and then climb a few small hills, through a pretty residential area, to return to Fort Wetherill State Park. The park, a popular launching spot for dive clubs, has picnic tables, seasonal restrooms, a boat ramp, and nice views from its granite cliffs.

For more information and an excellent street map of the island, contact the Jamestown Chamber of Commerce, P.O. Box 35, Jamestown, RI 02835, 401/423-3650, www.james townri.com. For more information on the state parks, contact Fort Wetherill State Park, 401/423-1771, www .riparks.com/fortweth.htm, and Beavertail State Park, 401/423-9941, www .riparks.com/beaverta.htm.

Options

This ride is just across the Pell Bridge from the Newport ride. Bikes are not allowed on the bridge, but the short

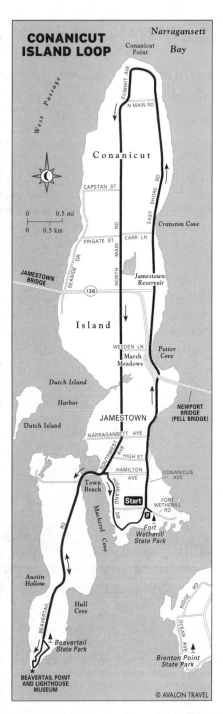

drive makes linking these rides viable. On the mainland across the Jamestown Bridge, the A Point, Two Towers, and the Pier ride is just a short drive away.

Locals' Tip: With no shortage of cute little places to dine or drink in town, a good bet is Chopmist Charlie's (40 Narragansett Avenue, Jamestown, RI 02835, 401/423-1020).

Places to Stay: The Newport Overlook (150 Conanicus Avenue, Jamestown, RI 02835, 401/423-1886, www.gonewport.com) offers great views across the bay of Newport and the Pell Bridge and is a comfortable, welcoming place to stay.

Driving Directions

Bikes are not allowed on either of the bridges to Conanicut Island, so you have to drive. From Newport, take RI-138 across the Pell Bridge. The toll is $4 each way. Take the first exit for Jamestown. Turn right off the exit, then left at the stop sign toward Jamestown village. Drive through town, on Conanicus Avenue, and go 1 mile. Turn left at a triangular intersection onto Fort Wetherill Road. Turn right into the first parking area for Fort Wetherill State Park. Parking is free and the park is open sunrise–sunset. From points west, take the Jamestown Bridge (RI-138) and take the Jamestown village exit as above. Supplies are available in Jamestown. The nearest bike shops are in Newport or North Kingston.

Route Directions

0.0 From parking area at Fort Wetherill State Park, go LEFT onto Fort Wetherill Road.

0.2 Turn RIGHT at triangle onto unmarked road (this becomes Conanicus Avenue).

1.1 Jamestown village. *Supplies available throughout town. Public restrooms are at the recreation center on the corner of Union Street and Conanicus Avenue.*

1.6 Turn LEFT at fork.

2.1 Turn RIGHT at fork to go under the bridge approach.

2.5 Continue STRAIGHT at stop sign on East Shore Road (unmarked).

7.0 Turn LEFT at stop sign, onto Summit Avenue (unmarked).

7.5 Turn RIGHT at stop sign, onto North Main Road (unmarked).

12.3 *Supplies available in Jamestown.*

12.5 Continue STRAIGHT at intersection onto Southwest Avenue.

13.0 Stay on Southwest Avenue as road curves to the right.

13.2 Town Beach. Proceed STRAIGHT on Beavertail Road (unmarked).

15.8 Enter Beavertail State Park. *Picnic tables are available.*

16.3 Pass Beavertail Point and Lighthouse Museum.

17.0 Exit the state park.
19.0 Pass Town Beach.
19.8 Turn RIGHT onto Hamilton Avenue.
19.9 Turn RIGHT onto Highland Drive (unmarked).
21.3 Turn RIGHT at triangle followed by an immediate RIGHT onto Fort Wetherill Road.
21.6 Turn RIGHT into parking area.

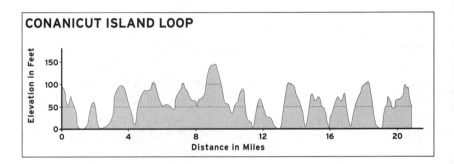

CONANICUT ISLAND LOOP

13 NEWPORT   BEST C
Fort Adams State Park, Newport

PAVED ROADS WITH MODERATE TRAFFIC

Difficulty: 2   **Total Distance:** 24.7 miles

Riding Time: 1.5-2 hours   **Elevation Gain:** 223 feet

Summary: This ride loops the southern half of the island, past mansions and cliffs and through historic areas.

If you've spent any time in downtown Newport, you know how crowded it can be. Tourists bump shoulders, cars jam city streets, restaurants book days in advance. But get outside the tight orbit of the downtown, and suddenly you're in a different world—one that's primed for exploring on two wheels.

There's much to see. The millionaires had good reason to build their mansions here at the turn of the last century. In places, Aquidneck Island has an end-of-the-earth quality and a rugged, natural beauty, and this ride highlights these. It also takes you past the much celebrated, over-the-top mansions along the water's edge, contrasting the accomplishments of man with those of nature. To avoid crowds and traffic, try doing this short ride very early on a summer morning, or wait until late fall to visit.

Starting from Fort Adams State Park, you'll make a loop on Ocean Drive, getting sprayed by the surf as you whiz past Brenton Point State Park, then passing by quiet landscapes of ponds, coves, and beaches.

Then it's on to the opulence of Bellevue Avenue, the main avenue of the Gilded Age mansions. Turning off Bellevue onto Ruggles Avenue, you'll travel through the lovely campus of Salve Regina University and ride to the end, where you'll get a good look at the Breakers mansion (built for Cornelius Vanderbilt in 1895) and have access to the Cliff Walk, a 3.5-mile National Recreation Trail. You could lock up your bike and do a 0.75-mile stretch of the walk, from

Riders in Newport will notice the route's pleasant mix of artificial and natural beauty.

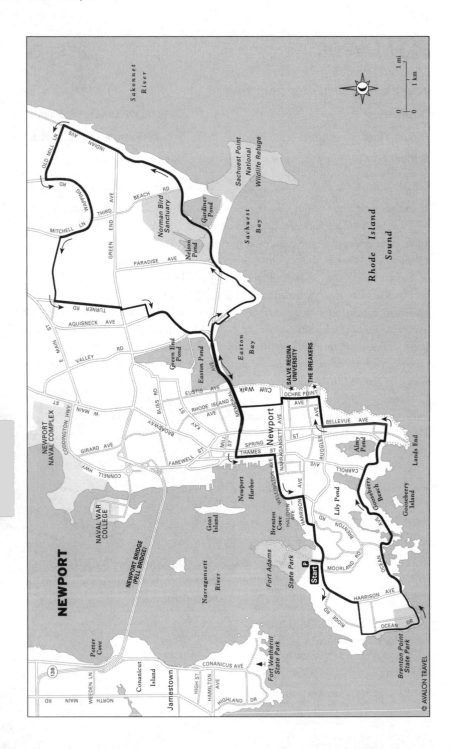

Ruggles to Narragansett Avenue, for the best mansion views and a taste of the spectacular path with its sheer drop-offs and breaking surf.

From there, you head east, past the easy-to-miss pulloff for Purgatory Chasm, a stop worth making for views from the rockface split by the ocean's relentless force, past a beach popular with surfers, and then between Nelson Pond and Gardiner Pond reservoirs. Then you loop back up through farmlands before heading back toward the start.

At nearly every point, this ride offers something to see, and at 25 miles, it's not likely to wear you out too much to enjoy a night bumping shoulders downtown.

For more information, contact the Newport County Convention and Visitor's Bureau, 23 America's Cup Avenue, Newport, RI 02840, 800/976-5122, www .gonewport.com. For more on Fort Adams State Park, contact Fort Adams State Park, Harrison Avenue, Newport, RI 02840, 401/847-2400, www.riparks.com/fortadams.htm.

Options

To cut this ride in half, at Mile 7.5, stay straight on Narragansett Avenue, turn right onto Thames Street, and make a quick left onto Wellington Avenue, rejoining the original ride at Mile 21.6.

This ride is just across the Pell Bridge from Conanicut Island Loop. Bikes are not allowed on the bridge, but the short drive makes linking these rides viable. Or on the mainland across the Jamestown Bridge, add the A Point, Two Towers, and the Pier ride, just a short drive away.

Locals' Tip: Newport offers an embarrassment of riches when it comes to meal choices, but a favorite is Busker's Irish Pub (178 Thames Street, Newport, RI 02840, 401/846-5856), where you'll see more locals than tourists.

Places to Stay: As a tourist destination, Newport abounds in options for lodging. Try the Newport Marriott (25 America's Cup Avenue, Newport, RI 02840, 401/849-1000, www.newportmarriott.com), which often offers off-season specials.

Driving Directions

From the center of Newport, drive south on Thames Street and turn right onto Wellington Avenue. The road bends left and becomes Halidon Avenue. Turn right at the stop sign, onto Harrison Avenue, left at the next stop sign, and right onto Ridge Road (unmarked). Drive 0.5 mile and turn right into Fort Adams State Park. Go past the entry booth and park in one of the large lots on the left. Parking is free and the park is open sunrise–sunset. Supplies, bike rentals, and bike shops are available in Newport.

Route Directions

0.0 Leave the main parking lot of Fort Adams State Park. *The park has free parking, restrooms, a pay phone, a visitor center and gift shop, a boating center, and a museum. Tours of the 19th-century fort are available during the summer for a small fee.*

0.4 Turn RIGHT on Harrison Avenue, past Newport Country Club.

1.2 Turn RIGHT on Castle Hill Avenue.

1.7 Turn LEFT on Ocean Avenue, passing through Brenton Point State Park. *You'll find picnic tables, park fields, and stunning views of waves breaking on rocks.*

5.5 Turn LEFT on Bellevue Avenue.

6.3 Turn RIGHT on Ruggles Avenue.

7.0 Turn LEFT on Ochre Point Avenue, passing the Breakers mansion, Salve Regina College, and access to the Cliff Walk.

7.5 Turn LEFT on Narragansett Avenue, and then make a quick RIGHT onto Annandale Road. OPTION: Stay straight on Narragansett Avenue and follow option directions.

8.1 Turn RIGHT on Memorial Boulevard, passing views of Easton Pond to your left and Rhode Island Sound to your right.

9.1 Bear RIGHT onto Purgatory Road, and then RIGHT again onto Esplanade, looping to the end and turning RIGHT onto Tuckerman Avenue.

10.7 Pass pulloff for Purgatory Chasm on your right. Bear RIGHT onto Hanging Rock Road, past a beach.

11.2 Bear LEFT on Hanging Rock Road, then pass Hanging Rock on your left.

12.0 Cross Third Beach Road and stay STRAIGHT onto Indian Avenue.

13.8 Turn LEFT on Old Mill Lane at dead end sign.

14.6 Turn LEFT on Wapping Road.

16.0 Turn LEFT on Wyatt Road.

17.0 Turn LEFT on Turner Road.

18.0 Turn RIGHT on Green End Avenue and immediately LEFT on Morrison Avenue.

18.3 Turn RIGHT to stay on Morrison Avenue, and then LEFT on RI-138A/Aquidneck Avenue.

19.2 Turn LEFT to stay on Aquidneck Avenue.

19.4 Bear RIGHT on Memorial Avenue.

21.1 Turn LEFT on Thames Street, heading back into downtown Newport.

21.6 Turn RIGHT on Wellington Avenue.

22.3 Bear LEFT onto Haddon Avenue/Brenton Road.

22.8 Bear LEFT on Brenton Road.

23.7 Bear RIGHT on Hammersmith Road.

24.2 Turn LEFT onto Harrison Avenue and immediately RIGHT onto Fort Adams Road.

24.7 END at parking area.

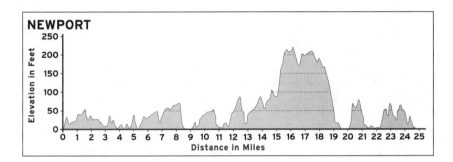

14 WATCH HILL
Westerly, Watch Hill, and Bradford

PAVED ROADS, MINIMAL TO MODERATE TRAFFIC

Difficulty: 3 **Total Distance:** 26.7 miles

Riding Time: 2-3 hours **Elevation Gain:** 430 feet

Summary: This moderately challenging ride explores Westerly and the upscale Watch Hill neighborhood, which is both scenic and impressive.

Though not on the scale of the Newport mansions, Watch Hill has its share of large, well-appointed homes. They're impressive and mostly beautiful, and almost to a one, they come with incredible views of the ocean. They're part of the appeal of this lovely little coastal ride.

Once Niantic Indian land, then a lookout for colonists during the French and Indian and Revolutionary Wars, Watch Hill later become a summer resort. It was redefined again as an exclusive neighborhood after a hurricane destroyed many of the area's structures in the late 1930s.

Technically, Watch Hill is a village in the town of Westerly, but in some ways the two are worlds apart. Downtown Westerly, where the ride begins, is cute and gives off that New England vibe, with a sprawling park, shops lined up along the

© KIM BERNARD

The roads of the Watch Hill ride are ideal for cycling, and you're likely to encounter other riders as you make your way along this route.

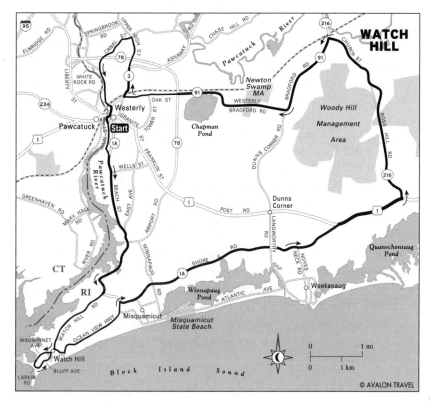

sidewalks, and pizza and chowder places everywhere you turn. But it's got more of a blue-collar feel to it, a lived-in town full of people you might know.

Pedal through Watch Hill, on the other hand, putting Westerly behind you, and you may wonder how far you've gone—and who, exactly, lives there. You'll pass the marina, with its megayachts and sailboats, and climb a small hill past mansions bigger than many shopping malls, exotic cars lined up in the driveways. You'll smell the salt air, and it will give you wings.

From there, you'll head back to the real world, meeting up with busy US-1 for a short distance—the bike lane is wide and smooth, but you do need to get over to the left lane for a turn—before hitting the only real ascent of the ride, up Ross Hill Road.

After that it's a breeze, through Bradford and into a different part of downtown Westerly, cutting the corner on a residential neighborhood and coasting downhill to the starting point. Grab a cold drink and a bite to eat, sit in the park, and imagine yourself in one of those houses or yachts.

For more information on this area, visit the Watch Hill tourism website at www.visitwatchhill.com.

Options

To expand this ride, turn right at Mile 10.2 onto Bayberry Road, and right again onto Maplewood Avenue. Turn left at the end, onto Atlantic Avenue, riding along Misquamicut State Beach. At the end, turn left onto Weekapaug Road, and right onto US-1A, rejoining the original ride at Mile 11.8.

This ride is near Oh, Chariho!, which it overlaps. To combine them, turn right at the stop sign at Mile 24.7 onto Potter Hill Road, joining Oh, Chariho! at Mile 14.4. Turn left onto Switch Road, then another left onto Woodville Road. In 5 miles, you'll cross RI-3; stay straight onto Clarks Falls Road and turn left onto Boom Bridge Road in about 2 miles. At Mile 9.2, cross RI-184 and turn right at Mile 11.8 onto Spring Brook Avenue. Turn left onto White Rock Road, paralleling the Connecticut state line. Turn right onto Canal Street, and rejoin this ride at Mile 25.5.

Locals' Tip: Perks and Corks (48 High Street, Westerly, RI 02891, 401/596-1260, www.perksandcorks.com) coffee and martini bar is a cool little hangout in town, with couches, Wi-Fi, good coffee, good drinks, and a good atmosphere. It's a few hundred feet from the ride's start.

Places to Stay: The Andrea Hotel (89 Atlantic Avenue, Westerly, RI 02891, 888/318-5707) is beachfront at Misquamicut Beach in Westerly, offering ocean views and amenities.

Driving Directions

From I-95, take exit 1 toward Westerly, and take Main Street/RI-3 about 5 miles. Bear left to stay on RI-3, and turn right after the Wilcox Arboretum onto Broad Street/RI-2. Parking is along the street. The ride begins at the corner of Broad Street and Main Street in Westerly.

Route Directions

0.0 Turn LEFT on Main Street.

0.6 Bear RIGHT onto RI-1A/Beach Street.

2.3 Beach Street becomes Watch Hill Road. Stay on RI-1A.

3.7 Bear RIGHT to stay on Watch Hill Road. RI-1A turns left.

5.5 Bear RIGHT on Westerly Road, and then RIGHT again onto Wauwinnet Avenue, which becomes Bay Street. *The harbor is a nice place to stop and watch the boats come and go. Facilities and water are available.*

5.8 Bay Street becomes Larkin Road as it turns LEFT.

6.2 Turn LEFT onto Bluff Avenue.

6.4 Turn RIGHT onto Westerly Road.

6.7 Turn RIGHT onto Ninigret Avenue.

6.9 Turn LEFT onto Ocean View Highway.

7.5 Pass Misquamicut Country Club.

8.3 Turn RIGHT onto RI-1A/Shore Road.

10.2 OPTION: Turn RIGHT onto Bayberry Road and follow option directions.

13.1 Turn RIGHT onto US-1 (divided highway).

15.5 Turn LEFT onto Ross Hill Road/RI-216. To make the turn, get in the left lane of traffic at the light (watch for cars). This is the only real climb of the ride.

18.3 Turn LEFT onto Bradford Road/RI-91.

20.0 Bear RIGHT to stay on RI-91.

23.3 Turn RIGHT onto RI-3/High Street, a short climb.

24.1 Bear LEFT to stay on High Street. RI-3 turns off to the right.

24.7 Turn LEFT at stop sign onto Canal Street. OPTION: Turn RIGHT onto Potter Hill Road and follow option directions.

26.7 END at intersection with Broad Street.

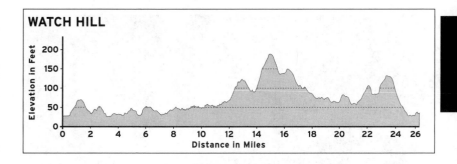

15 VIN GORMLEY TRAIL
Burlingame State Park, Charlestown

SINGLE-TRACK, PAVED ROADS, DIRT ROADS

Difficulty: 4

Riding Time: 2 hours

Total Distance: 8 miles

Elevation Gain: 315 feet

Summary: A popular, somewhat challenging trail, this ride explores the lakefront Burlingame State Park.

This is a popular trail, not just with mountain bikers but with hikers. In fact, all of Burlingame State Park—especially the picnic area by the lake—is often visited, and on a seasonable day you're likely to find a lot of people milling around, swimming, eating lunch by the lake, camping, or exploring the trails.

The state seems to allow mountain biking somewhat reluctantly in the park. Some trails are marked "Hikers Only." Respect the trail restrictions, and don't do anything to jeopardize biker access.

This trail ventures into deep woodlands and loops around Watchaug Pond. For the most part, it's well marked with yellow blazes and even, in some places, patterns to indicate turns. For general reference, or as a backup, refer to the trail map, posted at the Burlingame Picnic Area and in the campground and available at the campground office.

© CHRIS BERNARD

Mountain bikers will love the trails at Burlingame State Park, but on a summer day, expect to share the popular park with picnickers, beach-goers, anglers, and dogwalkers.

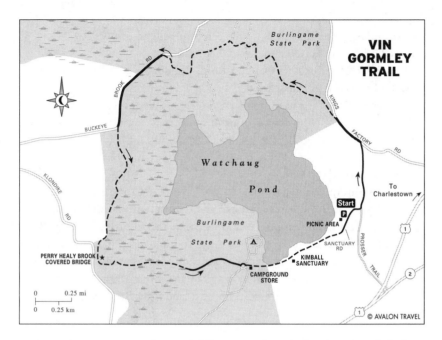

From the picnic area, this trail follows paved roads for about a mile before turning into the woods. The next 2 miles, across the north end of the pond, are technical and hilly, with some rocky sections, narrow rooty bits, and a few rocky places that pose the only real difficult stretch of this trail.

After a short stretch on another paved road, you head back into thick woods where marshy, wet areas have replaced rock ledges. There are several bridges, some quite long, and a sweet little covered bridge over the Perry Healy Brook. You'll ride on wide trails through pine forests and then along some rooty single-track before you enter the Burlingame State Park campground area.

After the campground, you'll pass through a very short stretch of the Audubon Society of Rhode Island's Kimball Wildlife Sanctuary, where you are required to walk your bike. Then there's a very bumpy gravel road to tackle before arriving back at the picnic area.

Burlingame State Park is a popular place and the campground has more than 700 sites; to avoid the crowds, try visiting after Labor Day. For more information, contact Burlingame State Park, US-1, Charlestown, RI 02813, 401/322-8910, www.riparks.com.

Options

This ride is near Oh, Chariho!, Worden Pond Loop, and Watch Hill. Rhode Island is small enough that all of these rides are relatively close to one another. If you're in the region for a few days, you can treat yourself to a variety of on- and off-road rides without riding the same route twice.

Locals' Tip: Cove (3963 Old Post Road, Charlestown, RI 02813, 401/364-9222) is known for its clam chowder.

Places to Stay: The nearby Surfside Motel (334 Narrow Lane, Charlestown, RI 02813, 401/364-1010, www.thesurfsidemotel.com) is walking distance from a beach, and close to Burlingame.

Driving Directions

From Westerly, drive about 5 miles on US-1 North. Pass the exit for the Burlingame Picnic Area and make a left exit and U-turn from the divided highway. From Wakefield and points east, take US-1 South and take the exit for the Burlingame Picnic Area. Drive 0.6 mile on Prosser Trail and turn left. The Burlingame Picnic Area has ample parking, picnic tables and shelters, seasonal restrooms, and a nice sandy swimming beach. There is a $2 fee in summer. Supplies are available in Charlestown, at convenience stores on US-1, and at the Burlingame State Park camp store in season. The closest bike shop is in Westerly.

Route Directions

0.0 Exit the picnic area parking lot.

0.2 Turn LEFT onto Prosser Trail.

0.7 Merge LEFT onto Kings Factory Road.

1.0 Turn LEFT into woods.

2.2 Jog RIGHT, then LEFT (cross a private camp road).

2.4 Cross a sandy, gravelly road.

2.8 Bear LEFT, following blazes.

3.0 Make a sharp RIGHT, following blazes.

3.3 Emerge and go LEFT on the Buckeye Brook Road.

3.6 Turn LEFT off Buckeye Brook Road into woods.

5.3 Arrive at stone wall and road. Follow trail LEFT back into woods.

5.4 Cross Perry Healy Brook covered bridge.

5.5 Turn LEFT at the T.

5.8 Trail curves to right.

6.4 Enter campground.

6.6 Continue STRAIGHT through rotary.

6.8 Continue STRAIGHT through rotary. Follow the right edge of the
playground and take a RIGHT at the end, heading back into the
woods. *The camp store is on the right, as are a pay phone and portable
toilets. The camp store hours are limited during the off-season.*

7.0 Enter the Kimball Wildlife Sanctuary. Walk your bike in this
section.

7.2 Resume riding on Sanctuary Road.

8.0 Return to Burlingame Picnic Area.

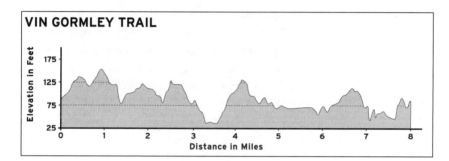

🔟🔢 ONCE AROUND THE BLOCK   BEST ◖
Block Island

PAVED ROADS WITH SOME UNEVEN PAVEMENT AND MINIMAL TRAFFIC

Difficulty: 2   **Total Distance:** 16.5 miles

Riding Time: 2 hours   **Elevation Gain:** 155 feet

Summary: A fun, beautiful ride for a lazy day exploring Block Island, this route does require a modicum of climbing.

Block Island is a popular place. How popular? Try to find cheap lodging during the summer and you'll find out. It's a splurge but worth it. And while this ride may not be the best ride judged on its own merits, like a lot of good rides, the context of its environment makes it better—much, much better.

In fact, it's hard to overstate just how much fun you can have biking around Block Island. This small island off Rhode Island's southern coast draws people with the unspoiled rugged beauty of its beaches, cliffs, and ponds. Even the constructed features appeal to people—the gray clapboard homes, a striking brick Victorian lighthouse, stone walls lining roads and fields.

You'll find fewer people on the island and better rooming rates in spring or fall. It's breezier, but you may have the back roads to yourself.

Along this ride, you'll pass many dirt side roads. A hybrid or mountain bike, or ideally, a cyclocross bike, will let you explore them while still making the most of the paved roads of the main route, which makes a counterclockwise loop around the island.

Heading north, you'll go to Settler's Rock at the tip and then back, with one steep hill at Sachem Pond to tackle. Three outstanding beaches on either side of the island are accessible by short rides along dirt roads, so leave plenty of time to poke around.

On the southern part, it's worth a stop at Mohegan Bluffs, near the end of the ride, even if you don't want to climb the 144 steps to and from the beach—you'll still get a fantastic view of the cliffs and the dramatic sweep of Crescent Beach.

For more information, contact the Block Island Chamber of Commerce, 401/466-2982 or 800/383-BIRI (800/383-2474), www.blockislandchamber.com.

Options
Ride this same loop clockwise instead of counterclockwise, which frontloads a

good, steep climb at the beginning of the route and renders the rest of the ride entirely downhill.

The Point Judith ferry terminal is also on the loop for A Point, Two Towers, and the Pier.

Locals' Tip: Deadeye Dick's (Payne's Dock, New Harbor, Block Island, RI 02807, 401/466-2654, www.deadeyedicksbi.com, open seasonally Memorial Day through Labor Day) offers waterside seating and a seafood-heavy menu with reasonable prices—and it's right on the ride.

Places to Stay: There are a plethora of downtown options at varying price ranges, but the Rose Farm Inn (P.O. Box E, Block Island, RI 02807, 401/466-2034, www.rosefarminn.com) offers a country setting on a former

working farm now home to deer, pheasant, and more, as well as an on-site bike rental facility.

Driving Directions

Two main ferries go to Block Island: a year-round car and passenger ferry that takes 55 minutes and arrives in Old Harbor (www.blockislandferry.com) and a high-speed catamaran (passengers only) that takes 30 minutes and arrives in New Harbor (www.islandhighspeedferry.com). Both leave from the main pier in Galilee. Ferries also travel from Newport, Rhode Island, and New London, Connecticut. On Block Island, you'll find several bike rental places, bike shops, supplies, public restrooms, bike racks, and lockers in Old Harbor.

Route Directions

0.0 From the ferry terminal in Old Harbor, go RIGHT onto Water Street, which hooks left and becomes Dodge Street.

0.4 Turn RIGHT onto Corn Neck Road, passing Block Island State Beach and heading north past Sachem Pond to the tip of the island.

4.2 TURN AROUND.

7.7 Turn RIGHT on Beach Avenue.

8.0 Turn RIGHT onto Ocean Avenue, and take it to the end of the road at the edge of the Great Salt Pond. TURN AROUND and turn RIGHT onto West Side Road.

11.0 Turn LEFT onto Cooneymus Road.

12.5 Turn RIGHT on Lakeside Drive.

13.5 Turn LEFT on Mohegan Trail, which becomes Spring Street.

16.4 Turn RIGHT to Old Harbor.

16.5 END at parking area.

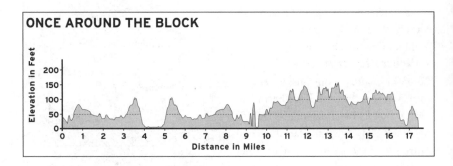

ONCE AROUND THE BLOCK

CONNECTICUT

© CHRIS BERNARD

BEST BIKE RIDES

The first sign that Connecticut is somehow different

from the rest of New England is the number of New York Yankees baseball caps worn by its residents. In any other New England state, the hometown heroes are the Boston Red Sox, and you'll see the team logo flown more proudly – and more frequently – than the state flag.

Connecticut, especially the crowded southwestern corner, is linked more to New York City than New England. But just a short drive into the state and you'll find yourself surrounded by rural country lanes, rolling hills, sharp ridges, and cow-studded fields. Welcome back to New England – enjoy your stay.

And you *will* enjoy it. Guarantee it by making plans to ride as many of the routes included here as possible, and then set out on your own to find more.

Start in the state's rural northwest corner, riding the long, rolling roads near Salisbury, the shady lanes around Lake Waramaug, and the blissful farm country of the Horse Heaven Hills ride in Washington. Make your way east, sampling the bike paths that leave Manchester, the country-side of Canterbury and Scotland, or the hilly towns around Barkhamsted Reservoir. Then head south to ride along the ocean's edge in Niantic and Madison or up the relentless hills from historic downtown Mystic into the sunflower-laden pasturelands of the countryside.

Connecticut has its share of off-road trails, too, and they hold their own against the best New England single-track. Rip it up at Case Mountain, where you'll find slick rock formations to test your skills or on the woodsy trails at Westwoods, on the Air Line Trail, or at Bluff Point or Huntington State Parks. Find it hard to believe a state so close to Manhattan, and with such dense urban areas as Bridgeport and New Haven, can have so much wild single-track? Get your tires dirty and become a believer.

With so many rides in Connecticut, where do you begin? The southeast corner of the state is packed with tourist attractions – including two major casinos and busy, touristy seaport towns. It's a good place to start, with access to many Connecticut rides (as well as most Rhode Island rides). But really, pick a part of Connecticut and you can't go wrong – you'll find places to ride nearby.

It's a popular state for cyclists, and its bicycle history goes way back; in the 1800s, a Civil-War-colonel-turned-businessman named Albert Pope created the country's first manufacturing plant for the modern bicycle in Hartford. Popular bike maker Cannondale has long been Connecticut-based. Today the state has its share of bike advocacy groups, and a good number of riding clubs. You'll see members on the roads and trails in matching kits. Stop and strike up a conversation with any of them – they tend to be tremendous resources. They'll sing the state's praises in terms of cycling, and if you spend any time on the routes in this chapter, you're likely to agree with them.

Enjoy Connecticut and all it has to offer. Just do yourself a favor and don't buy any Yankees hats.

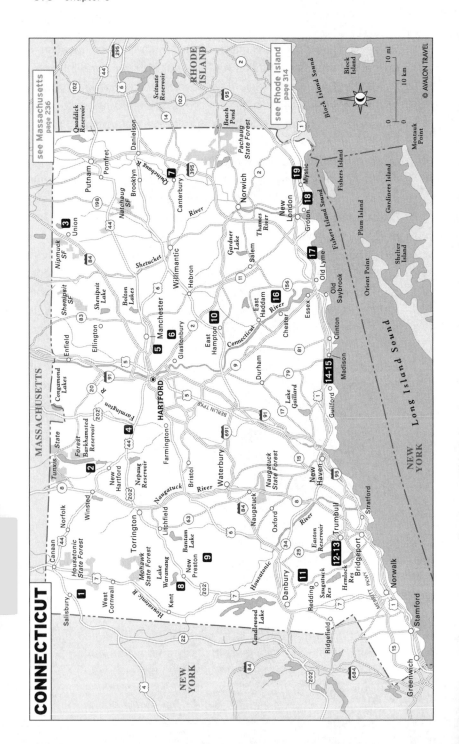

RIDE NAME	DIFFICULTY	DISTANCE	TIME	ELEVATION	PAGE
1 Salisbury Hills and Hollows	3	20.2 mi	2 hr	1,360 ft	378
2 Barkhamsted Reservoir Loop	4	23.6 mi	2-2.5 hr	2,200 ft	382
3 Breakneck Pond Loop	2	7 mi	1-1.5 hr	365 ft	385
4 Flora and Fauna Ride	2	30.6 mi	2 hr	535 ft	388
5 Charter Oak Greenway Sampler	3	31.8 mi	2 hr	883 ft	392
6 Case Mountain Scramble	5	11.4 mi	2-2.5 hr	780 ft	397
7 Little Britain Ride	2	24.4 mi	1.5-2 hr	761 ft	401
8 Lake Waramaug Ups and Downs	3	20.2 mi	1-2 hr	1,195 ft	405
9 Horse Heaven Hills	3	28.7 mi	2 hr	1,381 ft	409
10 Air Line Trail	2	21.4 mi	2-2.5 hr	1,315 ft	412
11 Huntington Sampler	3	7.9 mi	1-1.5 hr	615 ft	415
12 Fairfield Rural	3	39.4 mi	3 hr	945 ft	419
13 Pequonnock River Valley Ride	2	5.8 mi	1.5 hr	195 ft	423
14 Westwoods Trails	4	4.5 mi	1.5-2 hr	345 ft	426
15 Madison Beach	1	14.5 mi	1.5-2 hr	177 ft	429
16 Devil's Hopyard Loop	3	27.1 mi	2.5 hr	1,680 ft	433
17 Niantic Bay Loop	2	27.7 mi	2 hr	700 ft	437
18 Bluff Point Loop	3	7.5 mi	1.5-2 hr	425 ft	441
19 Mystic Birthday Ride	5	50 mi	3 hr	1,673 ft	445

1 SALISBURY HILLS AND HOLLOWS
Salisbury

PAVED ROADS WITH MINIMAL TO MODERATE TRAFFIC

Difficulty: 3   **Total Distance:** 20.2 miles

Riding Time: 2 hours   **Elevation Gain:** 1,360 feet

Summary: A hilly route through rural countryside, this ride is for cyclists with moderate levels of fitness.

The rolling green hills of the Berkshires reach into this pretty corner of north-western Connecticut, and the miles of quiet backcountry roads that run through farmlands make for nice bike outings. The starting point for this ride is the town of Salisbury, where you'll find cafés, markets, ice-cream shops, and tea rooms.

The first stretch, along Salmon Kill Road, follows gently rolling hills with views of the ridges on either side, past nicely manicured lawns, stone walls, split-rail fences, babbling brooks, and the occasional farm. Be careful as you ride a short stretch on CT-112, where traffic moves faster. Turning onto White Hollow Road takes you past Lime Rock Park, where traffic can be ridiculous when races are on. People pour in to camp on the fields and watch the NASCAR and Grand Prix races at the "Road Racing Center of the East"—check the schedule online at www.limerock.com before planning a trip.

After the track, you've got a few gentle hills before a steep climb up Calkinstown

This ride follows smooth, paved roads as they snake through the very rural northwestern corner of Connecticut.

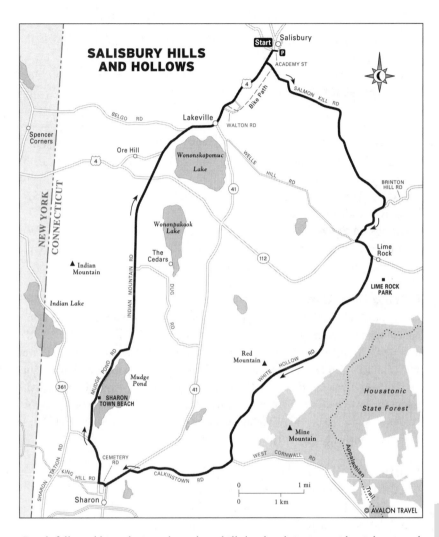

Road, followed by a glorious, long downhill that heads into a residential area and wraps itself into tight curves on the outskirts of Sharon. There's some fast traffic on CT-41, and then a sharp right to a steep descent on uneven pavement past a scenic cemetery.

It's downhill all the way on CT-361 before the poorly marked turn to Mudge Pond Road. After some nice views of the pond and an opportunity to stop and swim, you face a good-sized climb up Indian Hill with more pastoral scenes and nice mountain views. As you approach Lakeville, you'll get some good views of Wononskopomuc Lake.

If you've got thick tires or a hybrid, consider taking the bike path on an old railroad bed back to Salisbury, marked with a gate and a sign billing the Railroad Ramble.

For more information, contact the Litchfield Hills Visitors Bureau, P.O. Box 968, Litchfield, CT 06759, 860/567-4506, www.litchfieldhills.com.

Options

This ride is a reasonable distance from Barkhamsted Reservoir Loop. Both rides are similar, rural and hilly, and combined would make an excellent weekend of riding.

Locals' Tip: Tea at Chaiwalla (1 Main Street, Salisbury, CT 06068, 860/435-9758) is just what the doctor ordered after a cool spring or autumn ride.

Places to Stay: For more than 100 years, the White Hart Inn (15 Undermountain Road, Salisbury, CT 06068, 860/435-0030, www.whitehartinn.com) has offered comfortable rooms in a beautiful building.

Driving Directions

From Hartford, take CT-44 west approximately 47 miles to Salisbury. From Danbury and points south, take CT-7 to Kent. Continue on CT-7 for approximately 18 miles, past West Cornwall, and turn left onto CT-112 (Lime Rock Road). Drive approximately 7 miles and turn right onto CT-41. Drive 2.5 miles and turn right onto CT-44. Drive 2.5 miles into Salisbury. Turn right onto Academy Street, opposite the town hall, and park at Salisbury Marketplace. The route begins at the corner of Main Street and Academy Street, opposite Salisbury Town Hall. Supplies are available in Salisbury.

Route Directions

0.0 Ride south on Main Street (CT-44).

0.3 Turn LEFT onto Salmon Kill Road.

3.7 At fork, bear RIGHT on Salmon Kill Road.

4.0 Curve RIGHT and cross bridge.

4.5 Turn LEFT onto CT-112 (Lime Rock Road).

4.8 Turn RIGHT onto White Hollow Road.

5.1 Pass entrance to Lime Rock Park.

9.2 Turn RIGHT at triangle onto Calkinstown Road.

10.3 Make a sharp right, then left, curve.

11.1 Turn LEFT onto CT-41. *Supplies available in Sharon.*

11.6 Turn RIGHT onto Cemetery Road.

11.7 Turn RIGHT onto CT-361.

12.4 Turn RIGHT onto Mudge Pond Road (poorly marked).

13.8 Bear RIGHT at fork.

13.9 *Entrance to Sharon town beach on right, with small sandy beach, pay phone, changing rooms, restrooms, picnic tables, and playground.*

17.0 Continue STRAIGHT across CT-112, staying on Indian Mountain Road.

17.5 Turn RIGHT onto CT-44 (Millerton Road).

18.5 Continue STRAIGHT at fork with CT-41 in Lakeville. *Supplies available in Lakeville.*

18.8 Optional return route: Turn RIGHT onto Walton Road, ride to the end, and look for the signs for the bike path on the LEFT. The path starts paved but turns into a grassy narrow single-track, suitable for hybrid or mountain bikes. You come out onto Salmon Kill Road; turn LEFT, then RIGHT onto Main Street to return to Salisbury.

19.1 Continue STRAIGHT through traffic light.

20.2 Return to corner of Main Street and Academy Street.

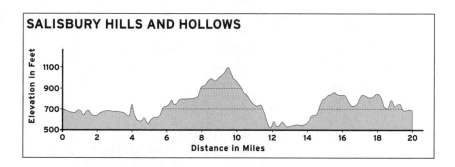

SALISBURY HILLS AND HOLLOWS

2 BARKHAMSTED RESERVOIR LOOP
Lake McDonough Recreation Area, Barkhamsted

PAVED ROADS WITH MINIMAL TO MODERATE TRAFFIC

Difficulty: 4   **Total Distance:** 23.6 miles

Riding Time: 2-2.5 hours   **Elevation Gain:** 2,200 feet

Summary: This scenic route puts serious demands on your legs with tons of climbing over not-a-lot of distance.

Barkhamsted Reservoir, the state's largest water supply, is surrounded by unspoiled, undeveloped, leafy countryside, much of which is state forest land—especially to the north and west. The forest is calming, the forest is peaceful. Which is good, because you'll need something to settle your stomach as you start the climbing.

Once it starts, it never ends. This is a ride for fit cyclists who want a fun, challenging workout along quiet, pretty rural roads. Most of the route is under heavy foliage, which means shade in summer and beautiful colors in autumn.

The route begins at the Lake McDonough Recreation Area, a place you can dip your quads and calves after the ride to put out the fire. It's a tricky start: turn uphill onto CT-219, then left across Saville Dam. With views of the reservoir on the right and Lake McDonough on the left, the dam offers some spectacular views.

Turn right after the reservoir, up a steep, bumpy, uneven side road to start the circuit around the reservoir. The climbing begins with one big hill, followed by

The Saville Dam gatehouse adds a measure of constructed beauty to the natural scenery of Barkhamsted Reservoir.

a series of smaller hills, one after the other, relentless, as you ride along this leafy, largely undeveloped road.

In West Hartland you get a break—the hills are only rolling ones—before one more big climb at Mile 5. Still more rolling hills take you along the northwest shore, allowing occasional views of the ridges to the east and the water below. At Mile 11, sneak a peek at the reservoir and take a break. Your legs will love you for it.

Two miles downhill, then two miles uphill at the northern end of the reservoir, bring you into East Hartland. There's a bit more traffic along this eastern side of the reservoir, especially on CT-219. The road has a wide, smooth shoulder, but like many shoulders, it can be sandy. Finish on a steep, long downhill—yes, a downhill—with a dangerous left turn at the end—heads up.

For more information, contact the Metropolitan District Barkhamsted Headquarters, 39 Beach Rock Road, Pleasant Valley, CT 06063, 860/379-3036, www.themdc.com/lakemcdonough.htm.

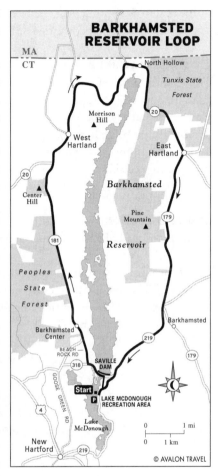

Options

Got some juice left in the legs? Add a 10-mile extension to the ride by turning left onto Ratlum Road around Mile 21. Stay straight, then turn left on CT-219. At New Hartford Center, turn right onto Prospect Street, then right onto Holcomb Hill Road, which becomes Goose Green Road. Turn right onto CT-319, Saville Dam Road, and cross the dam. Turn right on CT-219 to return to the parking area.

This ride is close to the Flora and Fauna Ride.

Locals' Tip: Chatterly's Restaurant (2 Bridge Street, New Hartford, CT 06057, 860/379-2428, www.chatterlysct.com) was built in the 1800s, and the building has some history to it—ask the bartender.

Places to Stay: Rest your tired legs in a tub at the Rose and Thistle B&B (24 Woodland Acres, Barkhamsted, CT 06063, 860/379-4744).

Driving Directions

From Hartford, take CT-44 west for approximately 18 miles to New Hartford. Turn right onto CT-219 and drive 3.6 miles along the shores of Lake McDonough. Turn left into the recreation area. The parking fee is $6; you can park at the boat launch or at the beach in season. You'll find several beaches with changing rooms and lifeguards, rowboat and paddleboat rentals, picnic sites, and nature trails. Supplies are available in New Hartford, but not at any point along the ride. Bike shops are nearby in Canton, Granby, and Simsbury.

Route Directions

0.0 From the Lake McDonough Recreation Area entrance road, turn LEFT onto CT-219.

0.4 Turn LEFT at triangle toward dam, and then make an immediate LEFT onto CT-318 to cross the dam.

1.3 Turn RIGHT onto Beach Rock Road (unmarked).

2.0 Bear RIGHT onto CT-181.

7.2 Continue STRAIGHT through intersection onto CT-20.

15.9 At stop sign, take a RIGHT and an immediate LEFT onto CT-179 (South Street) in East Hartland.

20.4 Stay to the RIGHT at intersection to continue on CT-219 (CT-179 veers to left).

21.0 OPTION: Turn left onto Ratlum Road and follow option directions.

23.0 LEFT turn at junction to stay on CT-219. (Caution: This is an extremely difficult intersection and turn. Come to a complete stop before turning.)

23.6 RIGHT to return to Lake McDonough Recreation Area.

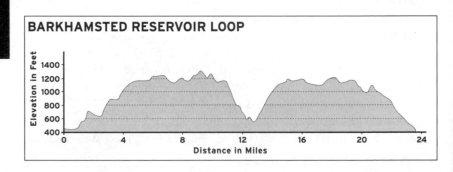

BARKHAMSTED RESERVOIR LOOP

3 BREAKNECK POND LOOP

BEST ☾

Bigelow Hollow State Park, Union

DIRT AND FIRE ROADS

Difficulty: 2

Riding Time: 1–1.5 hours

Total Distance: 7 miles

Elevation Gain: 365 feet

Summary: These fast, flat fire roads are well-suited to cyclocross bikes, beginner mountain bikers, or nature lovers.

Bigelow Hollow State Park and the adjacent Nipmuck State Forest encompass more than 9,000 acres, all entirely within the state's smallest town, Union. Bigelow Hollow is beautiful—the park is forested largely by hemlock and white pine, with a dense, low year-round canopy. Plenty of hilly, very technical single-track trails mean even strong riders may find some steep, technical hills that force them to their feet.

The state has worked to reduce the number of hikers and bike riders who manage to get lost in Bigelow by clearly marking trails and developing a detailed map of the area. The problem seems to have gotten better, but this is still a park where it's easy to get turned around. Everything looks alike.

The park's high water table means puddles and mud, as well as mosquitoes and deer flies. Locals have worked to solve the first problem by building log bridges and other stunts to cross the deeper waterholes. For the second problem, well, you're on your own, but DEET is a good start.

This route follows the dirt and fire roads around the shoreline of Breakneck Pond. Though it's a relatively easy ride, there are some difficult parts where the road is washed out and covered in rolling rocks. You'll pass many short side trips to the pond's edge, all worth exploring, and in the fall, when the leaves are brightest and reflecting in the water, this park seems like it's on fire.

Start at the dirt parking lot overlooking Bigelow Pond and continue around Breakneck Pond. The ride out

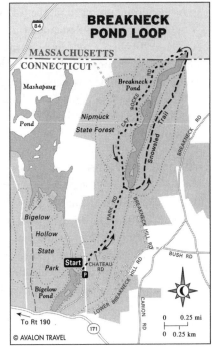

to the turning point is mostly flat on dirt roads. At the apex of the ride, the trail dips briefly into Massachusetts (look for the stone monument on the right side of the trail).

The return route is somewhat more hilly and technical, though still fairly easy. Several water crossings can be two or three feet deep at times, especially in spring. The logs across the water provide another option for those who don't want to get wet. Finish the ride along the same dirt roads you came in on.

If you're riding in the fall, be aware that hunting is allowed in the park, though not on Sundays. In the summer, a dip in crystal-clear Mashapaug Pond is an excellent way to end a warm ride. On summer weekends the park can get quite busy with boaters and swimmers, though once you leave the parking and swimming areas, it's likely you will encounter very few, if any, other people.

This ride is ideal for cyclocross bikes and well-suited to mountain bikes.

For more information, contact Bigelow Hollow State Park, c/o Shenipsit State Forest, 166 Chestnut Hill Road, Stafford Springs, CT 06076, 860/684-3430, www.ct.gov.

Options

The best way to extend this ride is to explore the trails. Grab a trail map at the park entrance or download one from the park website, and give yourself ample time.

Locals' Tip: Traveler Restaurant (1257 Buckley Highway, Union, CT 06076, 860/684-4920) offers an odd, pleasing mix of bites and books. One floor is packed with free books for diners to choose with their meal; another sells additional, high-quality used books for reasonable prices. It's definitely worth a stop.

Places to Stay: Give the Pond House B&B (19 Crystal Lake Road, Stafford Springs, CT 06076, 860/684-1644, www.pondhousebb.com) a call if you need a place to stay.

Driving Directions

From points west and south, take I-84 east to exit 73 and take a right onto CT-190. From points east and north, take I-84 west to exit 73 and take a left from the exit onto CT-190. Follow CT-190 east for 3 miles, and turn right onto CT-171. Drive 1.4 miles to Bigelow Hollow State Park; the entrance is on the left. Follow the access road 0.6 mile to the parking lot on the left. A parking fee, on weekends only, is $14 for Connecticut residents and $20 for nonresidents. The park has picnic tables and outhouses. Bike shops can be found in Putnam.

Route Directions

0.0 Take a LEFT out of the parking lot onto the paved road and take the first RIGHT onto the dirt road behind the park building onto Chateau Road.

0.3 Turn LEFT onto Park Road.

1.3 Turn RIGHT onto Snowsled Trail.

2.8 Stay to the LEFT at junction.

3.3 At the end of Breakneck Pond, turn LEFT onto Cat Rocks Road.

4.7 Turn LEFT.

5.0 Turn LEFT onto Breakneck Hill Road.

5.2 Stay LEFT at fork to remain on Breakneck Hill Road. (Caution: washed-out road.)

5.7 Turn RIGHT to return to Park Road.

6.7 Turn RIGHT onto Chateau Road.

7.0 Take LEFT onto paved road. The parking lot is on the right.

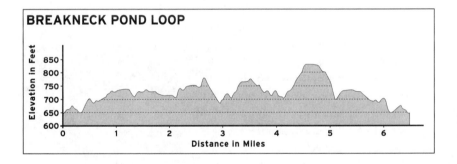

BREAKNECK POND LOOP

❹ FLORA AND FAUNA RIDE
McLean Game Refuge, Granby

PAVED ROADS WITH MODERATE TRAFFIC

Difficulty: 2   **Total Distance:** 30.6 miles

Riding Time: 2 hours   **Elevation Gain:** 535 feet

Summary: This mostly quiet, mostly flat ride with some nice country scenery will appeal to any rider.

The fauna in this ride's name refers to the animals of the McLean Game Refuge, 3,400 acres of land bequeathed to the state by Senator and former Governor George McLean. This refuge has grown by nearly 1,000 acres since then, and is home to fish, reptiles, birds, and mammals, including 16 rare or endangered species. The ride loops around the refuge, and while bikes are prohibited on its trails, you're welcome to walk your bike in to the pond and cabin for a scenic lunch break.

And the flora? Sure, there are more rural parts of the state where you'll see more trees, fields, and forests, but this ride scoots past two trees of note. First is the Constitution Oak, planted in 1901 to commemorate the Connecticut Con-stitutional Convention by local delegate Joseph Bartlett. This large, impressive oak sits in an island along Terry's Plain Road. Stop as you pass for a picture.

Second, and perhaps even more im-pressive, is the Pinchot Sycamore, the largest tree in Connecticut and one of the largest of its species in the coun-try. Named for former resident and first chief of the U.S. Forest Service Gifford Pinchot, this tree is estimated to be as much as 300 years old, nearly 100 feet tall, and more than 26 feet around. Perched over the banks of the Farm-ington River in the last miles of the ride, this is an excellent spot to stop for a rest—and a photo.

You'll also pass Simsbury's Bridge of Flowers, inspired by a similar bridge in Shelburne Falls, Massachusetts. Residents have developed landscaping

© CHRIS BERNARD

Towering over the Farmington River, the Pinchot Sycamore is the largest tree in Connecticut.

on and around the Drake Hill Bridge, including hanging flower planters and window boxes.

Aside from these notable sights, this ride follows a mix of roads ranging from minimal to moderate traffic. It's a fun ride that crosses a pair of interesting bridges, with the occasional long-distance view to catch your eye, including the ponderous Heublein Tower, a 165-foot observation tower in nearby Talcott Mountain State Park. It was built by the man who owned A1 Steak Sauce—a good bit of trivia for winning bar bets.

For more information, contact the McLean Game Refuge, 150 Barndoor Hills Road, Granby, CT 06035, 860/653-7869, www.mcleangamerefuge.com.

Options

If you don't have the time, or the legs, for a 30-mile ride, cut more than 7 miles out by skipping the McLean Game Refuge loop. At Mile 10.9, stay straight on Holcomb Street. At the stop sign, turn right onto Country Road, rejoining the ride at Mile 19.2.

This ride is near Case Mountain Scramble and Charter Oak Greenway Sampler.

Locals' Tip: Try the pizza at the First and Last Tavern (24 West Main Street, Avon, CT 06001, 860/676-2000, www.firstandlasttavern.com).

Places to Stay: The Simsbury 1820 House (731 Hopmeadow Street, Simsbury, CT 06070, 860/658-7658, www.simsbury1820house.com) is in a beautifully restored mansion and very plush.

Driving Directions

From I-84, take exit 43 and turn left at Park Road. Take the third right onto South Main Street, and after 2.3 miles, turn LEFT onto Albany Avenue/US-44. Stay straight for 5 miles, then turn right at CT-10/Simsbury Road/US-202. The parking area is your second right.

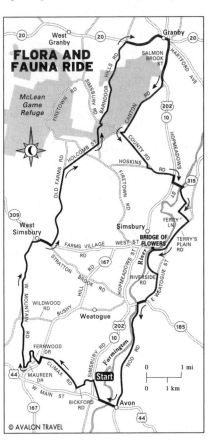

Route Directions

0.0 From the parking area, cross CT-10/202 onto Fisher Drive.

0.3 Turn LEFT onto Ensign Street and RIGHT onto Bickford Road.

0.7 At the stop sign, turn RIGHT onto Climax Road (unmarked).

2.0 At the end of the road, turn LEFT onto CT-167.

2.2 Turn RIGHT onto Fernwood Drive.

3.0 Turn RIGHT onto Maureen Drive.

3.2 At the end of the road, turn RIGHT at the stop sign onto West Mountain Road.

6.9 Turn RIGHT at the stop sign to stay on West Mountain Road.

7.1 Turn RIGHT onto CT-309. *Supplies available.*

7.4 Turn LEFT at the light, onto Old Farms Road.

9.7 Turn RIGHT onto Holcomb Street.

10.4 At the stop sign, stay STRAIGHT on Holcomb Street.

10.9 Turn LEFT onto Barndoor Hills Road.

11.5 Turn LEFT onto Simsbury Hills Road (unmarked), and then RIGHT immediately onto Barndoor Hills Road.

13.0 Pass McLean Game Refuge.

14.1 Turn RIGHT at stop sign onto CT-20. Watch for traffic.

15.4 Bear RIGHT at light onto CT-10/202.

16.4 Turn RIGHT into McLean Game Refuge for optional stop. TURN AROUND.

17.0 Turn RIGHT onto CT-10/202.

17.2 Turn RIGHT at light onto Canton Road, bearing RIGHT.

19.2 Turn LEFT at stop sign onto County Road.

20.4 Turn RIGHT onto Kilbourn Road.

20.5 Turn LEFT at stop sign onto Hoskins Road (unmarked).

21.0 At Y intersection, bear RIGHT to stay on Hoskins Road.

21.2 Turn RIGHT at stop sign onto CT-10/202. Watch for traffic, and get to the left when you can.

21.4 Turn LEFT at light onto CT-315, watching for traffic, and cross bridge.

21.7 Turn RIGHT onto Terry's Plain Road.

22.0 Turn RIGHT onto Goodrich Road, which loops and becomes Ferry Road.

22.8 Turn RIGHT at stop sign onto Terry's Plain Road. *The Constitution Oak is in the island with the stop sign.*

23.8 Turn RIGHT at Riverside Drive at the Farmington River.

24.4 Pass the Bridge of Flowers, on your right.

25.2 Turn RIGHT at stop sign onto East Weatogue Road.

26.0 Turn RIGHT at stop sign onto CT-185.

26.3 Turn LEFT on dirt road into small park. The Pinchot Sycamore is there, marked with a plaque, as well as access to the Farmington River. TURN AROUND and retrace your steps to the road.

26.4 Stay STRAIGHT at traffic light, crossing CT-185 onto Nod Road. The river is on your right, and views of the Heublein Tower and Talcott Mountain can be seen to your left.

29.7 Turn RIGHT at light onto CT-44. Watch for traffic. This road can be busy.

30.0 Turn RIGHT onto Mountain View Road.

30.3 Turn RIGHT onto bike path.

30.4 Turn LEFT before park bench onto path to Sperry Park.

30.6 END at parking area.

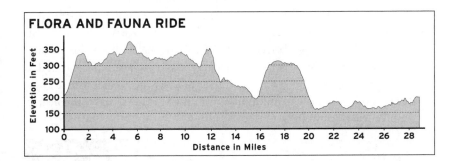

FLORA AND FAUNA RIDE

5 CHARTER OAK GREENWAY SAMPLER
Manchester to Bolton

PAVED OR HARD-PACKED BIKE TRAILS, PAVED ROADS, MINIMAL TRAFFIC

Difficulty: 3   **Total Distance:** 31.8 miles

Riding Time: 2 hours   **Elevation Gain:** 883 feet

Summary: A mix of wandering bike paths and paved roads suitable for riders who can handle a few small hills.

The East Coast Greenway runs throughout the northeast, appearing in fits and starts in different states as progress is made on its construction. It's an ongoing process, and progress is not made equally along its length. Similarly, the greenway runs throughout this book, appearing now and again on different trails that overlap the master route that someday will run from Maine to Florida.

This ride follows the Charter Oak Greenway, a section of the longer trail that connects East Hartford (and the Captain John Bissell Greenway) with Bolton. Built for commuters as well as recreation, this trail highlights all the things a good commuter route can be, with access to picnic areas, restrooms, athletic facilities, and playgrounds, as well as connections to major area roads. Bike lockers are provided at two locations along its length, as well, making it easy and convenient to leave bikes confidently and securely.

© CHRIS BERNARD

This ride begins and ends on the Charter Oak Greenway, part of the larger East Coast Greenway work-in-progress.

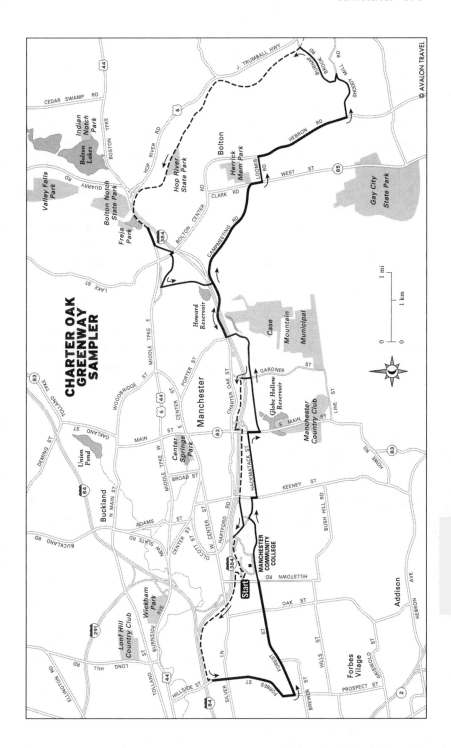

Beginning at Manchester Community College, this route follows the greenway for nearly eight miles on either end of the ride. In between, it makes a large loop to the east on mostly quiet roads to pick up the Hop River State Park Trail before making its way back west.

Be warned that at times, the trail parallels highways and major roads—it's not a peacefully quiet backwoods trail, and the sounds (and occasionally, smells) of exhaust are ever present. In addition, this isn't a flat rail trail. There are some good hills to climb, though nothing insurmountable for the average rider.

Parts of the path are paved and parts are a heavily compressed stone dust. Road bikes and hybrid bikes are suitable for the surface along its entire length.

The Charter Oak Greenway gets its name from a historical anecdote which may be, at least in parts, apocryphal. When King James II consolidated New England colonies, he sent Sir Edmund Andros to govern them. Andros made known his intention to physically retrieve, and presumably destroy, each colony's charter. Local Joseph Wadsworth stole the charter out from under Andros and hid it in a massive ancient white oak.

For more information or to download a map, visit the state of Connecticut online at www.ct.gov/dot/LIB/dot/documents/dbikes/020.pdf. This ride is suggested by Connecticut Bike Routes; contact them at www.ctbikeroutes.org for more information.

Options

Riders looking for an easier ride without the road portions can limit themselves to the bike path, turning around at any point.

This ride is very close to Case Mountain Scramble and a reasonable drive from Air Line Trail.

Locals' Tip: The Main Pub (306 Main Street, Manchester, CT 06040, 860/647-1551, www.mainpub.com) serves, among other things, excellent sandwiches. Get one up front and bring it along for the ride.

Places to Stay: The Mansion Inn B&B (139 Hartford Road, Manchester, CT 06040, 860/646-0453, www.themansioninnct.com) is stocked with hundreds of books and is a welcoming place to stay.

Driving Directions

From I-84, take I-384 east, then exit 1 for Spencer Street. At the end of the exit ramp, turn left at the traffic light onto Spencer Street. Just past the shopping center, turn right on Hillstown Road; 0.25 mile later, turn left on Great Path. In another 0.25 mile, turn right onto the Manchester Community College perimeter road, and then left into Parking Lot C. Proceed to the back of the lot to Emergency Pole Box 9. The ride starts from there.

Route Directions

0.0 From Emergency Pole Box 9, cross road and bear RIGHT onto bike path.

0.1 Cross Great Path Road, staying STRAIGHT on bike path, bearing LEFT on narrow bike path at ballfield, then make a quick RIGHT onto wider bike path.

0.9 Cross Spencer Street at light to stay on bike path.

1.4 Stay STRAIGHT past path to Wickham Park on right.

2.4 Turn LEFT at the end of the bike path onto Forbes Street.

2.8 Cross Silver Lane at light to stay on Forbes Street.

4.1 Turn LEFT onto Forest Street, which becomes Woodside Street.

6.1 Turn LEFT at end onto Hillstown Road, then make a quick RIGHT onto Wetherell Street path on a wide sidewalk over I-384.

7.3 Turn RIGHT onto Bidwell Street.

7.7 Turn RIGHT at end onto Keeney Street.

7.8 Turn LEFT onto Hackmatack Street.

8.9 Turn RIGHT at end onto South Main Street (CT-83), which becomes Horace Street.

9.0 Turn LEFT onto Spring Street.

10.8 Bear RIGHT to stay on Spring Street at Glen Road.

11.1 Turn RIGHT at light onto Highland Street, which becomes Campmeeting Road.

14.0 Bear RIGHT at West Street/CT-85 south.

14.2 Turn LEFT at Loomis Road.

14.6 Turn RIGHT on Hebron Road.

15.4 Cross School Street.

16.3 Turn LEFT onto Shoddy Mill Road.

17.1 Turn LEFT onto Skinner Road, which becomes Burnap Brook Road.

18.1 Turn LEFT onto rail trail.

20.6 Cross Steeles Crossing Road to stay on trail.

22.4 Stay STRAIGHT through US-6 tunnel. Caution: Bad road surface; walk bikes through tunnel.

22.6 Turn LEFT, heading through parking lot and out on the gravel road.

22.7 Turn RIGHT on shoulder of US-6/US-44 West, and bear RIGHT to continue when I-384 splits left.

23.0 Stay STRAIGHT to stay on the Boston Turnpike (US-44).
Commuter parking lot with bike lockers to your right.

23.3 Turn LEFT on Williams Street.

23.7 Turn RIGHT at stop sign onto CT-85 south.

23.8 Turn LEFT onto Carpenter Road, which becomes Bolton Center Road.

24.4 Turn LEFT sharply at stop sign onto Finley Street.

25.4 Turn RIGHT onto Campmeeting Road, which becomes Highland Street.

26.4 Turn LEFT at light onto Spring Street, passing over I-384.

26.6 Bear LEFT to stay on Spring Street at Glen Road.

27.5 Turn RIGHT onto Gardner Street.

27.7 Turn LEFT onto West Gardner Street, and take a quick LEFT onto bike path.

28.7 Turn sharply to the LEFT, following the path's 160-degree turn over the highway.

29.0 Bear LEFT to stay on the bike path.

29.7 At stop sign, cross road to stay on path.

30.3 Cross Keeney Street at stop sign and stay STRAIGHT on Wetherell Street.

30.8 Turn RIGHT at stop sign onto Bidwell Street.

31.0 Turn LEFT onto bike path next to Manchester Community College.

31.7 Bear LEFT past corner of athletic field.

31.7 Cross Great Path to stay on bike path.

31.8 Turn LEFT and cross road into parking lot. END at parking area.

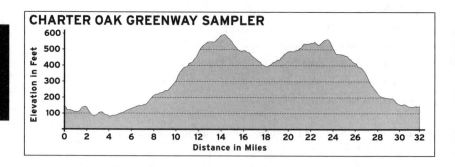

CHARTER OAK GREENWAY SAMPLER

6 CASE MOUNTAIN SCRAMBLE   BEST 〔
Case Mountain, Glastonbury

SINGLE-TRACK, DOUBLE-TRACK, FIRE ROADS

Difficulty: 5   **Total Distance:** 11.4 miles

Riding Time: 2-2.5 hours   **Elevation Gain:** 780 feet

Summary: Technically proficient mountain bikers will be right at home on these multisurface trails.

This area is popular with mountain bikers in central Connecticut, and it's no wonder, with more than 20 miles of very technical, mostly single-track trails to choose from. During the season, weekends bring lots of bikers and hikers to the mountain. A little courtesy toward other trail users goes a long way to keep multi-use trails like these open.

Case Mountain, as local riders call it, is actually land from three different areas—Birch Mountain, Case Mountain, and Manchester Water Company land. The town manages the Case Mountain area, and all trails are open to mountain biking. The top of Case Mountain on the Manchester side, at an elevation of 774 feet, offers a spectacular view of downtown Hartford and the surrounding area. Trail maintenance by the mountain bike community here has kept most trails within the system in pretty good shape, and some of the trails have been built specifically for mountain bikes.

© CHRIS BERNARD

Though the trails are marked on Case Mountain, the blazes aren't always easy to spot – especially at biking speed.

Once you make your way to Case Mountain proper, there's a seemingly unending network of trails. Having a guide familiar with the area is a definite advantage to get to the best trails. Ask around on online mountain bike forums, or find a group ride and ask politely if you can join.

The Case trails are extremely technical, littered with rocks of all sizes: these trails are best-suited for mountain bikes. The terrain is hilly, with some lung-busting climbs and long descents. A beginner rider will be able to walk the more difficult sections, but this is a place best enjoyed by intermediate or better riders. The streams you cross along the way are fed largely by runoff, so their intensity varies wildly throughout the year. During the early spring the streams can be a challenge to cross—even on foot. By late summer, however, most of the streams are barely running at all and easy to cross.

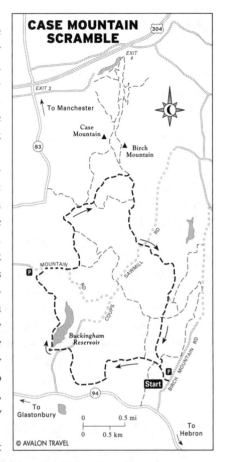

The route starts with an almost 3-mile-long descent on classic swoopy New England single-track, eventually landing on the shores of scenic Buckingham Reservoir. Although the water company is tolerant of mountain bikes on its property, it would not take much to change its mind, so tread lightly to ensure continued access to this section.

The trail progresses through hardwood forest, crossing the power-line access road several times. After doing some moderate climbing through the woods, you come upon a monster climb of three sections of "slick rock." If you've ridden in Moab, Utah, you'll be fine, but if your bike time has been limited to New England, hold on tight. After climbing the third section of slick rock, you'll reach a spectacular lookout spot under a canopy of white pines. The ride finishes with a roller-coaster ride out to the power lines, an incredibly steep and technical descent, and a final climb up the trail where you started.

For more information, contact the Town of Manchester, 41 Center Street, Manchester, CT 06040, 860/647-5235, www.townofmanchester.org.

Options
To get to the summit, at Mile 7.6 take a left onto the single-track marked blue/red. (Note that the trail markings vary here and aren't very clear.) Trails stretch and wind for miles throughout this area. Explore by following your whim or by following other riders. There's a pretty well established biking community, and on most days you can find someone on the trails—don't be shy.

This ride is near Flora and Fauna and Charter Oak Greenway Sampler.

Locals' Tip: There are burritos galore at Jalisco (103 New London Turnpike, Glastonbury, CT 06033, 860/652-0416), a family-owned Mexican restaurant well-loved by the locals—pile on the hot sauce.

Places to Stay: The Connecticut River Valley Inn (2195 Main Street, Glastonbury, CT 06033, 860/633-7374) is a good bet for overnighting, and it's run by friendly innkeepers.

Driving Directions
From Hartford, take I-84 to exit 4 and take CT-2 East. Drive approximately 8 miles and take exit 8. Take a left from the exit onto Hebron Avenue/CT-94. Drive 6.8 miles on Hebron Avenue and turn left onto Birch Mountain Road, at the top of the hill. Drive about 0.25 mile and look for the parking lot on the right, next to the radio towers. There are several other places to park to start a ride at Case Mountain. Many riders start at the abandoned Girl Scout camp parking lot in Manchester. Supplies and bike shops are available in Glastonbury and Manchester.

Route Directions
0.0 Turn RIGHT out of the dirt parking lot.

0.1 Turn LEFT onto blue/red-marked single-track.

0.4 Turn LEFT onto fire road after crossing under power lines.

0.7 Turn LEFT onto single-track.

1.7 Take the RIGHT fork in the trail.

2.6 Turn LEFT onto a dirt road, then immediately RIGHT onto single-track.

2.9 Cross a log bridge, and continue STRAIGHT across at top of the hill.

3.4 At a four-way intersection go STRAIGHT.

3.8 Turn LEFT at the T in the trail.

4.3 Turn RIGHT onto fire road, under the power lines.
4.6 Turn LEFT onto single-track (easy to miss).
4.9 Turn RIGHT onto single-track.
5.4 Turn LEFT at three-way intersection.
6.2 Turn RIGHT onto fire road.
6.5 Turn RIGHT onto hairpin to fire road.
6.9 Turn RIGHT onto yellow-marked single-track.
7.6 Turn RIGHT onto blue-marked single-track.
10.0 *Scenic lookout spot.*
10.7 Blue trail veers RIGHT.
10.8 Turn LEFT at the power lines.
11.0 Turn RIGHT onto blue/red-marked single-track (crossing back under power lines).
11.3 Turn RIGHT onto road.
11.4 Return to parking lot on left.

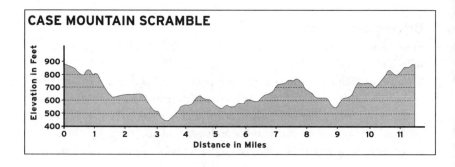

CASE MOUNTAIN SCRAMBLE

7 LITTLE BRITAIN RIDE
Canterbury to Scotland

PAVED ROADS WITH MINIMAL TRAFFIC

Difficulty: 2   **Total Distance:** 24.4 miles

Riding Time: 1.5-2 hours   **Elevation Gain:** 761 feet

Summary: This backcountry ride offers gorgeous rural scenery and hilly climbs.

Much of Connecticut's terrain consists of rolling hills, and this ride is no exception. Apart from the busy corner of the state nearest New York City and occasional urban centers, many of the state's roads are rural, backcountry routes, great for riding bikes. Again, this ride is no exception.

Sparsely populated, minimally trafficked, laden with natural features like brooks and streams and farms and forests, and well paved, the roads of this ride offer fantastic cycling. While they're hilly, the climbs are interlaced with descents and spread across the ride rather than stacked, and from Mile 18 or so, the ride's mostly downhill.

Small Canterbury is known primarily for resident Prudence Crandall, who, in the 1800s, opened a school for black students that brought the ire of the state, which outlawed it. Crandall persisted, and she was jailed before the case was

Cyclists treat themselves to mostly quiet, minimally trafficked roads in this rural part of the state.

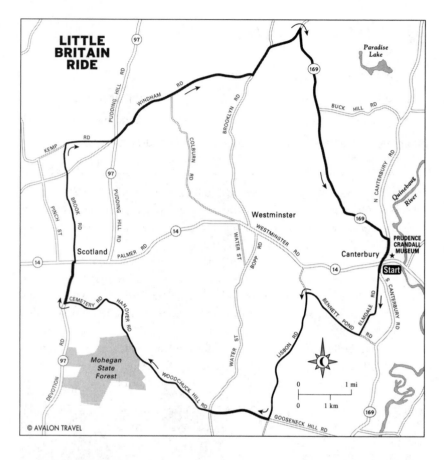

ultimately dismissed. But opponents took the law into their own hands and attacked Crandall and the school, forcing her to shut down. This footnote of civil rights is commemorated in the Prudence Crandall Museum on the town green, where this ride begins.

From there, the route heads clockwise past Mohegan State Forest and north to Scotland—named in 1700 by town father Isaac Magoon, who missed his mother country—climbing and descending, climbing and descending all the while. It's a beautiful ride and well worth the effort.

For more information on the museum or the town, contact the Prudence Crandall Museum, 1 South Canterbury Road (junctions of CT-14 and CT-169), Canterbury, CT 06331, 860/546-7800.

Options

To add 10 miles or so to this ride, at Mile 19.3 stay straight on Windham Road.

After 2.5 miles, turn right on Fairgrounds Road, crossing CT-169, and then turn right on Wauregan Road/CT-205. In 3 miles, turn right on Maynard Road, which becomes Wauregan Road. Turn left onto CT-169/North Canterbury Road, then make a quick right onto Buck Hill Road, which ends at North Society Road, joining the original ride around Mile 20.5.

This ride is near the Air Line Trail.

Locals' Tip: Reward yourself with a few slices at Martello's Pizzeria (200 Westminster Road No. 1, Canterbury, CT 06331, 860/546-6680).

Places to Stay: Spend the night, and not a lot of money, at the Plainfield Motel (66 East Main Street, Moosup, CT 06354, 860/564-2791), an unassuming place not far from downtown Canterbury.

Driving Directions

From I-84, take exit 59 onto I-384 east, toward Providence. After 8 miles, take US-6 east for 13 miles, and then take the exit for CT-32 toward Stafford Springs/Willimantic. Take CT-32 for 3 miles, then bear right onto CT-14 East/Main Street. After 13 miles, turn right into the parking area for the Prudence Crandall Museum at the junction of CT-14 and CT-169. If parking at the museum is tight, continue on CT-14 just past the junction and look for the small fenced commuter parking lot on the left.

Route Directions

0.0 Turn RIGHT out of parking area onto CT-14, and take a quick RIGHT at blinking light onto CT-169.

0.2 Turn RIGHT onto Elmdale Road.

1.0 Bear RIGHT to stay on Elmdale Road.

1.5 Turn RIGHT at stop, onto Bennett Pond Road.

2.8 Turn LEFT at stop, onto Lisbon Road.

5.5 Turn RIGHT at stop, onto Bates Pond Road.

6.7 Cross Water Street onto Woodchuck Hill Road.

8.1 Turn LEFT at stop to stay on Woodchuck Hill Road, over bridge. After the bridge, head uphill on unmarked Hanover Road, which enters from your left.

9.9 Turn LEFT onto Cemetery Road.

10.8 Turn RIGHT at stop, onto CT-97.

11.6 Turn LEFT at church, onto Brook Road.

13.4 Cross Brooklyn Turnpike at stop sign to stay on Brook Road.

14.0 Turn RIGHT at stop sign, onto Kemp Road.

14.9 Bear LEFT at stop sign, onto Brooklyn Turnpike.

15.0 Cross CT-97 at stop sign to Windham Road (unmarked).

15.5 Bear RIGHT to stay on Windham Road at fork.

16.1 Cross bridge and bear LEFT to stay on Windham Road.

16.8 Stay straight at stop sign to stay on Windham Road, which becomes Raymond Schoolhouse Road.

18.0 Turn LEFT at stop onto Brooklyn Road (unmarked; look for small red sign for Wright's Mill Farm).

18.7 At fork, stay STRAIGHT on Windham Road.

19.0 Bear RIGHT on unmarked Grass Road at fork.

19.3 Turn RIGHT at stop sign onto North Society Road (unmarked). OPTION: Stay straight on Windham Road and follow option directions.

23.9 Turn RIGHT at stop sign onto North Canterbury Road/CT-169.

24.4 Turn RIGHT at light onto CT-14, and then LEFT to END at parking area.

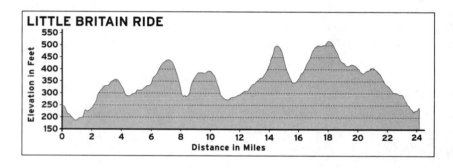

8 LAKE WARAMAUG UPS AND DOWNS

Lake Waramaug State Park, New Preston

PAVED ROADS WITH MINIMAL TRAFFIC

Difficulty: 3   **Total Distance:** 20.2 miles

Riding Time: 1-2 hours   **Elevation Gain:** 1,195 feet

Summary: Routes around the lake vary enough to let you pick and choose your challenge – from beginner to best-of-the-rest.

Riders of all abilities will enjoy this part of Connecticut. Beginners can take a scenic loop around the tree-lined lake, admiring the variety of summer homes with landscaped lawns and the beauty of rowing sculls unzipping the surface of the lake. Want a longer, hillier ride? Explore the backcountry roads to the northwest, where farm roads give views of the ridges that rise from this basin.

The route begins in Lake Waramaug State Park at the northwest tip of the lake. If you're camping at the state park, begin the route from the campground. Beginners, skip to the optional (and easier) 8-mile ride and go clockwise for the best views of the lake. Both West Shore Road and North Shore Road are twisty and narrow, so beware of cars. Though the lake is lined mainly with tasteful residences, you'll find a golf course, a vineyard, and a few inns as well.

© CHRIS BERNARD

Bike riders of all abilities will find the quiet roads around this scenic lake appealing.

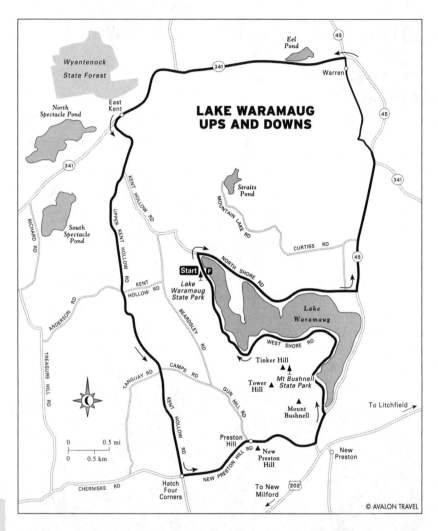

Once you're on Kent Hollow Road, traffic fades to nothing. You might encounter some uneven pavement, but the scenery is beautiful, with rolling hills, open fields and farmlands, a stretch of wild, undeveloped land, and views of mountains and valleys in the distance.

Prepare to face a long climb up the New Preston Hill Road, with a river valley running on the left. A distinctive stone church graces the hilltop, marking the start of a long, smooth downhill past horse farms into the village of New Preston. Check out the waterfall and antique shops in this former grist mill town before heading up CT-45 back to the lake.

For more information, contact Lake Waramaug State Park, 30 Lake Waramaug Road, New Preston, CT 06777, 860/868-0220, www.dep.state.ct.us/stateparks/parks/lakewaramaug.htm.

Options

Beginners—or any cyclists looking for a short, easy, and mostly flat route around the lake—can skip the main ride directions. From the park entrance, turn left instead onto West Shore Road and bear right onto North Shore Road. At Mile 2.5, turn right onto CT-45; then turn right onto West Shore Road in about 2 miles. In 4 miles more, turn left to return to Lake Waramaug State Park.

This ride begins just miles from Horse Heaven Hills.

Locals' Tip: Nine Main Bakery (9 Main Street, New Preston, CT 06777, 860/868-1879) makes some great lunch wraps that are ideal for lakeside picnicking.

Places to Stay: Tent up in one of the 77 wooded and open sites at Lake Waramaug Campground (Lake Waramaug State Park, 30 Lake Waramaug Road, New Preston, CT 06757, 860/868-0220, $26–36), open the weekend before Memorial Day weekend through September 30. Facilities include restrooms, showers, drinking water, a dumping station, picnic shelters, and a concession stand.

Driving Directions

From Litchfield and points east, take CT-202 west to New Preston. From New Milford and points west, take CT-202 east to New Preston. Once in New Preston, turn north onto CT-45 and drive 0.5 mile. Turn left at the intersection onto West Shore Road and drive 3.9 miles. Turn left into Lake Waramaug State Park. Supplies are available in Kent, Bantam, or New Milford. New Preston has one restaurant, but no other supplies are available there or along the route. The state park has a summer-only campground with showers and a concession stand, pay phones, picnic areas, restrooms, and a small sandy beach. On weekends and holidays, the parking fee is $14 for Connecticut residents and $20 for nonresidents. The nearest bike shop is in New Milford.

Route Directions

0.0 From the state park entrance road, turn LEFT onto West Shore Road.

0.2 Bear RIGHT onto North Shore Road.

2.5 Turn LEFT onto CT-45.

4.1 Turn LEFT at stop sign onto CT-341.

5.6 Continue STRAIGHT on CT-341 in Warren.

9.0 Turn LEFT onto Kent Hollow Road.

9.8 Turn RIGHT at fork onto Upper Kent Hollow Road.

11.4 At intersection, take a LEFT, then make an immediate RIGHT onto Kent Hollow Road.

13.9 Turn LEFT onto New Preston Hill Road.

15.9 Turn LEFT at junction, onto CT-45 in New Preston.

16.3 Turn LEFT onto West Shore Road at intersection.

20.2 Turn LEFT to return to Lake Waramaug State Park.

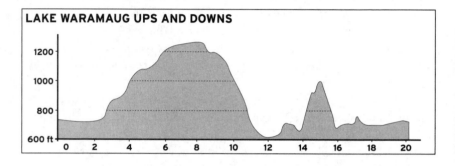

9 HORSE HEAVEN HILLS
Washington

PAVED ROADS, ONE DIRT ROAD WITH MINIMAL TRAFFIC

Difficulty: 3   **Total Distance:** 28.7 miles

Riding Time: 2 hours   **Elevation Gain:** 1,381 feet

Summary: A hilly ride on back roads through a beautiful, rural part of Connecticut, this route will tax your legs and lungs.

This ride leaves the Washington town hall for a hilly figure-eight around this rural region, exploring farmlands and woods on back roads with names like Horse Heaven, Hoop Pole, Grassy Hill, and Painter Ridge. The odd name is Transylvania Road, but that leads to Good Hill Road and redeems itself quickly.

You'll see a fair number of trees and fields on this ride, which begins with a steady 3-mile climb. That leads to rolling hills and a wicked descent, followed by another gradual climb that lasts from around Mile 17 until Mile 25. Just when your legs begin to question your relationship, everything changes again and you shoot down a long, fast hill to the finish.

There are several scenic viewpoints along this route. Early in the ride, look left from East Street to see why you're out of breath. Around Mile 10.5, take a look around from atop Grassy Hill Road.

Some rides are good for groups; others are good alone. This ride could certainly

© CHRIS BERNARD

The roads of this ride are quiet, scenic, and rural – a blast to ride, and for the most part, whimsically named.

be done either way, but something about the fresh air, the scenery, and the climbing makes it seem like moving meditation. It's a pretty part of the world. Get out there and enjoy it.

For more information, visit Connecticut Bike Routes, www.ctbike routes.org.

Options

To cut this ride a little short, at Mile 21.6 turn left onto Bee Brook Road/CT-47, which leads back to the starting point.

This ride begins just miles from Lake Waramaug Ups and Downs, and could be linked by bike—grab a map and plot a course to enjoy this beautiful part of the state.

Locals' Tip: Grab a post-ride panini and a cup of joe at Marty's Cafe (4 Green Hill Road, No. 1, Washington Depot, CT 06793, 860/868-1700).

Places to Stay: Get a room at the Hopkins Inn (22 Hopkins Road, New Preston, CT 06777, 860/868-7295, www.thehopkinsinn.com), on Lake Waramaug.

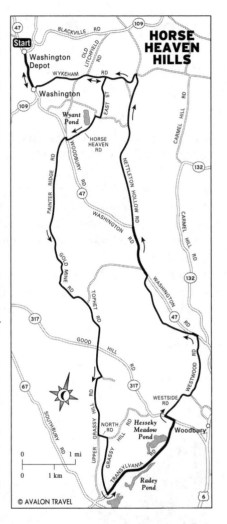

Driving Directions

From I-84, take exit 15 for US-6/CT-67, and bear right at the first fork to stay on CT-67/Main Street North/US-6. After about 5 miles, turn left at CT-47/Washington Road. Stay on CT-47 until it meets CT-109 after about 9 miles. Park in the Washington town hall parking lot.

Route Directions

0.0 From parking area, go STRAIGHT on CT-109.

0.3 Turn RIGHT to stay on CT-109.

2.1 Turn RIGHT at stop sign, onto Wykeham Road.

3.4 Turn RIGHT onto East Street.

4.4 Turn RIGHT at end of street onto unmarked road. *Scenic overlook to your left.*

4.5 Turn LEFT onto Horse Heaven Road.

5.3 Cross CT-47 and head up Painter Ridge Road (unmarked).

5.9 Cross Nichols Hill Road to stay on Painter Ridge Road.

7.5 Turn LEFT at end of road onto Painter Hill Road and stay straight through stop sign, onto Goldmine Road.

9.0 When Goldmine Road ends, stay STRAIGHT onto Tophet Road.

10.5 At stop sign, cross CT-317 onto Upper Grassy Hill Road.

12.5 Turn LEFT at stop, onto North Road.

12.7 Turn RIGHT onto Grassy Hill Road, which is a fast descent.

14.0 At stop sign, turn LEFT onto unmarked Transylvania Road.

16.4 At end of road, turn LEFT onto Good Hill Road/CT-317.

16.7 Turn RIGHT onto Westside Road.

17.5 Turn LEFT onto Westwood Road.

18.9 Turn LEFT at end of road onto CT-47, and take an immediate LEFT onto Hoop Pole Hill Road.

19.6 Turn RIGHT onto Sprain Brook Road, which is packed dirt.

20.7 Turn LEFT at end of road onto CT-47.

21.6 OPTION: Turn left onto Bee Brook Road/CT-47 and follow option directions.

21.8 Turn RIGHT onto Nettleton Hollow Road, which begins a gradual ascent.

25.2 Turn LEFT onto Wykeham Road, where the short climb turns steep.

26.5 Stay STRAIGHT to continue on Wykeham Road.

27.7 Turn RIGHT at end of road onto CT-47, a fast descent.

28.7 Turn LEFT into parking area to END.

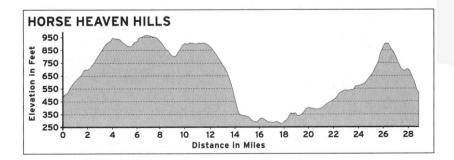

HORSE HEAVEN HILLS

 AIR LINE TRAIL   BEST **(**

Air Line State Park, East Hampton to Hebron

STONE DUST BIKE PATH

Difficulty: 2   **Total Distance:** 21.4 miles

Riding Time: 2-2.5 hours   **Elevation Gain:** 1,315 feet

Summary: The climb will challenge some riders, but the mostly smooth, off-road path is a great ride for all abilities.

Once upon a time, a railway ran from Boston to New York in almost a straight line. From 1873 to 1959, trains carried passengers along the Air Line at high speeds through Massachusetts and Connecticut. But the trains ceased to run, the railway bed was abandoned, and eventually the line was deeded to the state's Department of Environmental Protection. The story has a happy ending, because now the rail line is one of the region's loveliest multiuse trails, crossing high over rivers, giving dramatic views of lush countryside, and passing through areas rich with wildlife.

The state is developing the trail into two state parks, Air Line North (from Putnam to Windham) and Air Line South (from Windham to East Hampton). Not all the sections are completed, and the best-developed stretch is about 10 miles between East Hampton and Hebron. Here, the level trail is covered with stone dust and is suitable for road or mountain bikes, wheelchairs, horses, and walkers. It's wide, flat, and level and there are benches and picnic tables along the way as well as lots of interesting sights—adding up to a great family outing. Don't let the elevation gain fool you; the climbing is so gradual that you'll hardly notice it.

Starting in East Hampton, you'll quickly come to two viaducts, first Rapallo and then Lyman. These former viaducts drop off steeply on either side and give you great unobstructed views of rolling hills and lush green valleys. Built in 1873, the Lyman Viaduct was once a 1,000-plus-foot-long iron trestle bridge that loomed 137 feet above Dickinson Creek.

You'll pass through Salmon River State Forest, where the terrain drops steeply off to the right to a river bed. The total lack of development makes you feel you are deep in the woods. A new wooden bridge takes you high above Blackledge River. A short unfinished section means a 0.2-mile detour on the road, passing underneath CT-2, to return to the trail. Next you'll cross a beautiful bridge over the Jeremy River and then over the fast-flowing, waterfall-forming Judd Brook before coming to Grayville Road.

After crossing Old Colchester Road, you'll come to wonderful Raymond Brook

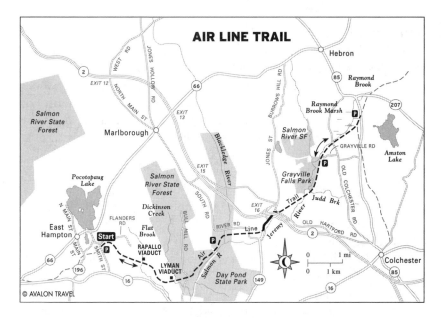

Marsh, a veritable trove of flora and fauna. In late spring, for example, you might see lady slipper orchids or dwarf ginseng, orioles or warblers, Canada geese, beavers, deer, or painted turtles.

Air Line trail maps and brochures can be picked up at the Town Office buildings in East Hampton and Hebron. (The map boxes at the trailheads may be empty.) For more information, contact the Department of Environmental Protection Eastern District Headquarters, 209 Hebron Road, Marlborough, CT 06447, 860/295-9523. The best website for trail information is http://pages.cthome.net/mbartel/ARRhome.htm.

Options

To view waterfalls and have a picnic, take a side trip into Grayville Falls Park by turning left onto Grayville Road and riding about 0.2 mile to the park entrance.

This ride is near the Little Britain Ride.

Locals' Tip: Shower up after the ride and show up at Rossini's (62 West High Street, East Hampton, CT 06424, 860/267-1106, www.rossiniseasthampton .com) for a good meal with homemade bread, or show up still muddy and get pizza to go.

Places to Stay: Rooms at the Riverdale Motel (1503 Portland Cobalt Road, Portland, CT 06480, 860/342-3498, www.riverdale-motel.com) are big and affordable, and they come with fridges to keep your post-trail beverages cold.

Driving Directions

From Hartford and points west or Norwich and points east, take CT-2 to Marl-borough and take exit 13 to CT-66 West. Follow CT-66 through East Hampton and turn left onto Lakeview Street (CT-196). Turn left onto Flanders Road, then right onto Smith Street. Drive 0.2 mile on Smith Street and turn left into the trailhead parking lot. No facilities are available along the trail. Supplies are available in East Hampton, Hebron, and Colchester, and there are bike shops in Hebron and Colchester.

Route Directions

0.0 START at trailhead in East Hampton.

1.4 Cross Rapallo Viaduct.

2.5 Cross Lyman Viaduct.

3.0 Cross Bull Hill Road. *Access to trail and parking lot on Bull Hill Road.*

5.4 Cross River Road.

5.9 Cross CT-149.

6.5 Arrive at park-and-ride parking lot. Turn RIGHT out of lot onto CT-149. (If you are on a mountain bike, you can ride along the short unfinished section of the trail.)

6.6 Turn RIGHT onto Old Hartford Road. *Access to trail and parking lots on Old Hartford Road.*

6.7 Turn LEFT at parking area to resume on trail.

8.9 Cross Grayville Road. OPTION: Turn LEFT for side trip to Grayville Falls Park.

9.5 Cross Old Colchester Road.

10.0 Pass Raymond Brook Marsh.

10.7 Arrive at CT-85 parking lot and trailhead. TURN AROUND.

21.4 Return to East Hampton trailhead parking lot.

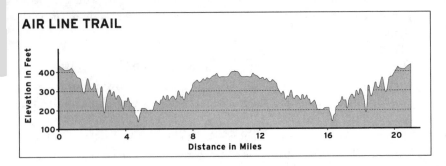

AIR LINE TRAIL

 HUNTINGTON SAMPLER
Collis P. Huntington State Park, Redding

CARRIAGE ROADS, SINGLE-TRACK

Difficulty: 3   **Total Distance:** 7.9 miles

Riding Time: 1-1.5 hours   **Elevation Gain:** 615 feet

Summary: These moderately challenging trails provide a getaway for urban bikers, offering verdant woods and quiet ponds.

The trails that wind through Huntington Park offer a good mix of single-track and easier smooth carriage roads, collectively adding up to a lot of great rides. Add in the fact that the trails snake through lush woods dotted with pristine ponds—all within an hour's drive of downtown New York City—and they're all the more impressive. These trails make a great respite for urban mountain bikers looking for some country dirt, but even riders spoiled by other New England trails will enjoy themselves here.

This route samples both kinds of trails, offering an almost equal mix of single-track and carriage roads. From the main parking area off Sunset Hill Road, the ride begins with a blast down a grassy hill. At the bottom of the hill, go left for about 50 yards and take a right onto the single-track at the blue blaze. This short, challenging, fun section dumps you on a dirt carriage road, where you continue up a slight incline for about 0.5 mile.

Look for the next section of single-track opening on your right. Eventually you will end up back on the carriage road. Stay right and hang on for a bumpy descent on the blue perimeter road. The road winds downhill, following a stream on the right, while several granite outcroppings crowd the trail to the left. Then it's time to pay for your fun with a long climb up the side of the ridge.

At the top of the climb, shoot between two ponds. Go straight across the wooden bridge and up just a bit more, then right on a chewed-up paved track called Dodgintown Road. This road is short and ends in an extensive network of single-track, where a little exploration will pay off with plenty of tight, twisting, rocky, rooty fun. You'll find trails, some sketchy drops, ramps, a teeter-totter, and at least one bridge across which you'll find hesitant riders walking.

Some trails lead to private property, so when you see No Trespassing signs, turn around.

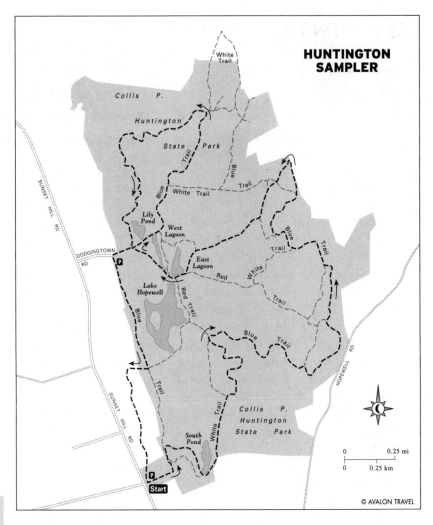

All trails eventually lead back to Dodgintown Road. At the top of the road, head left through a small dirt parking area and follow the carriage road past some stables. Look to the right for a mile-long stretch of smooth, rolling single-track through a beautiful meadow that will take you right back to where you began the ride.

If you're on a cyclocross bike, you'll want to limit yourself to the carriage roads, as the single-track can get technical at times.

For more information, contact Collis P. Huntington State Park, c/o Putnam Memorial State Park, 492 Black Rock Turnpike, Redding, CT 06896, 203/938-2285, www.dep.state.ct.us/stateparks/parks/huntington.htm (daily 8 A.M.–sunset, free).

Options

Riders with a sense of adventure will thrive on these trails, even without a sense of direction—many of the single-tracks lead back to the main carriage road, making it difficult to get lost. Follow your bike and ride where the spirit takes you to make a day of it.

This ride is reasonably close to Fairfield Rural and Pequonnock River Valley Ride.

Locals' Tip: Saddle up to the Georgetown Saloon (8 Main Street, West Redding, CT 06896, 203/544-8003, www.georgetownsaloon.com) for a funky Western decor and friendly service.

Places to Stay: Stay the night at the Stonehenge Inn (35 Stonehenge Road, Ridgefield, CT 06877, 203/438-6511, www.stonehengeinn-ct.com), just a stone's throw from the trails.

Driving Directions

From Danbury and I-84, take exit 5 to CT-53 south and drive 3.4 miles. At the junction of CT-53 and CT-302, take CT-302 east, through Bethel, for 1.6 miles. Turn right onto CT-58 South and drive 4.6 miles. Turn left onto Sunset Hill Road. Collis P. Huntington State Park is 0.8 mile on the right. There are outhouses but no other facilities. Supplies are available in Bethel, and there are bike shops in Bethel and Danbury.

Route Directions

0.0 From parking lot, ride past notice board onto trail.

0.1 Turn LEFT and immediate RIGHT at blue blaze.

0.7 Turn RIGHT onto single-track.

1.3 Turn RIGHT at fork.

1.4 Turn RIGHT onto carriage road and make an immediate RIGHT at fork in carriage road.

2.0 Turn RIGHT at blue blaze.

2.4 Turn LEFT at fork. (You will be riding straight between two ponds, Lake Hopewell and East Lagoon.)

3.8 Turn RIGHT at Dodgintown Road.

4.1 Turn LEFT on blue trail at the end of the road.

4.7 Turn LEFT onto single-track.

6.5 Turn RIGHT onto Dodgintown Road.

6.8 Turn LEFT onto carriage road at parking area.

7.3 Turn RIGHT on trail through meadow.

7.9 Return to main parking lot.

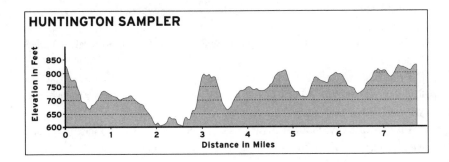

HUNTINGTON SAMPLER

12 FAIRFIELD RURAL
Fairfield, Monroe, and Newtown

PAVED ROADS WITH MINIMAL TO MODERATE TRAFFIC

Difficulty: 3   **Total Distance:** 39.4 miles

Riding Time: 3 hours   **Elevation Gain:** 945 feet

Summary: This hilly climb on country back roads offers opportunities to stop and enjoy a quiet part of Connecticut.

This ride is deceptively hilly: the total elevation gain is not as great as that of many other "hilly" rides, but the hills are relentless. They start right out of the gate, and they only let up twice for any real descents, though a third downhill, a quick one at Mile 7.5, is a welcome relief.

You'll begin in Fairfield, at the commuter parking lot off the exit ramp to CT-15, the Merritt Parkway, to head north in a counterclockwise loop. In the first mile you pass the Hemlock Reservoir, and at Mile 5 you pass the Aspetuck Reservoir.

The roads are shady, and you'll pass a mix of farm country, horse farms, and other features that will remind you this is rural country despite the major commuter turnpike running through the area. The high number of stop signs can be annoying, and you may be tempted to roll through them. Do the right thing

© CHRIS BERNARD

The roads of Fairfield and the surrounding towns are welcoming to cyclists.

and stop, both for safety's sake and to keep up bike riders' good reputations in the area.

At Mile 13 you'll pass the Stepney Green in Monroe. There are a few places to stop for food or a cup of coffee or just to sit on the green and watch the world go by as you rest your legs. You'll have more options another 7 miles or so into the ride if you haven't worked up an appetite yet.

You've still got to get up Brushy Hill, a long, slow climb with no respite from the wind, or worse, the sun, if you make the mistake of choosing a hot, bright day, and Sport Hill, which is brief but steep. There's some respite from the ascents after Sport Hill, followed by an especially relaxing roll down Valley Road, before the final push back to the start.

All told, this is the kind of ride that you'll enjoy riding and feel great about completing—a good solid effort, nothing too brutal, but fun every revolution of the pedals.

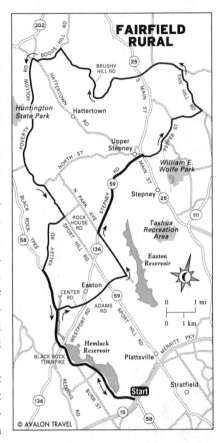

Options

To cut about 7 miles—and some of the climbing—from this ride, turn left at Mile 12.7 onto Hattertown Road (unmarked). Then turn left at Mile 17.9 onto Poverty Hollow Road, rejoining the original ride at Mile 24.3.

This ride begins not far from Pequonnock River Valley Ride.

Locals' Tip: Hot wings at Archie Moore's Bar and Restaurant (48 Sanford Street, Fairfield, CT 06824, 203/256-9295, www.archiemoores.com) go great with burning legs and a cold beer.

Places to Stay: It's not fancy, it's affordable, and it's very close to the ride—it's the Merritt Parkway Motor Inn (4180 Black Rock Turnpike, Fairfield, CT 06824, 203/259-5264).

Driving Directions

From I-95, take exit 38 for CT-15 toward Merritt Parkway/Wilbur Cross Parkway. From CT-15, the Merritt Parkway, take exit 44 toward CT-58/Fairfield/Redding. Turn left at Congress Street, and take the first left onto Black Rock Turnpike/ CT-58 South. Park in the commuter parking lot on your right.

Route Directions

0.0 From the parking area turn RIGHT on CT-58.

4.9 Turn RIGHT onto Center Road.

5.9 At the stop sign, stay STRAIGHT on Center Road.

6.2 At the stop sign, stay STRAIGHT on Center Road.

6.4 Turn LEFT onto Adams Road.

7.0 Cross CT-59 and stay STRAIGHT on Adams Road.

7.6 Turn LEFT at North Park Avenue at the stop sign.

9.5 Turn RIGHT on Stepney Road (CT-59) at the stop sign.

12.7 Turn RIGHT on CT-25, watching for traffic, and take a quick LEFT onto Pepper Street. OPTION: Turn left and follow option directions.

12.8 At the stop sign, turn LEFT to stay on Pepper Street (unmarked).

13.0 Stepney Green. *Supplies available.*

14.5 Turn RIGHT on Jockey Hollow Road, by the bridge.

15.6 Turn LEFT at the stop sign, onto Fan Hill Road.

17.3 Turn LEFT at the stop sign, onto Hammertown Road, which becomes High Bridge Road.

18.3 Turn LEFT on unmarked Botsford Hill Road at the stop sign.

19.0 At the light, stay STRAIGHT onto Meadowbrook Road.

19.9 Turn LEFT at the stop sign, onto Huntingtown Road.

20.6 Turn RIGHT at the stop sign, onto Brushy Hill Road, which begins a long, slow climb.

22.0 Turn LEFT on Platts Hill Road, which heads downhill and becomes Hundred Acres Road.

22.6 Turn RIGHT onto Palestine Road at the stop sign.

23.4 Turn LEFT at Boggs Hill Road (unmarked) at the stop sign.

24.3 Turn RIGHT on Hattertown Road (unmarked) at the stop sign.

24.5 Turn LEFT at the stop sign, onto Poverty Hollow Road.

29.2 Turn LEFT at Stepney Road and cross the bridge.

29.6 Turn RIGHT onto Sport Hill Road, and begin climbing. This is a short, steep climb that's over before you know it.

30.7 Turn RIGHT onto Rock House Road at the stop sign.
 31.5 Turn LEFT at the stop sign, onto Valley Road.
32.4 Bear RIGHT onto Valley Road at Staples Road.
33.0 Turn LEFT onto CT-58 (unmarked) at the stop sign.
39.4 Turn LEFT to END at parking area.

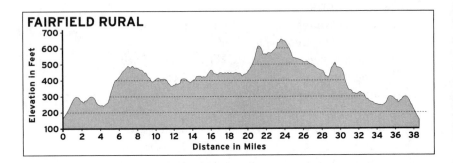

13 PEQUONNOCK RIVER VALLEY RIDE
Trumbull

UNPAVED RAIL TRAIL

Difficulty: 2   **Total Distance:** 5.8 miles

Riding Time: 1.5 hours   **Elevation Gain:** 195 feet

Summary: With smooth dirt trail on one side of the river and technical single-track on the other, riders can choose their own adventure here.

You might not expect to find these trails in this crowded corner of Connecticut, but just north of busy urban Bridgeport is a trail system confined to a scenic narrow river valley and gorge along the Pequonnock River. On the west side of the river, you'll find an unpaved but fairly smooth rail trail, on the east, a warren of hidden single-track as technical as any die-hard freerider could want.

The old rail bed climbs as it follows the river north for 2.6 uninterrupted miles. The gorge falls away short and steep to your right, and along the way you've got plenty of places to stop and take in views of the river below. At a gate, the trail briefly becomes a road, and it crosses another (Whitney Avenue) before becoming a rail trail again. A sign tells you when you're in Parlor Rock Park, an abandoned amusement park now barely even ruins. Soon after, the rail trail ends at the divided highway, CT-25.

Twisting, winding, and beautiful, this trail offers a choice of smooth dirt or single-track, giving riders options to fit any mood.

For an easy ride, turn around and retrace your route to the beginning. Or, review the option below for information on riding the single-track across the river. Cyclocross and hybrid bikes will suffice on the west side; mountain bikes are necessary on the east.

For more information about the area, visit the Trumbull Historical Society's website, www.trumbullhistory.org/written/prv.shtml, or contact the Trumbull Parks Department, Highway Garage, 366 Church Hill Road, Trumbull, CT 06611, 203/452-5075, www.trumbullct.com.

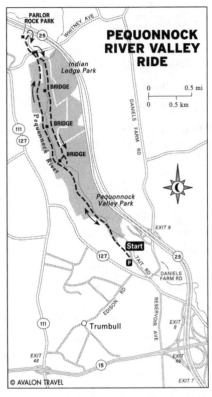

Options

For about 7 miles of challenging single-track, retrace your route to Whitney Avenue, turn left on the road across the river, and take the single-track to your right. Keep to the double blue-and single blue-blazed trails here, staying as close to the river as possible. Don't worry about getting lost; you'll hit highway or river if you stray too far in either direction. Some of these trails feature drops and stunts built by, and for, expert riders.

At Indian Ledge Park, you cross a bridge and pass a parking area. The trail continues to your right and works back toward the river. Look for the double blue blaze and follow it left. When you come to another bridge crossing the river, you can cross back to the railbed if you want. Or push on to a three-way fork in the trail. Follow the left branch to a bridge crossing back to the rail trail. There's a fast blast down the rail trail and your ride is complete.

Locals' Tip: Grab an excellent sandwich at The Main Pub (306 Main Street, Manchester, CT 06040, 860/647-1551, www.mainpub.com) and bring it along for the ride.

Places to Stay: Bibliophiles will love The Mansion Inn B&B (139 Hartford Road, Manchester, CT 06040, 860/646-0453, www.themansioninnct.com), a welcoming place to stay.

Driving Directions

From points east or west, take CT-15 (the Merritt Parkway) to exit 49 onto CT-25 north. From I-95, take exit 27 to CT-25 North. From CT-25, take exit 9 onto Daniels Farm Road. Drive 0.5 mile and turn right onto CT-127. Drive about 100 yards and turn right onto Tait Road. A small parking area is on the right, and the trailhead is just a few yards down Tait Road on your left. Supplies are available in Trumbull and there are bike shops in Monroe and Bridgeport.

Route Directions

0.0 From parking area, start at trailhead on left side of Tait Road and go LEFT through gate onto rail trail.

2.7 Cross Whitney Avenue.

2.9 TURN AROUND and retrace your route back to start.

5.8 Return to parking area.

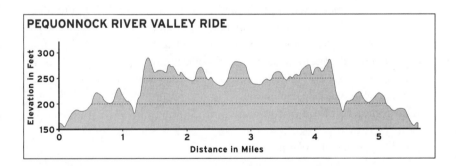

14 WESTWOODS TRAILS
Guilford

DOUBLE-TRACK, SINGLE-TRACK

Difficulty: 4   **Total Distance:** 4.5 miles

Riding Time: 1.5–2 hours   **Elevation Gain:** 345 feet

Summary: Skilled riders will thrive in this snakes' nest of technical trails winding through wooded, rocky landscapes.

Close to the Connecticut coast, just off I-95, lies a maze of trails some riders consider the best technical riding in the state. The Westwoods Trails mean lots of steep up-and-downs on granite-spined ridges, with some portage sections. This is not a place for an aerobic endurance workout, but it is a great opportunity to work on your technical mountain biking skills. The mix of single- and double-track is good, but even the double-track here is technical and does not ride like a leisurely fire road. These are mountain bike trails, and cyclocross bikes will be outgunned.

All the trails here are marked by shapes and colors: green rectangle, yellow and violet circle, red triangle. This route begins on Green Rectangle trail, which goes from single- to double- back to single-track, with some fun riding and one small stream crossing along the way. The trail has a long, steep climb that becomes more gradual as it tops out, eventually leading you to the Moose Hill Road entrance to the trail system.

Look to your left here for Violet Circle Trail, a solid single-track. Though not extremely difficult, it has enough in the way of obstacles to keep your interest. At the bottom of a steep, technical descent, you come to a fork in the trail. Take a right onto Yellow Circle Trail. You've descended into a gully and now will have to climb back out. Go left up a steep, rocky section on Yellow Rectangle Trail, or keep straight for two more options to climb out, each harder than the last.

Top out on a granite ridge that's a blast to play around on, with a view

The Westwoods Trails network begins adjacent to a fruit orchard and small, scenic Bishop Pond.

© CHRIS BERNARD

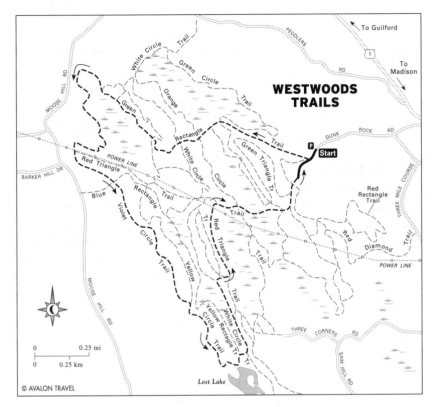

of Lost Lake below; several trails intersect here. Take White Circle to a left on Red Triangle. Stay left and work back toward Dunk Rock Road. Just after you cross under a power line, you will come to Blue Rectangle Trail. Turn right here and before you know it you're back where you started.

Westwoods covers 1,200 acres with 39 miles of trails crossing and recrossing, and it can get confusing. Trails marked with an X are connectors, so a red X, for example, will connect you to a red trail. Several trailheads touch on area roads, so if you become disoriented, you can always bail out and ride the road back to your starting point.

The Westwoods Trails area is owned in part by the state, the city of Guilford, the Guilford Land Conservation Trust, and private owners. Note that some trails close because of conditions. For updates on trail closures, help reading the blaze system, trail maps, or other information, contact the Guilford Land Conservation Trust, Box 200, Guilford, CT 06437, 203/457-9253, www.westwoodstrails.org.

Options

With so many trails in the area, you should be able to extend your ride as long as you want. Use a GPS unit if you have one or a trail map to keep from getting lost.

This ride is very close to the Madison Beach ride.

Locals' Tip: The freshest food you can find is across the street from the trail-head at Bishop's Orchards (480 New England Road, Guilford, CT 06437, 203/453-2338, www.bishopsorchards.com), where you can pick your own strawberries, blueberries, raspberries, peaches, pears, or apples, depending on the season.

Places to Stay: Start and end your day at the Bartlett Farm B&B (564 Great Hill Road, Guilford, CT 06437, 203/457-1657).

Driving Directions

From points east and west, take I-95 to exit 57 and follow CT-1 toward Guilford for 0.6 mile. Turn right onto Dunk Rock Road and drive 0.5 mile to the parking area across from Bishop's Pond, where you'll see a trailhead and sign. Several different parking areas allow access to the trails; this ride starts from the Dunk Rock Road area, which is the closest and easiest to find from the interstate. Supplies are available in Guilford; bike shops are in Branford and Clinton.

Route Directions

0.0 From Dunk Rock Road parking lot, ride up Dunk Rock Road.

0.2 Turn RIGHT onto Green Rectangle Trail.

1.5 Turn LEFT onto Violet Circle Trail at Moose Hill Road entrance.

2.4 Turn RIGHT onto Yellow Circle Trail.

2.7 Turn LEFT up steep, rocky section (you may need to carry your bike), onto Yellow Rectangle Trail.

2.8 Turn LEFT onto White Circle Trail.

3.1 Turn LEFT onto Red Triangle Trail.

3.8 Turn RIGHT onto Blue Rectangle Trail.

4.3 Turn LEFT onto Dunk Rock Road.

4.5 Return to parking area.

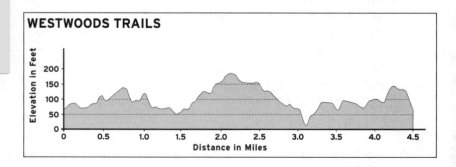

15 MADISON BEACH   BEST 【

Hammonasset State Park, Madison

PAVED ROADS WITH MINIMAL TRAFFIC

Difficulty: 1   **Total Distance:** 14.5 miles

Riding Time: 1.5-2 hours   **Elevation Gain:** 177 feet

Summary: This easy, flat ride meanders along the beach before ducking into the longest beachfront park in the state.

This ride won't challenge your legs, as it's flat and smooth the entire way. What it will do, however, is offer you a nice, lazy roll down back roads to the coast, from lovely Madison Beach into Hammonasset State Park.

Hammonasset is the state's largest shoreline park, and the more than two-mile-long beach is the longest in the state. Choose your ride day wisely, as this beach—and the park around it—is a draw during the busy summer months. You won't have to wait in traffic like everyone else if you're on a bike, but you don't want to have to fight for space on the roads, either.

Turn around at Meig's Point in the park, where you'll find facilities and a nature center. During World War II, American forces used the point as an artillery range, and residents would watch airplanes firing back toward the range from the bay. Oddly, this is not the first time the land was used in such a manner—Winchester, the firearms manufacturer, once tested rifles by firing them from boats back toward the beach. Despite its history, Hammonasset is now as peaceful a place as you could ask for. If you're so inclined, stop and visit the nature center.

© CHRIS BERNARD

Ocean views vie for cyclists' attention along much of the Madison Beach ride.

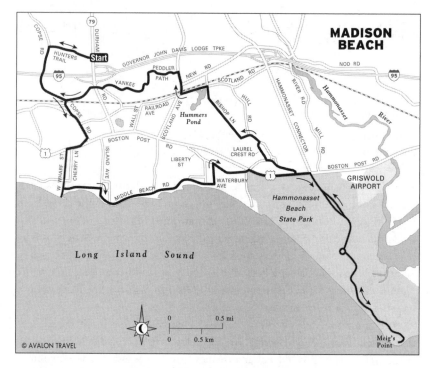

After turning around, the ride leaves the park and ducks through mostly residential neighborhoods back to the starting point for a short, flat, summer's day kind of ride that will please most anyone.

For more information, contact Hammonasset Beach State Park, 1288 Boston Post Road, P.O. Box 271, Madison, CT 06443, 203/245-2785, www.ct.gov.

Options

If you are on a mountain bike, or have on a cyclocross bike with you, combine this ride with Westwoods Trails. At Mile 10, stay on US-1 for about 4.5 miles, then turn left onto Dunk Rock Road. The trailhead is 0.5 mile down on the right.

This ride is also a reasonable drive from Devil's Hopyard Loop and Niantic Bay Loop.

Locals' Tip: Stately-looking Cafe Allegre (725 Boston Post Road, Madison, CT 06443, 203/245-7773) serves Italian and northern European food that won't break the bank.

Places to Stay: Spend a night at the Madison Beach Hotel (94 West Wharf Road, Madison, CT 06443, 203/245-1404), right along the ride at the ocean's edge.

Driving Directions

From I-95, take exit 61 for CT-79. Turn right from the exit and park in the commuter parking lot.

Route Directions

0.0 From the parking area, turn RIGHT onto CT-79. Watch for traffic, taking a quick LEFT onto Hunter's Trail Road. (This road may have packed gravel on it, depending on when repairs are finished.)

0.6 At the stop sign, turn LEFT onto unmarked Copse Road.

1.3 At the stop sign, turn RIGHT on Copse Road over railroad bridge.

1.5 At the stop sign, stay STRAIGHT on Copse Road.

1.8 Turn RIGHT on Britton Lane, opposite Madison Green, and turn RIGHT at the stop sign, onto US-1. Watch for traffic.

2.0 Turn LEFT onto West Wharf Road, at the Madison Country Club. Be careful turning.

2.3 At the stop sign, stay STRAIGHT on West Wharf Road.

2.5 Road ends at ocean and jetty. *Optional stop for scenic view of ocean and marina and a jetty popular with anglers.* Turn around and retrace route onto West Wharf Road, taking a quick RIGHT onto Middle Beach Road.

3.0 Turn RIGHT at stop sign onto unmarked road, then turn LEFT at curve as road becomes Middle Beach Road.

3.9 Stay STRAIGHT across bridge onto Seaview Avenue.

4.3 Turn LEFT as road becomes Waterbury Avenue.

4.5 Turn RIGHT at stop sign, onto Liberty Street.

4.9 Turn RIGHT at stop sign, onto US-1, watching for traffic.

5.5 Turn RIGHT at light, into Hammonasset State Park. Follow access road to rotary.

6.5 Turn LEFT at rotary (coming in at 6 o'clock, exiting at 9).

8.2 Road ends at Meig's Point pavilion. *Seasonal facilities and water available.* The Nature Center is on your right (10 A.M.–5 P.M. Tue.–Sat. Apr.–Oct., 10 A.M.–4 P.M. Tue.–Sat. Nov.–Mar.). TURN AROUND.

9.0 Turn RIGHT at rotary (coming in at 6 o'clock, exiting at 3).

9.8 Turn LEFT onto US-1, watching for traffic.

10.0 Turn RIGHT onto Signal Hill Road, and bear RIGHT at fork onto Laurel Crest Road. OPTION: Stay on US-1 for 4.5 miles and follow the option directions.

10.5 Take LEFT onto Saxon Road, which curves right and becomes Bishop Lane.

11.6 Turn LEFT at Scotland Road.

11.8 Turn RIGHT onto Horse Pond Road.

12.0 Turn LEFT onto Yankee Peddler Path.

13.0 Cross CT-79 onto Woodland Road.

13.4 Bear RIGHT onto Copse Road.

14.0 Turn RIGHT onto Hunter's Trail.

14.4 Turn RIGHT onto CT-79.

14.5 END at parking area.

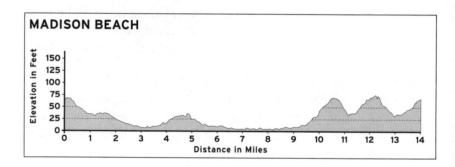

16 DEVIL'S HOPYARD LOOP
Devil's Hopyard State Park, East Haddam

PAVED ROADS WITH MINIMAL TO MODERATE TRAFFIC

Difficulty: 3   **Total Distance:** 27.1 miles

Riding Time: 2.5 hours   **Elevation Gain:** 1,680 feet

Summary: This ride will appeal to fit riders seeking moderately challenging hills and serene roads.

Nestled in southern Connecticut, this area teems with backcountry roads, rolling hills, brooks, and crumbling stone walls, and this ride makes the best of them. This is just plain good road riding, with two significant hills to tackle.

The route leaves Devil's Hopyard State Park for rural, thickly wooded, hilly roads to the north. It's worth spending time at the park to see Chapman Falls and the curious stone pothole formations; you can also begin the ride right from the campground if you are camping there. Next, loop around the southern end of Lake Hayward, where you'll hit some uneven pavement along the lake and then one killer half-mile hill as you climb away from it onto Mill Lane.

After crossing CT-82, turn onto Darling Road and you'll see Salem Valley Farms. This popular ice-cream stand, open in spring and summer only, makes a great regrouping or rest stop, with picnic tables, a pay phone, a large parking area, and excellent ice cream. The next stretch returns to rural roads, with a good downhill before a sharp right turn onto Holmes Road with another tough half-mile climb.

The next five or six miles are a joy. You'll ride on lovely lanes with smooth surfaces and downhill grades, past stone walls, horses in fields, old cemeteries, and pretty houses.

Turn onto CT-156 to see the library and school in Lyme, signaling an increase in traffic on this scenic highway through more open countryside with expansive fields and still more horse farms. For the finish, the narrow, winding Hopyard Road mimics the curves and bends of Eightmile River as you ride in deep shade back to the state park.

For more information, contact Devil's Hopyard State Park, 366 Hopyard Road, East Haddam, CT 06423, 860/873-8566, www.dep.state.ct.us/stateparks/parks/devilshopyard.htm.

Options

To shorten this ride by about 5 miles, bear right at Mile 11 to stay on Darling

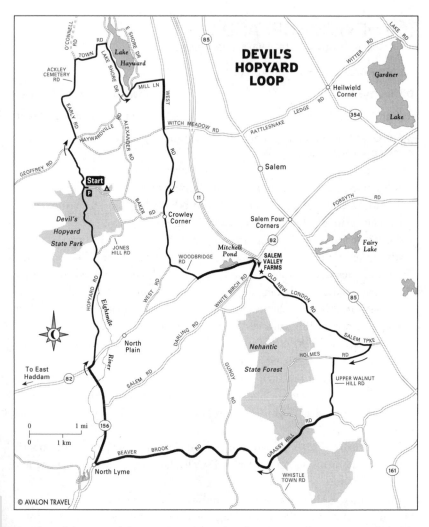

Road, and then turn left onto Gungy Road. When you reach Beaver Brook Road, turn right, rejoining the ride at Mile 18.5.

This ride is close to Niantic Bay Loop.

Locals' Tip: Butter up at Bagel Plus (25 Florida Road, East Haddam, CT 06423, 860/873-9448) before the ride.

Places to Stay: Spend the night at the Griswold Inn (36 Main Street, Essex, CT 06426, 860/767-1776, www.griswoldinn.com) and rest your weary pedal-pushers. Devil's Hopyard State Park also has a campground (860/526-2336, $22–32).

Driving Directions

From the south, take I-95 to exit 70 and drive north on CT-156 for approximately 9.5 miles. Turn right onto CT-82 and take the first left onto Hopyard Road, following signs for Devil's Hopyard State Park. Drive 3.5 miles and turn right into the Chapman Falls parking area. From the east, take CT-395 to Norwich and take exit 80 to CT-82. Drive approximately 13.5 miles and turn right onto Hopyard Road, following signs for Devil's Hopyard State Park. Drive 3.5 miles and turn right into the Chapman Falls parking area (the second entrance to the park). Devil's Hopyard State Park offers picnic areas, outhouses, a campground, a pay phone, and free parking. Supplies are available in Salem and East Haddam, but not along the route. A bike shop is nearby in Essex.

Route Directions

0.0 From parking lot, turn RIGHT onto access road and RIGHT onto Hopyard Road.

0.8 Turn RIGHT onto Haywardville Road.

1.1 Turn LEFT onto Early Road.

1.9 Turn RIGHT onto Ackley Cemetery Road (unmarked).

2.8 Bear RIGHT, staying on Ackley Cemetery Road (becomes Town Road).

3.2 Bear LEFT.

3.7 Turn RIGHT onto Lake Shore Drive.

4.7 Turn LEFT at junction, onto Haywardville Road.

5.1 Continue STRAIGHT on Haywardville (becomes Mill Lane).

5.8 Turn RIGHT at stop sign onto West Road.

6.7 Go STRAIGHT at stop sign, continuing on West Road.

9.3 West Road becomes Woodbridge Road.

10.0 Turn LEFT onto CT-82 at junction. (Caution: steep downhill just before the junction.)

11.1 Turn RIGHT onto Darling Road at flashing yellow light. OPTION: Turn left onto Gungy Road and follow option directions.

11.2 *Salem Valley Farms ice-cream stand.*

11.4 Turn LEFT onto Old New London Road at four-way intersection.

13.8 Old New London Road becomes Salem Turnpike.

14.3 Make a sharp RIGHT onto Holmes Road.

15.1 Turn LEFT onto Upper Walnut Hill Road.

16.2 Turn RIGHT at junction onto Grassy Hill Road.

17.8 Turn RIGHT at three-way intersection onto Beaver Brook Road (unmarked).

18.8 Continue STRAIGHT at stop sign, staying on Beaver Brook Road.

21.5 Turn RIGHT onto CT-156 at junction.

23.4 Turn RIGHT onto CT-82 at junction.

23.6 Turn LEFT onto Hopyard Road.

26.8 Pass first main entrance to state park.

27.1 Turn RIGHT into Devil's Hopyard State Park, Chapman Falls entrance, to return to start.

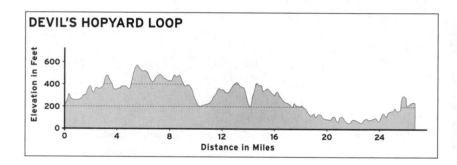

17 NIANTIC BAY LOOP BEST 🄲

Niantic, East Lyme, and South Lyme

PAVED ROADS

Difficulty: 2	**Total Distance:** 27.7 miles
Riding Time: 2 hours	**Elevation Gain:** 700 feet

Summary: This ride tours the waterfront village of Niantic and the rural roads of Lyme with moderate climbing.

Technically, Niantic is a village in the town of East Lyme, perched right on Long Island Sound. In some ways the village has a split personality. From one side, near the bridge across the Niantic River, it seems industrial, and the views of Millstone Nuclear Power Plant on the horizon across Niantic Bay don't help. From the other, near Rocky Neck State Park, the setting is serene, beautiful, and a world apart—while remaining just a mile or two away.

This ride leaves a municipal parking lot across the street from Niantic Bay Bicycles downtown and heads away from the industry up into the rural hills and quiet roads surrounding Niantic. The whole first half of the ride is basically a gradual climb, which gets steeper for a quick burst—and then you're over the top. After that, a few small uphills remain, but there's nothing you'd call a climb.

What you do get, though, is a pretty ride long enough to open up your legs and lungs a bit but not long enough to tax you. You'll ride past Rocky Neck, where

© CHRIS BERNARD

Though the Niantic Bay Loop runs into the more rural, residential neighborhoods outside town, it starts and ends near the waterfront.

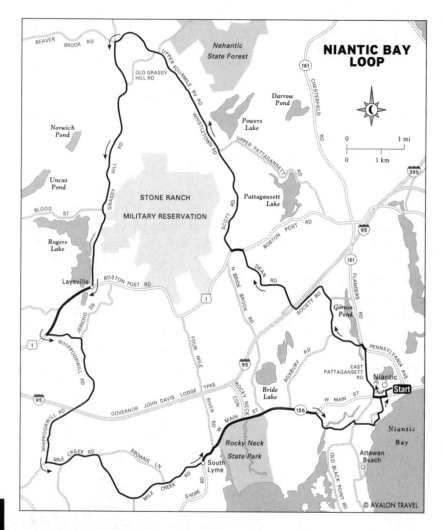

you can pull in and stop for a rest if you're so inclined. (There are some great hiking trails in the park, but bikes aren't welcome on them.) You'll head back toward Niantic, crossing the Pattaguanset River and riding past Crescent Beach at the base of Black Point, before rolling back down Main Street to the parking area.

There's some traffic on the main roads through town, which is worse at certain times of day, but most of these roads are quiet back roads in pretty good shape. Niantic Bay Bicycles recommends this ride; if you'd like company or a guide, check in with the owners to see when group rides are scheduled. The owners are friendly, experienced, and helpful.

After your ride, check out the mile-long Niantic Bay Boardwalk following the ocean's edge. It's a nice walk, but again, bikes are not welcome.

For more information, contact Niantic Bay Bicycles, 8 Methodist Street, Niantic, CT 06357, 860/691-0757, www.nianticbaybicycles.com.

Options

Cut two miles off the ride by turning left at the island at Mile 9.4 and left again when the road ends, rejoining the original ride at Mile 11.

If you're in the area for a few days and want to rides that explore further, try the Devil's Hopyard Loop, a slightly more difficult road ride, or Bluff Point Loop, if you have a mountain bike. Ridden in the same day, or on consecutive days, these trails are sure to please even jaded cyclists.

Locals' Tip: The Black Sheep Public House (247 Main Street, Niantic, CT 06357, 860/739-2041, www.theblacksheepniantic.com) is an outstanding Irish pub welcoming to cyclists.

Places to Stay: Fourteen Lincoln Street (14 Lincoln Street, Niantic, CT 06357, 860/739-6327, www.14lincolnstreet.com) is a very cool bed-and-breakfast in an old church.

Driving Directions

From I-95, take exit 74 and turn right onto CT-161, and then right onto CT-156/ Main Street. Less than 0.25 mile down, turn right onto Methodist Street. The municipal lot is on your right, across from Niantic Bay Bicycles.

Route Directions

0.0 From the municipal lot, turn LEFT onto Methodist Street and RIGHT onto Main Street.

0.4 Turn RIGHT onto East Pattagansett Road.

1.4 Bear LEFT onto CT-161.

1.6 Turn LEFT onto Roxbury Road.

2.0 Turn RIGHT onto Riverview Road.

2.7 Bear LEFT onto Society Road and pass under I-95.

3.5 Bear RIGHT onto Dean Road.

5.1 Turn LEFT onto US-1 and RIGHT onto Scott Road.

7.2 Turn LEFT onto Whistletown Road at island.

9.4 Cross Grassy Hill Road and climb Beaver Brook Road.

10.3 Turn LEFT onto Grassy Hill Road and descend.

15.1 Turn RIGHT onto US-1.

16.3 Turn LEFT onto Whippoorwill Road.

18.5 Cross over I-95.

 9.4 OPTION: Turn left at the island and follow option directions.

19.6 At the T intersection, turn LEFT onto Mile Creek Road (unmarked).

20.1 At the next T intersection, bear RIGHT to stay on Mile Creek Road (unmarked).

23.1 Turn LEFT onto CT-156 at T intersection.

23.4 Turn RIGHT to stay on CT-156, riding past Rocky Neck State Park. *Rest stop.*

25.5 Turn RIGHT onto Fairhaven Road.

25.9 Turn LEFT at T intersection.

26.5 Turn RIGHT onto Black Point Road.

26.6 Turn LEFT onto Crescent Avenue, riding past Crescent Beach.

 27.1 Turn RIGHT onto Columbus Avenue at T intersection. Use caution crossing railroad tracks.

27.3 Turn RIGHT onto CT-156/Main Street.

27.5 Turn LEFT onto Lake Avenue and RIGHT onto Hope Street.

27.7 Turn RIGHT onto Methodist Avenue. END at parking area.

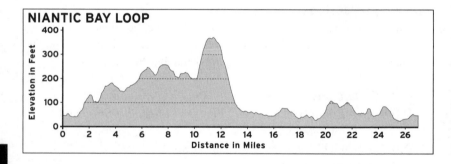

18 BLUFF POINT LOOP

Bluff Point State Park, Groton

BEST C

DIRT ROADS, SINGLE-TRACK

Difficulty: 3

Total Distance: 7.5 miles

Riding Time: 1.5-2 hours

Elevation Gain: 425 feet

Summary: These trails offer a mix of easy dirt roads and hard-core single-track, letting all off-road riders choose their own challenge.

Bluff Point Coastal Reserve is Connecticut's last remaining significant piece of undeveloped coastal land. It's also some of the best biking in Southern New England. The 800-acre peninsula—once a tombolo—juts out into Long Island Sound and offers a combination of wooded trails, spectacular views of the Poquonnock River, Mumford Cove, and Long Island Sound, and the opportunity to see wide-ranging wildlife.

These trails aren't exactly a secret—the after-work riding crowd is stocked with regulars—but they seldom get crowded. If you ride during off-hours, you may have them to yourself. Keep an eye out for horses, as these are shared trails. The trails are unmarked but because you're surrounded by water on three sides, it's hard to stay lost for long.

This loop begins on the main hard-packed gravel double-track that parallels

© CHRIS BERNARD

Scenic overlooks offer riders ample opportunities to rest while riding the mountain bike trails at Bluff Point State Park.

the Poquonnock River, and it offers short climbs and descents and technical rocky and sandy sections. The dirt-road loop is about 3.3 miles long and can be a nice ride for families. The single-track is mostly nontechnical, suitable for beginners taking it slowly or more advanced riders going faster. If you're riding a cyclocross bike, stick to the main gravel road. The park contains some protected research areas, so please stay on the trails.

Outhouses are available on the trail. Bugs can be bad, especially during greenhead season (July and August). Check yourself for ticks after each ride. After a good ride, you can walk the long, narrow beach, which was shaped by continental glaciers.

Maps are available at the trailhead. For more information, contact Bluff Point State Park, c/o Fort Trumbull State Park, 90 Walbach Street, New London, CT 06320, 860/444-7591, www.dep.state.ct.us/stateparks/parks/bluffpoint.htm.

Options

Follow signs along the way for trails that lead to Sunset Rock, a boulder where sunset religious services were once held, and to the former home of Connecticut's first governor, John Winthrop, dating back to the 1700s. From there, take the trail that says "picnic area" and follow the rocky descent back to the main trail.

This ride is within a half-hour drive of Niantic Bay Loop and Mystic Birthday Ride, both road rides. If overnighting in the area, expand your cycling horizons by giving these a shot. The Niantic Bay Loop is the easier of the two. The Mystic Birthday Ride is a very challenging ride that will test your climbing legs. Combined, these make a great cycling mini-vacation.

Locals' Tip: Build your own omelet at the 1950s-inspired Oh Boy! Diner (43 Gold Star Highway, Groton, CT 06340, 860/448-1000).

Places to Stay: Plenty of hotel chains are represented in Groton and nearby Mystic, including the Cedar Park Inn and Whirlpool Suites (85 Norwich-Westerly Road, at the CT-2/CT-184 rotary, North Stonington, CT 06359, 860/535-7829).

Driving Directions

From I-95, take exit 88 to CT-117 South. Turn right onto CT-1 South. Take a left at the first light, onto Depot Road. Park entrance is at the end of the road. Parking is free. There are picnic tables and outhouses but no other facilities at the park. The nearest bike shops are in Groton and Mystic.

Route Directions

0.0 START from the signboard at the south end of the parking lot with the map on it. Turn LEFT on first narrow trail, and then RIGHT at first fork.

0.3 Turn RIGHT at the T leading to the Winthrop Home site, then LEFT after 50 feet.

0.4 Stay STRAIGHT at intersection.

0.5 Bear RIGHT at Y intersection, then stay LEFT.

0.7 Turn LEFT, then veer RIGHT.

0.9 Veer RIGHT at the big rock at the Y intersection.

1.1 Continue STRAIGHT across at Upper Road intersection.

1.3 Turn LEFT at intersection.

1.4 Turn RIGHT at intersection, through gap in stone wall.

1.6 Turn LEFT as trail divides.

1.7 Continue STRAIGHT across at North Connector intersection.

1.8 Turn RIGHT at junction.

2.4 South Connector double-track intersection. Go RIGHT for 0.1 mile and take the trail on the left to Bluff Point. *Trail passes through wooded and open areas, and the view opens up as you approach the bluff. This is a perfect place to sit on the beach, eat a snack, and enjoy the view.* Retrace your route to the South Connector and follow trail uphill.

3.7 Turn RIGHT at trail entrance on right side of road (at meadow).

4.0 Continue STRAIGHT across the muddy river bottom.

4.3 Turn LEFT at Y intersection, then make another immediate LEFT.

4.5 Turn LEFT at Y intersection, then make another immediate LEFT.

4.7 Turn RIGHT at downhill.

4.9 Turn LEFT on East Side Trail at the big rock.

5.0 Turn RIGHT at Y intersection.

5.2 Turn LEFT at entrance to 0.3-mile stretch of challenging single-track. Enter, go 50 feet, then take a sharp LEFT and wind your way up to the top of the hill.

5.5 Turn RIGHT at intersection. The trail winds uphill back to the center of the park.

6.2 Turn LEFT, then make an immediate RIGHT.

6.3 Turn RIGHT (downhill).

6.4 Pass through the stone wall and turn RIGHT on East Side trail.

6.7 Turn LEFT, then go STRAIGHT for 50 feet and turn LEFT onto the road.

7.5 END at parking lot.

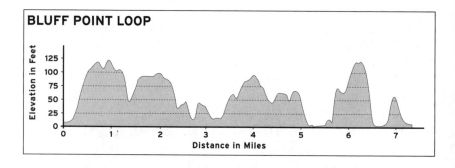

🔟🔟 MYSTIC BIRTHDAY RIDE **BEST (**

Mystic, Old Mystic, and North Stonington

PAVED ROADS WITH MINIMAL TRAFFIC

Difficulty: 5 **Total Distance:** 50 miles

Riding Time: 3 hours **Elevation Gain:** 1,673 feet

Summary: Even climbers will feel the burn on this relentlessly uphill ride, but the farmlands and scenery make it worth every inch.

Tradition at Mystic Cycle Centre dictates that the owner takes employees out for this ride on their birthdays. A brutally hilly route that never really leaves much time for recovery, the name could also refer to the fact that while on this ride, you may find yourself wishing you'd never been born.

But in the end, you'll be glad you persevered. As relentlessly uphill as this ride is, it's also beautiful from start to finish, and if you time it right, you'll ride past acres and acres of sunflowers in full bloom.

The ride starts and ends at the bike shop, traveling through downtown Mystic and turning north, through historic Old Mystic and up main roads toward Griswold. The roads are well paved and smooth, twisting and turning and shaded by trees, and they do see some fast-moving cars, but traffic is spaced out and not a major concern.

Continuing north, you'll pass the fields of Buttonwood Farm. Each year, from

This relentlessly hilly climbers' ride begins and ends along the Mystic River.

mid-July until the end of the month, the fields are alight with more than 300,000 sunflowers planted by the farm to sell as a fund-raiser for the Connecticut Make-a-Wish foundation. The brilliant yellow stretches almost to the horizon, and you can walk—or take a hayride—along paths between the thick stems. It's beautiful, and better yet, the farm—which you pass as you turn east on CT-165—sells sunflower-flavored ice cream made on site with milk from resident dairy cows. It's a good reward for all the climbing you've done.

About that—it's not over yet. And you may be making your own wish that it was. Heading south through more rural farmlands, by the time you reach Wyassup Lake, at the top of a sweet descent, the majority of the climbing is behind you, but two of the steepest (albeit shortest) hills still loom large. Back within sight of Mystic, you hit Whitford Road, a sharp uphill, and then one more uphill at Mile 44 that adds insult to injury, but it'll be over before you know it. And then you coast back across the Mystic Bridge into the

shop parking lot, sore, tired, smiling, and with serious bragging rights.

For more information on the sunflower fund-raiser, contact Buttonwood Farm, 471 Shetucket Turnpike, Griswold, CT 06351, 860/376-4081, www.sunflowers forwishes.com. For more information on this ride, contact Mystic Cycle Centre, 25 Stonington Road/US-1, Mystic, CT 06355, 860/572-7433, http://mysticcycle centre.com.

Options

Legs revolting in the first half of the ride? Cut eight miles by turning right onto Coal Pit Hill Road at Mile 19. Bear left at the intersection onto an unmarked road, and then turn left onto Legend Wood Road, rejoining the ride at Mile 27 by turning right onto CT-49.

Bring a mountain bike along with your road bike to turn this into a couple days of riding. This ride is close to Bluff Point Loop, which offers some fun, wooded singletrack. Or, stick to the pavement and drive to nearby Niantic for the Niantic Bay Loop.

Locals' Tip: Bike shop employees recommend a Middle Eastern place, the Pita Spot (45 Williams Avenue, Mystic, CT 06355, 860/415-4656), as the place to ingest much-needed calories after this ride.

This ride is close to Bluff Point Loop as well as several Rhode Island rides.

Places to Stay: There's no shortage of chains in the area, and you can find competitive pricing, or splurge a bit at the Whaler's Inn (20 East Main Street, Mystic, CT 06355, 860/536-1506, www.whalersinnmystic.com).

Driving Directions

From I-95, take exit 90 and turn onto CT-27 south. Pass Mystic Seaport, going all the way to the end of CT-27, then turn left at the light onto US-1. Mystic Cycle Centre is 0.25 mile up on the left—tell the owners you're there for the birthday ride. Parking and facilities are available.

Route Directions

0.0 From the parking area, turn RIGHT onto US-1/Stonington Road. Stay on US-1, crossing the Mystic Bridge.

1.1 After the bridge, take the second RIGHT, onto Pearl Street/Grove Avenue, along the water. The road becomes River Road.

4.0 Cross CT-27 and Shewville Road and stay straight onto North Stonington Road/CT-201. Stay on CT-201.

8.7 Turn LEFT onto Wintechog Hill Road.

11.6 Turn RIGHT onto CT-2/Norwich-Westerly Road.

13.8 Turn LEFT onto CT-201/Cossaduck Hill Road, which is a good long climb.

19.0 OPTION: Turn right onto Coal Pit Hill Road and follow option directions.

20.7 *If you're riding during the second half of July, you'll start to see the sunflowers first on your left, then on both sides of the road.*

21.0 Turn RIGHT onto CT-165/Shetucket Turnpike. *Buttonwood Farm is on your right.*

21.7 Turn RIGHT onto Kinney Road, bearing LEFT at fork to stay on Kinney Road.

23.2 Turn RIGHT onto CT-49/Pendleton Hill Road.

26.8 Turn RIGHT onto Wyassup Road, and climb to Wyassup Lake.

29.0 Begin descent at Wyassup Lake, staying on Wyassup Road into North Stonington.

32.7 Turn RIGHT onto Main Street.

33.3 Cross CT-2 onto Mystic Road/State Highway 627.

34.2 Bear LEFT to stay on Mystic Road as it merges with CT-201.

37.2 Turn sharply to the RIGHT onto Whitford Road.

38.2 Cross Lantern Hill Road to stay on Whitford Road.

38.7 Turn RIGHT onto Shewville Road.

39.6 Turn LEFT onto Town Farm Road.

40.5 When Town Farm Road ends, turn LEFT onto Gallup Hill Road, staying to the LEFT at the next intersection.

42.3 Turn RIGHT onto Shewville Road, which takes you across CT-184 into Old Mystic. After crossing CT-184, bear RIGHT onto River Road.

45.6 Turn RIGHT onto Bindloss Road.

45.8 Turn RIGHT onto Cow Hill Road.

45.9 Turn RIGHT onto Oral School Road.

46.6 Turn LEFT onto Cow Hill Road.

47.0 Bear LEFT to stay on Cow Hill Road.

47.5 Turn LEFT onto Bindloss Road.

47.6 Turn RIGHT onto River Road.

48.7 Turn LEFT onto Main Street/US-1. Cross the Mystic Bridge, and follow US-1.

50.0 END at parking area on LEFT.

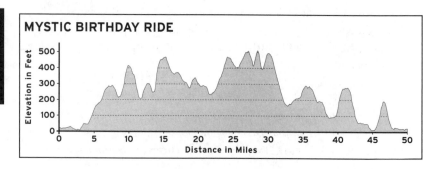

RESOURCES

BIKING ORGANIZATIONS

Following is a list of selected organizations, clubs, and bicycle shops in New England. While this is not a comprehensive list, you should be able to find a bike shop near most of the routes (though several are too remote to have any bike shops in the area).

Regional
East Coast Greenway
27B North Road
Wakefield, RI 02879
401/789-4625
www.greenway.org

Eastern Fat Tire Association
fax 603/529-0670
www.efta.com

New England Mountain Biking Association (NEMBA)
P.O. Box 2221
Acton, MA 01720
800/57-NEMBA (800/576-3622)
www.nemba.org

Maine
Bicycle Coalition of Maine
341 Water Street
Augusta, ME 04330-4627
207/623-4511
www.bikemaine.org

Eastern Trail Alliance
P.O. Box 250
Saco, ME 04072
207/284-9260
www.easterntrail.org

Maine Bureau of Parks and Lands
286 Water Street
Key Bank Plaza
Augusta, ME 04333
207/287-3821
www.state.me.us/doc/parks

Maine Department of Transportation
Child Street
16 State House Station
Augusta, ME 04333-0016
207/624-3000
www.exploremaine.org/bike

New Hampshire
New Hampshire Department of Transportation
Bicycle/Pedestrian Information Center
P.O. Box 483
7 Hazen Drive
Concord, NH 03302
603/271-1668
www.nh.gov/dot/nhbikeped

New Hampshire Division of Parks and Recreation
172 Pembroke Road
Concord, NH 03302
603/271-3556
www.nhparks.state.nh.us

New Hampshire Trails Bureau
Bureau of Trails
P.O. Box 1856
Concord, NH 03302-1856
603/271-3254
www.nhtrails.org

Vermont

Lake Champlain Bikeways Clearinghouse

1 Steele Street #103
Burlington, VT 05401
802/652-BIKE (802/652-2453)
www.champlainbikeways.org

Local Motion

1 Steele Street #103
Burlington, VT 05401
802/652-BIKE (802/652-2453)
www.localmotionvt.org

Vermont Agency of Transportation

1 National Life Drive
Drawer 33
Montpelier, VT 05633-0001
802/828-2657
www.aot.state.vt.us

Vermont Bicycle/ Pedestrian Coalition

P.O. Box 1234
Montpelier, VT 05601
802/279-7545
www.vtbikeped.org

Vermont Department of Forests, Parks, and Recreation

103 South Main Street
Waterbury, VT 05671-0601
802/241-3655
www.vtstateparks.com

Vermont Mountain Biking Association

P.O. Box 596
Waterbury, VT 05676
www.vmba.org

Massachusetts

Massachusetts Department of Transportation

Bicycle and Pedestrian Program
10 Park Plaza, Suite 3170
Boston, MA 02116
617/973-7000
www.mass.gov

Mass Bike

171 Milk Street, Suite 33
Boston, MA 02109
617/542-BIKE (617/542-2453)
www.massbike.org

Mass Parks

Division of State Parks
   and Recreation
251 Causeway Street, Suite 600
Boston, MA 02114
617/626-1250
www.massparks.org

Rhode Island

Bike Providence

www.bikeprovidence.com

Bike Rhode Island

Rhode Island Department
   of Transportation
2 Capitol Hill
Providence, RI 02903
401/222-4203, ext. 4042
www.dot.state.ri.us

Greenways Alliance of Rhode Island

Rhode Island Affiliate of the
East Coast Greenway Alliance
www.rigreenways.org

Providence Bike Network
City of Providence
Department of Planning and
  Development
401/351-4300

**Rhode Island Parks and
Recreation**
2321 Hartford Avenue
Johnston, RI 02919
401/222-2632
www.riparks.com

Connecticut
Appalachian Mountain Club
Connecticut Chapter
www.ct-amc.org/cycling

**Central Connecticut
Bicycle Alliance**
P.O. Box 270149
West Hartford, CT 06127-0149
www.wecyclect.org

**Connecticut Department of
Transportation**
Bicycle and Pedestrian Coordinator
Bureau of Policy and Planning
P.O. Box 317546
Newington, CT 06131-7546
www.ct.gov/dot

**Connecticut State Parks
and Forests**
Bureau of Outdoor Recreation
Department of Environmental
  Protection
79 Elm Street
Hartford, CT 06106-5127
860/424-3000
www.ct.gov/dep/site/default.asp

Farmington Valley Greenway
860/658-4065
rbd1414@hotmail.com
http://fvgreenway.org

**New England Mountain
Biking Association,
Connecticut Chapter**
www.ctnemba.org

BIKE CLUBS
Maine
Casco Bay Bicycle Club
www.cascobaybicycleclub.org

Maine Coast Cycling Club
Cape-Able Bike Shop
P.O. Box 581
Kennebunkport, ME 04046
207/967-4382
www.portcycle.com

Maine Cycling Club
Rainbow Bicycles
1225 Center Street
Auburn, ME 04210
207/784-7576
www.rainbowbike.com

Maine Outdoor Adventure Club
P.O. Box 11251
Portland, ME 04104
207/775-MOAC (207/775-6622)
www.moac.org

**Merrymeeting Wheelers
Bicycle Club**
P.O. Box 233
Brunswick, ME 04011
207/882-7206
www.merrymeetingwheelers.com

Mount Agamenticus NEMBA
P.O. Box 40
Cape Neddick, ME 03902
207/332-5497
www.mtanemba.org

Portland Velo Club
P.O. Box 15093
Portland, ME 04112
www.portlandvelo.com

Rage on Portland
www.ragemtb.com/mainiacs/

Southern Maine Cycling Club
Gorham Bike and Ski
1440 Congress Street
Portland, ME 04102
207/773-1700
www.gorhambike.com

New Hampshire
Friends of Massabesic Bicycling Association
P.O. Box 155
Auburn, NH 03032
www.fomba.com

Granite State Wheelmen
PMB 216
215 South Broadway
Salem, NH 03079-3309
603/898-5479
www.granitestatewheelmen.org

New Hampshire Cycling Club
www.nhcyclingclub.com

Seacoast New England Mountain Biking Association (NEMBA)
www.snemba.org

South Central New Hampshire New England Mountain Biking Association (NEMBA)
www.scnhnemba.org

Vermont
Green Mountain Bicycle Club
www.thegmbc.com

Killington Pico Cycling Club
www.kpccvt.org

Montpelier Area Mountain Bike Association
info@bikemamba.org
www.bikemamba.org

Massachusetts
The state has too many to list, but here is a sampling of Massachusetts bike clubs.

Boston Bicycle Club
www.bostonbicycleclub.org

Charles River Wheelmen
www.crw.org

Essex County Velo
P.O. Box 2246
South Hamilton, MA 01982
www.ecvcycling.org

Franklin-Hampshire Freewheelers
www.freewheelers.org

Minuteman Road Club
www.minutemanroadclub.com

Nashoba Valley Pedalers
www.nvpbike.org

New England Mountain Biking Association (NEMBA) Massachusetts
P.O. Box 2221
Acton, MA 01720
800/57-NEMBA (800/576-3622)
www.nemba.org

Northampton Cycling Club
P.O. Box 886
Northampton, MA 01061
www.northamptoncyclingclub.org

North Shore Cyclists
www.astseals.com/nsc

Rage on Boston
www.rageMTB.com

Seven Hills Wheelmen
P.O. Box 20232
Worcester, MA 01602
www.sevenhillswheelmen.org

Rhode Island
Narragansett Bay Wheelmen
P.O. Box 41177
Providence, RI 02940-1177
401/351-3055
www.nbwclub.org

Providence Velo Club
Providence Bicycle
725 Branch Avenue
Providence, RI 02904
401/331-6610
www.providence bicycle.com

Rhode Island New England Mountain Biking Association (NEMBA)
www.nemba.org

Connecticut
Hat City Cyclists
P.O. Box 1034
Bethel, CT 06801
www.hatcitycyclists.org

Pequot Cyclists
www.pequotcyclists.com

Sound Cyclists
P.O. Box 3323
Westport, CT 06880
203/840-1757
www.soundcyclists.com

Southern Connecticut Cycle Club
P.O. Box 51
New Haven, CT 06501-0051
www.ctcycle.org

Yankee Pedalers
http://yankeepedalers.home.att.net

BIKE SHOPS
Maine
Augusta
Auclair Cycle and Ski
64 Bangor Street
207/623-4351 or 800/734-7171
www.auclair-cycle.com

Bar Harbor
Acadia Bike
48 Cottage Street
207/288 9605 or 800/526 8615
www.acadiabike.com

Acadia Outfitters
106 Cottage Street
207/288-8118
www.acadiafun.com

Bar Harbor Bicycle Shop
141 Cottage Street
207/288-3886
www.barharborbike.com

Carrabassett Valley
Sugarloafer Shop at Sugarloaf USA
5092 Access Road
207/237-6718
www.sugarloaf.com
    (seasonal rentals only)

Ellsworth
Bar Harbor Bike
193 Main Street
207/667-6886
www.barharborbike.com

Freeport
L.L. Bean
US-1
207/552-7834
www.llbean.com

National Bike and Ski
308 US-1
207/865-0523
www.skimarket.com

Greenville
North Woods Outfitters
Maine Street
207/695-3288 or 866/223-1380
www.maineoutfitter.com

Kennebunkport
Cape-Able Bike Shop
83 Arundel Road
207/967-4382

Oakland
Mathieu's Cycle and Fitness
20 Main Street
207/465-7564
www.mathieuscycleandfitness.com

Peaks Island
Brad's Recycled Bike Shop
115 Island Avenue
207/766-5631

Portland
AllSpeed Bike and Ski
1041 Washington Avenue
207/878-8741
www.allspeed.com

Back Bay Bicycle
333 Forest Avenue
207/773-6906
www.backbaybicycle.com

CycleMania
59 Federal Street
207/774-2933
www.cyclemania1.com

Gorham Bike and Ski
693 Congress Street
207/773-1700
www.gorhambike.com

Rockport
Maine Sport Outfitters
US-1
207/236-7120 or 888/236-8797
www.mainesport.com

Rumford
Chase Cyclery
485 Prospect Avenue (US-2)
207/364-7946 or 800/834-7946

Southwest Harbor
370 Main Street
207/244-5856
www.southwestcycle.com

Westbrook
Ernie's Cycle Shop
105 Conant Street
207/854-4090

Woolwich
Bikeman
115 Main Street (US-1)
207/442-7002
www.bikeman.com

York
Berger's Bike Shop
241 York Street
207/363-4070

New Hampshire
Berlin
Crooker's Cycle Sports
240 Glen Avenue
603/752-3632

Concord
S and W Sports
South Main Street
603/228-1441
www.swsports.net

Dixville Notch
The Balsams Grand Resort Hotel
1000 Cold Spring Road
Dixville Notch, NH 03576
800/255-0600
www.thebalsams.com

Exeter
Exeter Cycles
4 Portsmouth Avenue
603/778-2331
www.exetercycles.com

Franconia Notch
Franconia Sports Shop
Main Street
603/823-5241
www.franconiasports.com

Hooksett
Goodale's Bike Shop
1197 Hooksett Road
603/644-2111
www.goodalesbikeshop.com

Keene
Andy's Cycle Shop
165 Winchester Street
603/352-3410

Norm's Ski and Bike Shop
62 Martell Court
603/352-1404

Lebanon
Omer and Bob's Sport Shop
20 Hanover Street
603/643-3525
www.omerandbobs.com

Manchester
Alternative Bike
616 Mast Road
603/666-4527
www.alternativebike.com

The Bike Barn
33 South Commercial Street
603/668-6555
www.bikebarnusa.com

Nault's Cyclery
30 Bridge Street
603/669-7993
www.naults.com

Milford
Souhegan Cycleworks
227 Union Square, Unit 3
603/673-1817
www.souhegancycleworks.com

Newbury
Outspokin' Bicycle and Sport
Junction of NH-103 and NH-103A
603/763-9500
www.outspokin.com

North Conway
Sports Outlet Shop
2420 White Mountain Highway
603/356-3133
www.sportsoutlet.org

Plymouth
Rhino Bike Works
1 Foster Street
603/536-3919
www.rhinobikeworksnh.com

Portsmouth
Bicycle Bob's Bicycle Outlet
990 Lafayette Road
603/436-2453
www.bicyclebobs.com

Papa Wheelies
653 Islington Street
603/427-2060
www.backbaybicycles.com

Vermont
Bennington
Roads and Trails
160 Benmont Avenue
802/442-8664

Bondville
The Startingate
VT-30
802/297-1213
www.startingate.net

Brattleboro
Brattleboro Bicycle Shop
165 Main Street
802/254-8644
www.bratbike.com

Burrows/Specialized Sport Shop
105 Main Street
802/254-9430
www.sover.net/~specspor

Burlington
North Star Cyclery
100 Main Street
802/863-3832

Old Spokes Home
324 North Winooski Avenue
802/863-4475

Royal Cycles
41 King Street
802/864-7059
www.royalcycles.com

Ski Rack
85 Main Street
802/658-3313 or 800/882-4530
www.skirack.com

Craftsbury Common
Craftsbury Outdoor Center
535 Lost Nation Road
802/586-7767 or 800/729-7751
www.craftsbury.com

East Burke
East Burke Sports
VT-114
802/626-3215
www.eastburkesports.com

Georgia
White's Green Mountain Bikes
1008 Ethan Allen Highway
802/524-4496
www.together.net/~wgmb

Ludlow
Mountain Cycology
3 Lamere Square
802/228-2722

Manchester
Battenkill Sports Bicycle Shop
1240 Depot Street
802/362-2734
www.battenkillsports.com

Middlebury
The Alpine Shop
Merchants Row
802/388-7547
www.alpineshopvt.com

The Bike Center
74 Main Street
802/388-6666
www.bikecentermid.com

Montpelier
Onion River Sports
20 Langdon Street
802/229-9409 or 800/894-7547
www.onionriver.com

Rawsonville
Mountain Riders at Equipe Sports
Junction of VT-30 and VT-100
802/297-2847 or 800/282-6665
www.equipesport.com.

Rochester
Green Mountain Bicycles
105 North Main Street
802/767-4464
www.greenmountainbikes.com

Rutland
Great Outdoors Trading Company
219 Woodstock Avenue
802/775-9989
www.joejonessports.com

Green Mountain Cyclery
133 Strongs Avenue
802/775-0869

Sports Peddler
162 North Main Street
802/775-0101

South Burlington
The Alpine Shop
1184 Williston Road
802/862-2714
www.alpineshopvt.com

Earl's Cyclery
2500 Williston Road
802/864-9197 or 866/327-5725
www.earlsbikes.com

Waitsfield
Fit Werx
4312 Main Street
802/496-7570
www.fitwerx.com

Stark Mountain Bike Works
VT-17
802/496-4800
www.starkmtnbikeworks.com

Winooski
Winooski Bike Shop
12 West Canal Street
802/655-3233

Woodstock
Woodstock Sports
30 Central Street
802/457-1568

Massachusetts
Amherst
Laughing Dog Bicycles
63 South Pleasant Street
413/253-7722

Valley Bicycles
319 Main Street
413/256-0880

Andover
Andover Cycle
26 Chestnut Street
978/749-3191

Barre
Country Bike and Sports
8 Exchange Street
978/355-2219

Belmont
Belmont Wheelworks
480 Trapelo Road
Belmont, MA 02478
617/489-3577
http://wheelworks.com

Brewster
Barbara's Bike and Blade
Route 6A
508/896-7231
www.barbsbikeshop.com

Brewster Bike Rentals
442 Underpass Road
508/896-8149

Rail Trails Bike Shop
302 Underpass Road
508/896-8200

Chelmsford
Chelmsford Cyclery
7 Summer Street
978/256-1528

Eastham
Little Capistrano Bike Shop
341 Salt Pond Road
508/255-6515

Gardner
O'Neil's Bicycle Shop
108 Main Street
978/632-7200
www.oneilsbicycles.com

Great Barrington
Berkshire Bike and Board
29 State Road
413/528-5555
http://berkshirebikeandboard.com

Greenfield
Bicycles Unlimited
322 High Street
413/772-2700
www.bikes-unlimited.com

Hadley
Valley Bicycle
8 Railroad Street
413/584-4466

Ipswich
Ipswich Cycle
5 Brown Square
978/356-4500
www.ipswichcycle.com

Lenox
Arcadian Shop
91 Pittsfield Road
413/637-3010
http://store.arcadian.com

New Bedford
Cesar's Cyclery
739 Ashley Boulevard
508/998-8777

Yesteryear Cyclery
330 Hathaway Road
508/993-2525
www.yesteryearcyclery.com

Newburyport
Riverside Cycles
50 Water Street
The Tannery
888/465-BIKE (888/465-2453)
www.riversidecycle.com

North Harwich
Bike Depot
11 Pleasant Lake Avenue
508/430-4375

Northampton
Northampton Bicycle
319 Pleasant Street
413/586-3810
www.nohobike.com

Orleans
Orleans Cycles
26 Main Street
508/255-9115
www.orleanscyclecapecod.com

Provincetown
Arnold's
291 Bradford Street
508/487-0844

Gale Force Bikes
144 Bradford Street Extension
508/487-4849
www.galeforcebikes.com

Nelson's Bike Shop
43 Race Point Road
508/487-8849

PTown Bikes
42 Bradford Street
508/487-8735

South Dennis
Barbara's Bike and Blade
430 MA-134
508/760-4723
www.barbsbikeshop.com

South Wellfleet
Black Duck Bike Shop
1446 US-6
508/349-9801

Idle Times Bike Shop
2616-A US-6
508/349-9161

Little Capistrano
1446 US-6
508/349-2363
http://capecodbike.com

Westport
The Bike Shop
1125 State Road (US-6)
508/636-1266

Williamstown
The Mountain Goat
130 Water Street
413/458-8445
www.themountaingoat.com

Worcester
Bike Alley
1067 Main Street
508/752-2230
www.bikealley.com

Fritz's Bicycle Shop
328 West Boylston Street
508/853-1799
www.fritzsbikes.com

Rhode Island
Block Island
Block Island Bike and Car Rental
Ocean Avenue
401/466-2297

Island Moped and Bike
P.O. Box 280
401/466-2700

Coventry
Greenways Cycles
585 Washington Street (RI-117)
401/822-2080

East Providence
East Providence Cycle
414 Warren Avenue
401/434-3838
www.eastprovidencecycle.com

Middletown
Pedal Power Bicycle Shop
879 West Main Road
401/846-7525
www.pedalpowerri.com

Newport
Newport Wheels
Brown and Howard Wharf, Unit 2
401/849-4400
www.newportwheelsports.com

Ten Speed Spokes
18 Elm Street
401/847-5609
www.tenspeedspokes.com

Narragansett
Narragansett Bikes
1153 Boston Neck Road
401/782-4444

North Kingstown
Ron's Bicycle Shop
7592 Post Road
401/294-2238

Providence
Providence Bicycle
725 Branch Avenue
401/331-6610
www.providencebicycle.com

Riverside
East Providence Cycle
Riverside (on bike path)
111 Crescent View Avenue
401/437-2453
www.eastprovidencecycle.com

Your Bike Shop
459 Willett Avenue
401/433-4491

Warren
Your Bike Shop
51 Cole Street
401/245-9755

Warwick
Caster's Bicycles and Fitness
3480 Post Road
401/739-0393
www.bikeri.com

Westerly
Ray Willis Toys and Bicycles
53 Railroad Avenue
401/596-1045

Connecticut
Bethel
Bethel Cycles
120 Greenwood Avenue
203/792-4640
www.bethelcycle.com

Berlin
Berlin Bicycle & Repair Shop
855 Mill Street
860/828-1132
www.berlinbicycle.com

Bloomfield
Bloomfield Bicycle
5 Seneca Road
860/242-9884

Branford
Branford Bike
202 Main Street
203/488-0482
www.branfordbike.com

Bridgeport
Spoke and Wheel Bike Shop
2355 East Main Street
203/384-8779

Canton
Benidorm Bikes and Boards
247 Albany Turnpike (US-44)
860/693-8891
www.benidormbikes.com

Country Sports
65A Albany Turnpike (US-44)
860/693-2267
www.countrysportsusa.com

Cheshire
Cheshire Cycle & Repair
471 West Main Street (CT-70)
203/250-9996
www.cheshirecycle.com

Colchester

Sunshine Cycle-Works
467B South Main Street
860/537-2788
www.sunshinecycleworks.com

Danbury

Bike Express
76 West Street
203/792-5460
www.thebikeexpress.com

Ski Market
61 Newtown Road
Plum Tree Plaza
203/798-6616
www.skimarket.com

Essex

Clarke Cycles
4 Essex Plaza
860/767-2405
www.clarkecycles.com

Glastonbury

Pig Iron Bike and Mountain Works
2277 Main Street
860/633-3444
www.pigironsports.com

Groton

Bicycle Barn
1241 Poquonnock Road (US-1)
860/448-4984
www.bicyclebarn.net

Hebron

Cycle Escape
50 Main Street
860/228-2453

Manchester

The Bike Shop
681 Main Street
860/647-1027
www.bikesboards.net

Middlebury

Bicycle Works, LLC
1255 Middlebury Road
866/462-0548
www.bicycleworksllc.com

Monroe

Cycle Fitness
612 Main Street
203/261-8683

Mystic

Mystic Cycle Centre
42 Williams Avenue (US-1)
860/572-7433
www.mysticcycle.com

New Milford

The Bike Express
73 Bridge Street
203/354-1466

Niantic Bay Bicycles

8 Methodist Street
860/691-0757
www.nianticbaybicycles.com

Putnam

Joe's Bike Shop
33 Memorial Terrace
860/928-6783 (repairs only)

Silver Bike Shop
6 Livery Street
860/928-7370

Rocky Hill

Cycling Concepts
825 Cromwell Avenue
860/563-6667
www.cyclingconcepts.com

Simsbury

Bicycle Cellar
532 Hopmeadow Street
860/658-1311

South Glastonbury
Bicycles East
2249 New London Turnpike
860/659-0114
www.bicycleseast.com

South Windsor
Bicycle South Windsor
978 Sullivan Avenue
860/644-0023
www.bicyclesouthwindsor.com

Stamford
Cycle Center
1492 High Ridge Road
203/968-1100
www.cyclecenterct.com

Vernon
Vernon Cycle
352 Hartford Turnpike
860/872-7740
www.vernoncycle.com

Index

Acknowledgments

Considering how much time I spent alone researching, riding, photographing, and writing this book, it's surprising how many other people I relied upon. All parties went above and beyond what you might reasonably expect, considering I had nothing to offer in return but some long bike rides and the occasional beer.

I could not have undertaken this book without the love, support, and understanding of my wife, Kim, known from here on out as "Book Widow." Her role in the successful completion of this manuscript rivaled mine.

Jeff Gibson, Adam Clough, Steve Hall, and Sea Sun Lee rode with me on more than one occasion, facing brutal climbs and raucous descents, tourist-clogged bike paths, bucolic rail trails, one massive bike-swallowing sandpit, and multiple cheap motels and dive bars. Dan Tuohy borrowed a too-big, too-old, and too-heavy bike and challenged himself on some very difficult single-track—during a thunderstorm that seemed, frankly, like overkill—just to keep me company, and got nothing but blood and bruises to show for it. Until now. Thanks, Dan. Thanks to HUP United, my cycling teammates, who set an example to strive for—these folks live biking. And thanks to Jon Bailey and BaileyWorks for the customized messenger bag that hauled my camera gear on the rides for this book.

Others supported me in ways that didn't involve long miles in the saddle, including James Norcott, Chris and Barbara Pukstas, Nicole Lagace and her wonderful family, Josh and Meggin Tuohy, and Doug Drown, Chris Lee, and Ben Stuart, who'd have ridden with me if they lived on the right coast. Thanks also to all the people I met on the roads, trails, and everywhere else along the way, like Ray Willis and Brendan Morgan. Thanks, too, to Sarah Braunstein for pointing me toward this opportunity when I needed a project, and to Melissa Kim for doing so much for the first edition that made this one easier and better.

Thanks to my editors, Nomi, Elizabeth, and Sabrina, each of whom helped tremendously in her own way, and to everyone else who worked on this project. An extra thank you to my photo editor, Elizabeth Jang, whose ongoing support, kindness, generosity, and patience made a lot of things much better—including, hopefully, this book.

And finally, thanks to my parents. One of the best things to come of this entire process was getting them back on bikes after a long absence—50 years in my Dad's case. First they rode a bike path with me, then they rode a few without me, and then they started riding every day, just for the fun of it. That's what brought me to biking in the first place, more than three decades ago, and that's what keeps them in my life now. If I'm correct, it's also what brought you, readers, to this book.

So thanks to all of you, too. Now, go ride.

www.moon.com

DESTINATIONS | ACTIVITIES | BLOGS | MAPS | BOOKS

MOON.COM is ready to help plan your next trip! Filled with fresh trip ideas and strategies, author interviews, informative travel blogs, a detailed map library, and descriptions of all the Moon guidebooks, Moon.com is all you need to get out and explore the world—or even places in your own backyard. While at Moon.com, sign up for our monthly e-newsletter for updates on new releases, travel tips, and expert advice from our on-the-go Moon authors. As always, when you travel with Moon, expect an experience that is uncommon and truly unique.

MOON IS ON FACEBOOK—BECOME A FAN!
JOIN THE MOON PHOTO GROUP ON FLICKR

OUTDOORS

COLORADO CAMPING

CALIFORNIA CAMPING

OREGON FISHING

CALIFORNIA HIKING

BAJA RV CAMPING

TAKE A HIKE NEW YORK CITY

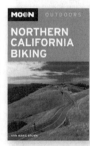

NORTHERN CALIFORNIA BIKING

UTAH CAMPING

"Well written, thoroughly researched, and packed full of useful information and advice, these guides really do get you into the outdoors."

—GORP.COM

MOON NEW ENGLAND BIKING

Avalon Travel
a member of the Perseus Books Group
1700 Fourth Street
Berkeley, CA 94710, USA
www.moon.com

Editors: Naomi Adler Dancis, Elizabeth Hansen,
    Sabrina Young
Series Manager: Sabrina Young
Copy Editor: Teresa Elsey
Graphics Coordinator: Elizabeth Jang
Production Coordinator: Elizabeth Jang
Cover Designer: Elizabeth Jang
Interior Designer: Darren Alessi
Map Editor: Mike Morgenfeld
Cartographers: Kat Bennett, Brice Ticen,
    Albert Angulo
Indexer: Sabrina Young

ISBN-13: 978-1-59880-026-5
ISSN: 1553-5657

Printing History
1st Edition – 2005
2nd Edition – May 2010
5 4 3 2 1

Some photos and illustrations are used by permission and are the property of the original copyright owners.

Front cover photo: The author rides in
    the Vermont woods © Chris Bernard
Title page photo: Mount Greylock in the Berkshire
    Mountains, Massachusetts © Chris Bernard
Page 4: Exeter, New Hampshire © Chris Bernard
Page 5: Willard Beach, Maine © Chris Bernard
Page 8: Battered sign, Massachusetts
    © Chris Bernard
Back cover photo: © Stockbyte Photography/Veer

Printed in Canada by Friesens

Keeping Current

We are committed to making this book the most accurate and enjoyable biking guide to the region. You can rest assured that every ride in this book has been carefully reviewed in an effort to keep this book as up-to-date as possible. However, by the time you read this book, some of the fees listed herein may have changed and trails may have closed unexpectedly.

If you have a favorite gem you'd like to see included in the next edition, or see anything that needs updating, clarification, or correction, please drop us a line. Send your comments via email to feedback@moon.com, or use the address above.